Third
Edition

CONSTRUCTION PROJECT MANAGEMENT

Frederick E. Gould, P.E., C.P.C.
Roger Williams University

Nancy E. Joyce
Art Gallery of Ontario

PEARSON
Prentice
Hall

UPPER SADDLE RIVER, NEW JERSEY
COLUMBUS, OHIO

Library of Congress Cataloging in Publication Data

Gould, Frederick E., 1954-
  Construction project management / Frederick E. Gould, Nancy E. Joyce.—3rd ed.
    p. cm.
  Includes index.
  ISBN-13: 978-0-13-199623-6 (pbk.)
  ISBN-10: 0-13-199623-1 (pbk.)
 1. Building--Superintendence.   2. Project management.   I. Joyce, Nancy (Nancy Eleanor)
II. Title.
  TH438.G62497 2009
  690--dc22

2008007792

Editor in Chief: Vernon R. Anthony
Editor: Eric Krassow
Editorial Assistant: Sonya Kottcamp
Production Manager: Wanda Rockwell
Cover Designer: Margaret Kenselaar
Cover Art: Getty Images, Inc.
Director of Marketing: David Gesell
Executive Marketing Manager: Derril Trakalo
Marketing Assistant: Les Roberts

This book was set in TimesTen-Roman by GGS Book Services. It was printed and bound by
Courier/Westford. The cover was printed by Phoenix Color/Hagerstown.

Pearson Education Ltd.
Pearson Education Singapore Pte. Ltd.
Pearson Education Canada, Ltd.
Pearson Education-Japan

Pearson Education Australia Pty. Limited
Pearson Education North Asia Ltd.
Pearson Educación de Mexico, S.A. de C.V.
Pearson Education Malaysia Pte. Ltd.

10 9 8 7
ISBN-13: 978-0-13-199623-6
ISBN-10:   0-13-199623-1

Preface

Over the past several years, the construction industry has seen enormous changes. From an industry steeped in conservative practices and narrowly scoped services, construction has moved to the forefront of the design and construction profession. From general contracting to construction management to project management and program management, the methods of servicing the industry have evolved to become more varied and comprehensive. This requires that practitioners and students alike understand the many aspects of the world of owners, designers, tenants, regulatory agencies, community groups, contracting lawyers, environmental lawyers, insurance providers, financial agencies, and subcontractors. Each participant brings political, professional, and personal motivations to the process, and each has the ability to place constraints on the project. To effectively navigate in this environment, the successful project manager must recognize the role of each participant, understand the nature of the project itself, and effectively utilize management tools to bring the project forward in a timely and cost-effective manner.

In addition to contending with the nature of each project and the individual participants, the project manager also has his or her own organization to navigate as well as those of the owner and the designer. As the major participants in any project, these organizations can support or hinder the process depending on the fit between organization and project as well as the fit among the individual organizations themselves. The recipe for success is indeed a complicated one. This book looks at the forms of organizations and some of the dynamics at play in them and outlines some methods of putting the right people and right organizations together for a specific project.

SCOPE OF THE TEXT

To address all of the aspects that a successful project manager needs to understand, this text is organized to explore the people involved in the design and construction process, the principle phases of a project, and the tools required to effectively manage the people and the project. It is intended primarily for students in a four-year construction management curriculum serving as an in-depth introduction to construction project management. The book will also benefit undergraduate or graduate civil engineering or architectural students who desire to better understand the construction process. It is also intended for older students or practitioners who are looking for an understanding of the changes in the industry and new tools and management methods available for dealing with those changes.

INSTRUCTIONAL TECHNIQUE

People learn in many different ways. While most people are able to absorb lessons through the written text, the concepts presented can be reinforced through other mediums. To that end, this book presents material in many different forms. The text is the major method employed, but the book also uses charts, illustrations, photos, and anecdotal sidebars. In addition, this book is coauthored by an academic and an industry professional. That combination fuses theory and practical reality in a dynamic interchange. Understanding pedagogy and how people learn is teamed with discernment regarding what information practitioners need to be successful in an increasingly competitive environment. In addition, many of the sidebars are authored by industry leaders, lending more real-world perspective to the book.

ORGANIZATION OF THE TEXT

The book is divided into three sections. The first section examines the industry and the profession by looking at the nature of the industry, future trends, and opportunities. It outlines the different sectors of the industry, explains the role of each participant, and looks at the variety of contractual arrangements available for particular projects. The second section focuses on the project itself, giving an in-depth overview of all aspects of the project from the very first concept to occupancy. This section emphasizes the recently expanded role of the construction professional during the design process and early construction. The third section focuses on the tools needed to manage the people and the project. Estimating and scheduling are two of the major tools used in construction management, but these combined with methods of control will ensure that an effective feedback system is established throughout the project. This section also examines what it takes to bring a project to completion, exploring the world of project administration with its documentation, procedures, and communication protocols. Lastly, a chapter on safety explains the importance of a good safety program to the financial and environmental health of the company and workers. The appendix provides a list of websites containing valuable construction-related information.

Throughout this text, the role of the owner, the designer, and the construction professional are interwoven. For a project to enjoy first-rate success, these three major participants have to be in perfect alignment with each other. Throughout the project, they each contribute to the project in a very specific way. To be in perfect alignment they must clearly understand and believe in the essential worth of each other's contribution and learn how to support each other for the mutual benefit of a successful project. The project manager is the key to creating an atmosphere where this support can be nurtured. This book gives project managers the tools that are essential to this task.

THIRD EDITION

The third edition of the book includes

- Updated statistics throughout—from newest cost information to industry sector breakdown—latest information on demographics, career choices, industry trends, and economic forecast.
- An overview of newest technologies being used in the industry and the advantages of each.

- Sustainability, with emphasis on Leadership in Energy and Environmental Design (LEED) that provides an overview of this new important trend in the industry, explaining in clear terms how to focus projects to be well positioned to qualify.
- An update of Construction Specification Institute (CSI) divisions that includes the new and revised 50 divisions, a description of the divisions and the rationale for the expansion. Also includes the list for reference.
- New project delivery methods including private/public partnerships and lean construction.

To access supplementary materials online, instructors need to request an instructor access code. Go to **www.pearsonhighered.com/irc,** where you can register for an instructor access code. Within 48 hours after registering, you will receive a confirming e-mail, including an instructor access code. Once you have received your code, go to the site and log on for full instructions on downloading the materials you wish to use.

Acknowledgments

With much appreciation, the authors acknowledge the contribution of Chapter 13, Construction Law, from Christopher L. Noble, Esq., and Heather G. Merrill, Esq., of Hill and Barlow, Boston, MA.

The authors gratefully acknowledge the following reviewers, who provided insightful criticism:

Third edition: Paula J. Behrens, Community College of Philadelphia; Allan D. Chasey, Arizona State University; Bobby Ensminger, University of Louisiana at Monroe; Henry Gaus, Lamar Institute of Technology; Paul E. Harmon, University of Nebraska; David Joswick, University of Houston; Daphene Cyr Koch, IUPUI; Kenneth J. Tiss, SUNY College of Environmental Science and Forestry; Wafeek Samuel Wahby, Eastern Illinois University.

Second edition: Terry L. Anderson, University of Southern Mississippi; David Bilbo, Texas A&M University; William W. Campbell, Montgomery College (retired); James A. S. Fatzinger; and James J. Stein, Eastern Michigan University.

First edition: Terry L. Anderson, University of Southern Mississippi; Naryan Bodapati, Southern Illinois University; and Joseph Gabriel, New York University and New York Institute of Technology.

The authors also thank Elizabeth Holmes, who compiled the original website listings in the appendix. (The authors updated the list for the third edition.)

The authors especially acknowledge Professor Dave Pierce, Southern College of Technology, for his early contribution to the format and content of the text.

Contents

CHAPTER 10 Project Planning and Scheduling   213

CHAPTER 11 Controlling Project Cost, Time, and Quality   239

1

THE CONSTRUCTION INDUSTRY

Chapter Outline

Student Learning Objectives

In this chapter you will learn the following:

1. The principle characteristics that define the construction industry
2. The four major sectors of construction projects
3. The nature of research and development within the construction industry
4. Current trends within the construction industry

INTRODUCTION

Although *construction* is principally defined by the concept of assembling materials and products, it is in fact multi-tasked. The construction of a building or infrastructure involves first an assembly of people, a definition of process, and creation of a site-specific work space. Just as divergent materials come together to form a structure, so, too, does a diverse group of people come together to make the project possible. To bring together numerous independent businesses and corporate personalities into one goal-oriented process is the peculiar challenge of the construction industry. The organizational cultures of architects, engineers, owners, builders, manufacturers, and suppliers may seem to work against the real need to forge a partnership that will ensure the success of a project. Yet, despite these very real challenges in the industry, construction projects do get completed. In fact, it is difficult to think of an industry that is more basic to our economy and to our daily lives. The highways we drive on, the bridges we cross, the water we drink, the fuel we burn: all are made possible by the activities of the construction industry. Likewise, where we shop, where we work, where we worship and learn, and where we live all exist because of the industry. Designers have visions; but until the contractor builds, those visions are just dreams on a sheet of paper.

    Construction is also very interwined with other aspects of our lives. It affects and is affected by developments in technology, computers, government policies, labor relations, and economic and political practices. Take, for instance, the technological leap of the skyscraper. Until the late 1800s, most buildings were four or five stories high. Masonry supported the structure from the ground. As the height of the building increased, the massing at the ground level also increased to support the additional load. Thus, if the building were built too high, the mass at the bottom would be too thick. Another limitation to height was that people could only practically climb four or five stories. Because floors on the upper levels were difficult to rent, owners had no economic incentive to build any higher. But with the development of cheap methods of producing iron and steel and the invention of the elevator, architects began designing higher buildings. This spurred construction activity: landowners were motivated to develop these new buildings because the return on their investment was higher. Over time, as technological advances have allowed, the skyscraper has gotten taller. Figure 1.1 contrasts older and newer skyscrapers.

    Innovations in robotics and computer modeling have also affected the construction industry. By using computers for modeling structures and imitating wind and seismic loads, architects and engineers can better anticipate nature's constraints and create

FIGURE 1.1   Technological innovation, if properly applied, allows projects to be built faster, bigger, and better

Source: Photo by Margot Balboni, Geoscapes.

FIGURE 1.2 The total station allows surveyors to collect, record, and transcribe surveying information with greater speed and accuracy

Source: Photo by Amos Chau. Courtesy of the Wentworth Institute of Technology, Boston.

better designs to counteract them. With robots directing equipment during construction, contractors can gain more control over processes that require precision for success, such as the construction of the underwater tunnel between France and England. The desire for such projects leads to the development of technologies to make them possible, which in turn encourages similar projects to go forward (see Figure 1.2).

TYPE OF INDUSTRY

Construction is big business in the United States. According to the Bureau of Labor Statistics, the industry employs 7.7 million people and represents 5.5 percent of the work force, making it the nation's largest single employer. The total value of construction in 2006 was $1,155 billion, which represents 9 percent of the gross domestic product (GDP). Opportunities in construction have increased significantly in the last

10 years. Construction employment has risen from 5.8 million in 1997 to 7.7 million in 2006. This is in contrast to employment as a whole, which has increased 21 percent. Although construction-related jobs are some of the best-paying in the country, they are often not a person's first career choice. Look at any construction company, and you will find people from a variety of backgrounds who, through experience and continuing education, have been promoted through the ranks. This profile is starting to change, however, with the professionalization of the field and the introduction of undergraduate and graduate construction management programs at colleges and universities. Both the American Institute of Constructors (AIC) and the Construction Management Association of America (CMAA) have initiated professional certification programs.

Construction projects can be awe-inspiring in their breadth and complexity—from the Egyptian pyramids and Gothic cathedrals to soaring skyscrapers and enormous bridges. Yet, the industry itself does not own these products, nor does it control their supply and demand. In fact, construction has relatively few assets compared with those of other industries. Its success or failure depends on the qualities of its people rather than on its technology or product. In this way, it is very much a service industry—one composed of many small businesses, especially in the residential and commercial building sectors. Construction does not require a patent or a large capital investment; anyone with motivation, technical skills, and a sufficient cash flow can start a business and be successful. However, because of the industry's cyclical nature, it inevitably has slow periods. Without capital to get them through these slow times, these small "mom and pop" businesses are at risk, and many are forced out of the market.

The risk factor is much higher in construction than it is in other industries because outside factors such as government funding, demographics, and market trends largely determine demand. Another reason for this high risk lies in the unpredictable nature of the work itself. Since construction takes place outside, it depends on weather conditions. Any extremes can affect productivity level, damage materials and work in place, create unsafe conditions, and even shut down the site entirely (see Figure 1.3). Moreover, the industry is custom-oriented, meaning that it is difficult to use mass-production techniques in either materials or methods. Each project has its own learning curve for both management and labor. Because all these factors make it difficult to accurately predict how much money will be necessary to complete the project, the industry has a higher risk of losing money than do industries that rely on more predictable factors.

Financial institutions, medical services, accounting firms, and real estate companies have all been involved in recent mergers, consolidations, and conglomerations. Construction, however, is a study of contrasts. At one time, general contractors constructed almost the entire project with their own work crews. But as buildings become more technically complex and the business of building them more sophisticated, the industry has turned increasingly to specialty trades. Thus, the contractor's role has evolved from boss to manager. However, in other aspects of the industry, the reverse is happening. While the technical complexities of projects have strongly influenced the trend toward subcontractor specialization, these same complexities are merging owners, contractors, and designers into more collaborative units. In a very real way, this trend is leading constructors back to their roots—as the master builders.

FIGURE 1.3   Unpredictable weather is just one of the many risks faced by the construction industry

Source: Photo by Margot Balboni, Geoscapes.

INDUSTRY SECTORS

Most designers and builders concentrate their business and build expertise in a specific sector of the construction industry, each of which is supported by separate material and equipment suppliers, manufacturers, and subcontractors. These distinct types have evolved because major differences exist in how projects within each sector are funded; in the building methods involved; and in the manner in which designers, builders, and owners interact. These sectors are usually separated into the following four categories:

- Residential
- Commerical building
- Infrastructure and heavy highway
- Industrial

Figure 1.4 shows the percentage breakdown of (a) private versus public construction and (b) the four industry sectors.

Private versus public construction

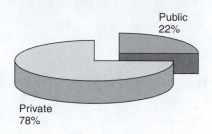

Public
22%

Private
78%

Breakdown by sectors

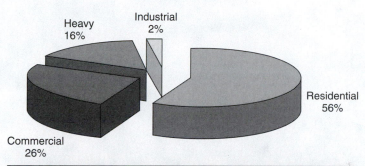

Heavy
16%

Industrial
2%

Residential
56%

Commercial
26%

FIGURE 1.4   Percentage breakdown of annual construction
put in place in 2004

Source: U.S. Census Bureau: 2004.

Residential Sector

The residential construction sector is comprised of individual homes, small condominiums, and apartment complexes (see Figure 1.5). What all these building types have in common (apart from the fact that they house people) are the conditions under which they are constructed. Such projects tend to be privately funded by individual owners for their own use or for speculation. They are typically designed by architects, although the plan may come from a mass-produced catalog. In some instances, the homeowner or the builder may design the structure. Within this sector, there has been some movement toward pre-manufactured homes and products. But despite the tremendous potential in developing pre-manufactured components for the residential market, the tendency is still to build most components on site.

As a site-built product, residential construction uses fairly low technology. Not surprisingly, most of the "mom and pop" operations are found in this sector. Because the technology needed to build residential buildings is readily available, the capital required to step into the business is fairly small: a pickup truck, some basic tools, and an understanding of construction. Supporting these operations are many other small businesses—lumberyards, tool and equipment rentals, specialty suppliers, and hardware stores. When the economy is strong, these small businesses do well; but because

FIGURE 1.5   Residential sector projects are usually privately funded, designed by architects, and strongly influenced by government housing policies and interest rates

Source: Photo by Margot Balboni, Geoscapes.

residential sector projects are privately funded and homogenous in type, many companies go out of business when money gets tight. Interest rates and government policy toward housing investment also influence the sector's health. In a good economy, about one-half of construction spending takes place in the residential sector.

Commercial Building Sector

This sector includes office buildings, large apartment complexes, shopping malls, theaters, schools, universities, and hospitals (see Figure 1.6). Like residential buildings, these structures tend to be privately funded, although some public funding is usually available for schools and hospitals. They are typically designed by an architect with support from an engineer and are built by general contractors as bid projects or by construction managers who assist during pre-construction and coordinate the construction. The technical sophistication necessary for success is greater than in the residential sector, as is the capital needed to enter the field. These factors lead to fewer players.

Within this sector, there is some specialization. Hospitals, which require a special knowledge of the activities that happen in them, tend to be technically complex to design

FIGURE 1.6   The commercial building sector includes privately funded projects such as retail malls and office towers as well as institutional buildings such as hospitals and college dormitories. The Der Neue Zollhof building in Düsseldorf, Germany, is one example—an office complex built speculatively with three separate towers joined by a common parking facility underground

Source: Courtesy of Frank O. Gehry & Associates, Santa Monica, Calif.

and require tight quality control during construction. Commercial structures such as shopping malls, office buildings, and theaters are built for quick turnaround and an eye to marketing and retail image. Firms build their reputations in these specialized fields, and owners choose designers and contractors based on their reputations. Larger firms tend to have various divisions that concentrate on specific segments of the market, meaning that they are generally able to weather economic ups and downs.

Annual construction expenditures are high for this sector, accounting for more than one quarter of the construction market. However, the sector is highly dependent on regional economic health. Houston in the 1970s, California in the 1980s, and the northeast in the 1990s experienced tremendous economic growth and construction success. But such success inevitably leads to overbuilding, which in turn leads to a real estate glut and very little continued construction activity as the economy slows and overbuilt real estate is absorbed. Such factors are part of the construction cycle.

Infrastructure and Heavy Highway Sector

Construction in this sector enables the distribution of goods and people. Examples include roadways, bridges, canals, dams, and tunnels (see Figure 1.7). These projects are designed principally by civil engineers and built by heavy construction contractors who

FIGURE 1.7 Typically, infrastructure projects are publicly funded and designed by civil engineers

Source: Photo by Margot Balboni, Geoscapes.

have engineering backgrounds or support. Because of the complexity of the projects and the importance of equipment and technical know-how, relatively few firms are involved, and those that are tend to be very large.

Most infrastructure projects are publicly funded because they serve the public's needs. Without a strong framework of infrastructure, the nation's productivity decreases, and our standard of living is affected. However, the current condition of infrastructure in the United States requires greater attention. Consider the following statistics from the 2007 U.S. Markets Construction Overview:

- The interstate highway system originally met the needs of the 170 million people in the United States in the 1950s but has not been updated sufficiently to meet the 2006 population of 300 million.
- The EPA estimates a national investment need of more than $390 billion over the next 20 years to replace existing sewage and waste disposal systems and to build new systems to meet growing demand.
- Most cities rely on water distribution systems that were built prior to World War I. These are deteriorating, have outdated water treatment, and have very little pollution controls.
- The Department of Transportation projects that total freight moved through U.S. ports will increase by more than 50 percent by 2020. Spending is needed to cover the overall modernization of cargo processing.

The need for building or rebuilding in this sector is great. Infrastructure projects tend to last for a long time and to continue despite regional economic ups and downs. Although they have traditionally been publicly funded, a growing trend toward partnership with private industries may offset their impact on taxes.

Industrial Sector

Steel mills, petroleum refineries, chemical processing plants, and automobile production facilities are all examples of industrial facilities (see Figure 1.8). These projects are defined by the production activities within the facility rather than the facility itself. The design and construction of the shell depend on the needs of the process and production equipment. In the United States, most of these facilities are privately funded. However, in other countries, money may come from public sources. Quality and time are extremely important in these projects; productivity and therefore return on investment depend on how well the facility performs. Because of the detailed complexity of each facility, this sector includes many specialties. Only a few designers and builders are qualified to work on any particular type of facility. Since the process technology is critical, designers and builders need to collaborate closely throughout the project. As a result, builders and designers often deliver services as a single company.

Opportunities in this sector have grown. The downsizing of the industry coupled with more efficient production processes has resulted in increased demand for U.S. products and therefore increased demand for new or refurbished facilities. In addition,

FIGURE 1.8 Industrial projects are characterized by the technological process housed in each facility. These projects tend to be privately funded and fast-moving

Source: Photo by Margot Balboni, Geoscapes.

the urgent need to clean up hazardous materials at old industrial sites has spawned the new field of environmental construction. This field combines the talents of scientists and engineers with specialized construction personnel. Presently, these sites are being cleaned using federal Superfund money or state funds. As of the end of fiscal year 2005, according to the Environmental Protection Agency (EPA) 966 sites have been cleaned up, which represents 62 percent of the highest priority sites. However, new sites are added to the high priority list annually—18 were added in 2005 and 12 in 2006.

RESEARCH AND DEVELOPMENT

Traditionally, construction focuses on cash flow and is almost completely driven by projects and their schedules. As a result, there is little incentive for individual companies to invest in research and development except in a propriety manner. The little investment that does exist is at the university level. Few U.S. engineering and construction companies have done any significant research aimed at improving construction processes. Not only are most projects pushed through with tight timetables, but new ideas risk failure and lawsuits. Thus, designers and owners tend to be very conservative when specifying products to be used on their projects. Moreover, even if a company does successfully invest in a new technology, it has no way to protect its investment. Most construction technologies are not patentable, meaning that a competitor could easily use them on its next project.

International companies are starting to challenge this profile—for example, Japanese companies, which spend up to forty times as much as the United States on basic research and development in construction. Organizations such as the Center for Building Technology and the Construction Industry Institute, which are aimed at fostering creativity, research, and innovation, are starting to influence changes. To be effective, however, labor, the academy, government, and business must work together.

PUBLIC PROFILE

The construction industry has an image problem. According to the *Jobs Rated Almanac* published in 2002, construction worker ranks 244 out of 250 possible career choices. The jobs were analyzed utilizing criteria such as environment, income, employment outlook, physical demands, security, and stress. Two other construction-related careers, roofer and ironworker, also appear in the 10 least desirable category. Whenever a contractor walks out on a homeowner before a job is completed, a person is injured or killed on a construction site, traffic is disrupted because of construction activity, or a labor action closes down a job site, the industry's image is further tarnished. Unfortunately, it has few positive images to counteract the negative ones.

In fact, construction is one of the noblest professions. Working with your hands, solving problems in the field, working collaboratively with many other disciplines to create a real product that will be handed down to future generations: this is construction. It is hard to imagine another profession that has such a physical impact on the quality of people's lives. The industry has much to be proud of, but it hasn't done a good job of letting others know about its accomplishments.

BOX 1.1

PROMOTING THE CONSTRUCTION PROFESSION

The construction industry faces an aging work force, declining numbers of eighteen-year-olds entering the industry, job entrants with lower literacy rates, and an industry with declining financial benefits. Construction is cyclical; that is, it has periods of boom and bust. The work is also dangerous, with one of the poorest safety records of any industry. Outdoors, the work force is exposed to dirt, rain, snow, cold, and heat. And workers are hired on a project basis: when a job ends, employment ends; the worker must look for another job.

This scenario describes a fairly bleak future for an industry seeking to build a work force from the best and brightest. Workers with strong technical, managerial, and organizational skills are necessary for the future, and this industry must compete against other industries for such people.

Why should a young person choose construction as a future career? As a construction professional, one is able to work on the world's largest projects. The Golden Gate Bridge in San Francisco, the Skydome in Toronto, the Sears Tower in Chicago, the English Channel Tunnel (Chunnel): all are examples of world-famous projects involving construction professionals.

Construction professionals work with more people from more disciplines than do most other professionals. On a typical project, a construction professional may work with people from as many as 30 different companies. Designers, owners, subcontractors, suppliers, testing laboratories, and government officials are all brought together for the purpose of building one project.

A career in construction has more variety than most. As a construction professional, one can solve technical problems, run meetings, meet the public, and negotiate changes and contracts. One estimates future costs, produces detailed schedules, and works as part of a sophisticated team—organizing, expediting, and dealing with change.

A construction career can certainly be rewarding and, for some people, very lucrative. Unfortunately, however, many people do not think of construction as a professional pursuit. They do not realize the amount of organizational and technical skill required to successfully complete a modern construction project. Young people who want to run construction projects should consider majoring in construction management or building construction, just as designers major in architecture or civil engineering. And just as architects and engineers seek professional registration, constructors should pursue certification from the American Institute of Constructors or the Construction Management Association of America.

One challenge for the future will be to educate people about the industry. Efforts at the high school level and even in the lower grades will help to attract youngsters to the field, as well as counteract negative images. Programs such as City/Build (which pairs high school students with design and building professionals) and Youth/Build (which pairs young people with construction projects through work apprenticeships and educational opportunities) are one way to start. They introduce students to the professions and emphasize the importance of getting involved in decisions about our

FIGURE 1.9   Construction professionals must promote a positive image of the profession to the public, particularly young people

Source: Courtesy of Historic Neighborhoods, sponsor of Boston's City/Build program.

built environment (see Figure 1.9). Professional organizations and professional registration of contractors will also create a new image of the constructor.

Construction Ethics

In recent years, the construction industry has become increasingly professional. Along with that professionalism is the realization that guidelines to expected professional behavior needed to be developed. Society governs behavior by written laws and unwritten moral and ethical codes. Many acts are allowed by law but considered unethical or immoral by a certain group's standards. In professional circles, expected ethical behavior is sometimes written out as a code of ethics. Here is the code of the American Institute of Constructors:[*]

> The construction profession is based upon a system of technical competence, management excellence, and fair dealing in undertaking complex works to serve the public with safety, efficiency, and economy. The members of the

---

[*]Courtesy of the American Institute of Constructors. Reprinted by permission.

American Institute of Constructors are committed to the following standards of professional conduct:

   I. A member shall have full regard to public interest in fulfilling his or her professional responsibilities.

   II. A member shall not engage in any deceptive practice, or in any practice that creates an unfair advantage for the member or another.

   III. A member shall not maliciously or recklessly injure or attempt to injure the professional reputation of others.

   IV. A member shall ensure that when providing a service that includes advice, such advice shall be fair and unbiased.

   V. A member shall not divulge to any person, firm or company, information of a confidential nature acquired during the course of professional activities.

   VI. A member shall carry out his or her responsibilities in accordance with current professional practice.

   VII. A member shall keep informed of new concepts and developments in the construction process appropriate to the type and level of his or her responsibilities.

Often it is difficult to discern if certain ways of acting are unethical or simply economic business practice. In construction, one example of unethical behavior is bid shopping. This can occur during the bidding period or after the bids are in. It can be instigated by contractors, subcontractors, or, in some instances, owners themselves. Basically, bid shopping involves letting a specific contractor or subcontractor know enough about the other bids so that he or she can bid below them to win the job. This practice hurts all the bidders. Bids cost money to put together and represent significant effort. It is unfair not to give everyone the same chance of winning the job. In the long run, bid shopping hurts the owner. The subcontractor who wins the job may have reduced his or her profit so significantly that the incentive to cut corners is high. Additionally, if the construction community learns about this practice, the contractor will find it difficult to get good bids on subsequent jobs.

Being able to trust the people we work with is a big part of putting our best effort into our work. On a construction job, people often do not know each other very well. They come together to do a project but may have no prior common working experience. A key to success is creating a trusting environment in which people feel comfortable with each other. If project participants adhere to a professional code of ethics such as the one you have just read, they already have a foundation for creating that trust.

Demographics

Demographics will shape the construction industry of the future. Today, the field needs 200,000 new employees each year. Because of the baby bust between 1965 and 1976, the industry's image problem, and the retirement of thousands of long-time craftsmen, these positions have been difficult to fill. Those who do take the jobs are not well trained and have inadequate levels of competency. However, the industry has taken steps to rectify these problems. Research and development should reduce the need for workers through better technology and productivity; better recruitment and retention will stabilize the work force; and the second baby boom from 1977 to 1994 is starting to populate the work force.

Demographics will also play a big role in the direction of construction. Americans are older, living longer, and living in smaller households; they are also more racially and ethnically diverse. "Their" demographics indicate future construction needs. Baby boomers, about 77 million people, have considerable influence over spending patterns. In their wake are the second-generation boomers, 72 million people, who will be the trendsetters of the twenty-first century. Their children are now pouring into aging schools that often need to be replaced. At the other end, people are living longer, which puts strains on health care facilities and creates additional need for assisted-living facilities.

Technology

Companies are increasingly using technology to help bridge the gap between home office and field office. Electronic communication and the ability to be plugged into the construction site through digital technology is starting to blur the lines between home office control and field office control. The larger construction home offices have incorporated accounting software, e-mail, estimating and scheduling, Computer-Aided Design (CAD) capability, electronic plan rooms, and other e-business models. Field offices have some of the home office capabilities depending on the size and duration of the project and may be utilizing web-based project management software, file transfer protocol (ftp) sites for exchange of drawings and other large storage documents, and advanced CAD packages such as Building Information Modeling (BIM). On the site, there may be handheld devices in use for communication, photography, punch lists, and timecards. There also may be robotics in use on some processes, electronically controlled survey equipment; Radio Frequency Identification (RFID) tags on hand tools and equipment. Some of the more common technologies being used for organizing and controlling the construction project are described below:

> *Computer-Aided Design* is a software used by architects, engineers, and increasingly by contractors to design and view the two- and three-dimensional components of buildings.
>
> *Electronic plan rooms* are secure web environments that allow owners, architects, and general contractors to invite subcontractors to bid on jobs. The subcontractors can access the site and view documents, and can either download them directly or through a copy vendor.
>
> *E-commerce* is an electronic platform for buying and selling material, products, and equipments, sometimes by auction, sometimes through an open exchange model that serves as a center for searching, evaluating, and procuring products.
>
> *File Transfer Protocol* are secure sites that are used to transfer files over the Internet. It is a common method of posting and downloading large files such as CAD documents.
>
> *Building Information Modeling* is a digital tool that supports the continual updating and sharing of project design information.
>
> *Radio Frequency Identification* is an identification and tracking system that consists of a transponder or tag, which is a microchip attached to an antenna, and a reader. The reader communicates with the tag through radio waves.

Opportunities

Increased productivity is the greatest untapped area for improvement in the construction industry. Companies that embrace new technologies, innovative processes, collaborative partnering, improved safety, and reductions in litigation costs through contract arrangements will have a significant advantage over others that continue with past practices. One of the barriers to greater productivity is the increase in government regulations targeted at construction. For instance, from 1970 to 2004 the number of people employed in the Environmental Protection Agency (EPA) increased from 4,000 to 18,000, and the budget itself went up from $1 billion in 1970 to $7.6 billion in 2004.

The ultimate success of the construction industry may lie in its ability to form a collective agenda. Competition from Japan, Germany, and other nations; liability costs; and computerization of the industry could all be rallying points. Every one of those issues has the potential to make or break the industry. If competition from abroad is allowed to continue unabated, if liability costs turn the industry reactive instead of proactive, or if the industry does not respond sufficiently to the electronic age, then the future will see an industry in disarray. On the other hand, these issues could spur great growth. Computerization can open up communication among companies and allow learning to take place across traditional lines. The industry can incorporate international successes while investing money in research and development to move into a better competitive position. By creating demonstration projects (projects not guided solely by budget and schedule), the industry can mitigate traditional risks while testing new products and processes.

BOX 1.2

BUILDING INFORMATION MODELING

Building Information Modeling (BIM) is a digital tool that supports the continual updating and sharing of project design information. This is accomplished by keeping the design information in digital form, easing updating and transfer. In addition, the design information can be modeled in real time with the full consideration of cost and schedule information increasing project productivity and quality. The term was first used by Autodesk and now more widely in the industry to describe 3D, object-oriented CAD.

A prime value of BIM lies in the technology's ability to support collaboration. Throughout the preconstruction stage of a project, professionals must continually balance project scope, quality, and cost with every design decision providing a positive or negative impact. At the design review stage every stakeholder needs to verify that their vision is being fulfilled. Users look to verify that the scope of the project is being met in terms of spaces, circulation, and relationships between spaces. Designer and subdesigners need to ensure consistency in design in terms of quality specified and in the relationship and coordination of building systems. Constructors look to the constructability of the design and to the cost and speed of construction. Because of BIM's ability to present the design digitally in 3D, users are able to clearly view the design to date. Spaces and relationships between spaces are evident; conflicts in mechanical, electrical, and structural systems

(*continued*)

BOX 1.2   Continued

can be seen; and through the inclusion of cost and productivity information, the constructor can produce a reliable estimate and schedule.

Since project designs evolve and each project review leads to adjustments in project scope and design, keeping the design in a digital format is a real plus. Design changes can be made quickly, encouraging the project team to investigate alternative approaches also called a "what if?" analysis. This is true value engineering; and with the full participation of the owner, designer, and constructor the team can really seek out the best approach to take. Systems decisions such as whether or not to utilize a concrete, steel, or wood structure can be evaluated early from the perspective of time, cost, and quality.

In fully utilizing BIM technology a BIM model is in the hands of many of the project participants. The architect has a BIM model to work out the floor plans, elevations, sections, and finishes. The mechanical electrical and plumbing (MEP) engineers use the model to design the building's heating, cooling, and plumbing systems. The structural engineer has a model to design the building structure. By "rolling" the engineering designs back to the architect's model, design coordination can be done efficiently. The builder also utilizes a BIM model to determine how the work will be phased and to study different construction approaches. The model speeds up quantity takeoff work and estimating. Curtain-wall subcontractors and structural steel fabricators can also use the BIM model to detail and fabricate their building components.

According to the Contractor's Guide to BIM published by the Associated General Contractors, the advantages of using BIM include identifying collisions, such as where piping may run into structural steel; studying what will be built in a safe, simulated environment; reducing errors and corrections in the field; having more reliable expectations of field conditions; being able to incorporate more prefabricated components and assemblies; and comparing "what if" scenarios for logistics, sequencing, hoisting, and other major moves.

The value of BIM does not end with construction. BIM is of great use to facility managers. It allows them to plan out their renovations and to provide a quick digital record of the work that was done. BIM includes project components, details, and quantities, so the preparation of the estimate, schedule, and the design for the renovation, should be a lot faster—there should be fewer unknowns and it should be easier for the designer and builder to match existing conditions. It also can be used as a basis for facility maintenance since the BIM documents hold information about manufacturers, part numbers, and their location in the building.

BIM can best be viewed as computer-aided design (CAD) with additional "layers" that allow for lifecycle management. It can also be viewed as an attitude, promoting the sharing of electronic design information with all of the key construction management participants. BIM keeps the design electronic and encourages every project stakeholder to look at the design from their own organizational perspective. Since the design is "electronically alive," project participants can continue to collaborate and perfect the design right into the construction phase of the project, and facility managers can utilize and modify the information to maintain and renovate the building throughout its useful life.

The most significant developments in construction center on the interrelations among the parties involved and the methods of communication that enhance those relations. The changes in relationships are a direct result of other developments in the field. Projects have become larger and more technically complex, government regulations have grown considerably, and public scrutiny has increased. Large, complicated projects require entities with strong financial backing and overall stability. Owners are breaking down barriers between traditional divisions because they need more shared information. Design/build, formal partnering arrangements, construction management, and program management are increasingly popular delivery methods that can provide stability and also cut back on litigation expenses.

Globalization has become a reality. Information, ideas, fashions, and money all stretch worldwide, unhindered by old boundaries. In addition, trade in the non-communist countries has eliminated tariff barriers with the creation of the World Trade Organization; the countries of the European Union (27 to date) have joined together to create a single market unit with a single currency; and the United States has created the North American Free Trade Agreement, binding itself with Mexico and Canada. These are examples of the opening up of economies to world markets. To compete in this new environment, U.S. companies must take several steps. A partnership with local companies is important, along with an understanding of the local economy, language, cultural differences, and knowledge of how work is procured. Strong technical skills and innovative processes are prerequisites for entering this market. Recent projects, such as Frank Gehry's Disney Concert Hall in Los Angeles, demonstrate such innovation. Computer technology was used to create unique shapes that would not have been possible to consider otherwise. The computer was also used to create three-dimensional structural models from the design models. These were then fed into a steel detailing program, which also drove the fabrication machines. In this way, there was an unbroken electronic chain from architectural modeling to the fabrication of parts. Figure 1.10 shows a similar process for fabricating the exterior wall system at the Der Neue Zollhof building.

Domestically, one of the greatest opportunities for construction is in the U.S. infrastructure—bridges, roadways, tunnels, airports, and water supplies—which are widely in need of refurbishment and replacement. Needs are great—the Department of Transportation says the price tag for all road and bridge projects alone is $61.4 billion annually. Natural disasters such as Hurricane Katrina, awareness of the need for increased security after the World Trade Center attack, and infrastructure failures such as the collapse of the bridge on Interstate 35W all put additional pressures on the government's ability to fund the huge infrastructure projects that will assure our continued safety and, if left unattended, the continuing degradation of services will affect all areas of the economy. To meet the challenge of updating the infrastructure without creating stress on taxes, government and private enterprises must create a partnership. This has the potential to create many construction jobs in the future. It is also an important investment in the health of the nation.

Conclusion

The construction industry will continue to play a key role in society. From the early days of building simple shelters, we have developed means and methods that have become a symbol of our sophistication and maturity. The industry began its life among master builders and seems to be returning full cycle to its roots. Although we still live

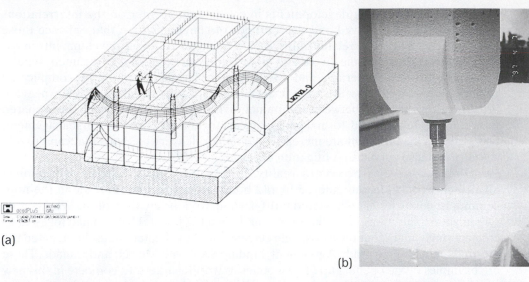

(a)

(b)

(c)

(d)

FIGURE 1.10   Frank O. Gehry & Associates used three-dimensional computer modeling in the design of the exterior wall system of the Der Neue Zollhof building in Düsseldorf, Germany. The sequence started with (a) the computer model and proceeded directly to (b) the cutting machine that transferred the design to Styrofoam form work. This was then (c) factory fabricated and (d) shipped to the field for installation

Source: Courtesy of Frank O. Gehry & Associates, Santa Monica, Calif.

in a world of competitive bidding, there is a trend toward more collaboration between designers and builders. Computer technology has created a bridge between the two industries. Owners' desire to avoid litigation is pushing them toward the design/build construction management model. Innovations in construction processes and methods are forging a partnership between design and building as well.

The opportunities in construction are endless. The industry spans small home projects and huge civil engineering feats. As each construction sector matures, the divisions among them become more pronounced. Each sector has its own specialty suppliers and subcontractors, and increasingly contractors build businesses solely in one of the sectors.

The future of construction is an exciting one. International markets, innovations in technology, and new relationships across disciplines are all avenues of development. To make best use of their opportunities, U.S. companies must invest in research and development; undertake public education about the field; and create new, nontraditional partnerships.

References

FMI Corporation. *2007 U.S. Markets Construction Overview*. Raleigh, NC: FMI Management Consulting, 2006.

Krantz, Les. *Jobs Rated Almanac: The Best and Worst Jobs 6th ed*. New York: Barricade Books, 2002.

Chapter Review Questions

1. Which of the following is not true about the future of the construction industry?
   a. The industry will become more global.
   b. There will be an increased demand for highly trained workers.
   c. The need for permits and regulations will decrease.
   d. Hazardous waste disposal and product recycling will become a greater factor.
   e. All of the above are true.
2. Which of the following categories of projects is often publicly funded and called *infrastructure?*
   a. Residential
   b. Commercial building
   c. Heavy engineering
   d. Industrial
   e. All of the above
3. Research and development expenditures are higher in construction than in other industries. True or false?
4. Compared with other industries, the construction industry has higher sales and assets. True or false?
5. Public sector projects are funded by tax dollars through cities, towns, states, and the federal government. True or false?
6. Which of the following industry sectors typically requires designs by a civil engineer?
   a. Residential
   b. Commercial building
   c. Heavy engineering
   d. Industrial
   e. All of the above

7. Which of the following best explains why research and development expenditures in the construction industry lag behind expenditures in some other countries?
   a. U.S. companies see little need to spend money since most competitors are not investing either.
   b. Owners and designers tend to be conservative in specifying new products, materials, and methods.
   c. New technologies are not time-proven and put the project at risk.
   d. It is often difficult to patent or protect from competitors new technologies that are successfully perfected.
   e. All of the above are true.
8. Poor professional salaries and benefits is one of the major reasons why people do not choose a career in the construction industry. True or false?
9. To compete internationally, what should a company do?
   a. Establish partnerships with local companies
   b. Become technically innovative
   c. Increase the cultural diversity of the company
   d. Ensure that professionals involved in the project speak the language of country
   e. All of the above
10. In the future, regulations that affect the productivity of the construction industry should decrease. True or false?

Exercises

1. Identify several new construction projects in your community. Decide which sector each falls within, and defend your reasoning. Are the projects funded privately or publicly? What differences can you identify among projects from different sectors?
2. Research several famous projects in history. Look at those that were successful as well as those that were not. Explain why each project succeeded or failed.
3. Identify a new technology that has been recently implemented in construction practice. What benefits does this new technology provide to the owner, contractor, designer, worker, or public?

CHAPTER

2 | PROJECT PARTICIPANTS

Chapter Outline

Student Learning Objectives

In this chapter you will learn the following:

1. The roles and responsibilities of the key construction participants
2. The division of labor within a designer organization
3. The division of labor within a construction organization
4. The common categories of construction labor
5. Professional registration and certification

INTRODUCTION

The product of a construction project can exist for hundreds of years. People occupy the buildings, maintain the refineries, operate the pipelines, and use the bridges. However, no one interacts quite as intimately with these facilities as those who dream of them, design them, and build them. Construction projects are born from ideas. For an idea to be realized, it must be translated into graphic form, which in turn must be transformed into a finished product. The idea is defined by the owner, developed by the designer, and produced by the constructor, who then turns it over to the owner. This circle defines the construction project.

This chapter concentrates on the people who fill the roles of owner, designer, and constructor. Who fills these roles and how they relate to each other are determined by many factors, including time, money, project uniqueness, and cultural environment. At first glance, the roles seem simple to define: the owner is the one with the deep pockets, the designer is the expert, and the constructor is the guy with the pickup truck and the backhoe. A closer look, however, reveals a more complex and interesting reality. Owners are often large organizations or institutions that are accountable to a board of trustees or a foundation that demands tight fiscal control. Designers depend increasingly on manufacturers, suppliers, and builders for technical expertise as technology and product design become more sophisticated. Constructors are professionals with advanced technical degrees who manage projects with sophisticated means and methods.

The closer you examine them, the more complicated and indistinct the roles become. As projects grow in complexity, owners are increasingly turning to outside consultants to represent their interests. These program managers and project managers may, in fact, be employed by design or construction firms that may or may not have a direct stake in the design or construction of the project. Owners, especially in large companies, may also be architects, engineers, or constructors by training; and experienced construction companies often employ architects and engineers as staff members.

If we consider how the management of the project is arranged, we see another layer of complexity added to these roles. Owners' increased need for tight financial control and quick project turnaround, coupled with concerns about the rising cost of litigation, are contributing to a change in the way in which the roles relate to each other. (See Chapter 4 for details on how project participants can interact.)

This chapter discusses the roles of owner, designer, and constructor as separate and distinct. In fact, it is their functions that are separate and distinct. Complexity develops from how those functions are configured and who carries them out.

OWNERS

Owners can be individuals seeking a home for their growing family, a large organization responding to a change in technology, a municipality seeking to improve its infrastructure, or a developer working to make money by filling a perceived market need. The motivation to build is as varied as the profile of the individuals and companies. Whatever the motivation, however, the owner is where the project is born. After identifying the need, the owner's most important function is to financially back the project; otherwise, there can be no project. The source of that financing partly defines the type of owner who enters into a construction process.

Public Owners
One-quarter of the construction in the United States is done with public money. The money can be from local, state, or federal sources, but in all cases the owner is the taxpayer. Some of these projects are done through public agencies that commission the construction—for example, the Army Corps of Engineers, the Department of Transportation, and the General Service Administration. They build military complexes, large public works projects, and courthouses, to name a few (see Figure 2.1). Because these agencies represent the public, they must follow specific methods of managing the projects. Public approval processes have to be figured into any schedule or budget. How the designer and contractor are selected is carefully spelled out. Negotiation of claims is well defined, as well as how payments are issued.

FIGURE 2.1   Most roads, bridges, and government buildings are public projects funded by taxpayers

Source: Photo by Margot Balboni, Geoscapes.

Some publicly funded projects are managed by private organizations such as universities or hospitals. The funding of these projects often combines public funding with private money for some or all of the construction. Thus, institutional owners may need to comply with public agency requirements while managing the pressures of private oversight boards.

There are special pressures on the team that is designing and building a publicly funded project. During design there can be multiple reviews by various agencies. Federal or state regulations that are not part of local building codes can be enforced. Bidding requirements may affect how specific building contractors are selected. The owner's representative must be well versed in all these special requirements to ensure that public money is well spent and that documentation supporting all actions is maintained.

Private Owners

Most construction is financed through private ownership. This category includes both the homeowner who builds only one house in a lifetime and the multinational company that owns numerous facilities (see Figure 2.2). Large companies often have a

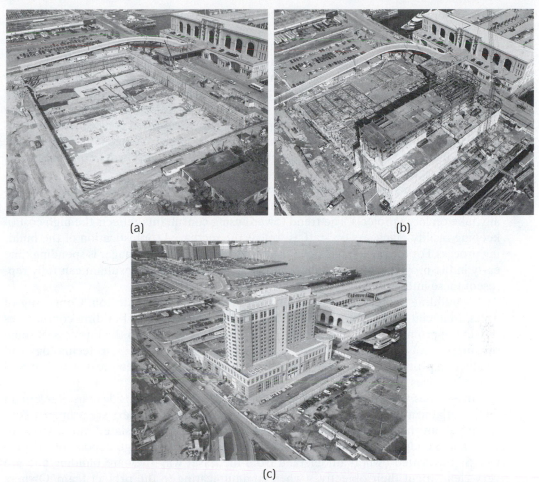

(a)   (b)

(c)

FIGURE 2.2 Privately funded projects are constructed for personal use or for the economic benefit of the investor. This figure shows the sequence of construction activity

Source: Photo by Margot Balboni, Geoscapes.

department of construction industry professionals who represent them during the design and building process.

A developer is a special type of private owner who often owns the project only for the duration of construction. The developer looks for economic opportunities and puts together a package that includes marketing, financing, location, and image. The goal is to make money, either through a quick sale or through long-term rentals.

Owner Representatives

Because owners can be any individual or organization that takes on a construction project, it is difficult to find a common profile. Facility managers are the most common professional owner representatives. They are found most often in large organizations and institutions, such as corporate offices with multiple facilities, military complexes, schools and universities, and hospitals. At one time, facility managers were the basement mechanics who oversaw the repair and maintenance of facilities. Now they are a more diverse and professional group. Facility managers view the facilities in a broader context than most of the other people in their organization and certainly more broadly than the other members of the project team. Their job is to understand the goals and objectives of their organization and ensure that the facilities are planned to support them. Therefore, they are often the people who determine when construction projects are necessary. Changing technologies, market competition, management innovations, organizational growth, and the natural aging of facilities all are factors that create the need for projects.

Organizations without large in-house departments often hire outside consultants to manage construction projects. This is especially true of owners who only occasionally take on large projects. The trend toward using consultants reflects the high cost of keeping facility managers on staff as well as the increased sophistication of the building process. For the owner, the key to success with an outside manager is spending time early in the project outlining organizational goals so that the consultant can fully represent these interests.

A building committee is another form of owner representation. Consisting of users, financial backers, and sometimes community residents, building committees reflect the prominent place of the design and building process in the business of some organizations. User representation is especially important because, as technology and production processes become more sophisticated, the link between the new facility and its use becomes more critical.

In all cases, whether represented by a facility manager, an outside consultant, or an ad hoc organization formed for the duration of the project, owners are primarily concerned about their needs and their money. This concern is translated into a scope of work and a budget, which, together with a timeline, become the guideposts of the project. Sophisticated owners understand from the onset why they are building and are very clear about their objectives when communicating to the project team. Owners who are not as familiar with the building process will sometimes be less clear about their motivations and may not fully understand them. Mixed motivations not clearly communicated can interfere with the design process and may cost the owner time and money.

Owners represent a specific interest during the project's life. While designers focus on functionality, aesthetics, and innovative use of materials, owners are additionally concerned about the durability of the design, storage and availability of materials, simplicity of operation, and ease of maintenance. While constructors are concerned with maintaining the schedule and budget through efficient methods of assembly and improved management techniques, owners are additionally concerned about a turnover process that ensures complete understanding of all systems in the project and a smooth startup transition. This focus can put them at odds with the other members of the project team, who are very narrowly focused on design and construction issues. In the best of teams, these diverging interests forge a creative tension that encourages all members of the team to incorporate the interests of the others as their own.

DESIGN PROFESSIONALS

Architects and engineers are the principal designers of construction projects. On most building and residential sector projects, the architect is the lead designer, laying out the concept on paper with the owner. The engineer is usually brought in after the basic concept is worked out but before the details are developed. The engineer designs the building systems: structures as well as mechanical, electrical, and plumbing systems. On infrastructure and industrial projects, the lead designer is usually an engineer; the architect is brought in to work on the aesthetics. For example, on a refinery project, the engineer designs the mechanical, electrical, and structural systems, while the architect handles the office spaces and building color schemes.

Each professional contributes to projects in different ways. When architects are given a design challenge, they respond by first identifying the important elements of the design. For some architects the physical context is the guiding feature, others are guided by the activities that will occur in the building, and still others focus on creating a unique image. Very good architecture responds to all three aspects (see Figure 2.3). The process is intuitive and subjective. Architects become known for the personal

FIGURE 2.3   Like many designers, Frank Gehry has developed a distinct architectural style that has become his trademark. The Nationale-Neverlander building, affectionately known as Fred and Ginger, links two historic buildings in Prague. The curved facade that helps the building turn the corner and the undulating window projections are stylistic expressions on recent Gehry buildings

Source: Courtesy of Frank O. Gehry & Associates, Santa Monica, Calif.

styles they develop over the course of their careers. Some architects tie their work to historic styles; others are more modern in their expression. They are hired to express those particular responses.

An engineer's approach to design is different from an architect's. Engineers tackle a challenge objectively, breaking it down into identifiable components and a series of questions to be answered. When engineers are the lead designers, the functional aspects of the work take center stage (see Figure 2.4). For instance, in the English Channel Tunnel Crossing (Chunnel) project, image was less important than the safe, efficient boring of many miles of tunnel, the removal of spoil, and the insertion of the tunnel liner.

Whether an architect or an engineer is the lead designer depends on the nature of the project. Architects tend to lead commercial building and residential sector projects. Engineers lead heavy engineering and some industrial sector projects. Architects and engineers may coexist within single companies called architectural engineering firms (A/Es). Both professions emphasize creativity, but whereas an architect may be asked to capture a corporation's image within the form of a new headquarters building that

FIGURE 2.4   Although engineers, like architects, develop identifiable styles, they must balance image with function

Source: Photo by Margot Balboni, Geoscapes.

provides convenient access for vehicles and a welcoming entrance for pedestrians, an engineer may be asked to replace and widen an existing five-mile interstate highway through a dense urban environment without adversely affecting the city's operations. Both designers must think mechanically, technically, and creatively, but the architect works in the artistic realm to solve a specific set of problems, while the engineer works in the technical realm.

Architects

Architects are the stars of the building industry, and many famous ones easily come to mind: Frank Lloyd Wright, Aalvar Alto, I. M. Pei. The profession has a certain mystique about it—romantic, artistic, and not entirely understood by people outside the field. Architects are the industry's image makers (see Figure 2.5). Traditionally, they have also been the primary representatives of owners' interests. Because owners usually hire architects first, they are the first people to hear the owners talk about their needs, and they are the ones who meet with the occupants and help define the budget and the schedule. Often they influence the choice of contractor and delivery method and act as an owner's representative throughout the construction phase of the job.

FIGURE 2.5 The Guggenheim Museum in Bilbao, Spain, designed by Frank O. Gehry & Associates, is an architectural masterpiece. It has created a tourist trade in this industrial city, with people coming from far away to view this beautiful building

Source: Courtesy of Frank O. Gehry & Associates, Santa Monica, Calif.

An architect's responsibilities are to translate and develop an owner's requirements and graphically represent them so that the contractor can accurately price, schedule, and implement the design. That responsibility is complex. In addition to understanding the requirements of the owner, the architect must have enough skill and expertise to choose appropriate systems and materials and the talent to formulate a design that is mathematically proportioned and aesthetically pleasing.

Architects today learn their profession in four- or five-year college programs and apprentice under a licensed practitioner for a certain number of years before they are eligible to take an exam allowing them to practice independently. The exam is intended to test an architect's abilities in a wide range of building-related topics. The field offers many opportunities. Architects can choose to practice as part of a large firm, a smaller partnership, or independently. They can specialize in one building type—for example, residences, health care facilities, universities, sports and recreation facilities, or museums. The list is extensive. In addition to practicing architecture, licensed architects have other alternatives, working in allied fields such as owners' organizations, government agencies, teaching professions, marketing, and sales.

Architects are usually the principal designers on building projects, but many other professionals contribute to their work, including specification writers, computer-aided design (CAD) operators, interior designers, and landscape architects. These specialized professions developed as the tasks facing architects became more complex. Sometimes, especially in larger companies, these professionals are employed full time by architectural firms. In other cases, they work independently and are brought in as consultants as needed. In addition, these professionals can have their own independent practices and can be brought in by clients to work directly as a principal consultant. Here are some examples:

- *Drafters/CAD operators.*   Until recently, drafting was done exclusively at drafting boards with mechanical tools of varying sophistication and using technical pens and pencils. Today, many companies use CAD software packages exclusively, and all drafting is done in front of a computer screen. Once drafters were junior architects paying their dues at the drafting table, but the complexity and changing technologies of the CAD systems have bred a new profession of people who produce construction documents in support of the architect's work. This profession has also become increasingly independent of architects. As communication among constructors, specialty contractors, owners, suppliers, and architects has evolved, the need for CAD operators has also evolved. A person choosing CAD operation as a career will find many opportunities in a growing field.
- *Specification writers.*   Architects produce the drawings that explain in detail what the design should look like. As part of the complete contract set, a specification writer prepares a written document called the specifications. Done in conjunction with the drawings, this document lays out the level of performance requirements and quality expected on the project. It may spell out specific products and methods to be used. Specifiers are often trained as engineers or architects, although they may not be licensed. Key to success in this field are keeping up with the latest products and maintaining a data base of how products perform on projects over time. To accomplish these goals, a specifier must meet

with manufacturer representatives and use sources such as the Construction Specification Institute (CSI). He or she must also be able to write clearly and concisely, be organized and methodical about material, and have an extensive understanding of construction processes. In addition to supporting the work of architects, specification writers may be employed directly by engineers and manufacturers—for example, to write the specifications for a particular roofing system.

- *Interior designers.* On large projects, architects sometimes use the services of interior designers. These professionals work on a project's nonstructural interior spaces. While the architect lays out how the exterior elevations will work, where the core systems in the building will be located, and what primary materials will be used, the interior designer works out interior finishes: paint, window treatment, flooring, ceilings, furniture, and signs. Most interior designers are trained in a two- or four-year program that provides a certificate or degree. In addition to working with architects, they may have their own independent client base and specialize in a specific type of interior. For example, when a company leases space in an office building, it often hires an interior designer to lay out the space. Homeowners hire interior designers to specify materials and products. Hospitals and museums need specific products and spatial layouts. Thus, interior designers require expertise in space planning, acoustics, lighting, and telecommunications and must have a good understanding of the latest products on the market.

- *Landscape architects.* Architects consult with landscape architects when a project involves significant outdoor space or indoor planting areas. Large firms have landscape architects on staff, but many are outside consultants with their own practices. Landscape architects also work directly with owners, government agencies, and homeowners. Their work includes identification of plant species and location of trees and shrubs. They set grades; establish walkways, walls, and fences; and specify paving types. They also get involved with site design, pedestrian and vehicular circulation, park design, and conservation measures. A landscape architect is usually a degreed professional registered by the state.

Engineers

With 25 to 65 percent of construction costs going to engineered systems, engineers play an important role on projects (see Figure 2.6). Sometimes they work within large A/E firms, but most often they are independent consultants. Engineers' responsibility on projects is varied, depending on their discipline; but in all cases they must understand an owner's requirements: budget, operations, durability, and intended use of space. All of these factors contribute to how an engineer chooses structural support, air conditioning, level of lighting and power, and plumbing capacity. Engineering tasks include specifying large equipment such as air-handler units and electrical switchgear. They then lay out the necessary distribution (ductwork, electrical conduit, and piping systems) and specify and locate the termination devices—for example, radiation units, electrical outlets, and sink faucets. Because their work is detailed, communication within the design team is critical. Adjustments are ongoing in the design to accommodate the dimensional requirements of the building systems, and sometimes the work of the engineer can influence large shifts in the design approach.

FIGURE 2.6 An engineer is responsible for the design of a project's structural, electrical, mechanical, and civil components

Source: Photo by Margot Balboni, Geoscapes.

Engineers are regulated by professional licensing requirements that include a four- or five-year college program; a specific number of years of experience; the successful passing of two exams and Fundamentals of Engineering; and, after proper documented experience, the professional engineering exam. Although engineers have many career options, here are the most common ones:

- *Structural engineers* calculate strengths and deflections, foundation sizes, beam thickness, and strength of floor slabs. They ensure that a building can withstand the forces of wind, gravity, and seismic activity.
- *Mechanical engineers* design heating, cooling, water supply, and sanitary systems. They work with architects to make sure that enough room is provided for ducts and fans. They share information about equipment weight with structural engineers and power requirements with electrical engineers.
- *Electrical engineers* calculate the overall electrical load required; size equipment accordingly; and supply drawings that show power lines, motors, transformers, switchgear, and telecommunications. They determine the amount of lighting required for the owner's intended use and design lighting layouts to meet an architect's criteria.
- *Civil engineers* determine the location of a project on a site by studying the subsurface soil conditions and the topography of the land. They design roads, bridges, tunnels, parking lots, storm water drainage, and sewage treatment plants.
- *Surveyors* measure distances and elevations of land surfaces. They locate natural features such as hills, valleys, vegetation, rock outcroppings, and water bodies. They also measure built features such as curbs, paved areas, utilities, structures, and property boundaries. This information is used as the basis for any site development.

CONSTRUCTION PROFESSIONALS

Constructors

Constructor is the general term used to define the professional responsible for all construction activities, whether he or she works as a general contractor or a construction manager. Of the three major participants on the project team, the constructor has changed most in terms of type and training of personnel. In the past, company executives rose through the industry's ranks, often starting as carpenters or laborers. Today, company heads are graduates of business schools or people with experience in the real estate or development industries. Their knowledge of the details of construction is supported by the expertise of specialty subcontractors. This trend is also working its way into the field management of jobs. Many project managers have been trained in construction management programs, and superintendents may be recruited directly from civil engineering programs. Such professionalization of the management of construction has allowed the industry to broaden the scope of services it can offer to owners. Once constructors came on the job after the design was complete, but now they may be brought in before the architect to advise an owner. Where once their responsibility was confined to construction, they now work as part of a design/build team responsible for delivery of the entire project from concept to completion or as part of a build, operate, transfer (BOT) team that takes on short-term responsibility for operation of a facility as well as design and construction. These capabilities are only possible with people who have expertise in areas outside construction combined with a solid base of construction knowledge.

Like the other professions, construction offers many options. The traditional path is to become a construction manager for a large company or to strike out on your own and become a general contractor. Inside large companies, other distinct career paths have evolved to meet the specialized needs of complex projects. This evolution is similar to what has happened inside the architectural profession. People in these positions support the work of the construction manager but may also be hired directly by owners or architects for independent consulting. Here are some examples:

- *Estimators* are pivotal to any construction company; jobs are won and lost by their efforts. Estimators work with design drawings and prepare a complete list of all job costs. They need to understand the construction process; be detail-oriented and well organized; and have a thorough knowledge of costs for labor, materials, and equipment. Estimating is a computerized activity; some companies have their own specialized programs, while others purchase estimating packages off the shelf and then customize them with their own data. Estimators come under considerable pressure when bids are due on a project because they must ensure good coverage on all sub-bids. This coverage can win or lose a job. Although estimators may come from a variety of back-grounds and learn on the job, many start out as engineers, constructors, or designers. Large companies have in-house estimating departments with cus-tomized data bases that combine historic data and information from subcon-tractors and material suppliers. Consulting companies specialize in providing estimating data, which is either developed for a specific project or provided as an off-the-shelf item. These companies may work for owners, architects, engi-neers, or constructors.

- *Schedulers* work between the home office and the field office. Before construc-tion begins, they are usually based at the home office but often move to the field during construction. Schedulers need to have a thorough understanding of the construction process as well as the ability to define distinct construction activi-ties and understand the relationships among activities. Although schedulers need a strong background in construction, they often learn the actual skill on the job. A person with knowledge of pertinent computer software has an advan-tage. Successful schedulers monitor job progress, coordinate subcontractors, analyze changes and the impact of delays, and solve problems. Although large companies may have in-house schedulers, the task is often outsourced to consulting companies. Scheduling consultants may also be hired by owners to represent them in a dispute.

- *Purchasing agents* buy subcontracts once a job is won. A person in this position negotiates to get the best price while ensuring that all contract requirements are met. Typically, a purchasing agent meets with a subcontractor to review the conditions and scope of the job. Their conversation sometimes leads to a change in the bid price. To successfully negotiate with subcontractors, a pur-chasing agent must understand building materials, prices, and the construction process; have broad business sense; and be persuasive. Because the function is tightly aligned with a constructor's ability to make money on the job, it is usually an in-house task.

Construction personnel are trained in a variety of ways. In the past, most started out in the trades and worked their way into management positions by either starting their own companies or joining others who had. As projects became more complex and companies larger, schools responded by offering degreed programs in related fields—for example, building construction and construction management. Supporting organizations also grew up, such as the American Institute of Constructors (AIC) and the Construction Management Association of America (CMAA). There is a movement toward professional certification similar to the registration process for engineers and architects.

Specialty Contractors

Generally known as subcontractors, these specialty firms include mechanical, electrical, excavation, and demolition contractors. They are usually hired by and work directly for a general contractor. Specialty firms supply most of the material and labor on the job. Once general contractors directly hired carpenters, laborers, bricklayers, ironworkers, and painters. Superintendents, foremen, and lead workers were on the permanent payroll and would hire, lay off, and rehire tradespeople as needed. Only the mechanical and electrical trades were subcontracted. Today, general contracting is very different. Builders hire specialty subcontractors to do all the tradework. A builder will typically carry superintendents on the permanent payroll to oversee the work and a small group of carpenters and laborers to perform general conditions work. Instead of directly hiring the trades, however, they bid the work out to subcontractors who carry the trades on their own payroll. This reduces a builder's financial risk and allows work to be done more economically in today's specialized markets.

The Trades

From the time the first pencil is laid to paper in the design process to the completion of shop drawings and coordination drawings, the goal is to instruct the people who actually perform the work in the field: the tradespeople. The trades form the core of the construction industry—a constant throughout its history. The ways in which projects are managed have changed over the years; but despite improvements in methods and materials and the introduction of robotics, buildings are still erected piece by piece. What *has* changed is the makeup of the trades. The number of trades needed on the job has grown with the complexity of the buildings. Where once there were electricians, there are now also specialists in telecommunications and security. Where once there were plumbers, there are now also pipefitters and sprinkler contractors. Most construction processes require specialized training. On complex building sites, as many as 15 different trades may be working on a given day.

People in the trades have a great deal of specialized knowledge. Most are attracted to their fields because of an early interest or aptitude often identified in high school. To address this interest, vocational high schools offer alternatives to the traditional liberal arts-directed classes. At these trade schools, students focus on learning skills that can be applied right out of high school or used as a foundation for further training at the college level. However, there are other methods of gaining the skills needed to practice

BOX 2.1

A COMPARISON OF UNION AND MERIT SHOPS

At one time, to work in any given trade a person had to be part of the trade union. After many years of organizing and fighting for fair wages and benefits, trade unions became well established in the United States. By assuring workers of good wages, providing good benefits, and establishing methods of training and promotion, unions were able to produce good-quality workers. But to ensure that work was steady, the unions limited the number of people who entered them. Thus, when demand was high, the unions couldn't produce the number of skilled workers needed, and people who were unable to get into the unions built up resentment toward them. In addition, there were territorial disputes inside the unions. Carpenters fought with laborers over the erection of scaffolding, with ironworkers over the setting of precast concrete, and with sheetmetal workers over the installation of metal trim. Local unions fought between themselves over geographic territory. This infighting focused unions' energies inward and created mistrust toward them in the industry.

In that climate, merit (nonunion) shops gained a significant foothold. Merit shops are able to compete with the unions on the issue of costs. Whereas the makeup of the typical union crew is heavily weighted toward skilled labor, with relatively few apprentices, merit shops have almost the reverse profile. These merit shops pay high wages to a few lead people and use semiskilled labor for the bulk of the work. For many projects, this profile is adequate and more cost-effective. Because open shops do not have territorial disputes, they are able to keep people working more steadily by shifting them to where the work is needed.

In the short term open shops are attractive options for tradespeople. Work is plentiful; it is easy to get hired; and if you are young and physically able, piecework pay is available. The story is a bit different over the long term. To maintain a competitive price edge, open shops have created a pyramid in which most of the workers remain at a low-paying level. There is little incentive to train people; in fact, most training programs are task-specific.

Unions have justified their higher costs by the difference in training and therefore the assurance of better quality. But with better management of open shops, the difference in quality will become less of an issue. Unions, in turn, have made some concessions in wages, so they are increasingly able to compete with nonunion shops. The future of the unions relies on their ability to compete for larger and more complex projects, which by their nature require a more skilled and specialized work force. The future for the open shops relies on creating long-term opportunities for their work force.

a trade. Contractors offer training programs, unions have apprenticeship programs, and the military trains recruits in specific skills.

The opportunities in construction are almost unlimited. The U.S Department of Labor lists the following job categories for construction trades:

Boilermakers
Brickmason, blockmason, and stonemasons
Carpenters
Carpet, floor, and tile installers and finishers
Cement masons, concrete finishers, segmental pavers, and terrazzo workers
Construction and building inspectors
Construction equipment operators
Construction laborers
Drywall installers, ceiling tile installers, and tapers
Electricians
Elevator installers and repairers
Glaziers
Hazardous materials removal workers
Insulation workers
Painters and paperhangers
Pipelayers, plumbers, pipefitters, and steamfitters
Plasterers and stucco masons
Roofers
Sheetmetal workers
Structural and reinforcing iron and metal workers

The following are descriptions of some of these trades:

- *Construction equipment operators* use machinery to move construction materials, earth, and other heavy materials at construction sites. From backhoes to bulldozers to tower cranes, the skills needed to run this equipment are learned over many years of experience. This is a highly skilled job that is becoming more complex as computers and Global Positioning System (GPS) technology become integrated in its processes. Equipment operators also take care of their equipment for maintenance and repair.
- *Ironworkers* put together the steel skeleton of a building or a bridge over a foundation. They also install metal decking and steel reinforcing bars in concrete slabs and assemble grills, canopies, stairways, and ladders. The job may involve climbing as well as welding.
- *Cement masons* pour concrete; lay concrete slabs, reinforcing walls, steps, and paving; and apply leveling and finishing techniques. They must have a good understanding of the properties of concrete and how temperature and humidity can affect the final product.
- *Sheetmetal workers* fabricate and install ducts for heating, ventilating, and air conditioning. They must be able to follow instructions from shop drawings. Much of their fabrication work is done at the shop rather than the site.
- *Plasterers* fireproof steel beams and finish ceilings and walls using plastering material on the interior and stucco material on the exterior.

- *Plumbers and pipefitters* install all types of piping systems, including water, gas, steam, processed chilled water, and sprinkler lines. This trade depends on a licensing process. The work involves welding, work on high-pressure systems, and the use of a variety of tools.
- *Electricians* assemble and wire the systems needed to provide electricity for heating, lighting, power, and air conditioning. They also install the conduit for running wires and hookup equipment. They must be licensed because high-quality work is critical to a safe environment.
- *Bricklayers* build walls, chimneys, and pavement using unit masonry such as bricks or concrete blocks. The process is basic but requires careful, accurate work to function and look right.
- *Glaziers* install all types of glass, whether on storefronts, in windows, or as display cases. The work involves sizing, cutting, fitting, and sealing the glass.
- *Roofers* weatherproof roofs using a variety of materials, including tar and gravel, rubber, PVC, asphalt shingles, clay tile, and slate. Most of this work is performed high off the ground.
- *Carpenters* make up the form work for concrete pours, install metal and wood studs for walls, apply gypsum sheathing for walls and ceilings, install hung ceilings, hang doors, apply trim, install hardware, make up wood cabinetry and shelving, and install landscape office furniture. This work requires precision and the ability to work with a variety of hand and power tools.

To practice a craft is to create a legacy for generations to come. Manipulating materials, assembling parts, creatively using knowledge and skills to create better conditions for people—these are all part of practicing a craft. At the end of the work day, an observer can see how those hours were spent. At the end of the job, there is something new left behind for others to enjoy and use for many years, sometimes for generations. Few jobs offer such a tangible measure of success.

Material Suppliers

A project may have talented designers, innovative constructors, and wealthy, sophisticated owners; but without materials to build with, the project would be only a dream. Materials and building components are manufactured, fabricated, and installed by suppliers. A user's choice of materials is based in part on performance, durability, and aesthetic appeal. But without the help of suppliers and their trade associations, architects and engineers would be daunted by which materials to specify, constructors by which methods of material assembly to use.

To promote their industry and provide information about material characteristics, suppliers have formed trade associations that establish a level of quality for each product and standardize certain characteristics (for example, dimensions). The American Plywood Association is a trade association, as are the American Concrete Institute and the National Electrical Manufacturers Association. Manufacturers of materials that fall within their categories support these groups. Through research, the associations develop criteria that members then agree to use. To ensure that the criteria have been followed, the associations provide oversight methods, using seals or some other mark as a stamp of approval. Although they have no regulatory function, trade association standards are often adopted by other groups, such as the American

TABLE 21
Recommended Uniform Roof Live Loads for APA RATED SHEATHING(c) and APA RATED STURD-I-FLOOR
With Long Dimension Perpendicular to Supports(e)

Panel Span Rating	Minimum Panel Thickness (in.)	Maximum Span (in.)		Allowable Live Loads (psf)(d)							
		With Edge Support(a)	Without Edge Support	Spacing of Supports Center-to-Center (in.)							
				12	16	20	24	32	40	48	60
APA RATED SHEATHING(c)											
12/0	5/16	12	12	30							
16/0	5/16	16	16	70	30						
20/0	5/16	20	20	120	50	30					
24/0	3/8	24	20(b)	190	100	60	30				
24/16	7/16	24	24	190	100	65	40				
32/16	15/32	32	28	325	180	120	70	30			
40/20	19/32	40	32	—	305	205	130	60	30		
48/24	23/32	48	36	—	—	280	175	95	45	35	
60/32	7/8	60	48	—	—	—	305	165	100	70	35
APA RATED STURD-I-FLOOR(f)											
16 oc	19/32	24	24	185	100	65	40				
20 oc	19/32	32	32	270	150	100	60	30			
24 oc	23/32	48	36	—	240	160	100	50	30		
32 oc	7/8	48	40	—	—	295	185	100	60	40	
48 oc	1-3/32	60	48	—	—	—	290	160	100	65	40

(a) Tongue-and-groove edges, panel edge clips (one midway between each support, except two equally spaced between supports 48 inches on center), lumber blocking, or other. For low slope roofs, see Table 22.

(b) 24 inches for 15/32-inch and 1/2-inch panels.

(c) Includes APA RATED SHEATHING/CEILING DECK.

(d) 10 psf dead load assumed.

(e) Applies to panels 24 inches or wider applied over two or more spans.

(f) Also applies to C-C Plugged grade plywood.

Note: Shaded support spacings meet Code Plus recommendations.

FIGURE 2.7 Manufacturers' associations establish criteria for the proper use of their products. These standards are often included in a project's specifications

Source: Courtesy of the Engineered Wood Association.

National Standards Institute (ANSI). These standards, in turn, often are incorporated into architectural specifications, government regulations, and building codes (see Figure 2.7).

Equipment Suppliers

Depending on the project, equipment can play a very big role in construction. Highway jobs, large excavations, bridges, tunnels, and tall buildings all rely heavily on the use of equipment to carry out the work (see Figure 2.8). The people who supply this equipment offer it for sale or rent. Rental arrangements can vary on points concerning who maintains the equipment and whether it comes with an operator. Construction companies decide to buy or rent based solely on economics and whether there will be a later use for the equipment. Small hand tools, portable generators, huge tower cranes, excavators, backhoes, and scaffolding are all examples of equipment used on construction projects. A major difference between equipment and material is that the equipment does not become part of the project at the end.

Equipment types break down into six loose categories:

- Earthmoving excavators, loaders, and trenching machines
- Lifting—cranes, aerial lifts, and boom trucks
- Light equipment—breakers, saws, generators, pumps, compressors
- Bituminous machinery—cold planers, asphalt pavers, rollers, and soil stabilizers
- Concrete and aggregate—crushers, screens, feeders, conveyers, rock drills, mixers, pavers
- Components and attachments—buckets, blades, demolition tools, hydraulic and electric components

FIGURE 2.8   Equipment suppliers are an important part of the construction industry

Source: Photo by Margot Balboni, Geoscapes.

OTHER PARTICIPANTS

Behind all the people who interact directly with the construction is a host of others who are involved. Before a project even starts, many issues must be resolved. Financing is certainly one of the biggest. Where the money comes from, how the funding is set up, and the terms and conditions of the funding all play a direct role in how the project will be managed. Many financial institutions are involved in funding construction companies, and some of the funding may come from government agencies as well. Certain public agencies are interested in the project from a regulatory perspective. They have the authority to rule on the conditions of building and can deny the right to build if the project is deemed not in the public interest. These agencies include zoning boards, planning boards, historical commissions, and building code officials—all locally administered and controlled.

The project also must be insured. Insurance comes from many sources. Some companies provide property insurance to the owner, liability insurance to the designer, and bonding insurance to the constructor. Insurance issues will be discussed in detail later in the book.

When contracts are being prepared, companies often consult with lawyers before agreeing to any conditions. Lawyers advise their clients on ways to minimize liability, risk, and dispute resolution and help their clients negotiate these issues through contract language. When disputes emerge that cannot be solved by the project team members, the lawyers will often get involved again to interpret contract language and offer suggestions for resolving the conflict.

ORGANIZATION OF COMPANIES

The roles of design and construction firms are certainly different; but because both participants are project-based, they have some similarities in the ways in which they are organized. Both types of companies are internally organized to support technical people such as marketing managers, accountants, information systems, technical support, and human resource personnel. For instance, a marketing manager's position would be described in a similar way in both companies, varying only in details. A marketing manager's principal job is to generate business, establishing the proper mix of work among the company's different specialties. He or she must understand the language and processes of the design and construction industry, translating technical language into lay terms. The position requires research, advertising, public relations, and client service. The person in this position is usually part of the upper management team that understands and contributes to the strategic business plan.

At the project level, the profile of company roles varies to some degree. Both design and construction companies hire outside help to complete a good portion of the work: for designers, this means consultants; for contractors, this means subcontractors or specialty contractors. To manage both in-house resources and outsourced specialties, each firm (depending on size and discipline) organizes its project teams a little differently.

Here are some common staff positions in design companies:

- *Project manager.* As soon as the company agrees with an owner to perform the work, a project manager is formally assigned to the project. The project manager was probably introduced to the owner during the interviewing process, and in most cases the project is awarded with the understanding that this person will be assigned to the project. The project manager is the owner's primary contact, responsible for scheduling in-house work and identifying necessary staffing levels for both in-house personnel and outside consultants. He or she also helps the owner get bids from contractors and negotiate the construction contract. Sometimes the project manager is also the principal designer—the person with the ideas and the vision for turning the client's requirements into reality.
- *Clerk of the works.* This person is usually an architect or an engineer employed by the designer to enforce the terms of the contract and to interpret the plans and specs. He or she may assist with problem solving, approve of or reject materials, approve or disapprove of methods and quality, and review contractor payment requisitions.
- *Job captain.* This person organizes the drawings required to complete the job, manages the personnel resources, communicates with the engineers and other consultants, and details the schematic designs.

In construction companies, project-related positions might be located in the field. Therefore, people in these positions must be able to make decisions independent of upper management. Here are common positions:

- *Construction project manager.*   Similar to the design firm's project manager, this is the first person assigned to a project. The primary responsibility of the construction project manager is to configure the project team, schedule the job, and set up a cost-control system. If there are changes on the job, this person negotiates the costs with the various parties. The position requires many years of experience and a solid knowledge of project administration, good verbal and written communication skills, knowledge of labor union issues, and technical construction knowledge. People filling the position have often graduated from a construction management program, served in other positions in the home office, and worked under the guidance of more senior project managers.
- *Superintendent.*   Superintendents on the job site interact with the specialty subcontractors, coordinating the flow of workers, supplies, and equipment to ensure that the schedule is met. They also prioritize work and negotiate disputes between trades. Because of their relationship with the subcontractors, superintendents are usually the first to know about problems on the job and are often in the best position to offer solutions. Traditionally, people in this position were from the trades themselves, working their way up to a management position. Recently, however, superintendents have been hired out of college engineering or construction management programs.
- *Field engineer.*   A field engineer is usually a young construction engineer who has graduated from a four-year college program and takes this entry-level position on the track to becoming a project manager. The person is typically assigned to handle the various documents that flow through a field office. He or she may also follow up on owner requests and communicate with tenants. An important function in the field, the job offers an overview of how a project is administered and constructed.

Conclusion

The people in construction cover a wide range of skills and experience. From apprentice carpenters to company executives, the one thing that they share is their passion for the built environment. The building industry is tough: risks are high, working conditions are often harsh, conflicts arise because of financial pressures, and safety is always a concern. Interactions among the people on the job can determine whether the project succeeds or fails. Thus, it is important to understand who these people are and what their motivations will be when they come to the job.

The industry is changing. No longer are the roles of individuals distinct and understood by all participants. Because of the sophistication of some modern projects, owners' desire to minimize risk, and the professionalization of the construction industry, these roles are shifting and merging. Owners can have large in-house design and construction groups. Designers and constructors can come together to offer services under one company heading. Both can act as representatives of the owner. Chapter 4 examines some of these relationships and how they are configured through formal delivery methods and contract arrangements.

Suggested Reading

AIA Press. *The Architects Handbook of Professional Practice*. Washington, D.C.: AIA Press, 1994.

Erlich, Mark. *With Our Hands: The Story of Carpenters in Massachusetts*. Philadelphia: Temple University Press, 1986.

Olin, Harold B. *Construction Principles, Material and Methods*. Chicago: Institute of Financial Education, 1983.

Rice, Peter. *An Engineer Imagines*. London: Ellipse, 1994.

Chapter Review Questions

1. A private sector owner has more flexibility in designer and builder selection and choice of delivery method than does a public owner. True or false?
2. Both public and private sector owners hire architects first; the architects are responsible for hiring appropriate engineers. True or false?
3. Although a designer's and a constructor's responsibilities on a project differ, the financial, marketing, and personnel functions of their home offices are relatively similar. True or false?
4. Which project participant is responsible for establishing the project objectives?
   a. The owner
   b. The architect
   c. The engineer
   d. The constructor
   e. All of the above
5. A constructor may be brought into a project before the designer to provide early estimating, scheduling, and project control support. True or false?
6. Who is responsible for contracting for subcontractor services on a project?
   a. The field engineer
   b. The estimator
   c. The superintendent
   d. The purchasing agent
   e. All of the above
7. Who is responsible for the correct positioning of a building on a site?
   a. The structural engineer
   b. The surveyor
   c. The civil engineer
   d. The constructor
   e. None of the above
8. Which project participant is responsible for the physical construction of the project?
   a. The architect
   b. The engineer
   c. The constructor
   d. The construction trades
   e. None of the above
9. Through their respective trade associations, material suppliers often provide standards that may be incorporated into a project's technical specifications. True or false?
10. Which of the following professions does not require state registration?
    a. Architecture
    b. Construction
    c. Engineering
    d. Surveying
    e. All of the above

Exercises

1. Identify a new project that has been constructed in your area. Who was the lead design firm? Identify the subconsultants/designers hired by this firm. Identify the training and/or registration of the key designers that were used on the project.
2. Identify the local professional architectural, engineering, and construction chapters that exist in your area. Contact one of these societies, get copies of their publications, invite a guest speaker to your class, and/or attend a meeting.
3. Visit a job site and identify the trades that are presently working there. Write up a description of work for each trade. Is the job union or nonunion?

CHAPTER

3

ORGANIZING AND LEADING THE CONSTRUCTION PROJECT

Chapter Outline

Student Learning Objectives

In this chapter you will learn the following:

1. The three basic models for organizing project teams
2. The importance and methodology for continuous quality improvement
3. The three forms of business ownership
4. The characteristics of an effective leader

INTRODUCTION

The construction industry, like most industries, needs leaders. The construction projects of today are completed at such a quick speed that people and organizations are in a continuous state of flux. The industry desperately needs people who can make solid decisions with imperfect knowledge, without precedent, and without well-defined operational procedures. Today's successful project manager establishes a clear vision for the project, communicates that vision, and continually reinforces it throughout the project's life. Dialogue and discussion are nice, but timely decisions are a necessity.

Leading a significant construction project can be compared to going into battle. The project manager must exude confidence and command the respect of all members of the project team. Allegiance to the project—not the home office—is imperative. Frank Moolin, who was the project manager of the Trans-Alaska Pipeline System project, advocated the hiring of what he called the *managerial elite*. Moolin defines the managerial elite as follows:

Basically, I define a "Managerial Elite" as "a small," 5 to 20 person team, put together in a "salt-and-pepper" organization, composed of the best possible talent that exists, highly paid, highly motivated by dollar incentives that relate to the cost and schedule performance of the project, that are organized in a highly compact and unstructured team reporting directly to the owner, that will lead, plan, motivate and direct others, make the basic decisions essential to the project, and take ultimate responsibility for the bottom-line performance of the project.

A big difference exists between corporate management and project organization and management. "Projects," Moolin states, "are in business to go out of business; corporations are in business to perpetuate themselves. . . . Large numbers of people are involved in projects for very short and intense periods of time. . . . Frequent and often brutal organizational changes are essential to the success of giant projects." Through all of Moolin's comments runs the unifying idea of the overwhelming and overbearing emphasis on time—the short, intense, activity-filled, hectic time in which one has to complete a project. Dedication to the project—and only to the project—is mandatory to its successful and timely completion.

Due to the time, cost, and organizational pressures a project manager faces, his or her looks, stature, and personality may be just as important as his or her understanding of theoretical managerial principles. As Bill Parcells said in his book *Finding a Way to Win:*

There's a big difference between *leading* and *managing*. You can manage inventories, but you lead people. You can manage from afar, with a fax machine and a cellular phone, but you better be up close and personal when it comes to leading.

The construction industry is the single largest employer in the United States. It is an industry that is fragmented with a large number of small firms, that is, firms with fewer than 10 employees. The industry is challenged by fluctuating demand for its products, a continuously changing technology, and a custom-built nature that makes mass production difficult. Because entry is relatively easy in that it requires a fairly low level of investment, many firms are created and led by managers without adequate managerial or leadership skills. This helps explain the high level of industry failures, most often due to managerial inexperience or incompetence. To survive and prosper, construction companies need well-thought-out policies and procedures, training, work coordination, and communication. Project managers must provide aggressive management, discipline, and motivation to the project team.

This chapter discusses the managerial and leadership skills important to today's professional constructor. Employees, materials, and equipment must all be organized, supervised, and brought to bear on the project in a timely and cost-efficient manner. Project managers need the integrity, vision, and confidence to direct and lead their project teams through the entire design/build process.

ORGANIZING AND MANAGING

Before projects can be effectively led they need to be effectively organized. Although leadership and management are certainly interrelated, the field of management sciences focuses on the scientific study of decision making. As a science it is progressively moving away from guesswork to the establishment of set methodologies for making intelligent decisions. Creating policies, planning, organizing, and the committing of resources are all aspects of management. Good management systems help good leaders become even better.

Levels of Specialization and Authority

First and foremost, the construction process must be correctly compartmentalized to allow people to specialize in their specific areas of expertise. The more specialized the function, the fewer issues a specific worker has to pay attention to. By dividing work more narrowly, workers should be able to produce a better product at a faster rate. Narrow compartmentalization is not a panacea, however, because too many specialists creates a cumbersome organization, slowing down communication and decision making. The challenge is to establish the appropriate level of specialization.

Closely related to compartmentalization is providing the correct level of authority to the members of the project team. Authority can be defined as decision-making power, or position power. It is the power to exact obedience, which comes with the position established by the organizational structure. Position power should be discriminated from personal power, which is based on an individual's intelligence, résumé, or charisma. The natural corollary of authority is responsibility. Responsibility is the reward or the penalty that comes with the authority. In establishing an organizational structure for a project, managers should strive to match authority with responsibility within their project teams. Being held responsible for work that one does not have the authority to accomplish is a real demotivator.

Every employee should have only one direct supervisor. Multiple bosses wreak havoc on an organization as workers become confused about who their "true" boss is. This situation undermines the authority of the real boss (if there is one) and creates confusion and animosity throughout the organization. Organizations need to be careful to establish clear lines of authority at all times.

Decision Making

Organizations should also strive for the proper balance between centralized and decentralized operations. Small firms are naturally centralized because all decisions come from the president, but as firms grow all decisions can no longer effectively be made at the top. Some decisions need to be shifted elsewhere in the organization. Which decisions get shifted and to whom is a critical management issue. Firms that tend toward decentralization shift more decisions to the field, whereas centralized firms retain the bulk of the decision-making power at the home office. Each strategy has its advantages.

Decentralized firms tend to be more nimble because decisions can be made faster and control systems can be set up that are particular to the project. These firms have a flatter organizational structure and are less bureaucratic. "Take-charge" managers relish this type of structure because they become their own boss and do things their own way.

Centralized firms allow the support activities that are common to every project to be standardized. This creates an increased economy of scale and allows people with specialized skills to be brought into the organization. Centralized organizations tend to run projects in a more methodical and consistent manner because more decisions are elevated to the same people. People tend to get good at what they do when they repeatedly do the same thing.

The ultimate goal of every organization is to fully utilize the skills and creativity of its people. Organizations should not get locked into either one philosophy or the other, but should continue to evaluate their people and establish the appropriate system of control to support their leadership style. If a manager possesses the intelligence and experience to manage a wide range of activities and consistently make good decisions, then the decision may be to move that manager into a more decentralized situation. Conversely, if the field manager values and seeks the opinions and experience of the home office, then that manager may need a more centralized structure. Likewise, if the organization possesses a particularly talented estimating, scheduling, or software team, then these skills should be used for each project. Talented people are one of the most valuable resources that a company possesses and utilizing this resource effectively will provide the company with a competitive edge.

Organizational Structure

As construction projects move through the phases of design and construction, the tasks and people involved change. For that reason, the organizational structure may also need to evolve to reflect these changes. When most projects begin they require a strong centralized structure, often with continual guidance from the company's upper management. Client relations are being established; the team is being identified; the work plan is being developed. These tasks require the contribution of a wide sector of the company. However, once the project moves into construction and the field office is set up, the focus narrows to construction activities. At this point, a shift to a more decentralized project management style is more effective. Decisions need to be made quickly; the team is acting and reacting to a set of circumstances that can change on a daily basis. Waiting for guidance from the home office would slow down decisions and could cause a failure on the job because of this slow turnaround.

Work Breakdown Structure

The process of establishing the most effective organizational structure for a project begins with a complete analysis of the scope of work and a subsequent organization of that work into the Work Breakdown Structure (WBS). WBS is a deliverable grouping of work elements that subdivides the work of the project into manageable parts. These parts or activities have some common characteristics.

- They can be readily understood by project participants
- They are unique units of work
- They are the responsibility of an individual
- Time durations, costs, and resources can be assigned
- Progress against them for time and cost can be measured
- Flexibility is built in so that changes are easily incorporated

The WBS defines the project's contractual elements as well as the tasks and subtasks and their interdependencies. Labor, material, equipment, and other resource allocations are identified along with a clear understanding of the schedule and cost estimates. It is a critical tool for organizing work, building realistic schedules and costs, and setting up mechanisms for controlling and tracking the progress of the project. It establishes the contract, task, and time constraints for the project, that leads to the design of the organizational structure.

Workflow

As mentioned earlier, specialized tasks that are common to all projects are most efficiently handled if they are centralized by positioning these people together and pooling resources. This streamlines these tasks, allowing standardized procedures to be developed that ultimately allow this work to be done quite efficiently. Other tasks need to be done in an interdisciplinary fashion, face-to-face or on the telephone. These types of reciprocal actions may require the establishment of a committee or task force. Other actions need to be handled sequentially as defined in the CPM schedule (see Figure 3.1). The organization design should become clear as a result of the above analysis because organizational positions follow the manner in which the workflow needs to occur. The design establishes project teams as well as the physical location of the people. Form should follow function. The above analysis leads to a "bubble diagram" (see Figure 3.2).

Allocation of Authority and Responsibility

The next step involves the allocation of authority and responsibility. In this step the line of authority is established from the president to the lowest supervisor. This is defined as the *chain of command* and is the formal route by which orders and directives are issued. Care should be taken so that each worker has one and only one supervisor. As people are assigned to positions with varying levels of responsibility, consider the following:

1. Does the worker have the managerial and technical skill set to add supervisory value?
2. How many people, if any, will this person be supervising?
3. Does the organization benefit by creating this hierarchical level?

Each hierarchical level created should add value since it provides an additional decision-making level in the organization. Each additional level makes the organization more centralized, while providing additional levels of formal review. More levels,

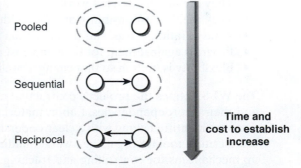

FIGURE 3.1 Organization design begins with an understanding of the working relationships necessary to complete the project

Pooled

Sequential

Reciprocal

Time and cost to establish increase

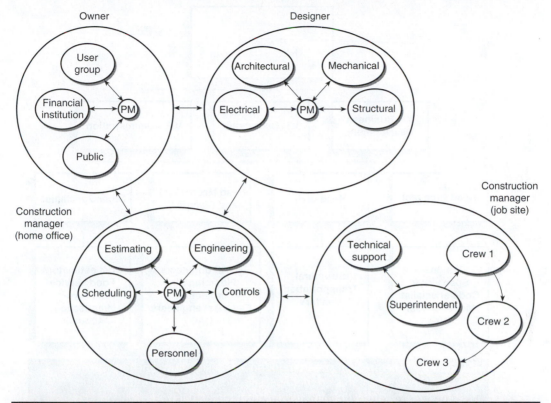

FIGURE 3.2 In a construction management (CM) delivery method, the owner, designer, and construction manager work in a reciprocal manner throughout the design stage. As construction begins, the CM superintendent directs the work of the trade contractors who operate sequentially

however, slow decisions and provide additional separation between the top decision maker and the core business (see Figure 3.3).

Organization Chart

The result of the allocation of authority and responsibility is the establishment of an organizational chart that will fall into one of the basic forms: generalist, departmental, or matrix.

The generalist organization is the most basic organizational structure (see Figure 3.4). It represents both line authority (represented by the vertical line) and staff authority (represented by the horizontal line). Line authority means giving orders "down the line" about production. Line supervisors direct, supervise, and evaluate the work of their subordinates. Staff authority means advising or assisting those with line authority. A person in a staff position, in contrast to a line position, does not directly supervise staff. He or she provides advice, conducts studies, and provides the information necessary to allow line supervisors to make better decisions. Note that the ultimate authority for the project resides with the principal, who has a line relationship with the technical

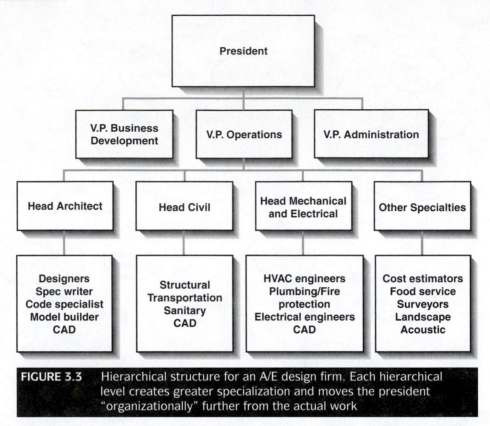

FIGURE 3.3 Hierarchical structure for an A/E design firm. Each hierarchical level creates greater specialization and moves the president "organizationally" further from the actual work

staff. The technical staff is the operational arm of the organization—where the physical work is accomplished. The support staff members have a staff authority relationship with the principal.

Span of Control

A concern of every organization is the number of people that any one manager has control over. This is called *span of control* (see Figure 3.5). Narrowing one's span of control creates additional organizational hierarchy. A narrower span of control provides more supervision and control, but also tends to create more departmentalization (specialization). Such specialization can be formalized in a departmental organization (see Figure 3.6). Here each unit focuses on a specific technical or production area, grouping people by discipline, expertise, and technical training and thereby promoting technical teamwork.

Matrix

When interdisciplinary teams are needed, for instance, for a major project, the departmental structure is not sufficient. Communication among the involved departments must be sound and relatively swift. Links (sometimes called *planks* or *gangplanks*)

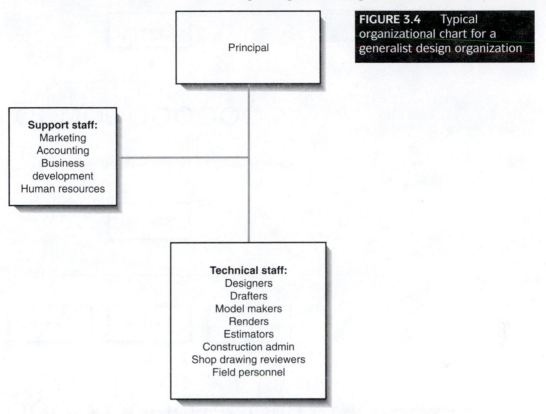

FIGURE 3.4   Typical organizational chart for a generalist design organization

must be made between the working levels of the involved departments (see Figure 3.7).

When these links are required for extended periods such as in a major project, they need to be formalized and directed by a project manager. This leads to what is called a *matrix* organizational structure (see Figure 3.8). In a matrix-type organization, the project manager takes responsibility for the budget, schedule, day-to-day coordination, and reporting on the project's status to the client and organization principals. The matrix organizational structure allows project teams to communicate effectively. Without this overlaying structure, all formal communications would have to go through the respective supervisors.

Formal lines of authority and communication (information) move along the organizational lines, vertically in both the generalist and departmental organization. The exception is the matrix organization, which appears to violate the "one-boss" tenet. For a matrix organization to work, clear rules of authority and a respectful relationship need to be established between the functional head and the project manager.

The line of authority just discussed forms the basis of control and communication for the organization and should be honored to the best of the organization's ability. At times, however, urgent decisions will need to be made and it might be impossible

FIGURE 3.5   Span of control

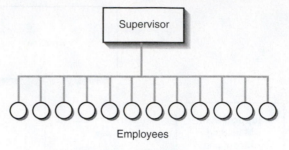

(a) *Wide* span of control—12 employees to supervise.

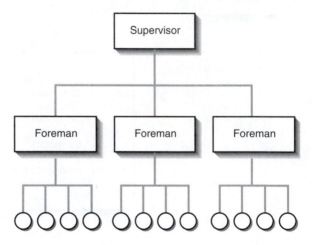

(b) *Narrow* span of control, as now the supervisor oversees only three people and each foreman oversees four people.

(due to time constraints, illness, vacation, and so on) to reach the appropriate supervisor. In this case, the worker needs to have the confidence and the knowledge to make the decision in accordance with the organization's philosophy. This internalization of the company's goals and objectives comes with organizations run by effective leaders.

Quality Management

One factor that is contributing to the success of organizations and their need to sometimes span across traditional corporate boundaries is the evolution of internal quality management. Internal quality management breaks down barriers among organizations because customer satisfaction is the focus of work and the measure of success. The idea has taken serious hold in the United States during the past 20 years.

To address both the opportunity to work globally and owners' concerns about quality assurance, many companies are incorporating re-engineering, Total Quality Management (TQM), and business process improvement (BPI) methods into their

Departmental organization

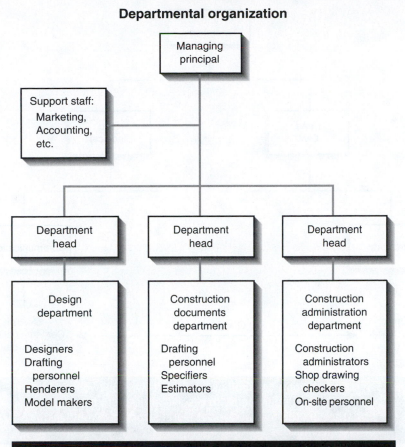

FIGURE 3.6   A design organization with the operational arm
divided into three departments

business environments. They use standards such as ISO 9000 to ensure customers worldwide that quality will be consistently high. Although each approach assumes a slightly different perspective about how to adapt a work environment for quality services and products, the goal is the same: to deliver consistent high quality to the client at a reasonable profit.

All of the methods focus on business processes versus tasks. This focus puts the process itself on center stage and redefines the role of the worker. It assumes a high level of involvement from upper management and participation by everyone in the organization. The fulfillment of client needs defines success, and the client's voice is included in all organization decisions. All of these systems assume a feedback loop, either through internal methods or through customer surveys. When a company changes its focus in this way, methods of reward within the company change. Measurement of performance is weighed against the whole process, not the assigned task.

Although many of these systems were developed originally for product-oriented organizations, they have been successfully applied to construction. In some construction

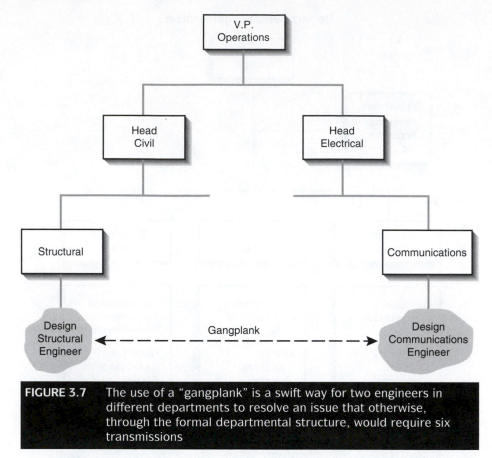

FIGURE 3.7 The use of a "gangplank" is a swift way for two engineers in different departments to resolve an issue that otherwise, through the formal departmental structure, would require six transmissions

companies, bonuses, for instance, are given at the end of a project after feedback is solicited from the customer. The bonuses are given to the team in equal proportions without preference to one individual. This encourages people to look out for each other and focuses attention on successful completion of the whole job, not just one isolated task.

Many rewards are reaped when a customer-focused organization is created. Creating such an organization means building long-term relationships and learning to understand, on a deeper level, the needs of the customer. This can be personally satisfying and, if successful, mean repeat business and more negotiated work. It also means more opportunities to help clients (more business) in other ways. For instance, a large owner may call a construction professional for assistance in reorganizing a facilities group. Or an owner may want to outsource some of his or her own processes, essentially using the construction professional's organization for additional staff when needed. If the company has good processes in place and has developed a good relationship with the customer, the opportunities for continued and broadened business are numerous.

The foundation of total quality is continuous improvement. One way to measure improvements is through involvement with ISO 9000. [The ISO is the International

Matrix organization

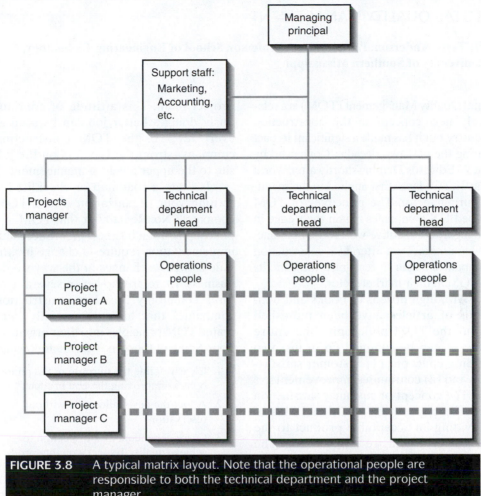

FIGURE 3.8 A typical matrix layout. Note that the operational people are responsible to both the technical department and the project manager

Organization for Standardization.] This group publishes international standards that define comprehensive quality management concepts and guidance. The standards describe what elements quality systems should encompass but do not specify how to accomplish them. The specific methods are left to the particular culture of the organization. Registration with the ISO means that a third-party accredited auditor will examine a company's practices to ensure that it meets the appropriate standard. Focus is on continual improvement of processes. Many companies have joined the ISO with the hope of increasing their competitive advantage worldwide. Owners concerned about standards of quality are asking contractors about internal programs such as TQM and adherence to standards such as ISO 9000. Involvement in these methods and adherence to these standards can mean more satisfaction internally, more consistent quality of service, and more business and profits.

BOX 3.1

TOTAL QUALITY MANAGEMENT

by Terry Anderson, P.E., Assistant Professor, School of Engineering Technology, University of Southern Mississippi

Total Quality Management (TQM) is a relatively new concept in the construction industry, but it has made a significant impact during the past two decades. Conceived by Dr. W. Edwards Deming shortly after World War II, TQM was first applied in the manufacturing sector. The principles of TQM helped U.S. companies regain their edge in the highly competitive worldwide manufacturing arena. Soon after, U.S. construction companies began to recognize the benefits of TQM in their market sector.

Although dozens of books and hundreds of articles have been published about the TQM philosophy, the entire concept can be summed up in just two guiding concepts: (1) customer satisfaction and (2) continuous improvement.

The concept of customer satisfaction goes far beyond the traditional idea of providing an acceptable product to the owner for whom we are working. The "customers" are considered to be everyone involved in the building process from designers to subcontractors and employees. With the goal of developing an atmosphere of pride, trust, and profitability in the construction process, the TQM concept does away with traditional hierarchical barriers and encourages innovation and cooperation. Ideas flow more freely, and decisions are made with more input from all of the parties involved.

Continuous improvement means making every job better than the last one. Ask "Is there a better way to perform this task?" If so, learn from the experience and share it with other members of the project team. This attitude of continuously doing a better job can be seen at every level in the TQM construction company—from the laborers on the job site to the upper levels of management.

Is there a roadmap or checklist for turning your organization into a TQM company? No. Remember that TQM is a philosophy, not a business plan. Successful implementation requires a change in attitude as well as changes in the way we do business. There are, however, several features commonly found in construction companies that have successfully integrated TQM principles into their organizations. Some of these include the following:

1. Clearly define the purpose of the philosophy as improving the end product.
2. Adopt the new philosophy without reservation.
3. Cease dependence on inspection to achieve quality. Expect a quality product in the first place.
4. Build long-term relationships with suppliers and subcontractors based on trust.
5. Constantly improve quality and production, thus reducing costs.
6. Initiate training throughout all levels.
7. Train leaders to help people do a better job.
8. Eliminate fear and encourage new ideas.
9. Have the company work as a team instead of as individual departments.
10. Eliminate targets for the work force demanding zero defects and unreasonable levels of productivity.

11. Eliminate management by numbers stressing quotas. Substitute leadership instead.

12. Instill pride of workmanship in hourly workers.

13. Institute vigorous programs of education and self-improvement.

14. Put everyone in the company to work accomplishing the transformation.

TQM is everyone's responsibility and everyone's reward.

Does TQM work? Studies by the General Accounting Office of some of the most productive U.S. companies found that TQM organizations consistently achieved better employee relations, higher productivity, greater customer satisfaction, increased market share, and improved profitability. These benefits do not always come easily or quickly—every level in the company's organizational structure must adopt the TQM concept. Typical time frames for complete incorporation of TQM principles range from one year to eighteen months.

Is it worth it? More and more construction companies are adopting the principles of TQM because of the associated benefits. As always, the "bottom line" is the bottom line. Total Quality Management means increased productivity, profitability, and a better corporate image. If you would like to see for yourself, try an Internet search of "Construction TQM" (or something similar). You will find that many of America's foremost contractors include this concept in their corporate mission statement.

LEGAL FORMS OF ORGANIZATIONS

There are many factors that determine a particular organizational culture. How the home office is organized, how flexible the administration is, and the administration's impact on decision making depend in part on the legal form of the organization. Three forms are common in businesses: the sole proprietorship, the partnership, and the corporation. Each has advantages and disadvantages in addressing taxes, up-front costs, risk and liability, management flexibility, and the ability to attract capital.

Sole Proprietorship

Proprietorships are single-person ownerships. This person owns, operates, and makes all major decisions for the company. There may be many employees, but the only responsible person is the one proprietor. This is by far the simplest form of ownership. It can be started with no formal documents and ended with no formal documents. It is whatever the person wants it to be.

The disadvantage of a sole proprietorship is the high risk involved for the person who owns the company. All losses are personal losses to the owner. Debts need to be paid back with private funds if the company assets are insufficient. Also, because only one person has collateral, a proprietorship may have difficulty raising money.

Partnership

A partnership, by definition, must include at least two people to be legal; but there may be many more than two in the partnership. The percentage of ownership varies. It sometimes depends on how much money each partner contributes to the firm but may also depend on other assets or skills—for example, land, equipment, or expertise. Assets are still considered personal but are the sum of the partners; therefore, the line of credit is greater.

Partnerships, like proprietary arrangements, are not separate legal entities that exist apart from the individuals. Partners are each fully responsible for all debts incurred by any one member. Although these debts are normally shared by legal agreement, one or more partners may default. The others, in this situation, are responsible for the debt share of the defaulting partners.

A partnership dissolves according to a prior agreement about how to dissolve it. The reasons for dissolution are varied. For example, one member may die or be terminated for just cause, the partners may reach a mutual decision to quit, or a predetermined time frame for dissolution may have been reached. In the case of a death, the partnership is legally terminated. There can, however, be provisions for others to continue by buying the shares of the deceased partner. Such terms should be determined on formation of the partnership. In the case of a bankruptcy or financial loss, general rules apply regarding how debts are paid off. Outside creditors are paid first. If the assets of the business are insufficient to cover these debts, then the partners are personally and equally responsible for payment. After these outside obligations are met, any investments made by the partners are reimbursed. Then the initial investment of each partner is repaid; and if there is any money left over, it is distributed according to prior agreements.

A variation on partnerships is the limited partnership agreement. People who invest a certain amount of money in a business but do not contribute to the management of the firm are called *limited partners*. A limited partner is only liable to the extent of his or her investment, even if the percentage of ownership is greater. The difference between general and limited partners is this limit of liability and their involvement with business decisions.

General partners may take on limited partners to increase their ability to raise capital and increase their credit base while retaining control over the firm. For the limited partner, the advantage is sharing in the profits of the firm while retaining limited liability. For such a partnership to be legal, a firm must have at least one general partner.

Corporation

Corporations are the most complex of the three forms of organizations. To form a corporation, a company has to apply for a charter from the state in which it does business. The services of a lawyer are required to prepare documentation; fees are paid to the state to cover its work in drawing up the charter. Once the corporation is formed, formal meetings must be held for any major decision.

As in partnerships, each member of the corporation contributes a sum of money or other assets. The percentage of ownership is recognized in the amount of stock given to this individual. The number of shares first offered is sometimes arbitrary, meant essentially to establish ownership. Each share is given a par value and a book value. The par value is a simple unit of measure—say, $1. The book value represents the actual amount contributed by each owner and is arrived at by dividing the amount of stock by the total net worth of the company. For instance, imagine that four owners decide to incorporate. The net value of the company is $2,000,000, and the initial offering is 1,000 shares. The percentage of shares might look like this:

Owner	Investment Sum	Percentage of Whole	Number of Shares
A	$200,000	10	100
B	$500,000	25	250
C	$300,000	15	150
D	$1,000,000	50	500

The number of shares also determines the number of votes each person has in the company.

A corporation has many advantages over other forms of business. Unlike proprietorships or partnerships, it has continuity independent of the stockholders. The corporation is perpetual. If a stockholder dies, the heirs offer that stock to other stockholders before selling it outside the company or retain the stock themselves. Also, because the company itself is a legal entity, only assets that belong to the firm are attachable for settlement of claims. Therefore, stockholders are only liable up to the amount they have invested in the company. If the corporation wants to raise additional capital, it can sell more shares of stock, which do not have to be paid back, instead of borrowing money, which would then be a debt. However, a company should be careful about the sale of stock because this will affect stockholders' ability to manage the company. Construction companies tend to be closely held corporations, which means that only a few people hold all of the stock in the firm. This offers risk protection and allows a small group of principals to control company policies and functions.

Corporations do have disadvantages. Some management decisions about dividend levels paid out or the selling of additional stock, for instance, must be approved by all stockholders. Obviously, the more stockholders there are, the slower the process of making decisions will be. Another disadvantage involves taxes. Profits from corporations are taxed twice: once on the corporate level and once on an individual level when the profits are paid out as dividends. Also, since corporations are chartered by states, they are considered foreign entities in other states. Sometimes individual states that want to encourage local business growth put restrictions on corporations. Proprietorships and partnerships do not have the same problem with other states since they are not legal entities separate from the individuals.

If a corporation is dissolved, outside creditors are paid first and shareholders last. Corporations are dissolved by simply surrendering the charter. Of course, getting to this point is not simple because it must be done via a vote by all shareholders. Sometimes there may be a predetermined expiration date for a corporation or an involuntary closing through the courts or a bankruptcy.

LEADERSHIP

Leadership is at the core of the construction management profession. Because most projects are in a constant state of flux and tend to move from one crisis to another, project success is dependent on the leadership of the construction manager. It is through the project manager's leadership that the project team stays focused on the task at hand, supports each other, communicates, and continues to subordinate individual needs in the best interest of the project. Effective project leaders stay true to their own values and are flexible, resourceful, and confident. They continually demand loyalty in their team, insist on preparation, and are always training and grooming future leaders. Good project leaders are clear and honest communicators who watch out for and care about their subordinates. Effective project leaders are teachers, not drill sergeants.

Effective leadership starts with a clear understanding of the project, the project environment, and the resources available. The project leader needs to establish the standards for the project—call it the philosophy for success—and communicate it throughout the organization. This vision for success must be continually articulated and reinforced. It helps to recruit people who share this vision. The project leader needs to be patient and allow adequate time for his or her vision to permeate the team, but also needs to be flexible enough to make adjustments.

Flexibility

As the project moves forward and personnel change, leaders need to adjust their strategies. As an example, alternate design ideas are encouraged early in the life of the project, but during peak construction it is normally too late for the incorporation of any major design innovations. The focus needs to be on production. A leader's tone, message, and timing need to change continually depending on the situation and the audience. Consistency is not nearly as important as taking advantage of opportunity.

High-risk projects, like construction projects, are very unpredictable and require a management and leadership style that is flexible enough to respond to the daily changes that happen on a construction site. Managers need to move with the flow of the project, the team's mood, the weather, the current technical skill and experience of the team, and public sentiment. They need to respond to daily events, delivery delays, the changing culture of the work force as trades come and go on the site, field changes, owner requests, and budget crunches. At the same time, they need to keep the home office happy with status reports, paperwork, and assurances that the project is under control.

Morale Building

Division from within can be disastrous to a project team, and project managers need to be ever vigilant to the mood, cooperation, and politics of the project team. It is the job of the leader to enforce the collective loyalty of the team and build what is often called *esprit de corps*. Dividing the enemy to weaken them is clever, but dividing one's own team is a mistake. Rewarding each subordinate's efforts on his or her own merit without arousing any petty jealousies or disturbing the team's internal relationship is important. [Encouraging the personal and professional growth of each member bolsters the morale of not only that person but of the whole team as people perceive themselves to be part of a "go-getter" organization.]

One of the quickest ways to build esprit de corps is to achieve success. Project milestones and team achievements are good reasons for celebration. Safety is one very measurable achievement and an accident-free site provides many benefits to the team and the project itself. Be on the lookout for any and all project achievements and call attention to them.

Look to cultivate a "team first" mood. Team first employees are always on the look out to do what is best for the project. Encourage this type of behavior and get rid of people who refuse to cooperate with team members or who act selfishly. For a project to be successful, workers need to keep expanding their skills and need to be willing to work outside of their job descriptions. Supervisors need to treat all of their subordinates kindly and equitably; to do otherwise is to destroy team loyalty.

It is also important for project managers to successfully represent the group at the next hierarchical level. Successful representation gives the team the confidence that their group is important within the overall organization. Harnessing resources from the home office can be a bit of a challenge because all projects are vying for the same resources. Effective project managers know how to work within the larger organization to get the level of resources that their project requires. This frees up those working under them to concentrate on the project itself and not worry about the availability of home office support.

Order and Discipline

Order and discipline are also important to a project. Both material (a place for everything and everything in its place) and social (a place for everyone and everyone in his or her place) order must be maintained. Material order is necessary to prevent waste and to support the work of the organization. This includes a well-laid-out site with specified areas for different subcontractors and rules about the handling and storage of material and equipment. It also includes good housekeeping practices with all workers responsible for their own material.

Social order means that every worker has a clearly defined job and job description. This includes safety training, job site orientation, identification of the immediate supervisor, and a broader understanding of the hierarchy on the site. It means that every worker is given instructions about the daily work environment and a sense of the other work that will be going on around him or her.

Without both material and social order, accountability would be impossible. Just like every project is made up of defined deliverables, each organizational worker must also deliver. To ensure peak delivery, it is important to provide the proper environment.

Goals and Accountability

It is the job of the project leader to set standards and ensure that they are being met. Establishing high standards of excellence begins with the example that the leader sets. A group is highly perceptive of its leader's behavior and reacts quickly to it. An accountable organization begins with an accountable leader. Leadership is hard work and visible; leaders need to work harder than their subordinates do. Leaders need to practice what they preach.

Leaders are clearly accountable for the success and failure of their unit. But the people working for them need to be held accountable as well. To help establish this accountability, leaders should set clear expectations and goals for their people and monitor their performance. Good monitoring will allow for correction if a worker is going off course. The monitoring system should be customized to the job situation and to the skill level of the worker, and it should provide enough room so the worker can operate as independently as possible.

In life safety situations, there is no room for tolerance and project leaders may need to step in very quickly and provide direct reprimands and even dismissal if necessary.

In normal situations, however, especially with senior, experienced people, leaders may need to back off, observe, and subtly guide their subordinates. In other cases it may be best to let people learn through self-correction, like the instructor pilot who lets the trainee try to right the aircraft until the very last minute before grabbing the stick. Although corrections and even reprimands are part of a team leader's responsibilities, they should be done in a way that corrects faults, but does not erode the confidence of the team or the individual.

Successful project teams are organized, prepared, and made up of people who are confident in their abilities. Workers develop confidence from a demonstrated ability and success in their assigned duties. Project leaders can support this confidence building by ensuring that each worker is appropriately supported, that the scope of each job is clear, and that measurements for success are understood. Reinforcing successful behavior through praise and discouraging unsuccessful behavior through criticism is also key. A confident team does not get created in an instant. It is an effort that has to be consistent over the life of the project. But the effort is well worth it and the results will be their own reward. Confidence promotes a positive risk-taking attitude, which is important in construction, an inherently risky industry. Healthy, confident organizations are resilient. These organizations can absorb failure and learn from mistakes. Confidence is infectious though it takes time to instill.

Organizational confidence like most of the other qualities of effective leadership starts with the leader. It is often said that it is better to decide wrong strongly than to decide right weakly! Projects need leaders—people who look and act confident. The way people hold themselves, their stature, and the confidence in which they give commands are all important. Leaders need to keep their doubts to themselves. They can and should accept guidance, but when it is time to make a decision, the discussion ends and the organization follows the leader's decision.

Confidence comes with preparation. The better prepared a project team is, the more creative, resourceful, and confident it can be. This preparation starts with the project leader. Visionary planning, anticipation of the future, and preparing for contingencies are critical tasks for the project team leader. Project teams need to be trained, drilled, and instructed as to all required procedures so that when the pressure is on, the team will perform well. Because every construction project is different, it is impossible to prepare for every contingency. However, if the team members are cooperative, loyal to the project and each other, and confident in their abilities, they will rise to meet the challenges in a resourceful manner.

Mentoring

Good leaders develop organizational stability and are always on the lookout to develop and train future leaders. People function best when they operate within a stable environment and are knowledgeable and confident as to how their colleagues will perform. People need time to learn the system, perfect their skills, and develop working relationships with others in the organization. Most organizations are better off with an average manager who stays on for the life of the project than an outstanding manager who comes and goes.

Because projects require leadership at various locations and points in time, it is close to impossible for one person to be physically present on every occasion. Also, as is the case in today's "mega-projects" the organization is too large to be directly led by one person. Leaders must still provide the direction, but they must also select, develop, and train the appropriate number of subleaders for the project. Organizations that develop their future leaders from within are inherently stable because they allow people to progress in their careers without leaving. People appreciate an organization that is committed to the advancement of its people. As organizations "grow" future leaders they gain flexibility; they become more confident, capable, accountable, and prepared for the future. These organizations are establishing the groundwork for expansion, and the leader who develops his or her replacement is now in a position to advance himself or herself. Equally important to developing staff from within is the need to search continually for new blood to add to the organization. Effective leaders maintain relationships in the industry and with academic institutions to identify good people who are looking for a move or good, young prospects coming out of educational programs. By feeding the organization with new people, companies can keep themselves competitive and up to date on changes in thinking in the industry and in the research environments. New people can reinvigorate an organization with their fresh perspective and new energy.

Communication

A discussion on leadership would be incomplete without addressing the topic of communication—good, clear, honest communication. Many forms of communication occur on a project and within an organization. Leadership communication is a different animal—it is up close and personal. Whether the message is inspirational, criticizing, or crisis driven, the form and the timing of the message are important. In communication, timing is everything.

For real communication to occur, the message must be delivered *and* received. The receiver has to be in a frame of mind to hear the message. Therefore, leaders must be very careful about when they transmit their message, particularly when it comes to communicating criticism. They must also be explicit in the scope of their words. Not everyone needs to know the big picture, only what is pertinent to do the job. Too much information can hide or distract the intended message. Timely and precise communication can correct a problem before it becomes serious. This model for communication is effective not just down the chain of command but also between co-workers and even up the chain of command. Everyone can benefit from timely and accurate assessments of their performance.

Leaders must not only communicate, they must also inspire and motivate their teams. As stated in the U.S. Department of Defense publication "The Armed Forces Officer":

> Other things being equal, a superior rating will invariably be given to the officer who has persevered in his studies of the art of self expression, while his colleague who attaches little importance to what may be achieved through working with the language will be marked for mediocrity. . . . Battles are won through the ability of men to express concrete ideas in clear and unmistakable language. All administration is carried forward along the chain of command by the power of men to make their thoughts articulate and available to others. . . . [The ability to communicate] is more essential to military leadership than knowledge of the whole technique of weapons handling.

Basic communication loop

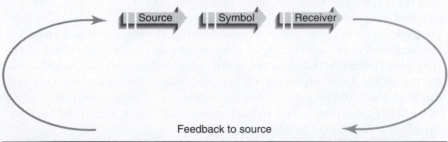

FIGURE 3.9   Effective communication requires that the sender and receiver "connect" and that the correct code and channel be selected

At its most basic level, communication contains three components: a source, symbols to impart a message, and a receiver (see Figure 3.9). The source could be the project leader, the symbols a written memo or a verbal announcement, and the receiver a subordinate. The obligations of the source are to formulate an accurate message, select an effective medium (i.e., oral or written), and deliver the message in a manner appropriate for the audience. The symbols of communication involve the message and a channel. The sender utilizes codes common to the organization and selects a channel such as the receiver's eyes (written message) or the receiver's ears (oral message). The codes reflect the culture of the organization both in the words that are used and in the format that is chosen. The channel is chosen for its appropriateness depending on the message.

For successful communication, the receiver must also be considered. The receiver's background, experience, and education must be compatible with the symbols and channel selected. A written message sent to an audience that cannot read would be an ineffective method of communication. On the other hand, a message meant for one person that is announced in a group could do a lot of damage. The receiver is also an active participant in communication. It is the obligation of the receiver to empathize, work with the sender, and try to connect and understand the message. Receivers need to indicate to the source that they understand the message. This will satisfactorily complete the transaction.

Leaders must understand that even when everything on a project seems perfect—the team is focused, morale is high, the job is on schedule, productivity is high, and costs are down—a letdown might be right around the corner. Effective leaders never let their project team lose focus because they know that success is fleeting and that it takes a mature organization and leader to stay sharp. Leaders need to foster an attitude of constant improvement and also provide reality checks. New technologies and innovations appear every day and any company that remains static is in reality dying. Leaders need to reward and acknowledge team success, but at the same time not allow complacency. Remember the saying, "The taller you get, the greater the fall." Leaders must help their teams remain humble and keep them away from the slippery slope.

Conclusion

This chapter has examined both the science and art of organizing and leading a construction project. The numerous challenges the construction industry and the typical construction project face necessitate a well-thought-out scientific plan. History and academia provide industry with the background theory and workable models that can help them structure a typical project. As was explained in this chapter, material order and social order are important to success and companies can find numerous organization examples to guide them.

For efficiency's sake, companies need to arrive at the correct level of centralization and give their project leaders the appropriate level of organizational support. Projects and project leaders need to begin with a stated organization mission and with adequate authority to direct their project teams and successfully complete the project.

Organizational design and structure, however, do not guarantee success. Projects need leaders, people whom the team can rally around and trust to bring the project success. When times get tough and the unexpected occurs, the leader takes charge and makes the hard decisions. Leaders keep the team focused and establish and maintain a positive team attitude. Leaders watch out for their people and support their subordinates' personal and professional growth. Leaders coach their people and are always looking for opportunities to pat them on the back and build their confidence.

Leaders are patient and recognize that every person is different. Because every worker operates under a different value system and brings to the project different strengths, leaders must know how to meld this talent to get these disparate workers to function as one. Leaders establish and insist on a unity of direction for their project. They are strong, effective, honest communicators and have an excellent sense of timing. They know how and when to motivate and provide corrective criticism. A perfect leader is almost impossible to find, a good leader a rarity, but maybe possible.

Chapter Review Questions

1. In a departmental organization, "gang planks" are formally established to link interdisciplinary teams. True or false?
2. Corporations exist independent to the interests of the stockholders. A corporation is perpetual. True or false?
3. When leaders establish *esprit de corps*, they are addressing which of the following leadership characteristics?
    a. Flexibility
    b. Morale building
    c. Order and discipline
    d. Goals and accountability
    e. Mentoring
4. TQM is best described as a business philosophy, not a business plan. True or false?
5. What is the term used to categorize the number of people that a manager supervises?
    a. Gangplank
    b. Matrix
    c. Span of control
    d. Work breakdown
    e. Pooled

6. Managing (as opposed to leadership) speaks to the establishment of a clear project vision, timely decision making, and clear inspirational direction. True or false?

7. A person in a staff position provides advice to a line supervisor who makes decisions and directly supervises staff. True or false?

8. Which of the following is *not* a basic component in the communication process?
   a. Noise
   b. Message source
   c. Message receiver
   d. Symbols

9. Which of the following organizations has attempted to formalize the usage of "gang-planks" to create effective interdisciplinary teams?
   a. Generalist
   b. Departmental
   c. Corporation
   d. Matrix

10. Which of the following should be considered in establishing an organizational structure for the management of a construction project?
   a. How work functions will be compartmentalized
   b. The number of resources to be committed to the project
   c. Whether decisions should be made in a centralized or decentralized manner
   d. The degree of need for interdisciplinary work
   e. All of the above

4

PROJECT DELIVERY METHODS

Chapter Outline

Student Learning Objectives

In this chapter you will learn the following:

1. The principal challenges that successful projects overcome
2. The four major categories of project risk
3. The three primary delivery method arrangements, with their advantages and disadvantages
4. The three major types of contracts

INTRODUCTION

An owner's primary goal in choosing a delivery method is to ensure that it will meet the project objectives and at the same time allow the project to be delivered on time and within budget. In a risk-free, predictable world, this would be a relatively simple task. The world, however, is full of unpredictable forces and undesirable outcomes. As a consequence, an owner must monitor the process to prevent unpleasant outcomes along the way.

Construction projects have many unique characteristics. Creating a large facility takes a long time and usually involves a large capital investment. Cost overruns, delays, and other problems tend to be proportionally monumental. The process of building is complicated by the large number of components that are provided by different suppliers. Furthermore, the process only occurs once. Even if an owner builds repeatedly, the nature of the product and the parties involved in building depend on time, site conditions, user needs, and economic health. Compared with professionals in other industries, designers and constructors have less opportunity to transfer lessons learned from project to project. All of these factors combine to create uniqueness, which carries with it heightened risk.

A building not delivered on time usually costs more than planned, and a late delivery can have cascading effects throughout an owner's organization. For example, a microcomputer chip manufacturer may need a new facility to manufacture the latest version of a chip. If the facility is late, the manufacturer may miss the market and allow a competitor to get its chip on line sooner. This will affect the entire organization and may cause serious economic setbacks. An owner's primary goal is to avoid such pitfalls.

One method to avoid these pitfalls is to put together a team of people whose skills match the type of project envisioned and who have a proven record of delivering such projects. Before this team is put together, however, an owner should decide how the members will interact with both the owner organization and each other. This approach is called the *project delivery method:* a particular combination of professionals and contract arrangements that assigns responsibilities and risk in a certain way. The three most common delivery methods are design/bid/build, design/build, and construction management. Within each of these methods there is a choice of contract arrangements, and each has its own set of risks and capabilities. Early on, the owner must decide which type will best suit the specific circumstances of the specific project.

MANAGING PROJECT RISKS

Lessons from History

An owner may choose a particular delivery method after studying why construction projects throughout history have failed. The task is not as daunting as it may seem. A number of recurring problems account for the vast majority of construction project failures. Here are the most common:

Separated Functions

The two primary professionals on the project are the designer and the constructor. Their communication during the entire project life cycle is key to project success. Projects tend to be large, complex undertakings, and each is unique. The actions of one professional can have a major impact on the concerns of the other.

For example, a design change after construction has started can adversely affect construction sequencing, thus causing considerable increases in cost due to lost efficiency. Early information about these changes gives construction personnel time to anticipate how to integrate them into the overall schedule. The longer the designer waits to inform the contractor of the change, the more money will be spent making the change. Conversely, if a contractor makes a field change and does not include the designer in the decision loop, design elements could be adversely affected and the building may not function as well as intended. In both cases, consultation between parties is important to maintain quality, budget, and schedule.

Scope Creep

The scope of work on a project can be defined as the product of the quantity of the work and the character of the work. For instance, imagine that 10,000 square feet of ⅜-inch gypsum wallboard defines the work of a drywall subcontractor. If the quantity increases to 11,000 square feet or the thickness to ⅝ inch, then the scope of work increases. Scope of work is the primary determinant of costs on a project. If scope increases, costs also increase.

Maintaining the scope of work as budgeted on a project can be a difficult aspect of managing the project since it is often beyond the control of any one member of the project team. Many factors can cause scope to increase. Today's large projects often involve complex and highly political organizations. Getting 100 percent consensus of what constitutes the entire project can be time-consuming. Most projects have tight timelines and often do not take into account the time needed for up-front consensus. Therefore, projects often go forward without total consensus. This usually creates a backlash somewhere further into the project. Often the only way to resolve it is to incorporate more scope.

Scope may also grow when a critical user is left out during the early needs analysis stage and must be accommodated later in the process. Sometimes this user was not available during the planning stages or became critical because of a new influx of money or other requirements. The change may be necessary, and the job of the project team is to minimize its impact on money and time.

Another cause of scope growth is miscommunication among the user, the designer, and/or the constructor. In complex projects, a tremendous amount of information moves among the different organizations. Controlling this information flow and ensuring that each party knows and understands critical information are major considerations when choosing delivery methods. It is the task of the project team to clearly identify the scope of work that was budgeted in the project and note any time that scope changes.

Project Acceleration

Buyers of construction services prefer to have projects delivered quickly. Finishing early lowers some costs, puts the building into service sooner, and can cut interest costs on construction loans considerably. Early completion also has a psychological impact, making owners, designers, and constructors alike happy. There is enthusiasm when closing out the job. Changes are easier to settle, inspectors are less rigid, and in general other aspects of bringing in the project flow smoother.

There are, however, real risks associated with going too fast. The biggest is that the project team will proceed into construction without having thoroughly considered all the elements of the design. As a consequence, the end product may not serve the needs of the owner as well as it could have with more planning. Another major risk is the problem of incomplete documents. A construction team faced with this situation can be well into construction only to find that the drawings are not detailed enough to accurately calculate the real costs. It is also possible that construction may have to be stopped or slowed to fix design problems, wasting rather than saving time.

BOX 4.1

DELIVERING A PROJECT FAST

Getting a project to market fast is important to project owners for many reasons. The sooner a project is completed, the sooner it can begin to provide benefits to the owner. Private sector projects become assets and can be refinanced at lower interest rates, thus reducing an owner's liability. Completed projects also begin to produce income. Some projects are necessary for the design and manufacture of products that have tremendous value but short useful lives—for example, computer-related products. Getting to market fast is essential for both reclaiming the initial investment and beating the competition. Understandably, owners often offer substantial bonuses for early completion and correspondingly stiff penalties for late completion.

Public sector projects also carry early completion incentives, not necessarily because of an incentive to beat the competition but because of the need to reduce debt and provide early public benefits. Examples might be the completion of a school by the start of fall classes; the timely construction of sewage treatment facilities to match population growth; and the quick repair and construction of road, rail, and other transportation projects.

For example, consider the road repairs that were necessary after the January 17, 1994, Northridge earthquake in southern California. A roadway that supported 217,000 car and truck trips a day was severely damaged by the quake. The California Department of Transportation awarded an incentive-laden contract to C. C. Myers of Sacramento. The company's base bid was $14.9 million, with an incentive of $200,000 per day for every day it completed the project under the 140-day deadline. Myers accelerated construction, using multiple shifts, expediting materials, and keeping key equipment constantly on standby. In the end, it successfully completed the project in 84 days, earning a huge bonus; and the public received a working roadway in record time.

Poor Working Relationships

It is difficult enough for companies that perform the same tasks year after year to build effective organizations. The unique character of construction makes the task doubly difficult. The project team hired and assembled by the owner will probably be together only for one project. There simply is not enough time to work out all the relationships necessary to perform difficult interconnected work. Personal work styles as well as corporate cultures can be very different from one another. Personal chemistry between individuals plays an important role, and good working relationships at the personal level are often a matter of luck.

It is also true that contract forms, which are used in construction, can work against good teamwork. A construction contract has been called an exercise in risk allocation. If one party or team member attempts to unfairly or unrealistically put most of the risk on another party, then the effect on team performance can be dramatic. Most professionals in construction have heard horror stories in which project participants communicated only through formal means, using memos or (even worse) lawyers. Establishing good, informal rapport with other project participants is one of the most effective ways of ensuring that vital information will be exchanged early and often.

These examples are certainly not the only lessons that can be learned from the history of construction failures, but they are among the most important. Throughout this chapter we discuss ways to mitigate these pitfalls through organization of the team, contract choice, partnering sessions, and delivery methods.

ASSESSING PROJECT RISKS

Selecting a delivery method and a contract type involves sequential decision-making in which the owner, usually with professional advice and sometimes after the designer is selected, examines the specific circumstances of the project and chooses the best fit. Perhaps the project requires a fast turnaround, the scope is technically complex, or the work is a renovation with many unknowns. Whatever the important drivers, the steps to the decision are essentially the same.

General Risks

The general risks that occur on any project can be classified into four major areas:

- *Financial.*   The project will cost more than the money that has been allocated to it, or it will cost more than the product itself is worth.
- *Time.*   The project will not be completed within the planned time. Worse, it will be completed so late that it has an adverse effect on other parts of the owner's work.
- *Design.*   The project will not perform the function for which it was intended or, more commonly, will perform the function in a degraded manner.
- *Quality.*   The project will have poor-quality materials or workmanship, or the work will be incomplete in some way.

A project team experienced with the building process will address these risks during project development. The risks are approached differently, depending on whether the team is in the preconstruction or construction phase of the project.

Preconstruction is often thought of as the design phase, but in reality it goes beyond the design tasks of working out the functional, aesthetic, and material requirements of the job. In this phase the project team (owner, designer, and constructor) starts to deal seriously with balancing the design/cost equation. This equation is not a formalized mathematical expression but an understanding that increased function and quality equal increased costs (see Figure 4.1). By factoring in this understanding while the design is being developed, team members play off one element (function and quality) against another (costs). The designer must take the lead here—identifying changes in scope, engineered systems, level of quality, or any other elements in the design that could increase costs. If the owner has this information early enough, then he or she can make informed decisions before too much money or time is spent. The risk occurs when realistic assessments of costs are not part of the design process, leaving the owner vulnerable to some unpleasant choices when these costs are finally identified.

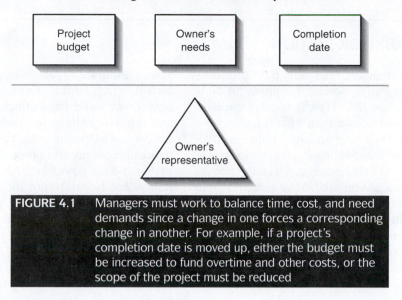

Balancing the needs/cost/time equation

| Project budget | Owner's needs | Completion date |

Owner's representative

FIGURE 4.1 Managers must work to balance time, cost, and need demands since a change in one forces a corresponding change in another. For example, if a project's completion date is moved up, either the budget must be increased to fund overtime and other costs, or the scope of the project must be reduced

During the actual field construction process, the emphasis shifts from design/cost tradeoffs to executing a project within the constraints defined by the contract documents, schedule, and budget. Risks in this phase involve time and external unknowns. One serious problem is that the early estimates are only that—estimates. They are not purchase prices. There are no guarantees when the estimates are prepared that the same conditions will prevail when materials are bought or labor hired. A sudden shift in lumber availability or a new union trade contract can alter prices. There are also many other risks. Community disapproval of a certain project can put pressure on local officials and cause delays. Labor actions, adverse weather conditions, and site accidents are all risks that are difficult to predict and hard to control. All can cause serious overruns in time and money during construction.

Project-Specific Risks

In addition to general industry risks, there are specific risks that all owners and designers must take into account during their work.

Site Risks

Every project has neighbors who may or may not be pleased with the idea of a new facility in their community.

There will always be a regulatory environment. Some are stricter than others, but the rules are usually unique to the locale and must be understood and factored into the design and construction plan. Each region of the country has local geological characteristics. Specific conditions of the site, especially underground conditions, are difficult to predict. Finally, every site is located within a specific economic region. Economic conditions can change more rapidly than any other site factor.

BOX 4.2

SEABROOK STATION

In September 1988, the past president of the Public Service Company of New Hampshire (PSNH) was asked, if the company had known then what it knows now, would it still have undertaken the construction of the Seabrook power plant (see Figure A)? His response: "Of course not. . . . How could you ask? We're bankrupt." He added that the company had probably paid too little attention to "what's on the minds of the people" (Bedford 1990: 163).

The Seabrook power plant was conceived in the 1960s at a time when the United States was looking for alternative power resources to reduce its dependence on oil, a depletable resource. Nuclear power was viewed as both clean burning and relatively cheap to produce. PSNH, the project's developer, looked at a stable national economy and a projected increase in demand for power in the New England region and began to put together a plan for an 860-megawatt power plant. Plans for the project fluctuated as financing was arranged. Ultimately, the project was formally launched in March 1973, when PSNH formally applied to the Atomic Energy Commission for permission to

FIGURE A   The construction of Seabrook Station illustrates the importance of maintaining proper corporate leadership, understanding goverment regulatory and bureaucratic procedures, and educating and attaining the support of the local community

Source: Courtesy of Margot Balboni, Gooscapes.

build two 1,100-megawatt reactors. The financial partners for this undertaking were Northeast Utilities (10%), United Illuminating (20%), several other New England power companies (20%), and PSNH (the principal owner at 50%). The project's budget was set at $850 million.

Initially, the project went along well. United Engineers and Constructors were hired to design and construct the facility. The construction phase began in 1975, with Seabrook I scheduled to become operational in 1979, Seabrook II in 1981. Plans were also made for the purchase of the uranium that would fuel the reactors. However, in 1976 fate stepped in when the Atomic Energy Commission voted two to one to approve construction. Although the plant was approved, the decision was the first split vote in the history of nuclear power regulation ("Seabrook Chronology," March 2, 1990).

Many reasons have been cited for why the power plant failed to materialize as it was originally budgeted and scheduled: poor management of the design and construction process, poor emergency planning, inadequate planning for the disposal of nuclear waste, inadequate safety provisions for residents and plant workers, inadequate project financing, proper protection of the seacoast environment. Every one of these issues was debated throughout the course of the project, delaying construction and increasing cost. Ultimately, one reactor was finished, the second partially, at a published cost (when the reactor finally received its full power license in 1990) of $6.4 billion.

The reasons for the increase in budget and time were clearly not unique to Seabrook; they also pertain to every nuclear plant ever constructed. In Seabrook's case, unfortunate timing and the mood of

the country got in the way. People began to fear centralized power, damage to natural balances, corrupt government, technical incompetence, and human arrogance (Bedford 1990). The Three Mile Island disaster in 1979, the Chernobyl disaster in 1986, and the release of the movie *The China Syndrome* in 1979 all occurred at the peak of construction. Groups such as the Seacoast Anti-Pollution League, the Audubon Society, the Society for the Protection of New Hampshire Forests, and the Clamshell Alliance diligently worked to confront and question the project and keep the public involved. Public forums, protests, and lawsuits forced delays and occupied managers.

Even as the project neared completion, low power testing and operation were delayed for years as battles over emergency evacuation and planning and the costs of decommissioning and storage of hazardous waste were fought in court.

Almost everything that happened at Seabrook over the last 17 years has received intense scrutiny, making it what almost surely is the most controversial nuclear power plant in the nation. First there were concerns that discharges of super-heated cooling water would kill nearby marine life. Then there were doubts about whether plant owners could afford to complete it. Seabrook also came under attack for drug and alcohol use among workers, alleged deficiencies in welds and other construction work, supposed security breaches. . . . The grass-roots antinuclear movement also began at Seabrook, with more than 2,500 protesters arrested at peaceful sit-ins staged by the Clamshell Alliance and more than 50 lawsuits filed by a variety of critics. The Clams, as they were called, inspired the founding of similar alliances across the nation that are credited with turning the public against nuclear power and forcing utilities to cancel plans for scores of reactors. (Tye 1990: 12)

(continued)

BOX 4.2   Continued

In the end, one reactor was completed at a cost more than six times greater than what was budgeted for both. The principal owner went bankrupt, and the project became operational 11 years late. Electrical rates across New England were forced up substantially to pay off the huge budget increase. The rates of customers of the bankrupt PSNH went up 5.5 percent for seven years, and United Illuminating of Hartford, Connecticut, raised its electric rates 9 percent a year for three years to compensate for its additional costs (Tye 1990).

Technically, the design and construction of the Seabrook power plant was typical of nuclear plants built at many locations throughout the world. What made this project different and ultimately a financial failure was the political climate of the country and, in particular, the region. If the backers of Seabrook had understood public sentiment and sought regional cooperation early on, issues may have been smoothed out, and the project might have been a success. Instead, the region fought the project for its entire duration, tying it up in the expensive and time-consuming regulatory processes that led to its failure.

References

Bedford, Henry F. *Seabrook Station*. Amherst: University of Massachusetts Press, 1990.

"Seabrook Chronology." *Boston Globe*, March 2, 1990.

Tye, Larry. "NRC Approves Licensing of Seabrook Plant Called Safe; Ruling Effective This Month." *Boston Globe*, March 2, 1990.

The Project Itself

Because each project is unique, the risks associated with each are also unique. Many factors can influence the levels of risk. Complexity is a major factor because complex projects tend to be more difficult than simple projects. Complexity is related to the level of technology employed. New technologies of materials and assembly are more likely to be used on complex projects, but they also carry more risk than do proven technologies. For example, constructors working on the tunnel between England and France used a tunnel-boring technique that had never been used at this scale before. In building projects, using a brick facade is a known and proven technology; but if project members want a different look, they may use a new configuration of a curtainwall system. Details of this system might be designed for the first time on this particular project and may be troublesome both to install and maintain. Recently, there has been an increase in risk associated with "smart systems"—the use of computer technology to run operating systems in, for example, a building, a hydroelectric plant, or a nuclear reactor. This technology is continually developing, which increases potential obsolescence, incompatibility of parts, and installation glitches.

Other Risks

In addition to technical concerns, there are organizational and financial risks. An owner's level of knowledge about the building process varies from person to person. To minimize risk, project members should match the delivery type with this level. Great danger lies in putting an unsophisticated owner into a delivery mode and contract arrangement that require knowledgeable involvement.

Financial changes can also upset the success of the project. Many projects have been technically feasible only to fail due to inadequate capital for paying the bills as the project proceeds. Tightening the schedule can also create considerable risk. If the team is not assembled for an accelerated schedule, errors and inefficiencies can occur as the team races to accommodate it.

MINIMIZING RISK

Once the general and specific project risks have been assessed, the owner must build a team that is matched to the project and therefore has the best chance of minimizing the risks. Among the many members of this team, the two primary ones are the design professionals and the construction professionals. These team members are usually corporate entities who assign appropriate, qualified personnel to the project organization for the life of the design and building effort. These primary members influence the inclusion of other participants such as consultants, specialty contractors, and suppliers. Both the firms and the individuals must have qualifications and experience that are suited to the particular demands of the unique project.

The demands of the project can be categorized in many ways. Technically, each project can be categorized as a type—bridge, tunnel, biotech production facility, highway project. Design and construction firms often specialize in a type of project, so these qualifications are easy to fill. The makeup of the owner organization also puts demands on the project. Government agencies and private owners require different criteria to be met. Institutional owners often have specialized needs not required by the government. Design and construction firms often work primarily with one type of owner and understand these specific requirements quite well. No matter what the case, the owner wants to match the team with the project. The project delivery method should also have some bearing on the makeup of the team. Some firms specialize in specific delivery methods. They set up their internal organization to meet the demands of the delivery method and are able to perform efficiently and effectively.

Choosing the Right Delivery Method

Ideally, before choosing the members of the project team, an owner will choose the delivery method. Sometimes the designer is on board before the method is chosen. In that case, the designer helps the owner determine which method will work best under the conditions of the project. But regardless of when the method is chosen, it must be appropriate to the project. The nature of how the team members interact depends on the delivery method.

The dilemma for the owner in choosing delivery methods is one of price versus performance. Each project has distinctive requirements for problem solving, and some methods work better than others in solving problems. If the project is highly complex, such as a hospital, it requires close cooperation among the project participants. In this case, the owner wants to choose a method that emphasizes cooperation and performance. If the project is a relatively simple one, such as a warehouse, then the owner can opt for an approach with a lower price or an earlier completion date.

Choosing a Contract Type

At this point the owner must choose a contract type. The goal here is to purchase the actual construction service for the lowest price possible without creating undue risk for the owner. The three major types of contracts are *lump sum, unit price*, and *reimbursable*, also called cost plus a fee. These types and their variations will be discussed later in the chapter.

Monitoring the Entire Process

As the process proceeds, the owner must devise mechanisms to ensure that budget is monitored, schedule maintained, and quality ensured. There are several mechanisms for accomplishing these tasks that will be covered in greater detail in later chapters.

Partnering

During the 1980s the construction industry went through a period of considerable litigation. Although many of the disputes were minor, they were blown out of proportion once they entered the court system. In an effort to save itself, the industry adopted a more structured approach to working together. This approach, called *partnering*, was developed by the Army Corps of Engineers for use in its relationships with contractors. Its primary goal is to encourage people to look beyond traditional adversarial roles toward cooperation and open communication. For partnering to work, all stakeholders must make a serious commitment. Issues of ethics are also taken very seriously.

Partnering usually begins with the owner. When hiring the project participants, he or she introduces the concept. There must be a commitment from the top management of all stakeholders and a designated managing partner who nurtures the project participants throughout the project. Partnering is a project-length commitment and does need continual renewal, which should be part of the original charter of the partnering exercise.

Usually partnering involves a workshop in which all participants, through a facilitator, discuss and agree to mutual goals. A charter is developed that identifies those goals. Then a formal organization is established to help carry them out. This organization lays out lines of communication, dispute-resolution methods, and decision-making and problem-solving procedures. Follow-up and support are important components of the plan. Like any plan, however, its strength lies in its ability to evolve with time and need. This can happen only through vigilance and continual evaluation. The rewards of partnering are a decrease in litigation costs; collaborative problem solving; and equity in the development of goals, personal job satisfaction, and a job well done.

DELIVERY METHODS

The term *delivery method* refers to the owner's approach to organizing the project team that will manage the entire design and construction process. This selection process is governed to a large extent by risk but also by the owner's desire to find a method that will deliver the project on time, within budget, and in a form that will meet the owner's needs most effectively.

A number of proven strategies can be used to accomplish these ends. The three most common are *design/bid/build, design/build*, and *construction management*. Combinations of these strategies may be employed as well. Each has its distinct advantages and disadvantages, but the choice is not always clear and simple. The owner must carefully weigh his or her options to ensure the right choice for the specific project.

Design/Bid/Build

In this arrangement, the owner first hires a design professional, who then prepares a design, including complete contract documents. The design professional is typically paid a fee that is either a percentage of the estimated construction cost or a lump-sum amount, or he or she is reimbursed for costs at an agreed-upon billing rate. With a complete set of documents available, the owner either conducts a competitive bid opening to obtain the lowest price from contractors to do the work or negotiates with a specific contractor. The contractor is then responsible for delivering the completed project in accordance with the dictates of the contract documents. The contractor may choose to subcontract much of the work or may have the forces in house to accomplish the task. That choice usually depends on the complexity of the project. No matter how the work is done, however, the contractor remains solely responsible for execution of the work. This delivery mode became popular near the turn of the twentieth century in response to the increasing specialization of the various building professions, and until recently it was the predominant mode of delivery. Figure 4.2 illustrates the traditional approach.

During the construction process, the owner may hire the architect to administer the contract or may choose to have in-house employees do this task. Administering the contract consists of observing the work to monitor quality, carrying out the change order process, certifying payment to the contractor, and ensuring that the owner is

FIGURE 4.2   Information exchanged between the designer and the contractor formally flows through the owner

Design/bid/build approach

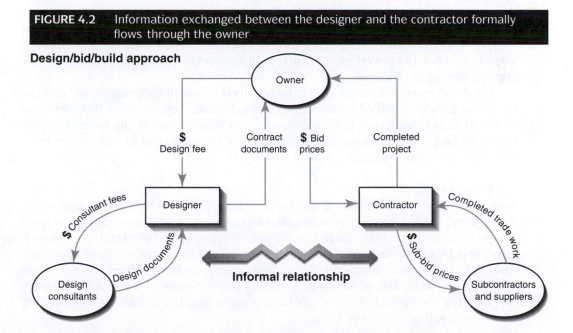

receiving the product called for in the contract documents. If the owner hires the architect, he or she does so through an agency relationship—that is, the architect is bound by the legal rules of this relationship and as such is empowered to act in the owner's name. The contractor, on the other hand, is hired in a simple commercial contract and as such is charged with carrying out the terms of the construction contract. There is no contract between the architect and the contractor. The relationship is one in which the architect acts for the owner during any dealings with the contractor. Nor are there contract agreements between the architect/owner and the specialty subcontractors. The relationship exists only with the contractor, who is solely responsible for the subcontractor's performance.

Advantages

The design/bid/build approach is a known quantity to owners, designers, and constructors. This is probably its greatest strength. For many years, the mode of delivery was the predominant one for construction in the United States. The procedures and contractual rules of conduct have been worked out and are well understood. Many professionals prefer this well-defined relationship, which reduces their level of risk because it reduces uncertainty. Under the right circumstances, this means that a project is more likely to proceed smoothly from beginning to end.

The mode also contains considerable contractual protection for the owner. The allocation of risk for construction performance rests almost completely on the contractor and the subcontractors. The owner is insulated from many of the risks of cost overruns, such as labor inefficiencies, nonperforming subs, inflation, and other vagaries of the larger economic picture. In most instances, the owner knows the final cost at the beginning of construction, and the risk of cost overruns are borne by the contractor. However, the risk of cost increases depends to a large extent on the accuracy and completeness of the contract documents. If they are unclear or not well done, the changes that must ensue can raise the owner's costs considerably.

Additionally, this method provides the owner with all the benefits of open market competition. The open bidding procedure, in which the lowest bidder is the "winner," gives the owner the lowest price available in the marketplace and presumably the greatest economic efficiency.

Finally, the owner does not have to be heavily involved in the construction process. He or she must be involved in the design process to make key decisions about whether or not to accept the design; but once construction actually begins, the owner is represented by professionals empowered to act in his or her name and to make recommendations. Day-to-day interaction is not necessary.

Disadvantages

Nevertheless, several elements of the design/bid/build approach can work against the owner. First, the construction professional does not enter the process until the design is complete, meaning that the design is not usually reviewed for constructability before it is finished. Design features that could have been built more economically or effectively often result in higher costs. Some design firms overcome this problem by hiring preconstruction consultants or having construction professionals on their staffs. Although this benefits the project, it is not as effective as having the design reviewed by the person who will actually have to build it.

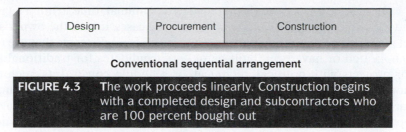

Conventional sequential arrangement

FIGURE 4.3 The work proceeds linearly. Construction begins with a completed design and subcontractors who are 100 percent bought out

Second, with the traditional approach it is difficult to reduce the time required to do both design and construction. As Figure 4.3 shows, the process is sequential and linear; there is no opportunity to overlap tasks and thus reduce overall time. This may raise interest expenses on construction loans and other costs and can expose the project to greater risks of inflation. The time element problem is one of the primary reasons for the recent decline in the use of the traditional method.

Finally, all parties work autonomously in this mode. The designer designs the project based on the owner's instructions. The general contractor prices and schedules the project based on the construction documents alone. This approach provides little opportunity for interaction and team building among the participants and can lead to major breakdowns in relationships.

For example, when the contract must be interpreted, the parties involved view the situation from fundamentally different perspectives. A firm, fixed-price contract can considerably exacerbate the problem because the contractor had to competitively bid for the job and thus interprets details as cost-effectively as possible. The owner and the designer, on the other hand, want to receive the most for their money. Such differences in interpretation lead to conflicts that can quickly escalate, creating adversarial relationships.

Unforeseen conditions on a job can also be a source of conflict and may lead to changes in the contract. A thorough design process and a complete set of drawings attempt to minimize these conditions. Conducting additional soil borings or opening up walls in renovation work can help to properly identify actual conditions and avoid future conflicts. Unfortunately, not every condition can be identified; and when unforeseen conditions or events occur, the contract may have to be renegotiated. This takes away any advantage to the owner in terms of known costs when construction begins.

Summary

The traditional design/bid/build approach has distinct advantages and disadvantages. In choosing this method, the owner must make tradeoffs. One major advantage is the fact that the owner knows the cost when construction begins; however, he or she must give up the potential cost savings of fast track to obtain it. The owner also gives up the design–construction collaboration that could improve the design and lower the overall price. This certainty of cost is only as good as the quality of the documents. If there are a large number of change orders to cover work not specified or detailed properly or to increase the scope, the costs may be significantly different from those anticipated and the advantage lost.

On many projects, the risk of changes is minimal, time is not a significant factor, and the project scope is well defined. In these cases, it is to the owner's advantage to get good price competition and a fixed price up front. Projects that are not technically complicated or have been built before are candidates for traditional arrangements. For projects with political, technical, or schedule constraints, such arrangements should be examined more closely. A road paving operation, a single-family home, or a warehouse could all be built using a design/bid/build approach. An emergency bridge repair or a large commercial project would be more successful using another delivery method. It is also worth noting that the selection of this delivery method may be mandated for some owners. For instance, public agencies are often required by law to use the traditional method.

Design/Build

For the owner, the design/build method provides a single point of contact and responsibility throughout the life of the project (see Figure 4.4). The firm hired by the owner will perform both design and construction. Entities offering this service may be design/build firms with in-house employees or joint-venture firms that come together contractually to perform a single project. In either case, the design/build entity can hire subcontractors who perform the actual construction in the field.

FIGURE 4.4   Information exchanged by the designer and the constructor flows directly between them

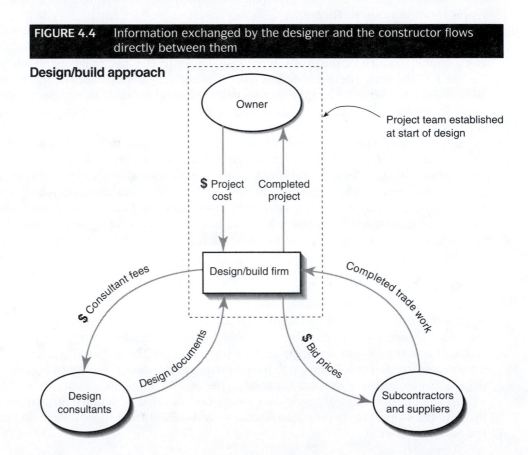

Design/build approach

This mode is used extensively in certain industries, particularly industrial construction. The complexity of industrial projects such as oil refineries and power plants makes them a good candidate for design/build. Before the design/bid/build method became popular, design/build was actually the preferred mode of delivery for almost all projects, although it was not named as such. An owner hired a master builder, who designed the project, acquired the materials, and hired and supervised the craft workers on the site. This mode of delivery became less popular as professional tasks became more specialized.

Advantages

One major reason for choosing a design/build arrangement is to benefit from the good communication that can occur between the design team and the construction team. Many of the largest design/build companies specialize in particular areas and have developed a smooth flow between the design and construction phases of the project. This collaboration allows the project to be easily fast-tracked, cutting down on overall schedule for the project (see Figure 4.5).

Good communication between the designers and the construction professionals also allows construction input early in the design phase. Such input includes constructability analyses, value engineering, and subcontractor pricing. Cost estimating, scheduling, long lead item identification, and ordering all become part of the overall project planning.

In general, this arrangement allows easier incorporation of changes due to scope or unforeseen conditions since their coordination occurs within the same contractual entity. The owner is less heavily involved and sits outside the direct day-to-day communication between designer and constructor. This keeps owner staffing to a minimum and puts the full responsibility for good communication, problem solving, and project delivery on the design/build team.

FIGURE 4.5 Fast tracking allows a project to be completed earlier than is possible in a conventional sequential approach by designing it as a series of work packages

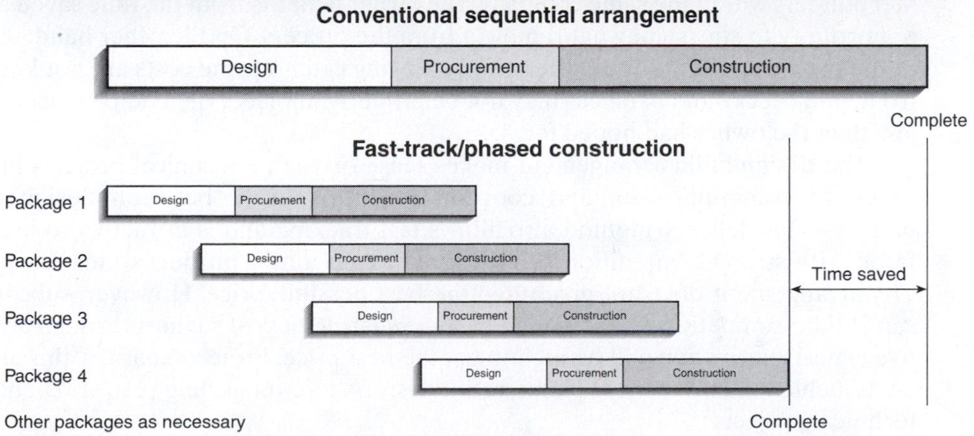

Disadvantages

Although it is possible to give the owner a fixed, firm price before the project begins, this generally does not happen in a design/build arrangement. Because the firm is hired before the design has started, any real pricing is not possible. Instead, an owner usually enters this arrangement with a conceptual budget but without the guarantee of a firm price. Firming up the price too soon puts the design/build team in the position of making the scope fit the price, which carries the risk of sacrificing quality to protect profit. If the project is fast-tracked, the owner may not have a good idea about the final price until part of the project, such as the foundation, is complete.

The owner's ability to remain marginally involved can be both an advantage and a disadvantage. When a design/build company has an organization that is efficient at performing the work, the project can move very fast. If the owner does not stay consistently involved throughout the process, he or she may have to make decisions without fully understanding the issues. Once a project develops a rhythm, it is difficult to change that rhythm. If the owner is not moving to the same rhythm, the project may take a direction that he or she does not want but is not aware of until too late.

Another disadvantage is the lack of checks and balances. In a design/bid/build approach, the designer prepares a complete set of contract documents, which is then used to measure and evaluate the performance of the contractor in the field. The owner often hires the designer to oversee the work of the contractor and to ensure that deficient work is identified and corrected. But in the design/build arrangement, the designer works for the same company as the builder. Similarly, during construction the builder sometimes uncovers certain design deficiencies, errors, or omissions. The designer is bound by contract to correct these deficiencies without additional costs to the owner. In design/build, the design and construction professionals are put in the position of critiquing their co-workers and perhaps affecting their bottom line by that critique. The owner must rely more heavily on the quality and ethics of the firm since most of the checks and balances will likely take place behind the company's door.

Summary

The design/build process benefits from the smooth coordination between the designers and builders within the same company. The owner benefits from the time saved and the opportunity to stay somewhat removed from the process. On the other hand, the pace of the project can leave the owner always playing catch-up, the costs are not known up front, and checks and balances may not be properly in place. The end product could be less than the owner had hoped for.

The design/build arrangement makes sense on highly technical projects in which excellent communication and coordination must occur between designers and builders. This delivery method also allows fast tracking and is attractive to industries faced with strong competition and the need to get a new product to market quickly. The arrangement does not guarantee the best possible price. However, subcontracts can still be competitively bid; and with some sharing of cost savings through an incentive clause, motivation will be high to get the best price. Projects that use this arrangement include manufacturing plants, refineries, offshore oil drilling platforms, and other technical projects.

Construction Project Management

In this delivery method the owner hires both a design firm and a construction project management firm early in the preconstruction phase of a project (see Figure 4.6). Which firm is hired first as well as which specific responsibilities each firm will handle varies, depending on the owner's level of involvement as well as the expertise of the designer and the construction professional. This delivery method has a number of variations, including program management, professional management, construction management, and professional construction management. The differences among these arrangements reflect the expertise of the management team, at what point the team is hired, and the particular needs of the owner. For instance, the company may be a designer, a builder, or a management consultant. The team may be put into place at the conceptual stage, the design stage, or the procurement stage. The owner may not have in-house support and may need services from the team that include coordination of the move, purchase of furniture, or working with users. This last variation is typically called a *program management delivery method*. In a construction management delivery method the owner does much of the programming and designer selection himself or herself and looks to the construction manager to do the work directly associated with construction.

Advantages

A major advantage of this arrangement is that good communication among the owner, the designer, and the constructor is established early in the design and construction process and continues through the completion of the project. The process encourages collaboration and allows the construction people to critique and influence the design

FIGURE 4.6 One advantage of construction management is that the builder, because he or she is paid a fee, becomes an advisor to the owner

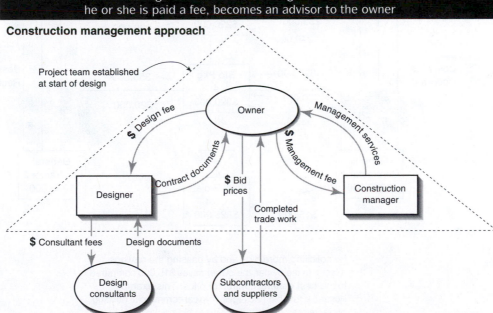

Construction management approach

of the project before it is bid. The designers have a say in selecting the contractor and reviewing the work in the field. Problems are worked on collaboratively because the incentive is to produce the best product for the owner. Both the architect and the contractor work on a fee basis and are paid for their professional expertise throughout the entire project.

This arrangement allows for good value-engineering because of the early involvement of the contractor. It also allows for fast tracking since the design and construction people work together early enough to develop the necessary coordination schedules.

Another advantage is that the owner receives the cost benefit of the competition among the subcontractor bids. The subcontractors are under contract to the owner; so if the project is broken into bid packages with five bidders per package, the owner receives the benefit of one hundred competitive bids. The designer and the construction

FIGURE 4.7 Cost savings due to competitive bidding

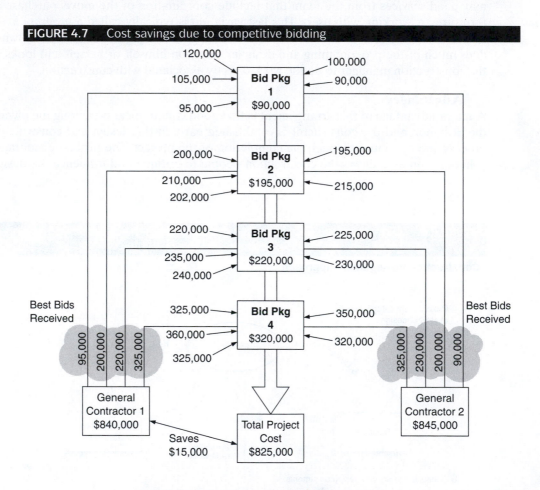

By soliciting more bids and by passing the savings directly to the owner, the owner saves $15,000 compared to the best general contractor price. This example illustrates four bid packages. Typical commercial building projects may have thirty or more bid packages.

manager review and recommend the contractor; but because they are simply being paid a fee, the owner receives any financial benefits (see Figure 4.7).

The implementation of changes during the course of construction is not as difficult as it is in the design/bid/build method since the designer and the construction manager are in close communication. Many times changes can be first worked out informally, thereby saving time and wasted effort in the field. Ideally, the team should be able to anticipate changes, minimizing their impact on the project.

Disadvantages

For this arrangement to work well, good communication and cooperation must exist among owner, designer, and construction manager. If any of the players become inflexible, uncooperative, or uncommunicative, all of the advantages of construction project management can quickly become disadvantages. This delivery method depends heavily on shared, mutual respect among the players, and this requirement is repeatedly tested during any project.

High owner involvement is necessary for this delivery method to work. In principle, the designer, the construction manager, and the owner form a team, with each taking on shared and individual responsibilities. The arrangement requires a more sophisticated owner than do the other two delivery methods. If the owner is unable to fulfill this function, program managers or project managers may be options. The project manager essentially becomes the owner and in some cases may even hire a construction management company, creating a second tier.

Construction project management tends to encourage fast tracking since the construction management team gets involved early in the process. However, because the firms may not have the organizational sophistication to handle fast tracking or the owner may not be ready for acceleration of the schedule, fast tracking can be risky. If the team ignores the risk and pushes the project into construction anyway, the owner may incur significant financial penalties.

BOX 4.3

INNOVATIONS IN PROJECT DELIVERY

PUBLIC/PRIVATE PARTNERSHIPS

As we look to the future and a public infrastructure that needs considerable attention, innovative approaches are being developed to jump start the reconstruction effort. Public/Private Partnerships (3P) are being formed as a way to finance these large infrastructure projects. Build–own–operate (BOO), design–build–operate (DBO), and design–build–finance (DBF) are just a few of the many examples of 3P that have emerged.

The concept is relatively simple. The designer, builder, or developer funds, designs, and builds the project and then collects a usage fee, rent, or toll, for a set period of time. At the end of this period the project reverts to the public.

The advantages are many—more projects can be initiated since up-front funding is available, the designer and builders get work, and the public in the end gets new infrastructure without the usual resulting increase in taxes. The arrangement is particularly attractive to developing countries or in regions that are experiencing rapid growth with a backlog of necessary projects.

(continued)

BOX 4.3   Continued

The disadvantages to the 3P devloper is that attaining a commitment for a project is a time consuming, expensive, and very political. Whereas some see this as an excellent approach to attain the necessary infrastructure, others see 3P as "outsourcing" with the government and public the losers. However, as the need for infrastructure repairs becomes more critical and the public funding continues to stuggle to keep up, this will likely be a more common form of moving projects forward and, therefore, the iniration process less costly.

LEAN CONSTRUCTION

Lean construction is derived from the manufacturing industry and more specifically from a system of production that Toyota developed in the later part of the twentieth century that continues to be refined. Known as Toyota Production System, the goal of it is to maximize value and minimize waste. The system identifies value as something that the customer will pay for and waste as those things that do not contribute to the value. Examples of waste are lags in production time, unnecessary transportation, and defects.

Lean construction is an approach to project delivery that incorporates some of the attributes of Lean manufacturing. The development of electronic forms of communication has enabled the many players in construction to collaborate on projects much earlier and much more consistently than has been possible in the past. Lean principles applied to construction include the simultaneous design of both the facility (the product) and the process of production. Review and analysis of the design is incorporated at an earlier phase and involves a much wider range of specialists than has been the traditional approach. Construction scheduling shifts from improved productivity to a more reliable system of work flow, creating continuous work for work crews. Materials arrive on site as they are needed; defects are identified and fixed at the source. And both during and at the end of the project, a defined feedback informs both the ongoing project and follow-on projects.

Summary

Construction project management offers significant advantages to the owner as long as he or she is willing and able to stay active in the process and select a good designer and construction project manager who are willing to work as team players. This delivery method provides cost advantages to the owner: both competitive bidding and the opportunity to fast-track the project.

Real estate developers in the commercial building industry commonly use this delivery method. In some cases, the project starts with a construction project management arrangement. Then as the design nears completion, the construction manager negotiates a fixed price with the owner, and the project becomes a traditional arrangement. On "mega" projects such as the Alaskan pipeline, the owner hires a program manager to oversee the entire program. The manager's job is to break the large project into smaller packages that will be designed and constructed by separate design and construction companies.

For a construction management arrangement to be successful, all parties must be fully committed to it from the beginning. Some general contractors sell themselves as construction managers when in fact they approach the project as if it were a lump sum arrangement with preconstruction estimating and scheduling thrown in. Some architects have a difficult time letting go of control in the construction phase and resent the elevation of the contractor as an equal player. Owners need to set aside the time to be involved with the project on a day-to-day basis, truly functioning as the third leg of the stool.

CONTRACT TYPES

In addition to choosing a delivery method for a project, the owner must decide what type of contract to use. A contract is simply an agreement between two or more people in which a person agrees to perform or provide a specific task or service to another person in exchange for something in return. The contract type, like the delivery method, is an important choice for the owner because it addresses project risk. Here we discuss three basic types of contracts: *single fixed price, unit price*, and *cost plus a fee*.

Single Fixed Price
In a single fixed price contract, also called a lump sum, the contractor agrees to provide a specified amount of work for a specific sum. Both parties try to fix the conditions of the project as precisely as possible because once the contract is signed, both parties must live with its terms.

The advantage of this contracting method is that the owner knows before the work begins what the final cost of the project will be. It is usually used with the design/bid/build delivery method. The designer prepares a complete set of contract documents, which the owner then either bids out or negotiates with a contractor. A final contract amount is agreed to, and the work begins.

The risk for the owner is that the contract is only as good as the accuracy of the contract documents. If the scope of the project changes or if errors exist in the documentation, the contract will need to be renegotiated, possibly exposing the owner to increased costs. Moreover, negotiating or bidding a complete set of contract documents takes time and prevents construction from beginning until the design work is complete, a problem endemic to the design/bid/build approach. This eliminates the possibility of a fast-tracked project.

In sum, this contracting method combined with a design/bid/build delivery method allows the owner to define and commit to an agreed-upon project description and dollar amount before the work begins. For owners who want to minimize risk on a project that can be clearly defined (that is, has few unforeseen conditions), this type of contracting method is a good fit. The owner must understand that the process will take longer and that changes caused by mistakes, unknowns, or changes in owner requirements will jeopardize the agreement.

Unit Price Contract

In a unit price contract the owner and the contractor agree on the price that will be charged per unit for the major elements of the project (see Figure 4.8). The owner/designer typically provides estimated quantities for the project, asking contractors to bid on the job by figuring unit prices for these items and calculating a final price. Contractor overhead, profit, and other project expenses must be included within the unit prices. The owner then compares the final price and selects the low bidder.

The advantage of this contracting method is that in many projects (for example, heavy engineering projects) it is difficult to accurately quantify the work necessary. In excavation work it is often difficult to figure the actual amount of rock versus earth that must be excavated. To eliminate risk to both the owner and the bidders, the designers estimate quantities and then ask the bidders to provide a unit price for each type of excavation. Payments will be based on multiplying the actual quantities excavated by the unit price.

This contracting method provides the owner with a competitive bid situation that allows for a fair price for the work. It also eliminates the risk of negotiating a fixed price but then having to renegotiate because of unexpected site conditions. With this contracting method, work can begin before the design is complete, thus speeding up the project.

However, if actual quantities are significantly different from estimated quantities, the owner's financial commitment may be greater than planned. Mistaken quantities also expose the owner to an unbalanced bid, increasing the project's costs (see Figure 4.9). Significantly unbalanced bids border on being unethical and in some cases can be rejected, or the unbalanced work items can be deleted by a change order.

With a unit price contract, actual quantities must be measured in the field, requiring the owner's presence on the site to work with the contractors. Delivery tickets and other invoices must be checked and validated. Final contract price is not known until the last item of work is measured and invoiced by the contractor.

FIGURE 4.8   Unit price example

Work Items	Unit	Estimated Quantity	Bidder 1		Bidder 2	
			Unit Price	Bid Amount	Unit Price	Bid Amount
Soil excavation	Cubic yard	10,000	5.50	55,000	2.00	20,000
Rock excavation	Cubic yard	3,000	25.00	75,000	25.00	75,000
60" pipe	Linear foot	600	17.00	10,200	18.00	10,800
Crushed stone fill	Cubic yard	4,000	21.00	84,000	20.00	80,000
Fill material	Cubic yard	6,000	14.00	84,000	20.00	120,000
Topsoil 40" deep		400	5.00	2,000	6.00	2,400
Total				$310,200		$308,200

Bidder 2 wins the job with the $308,200 total price.

	Estimated Quantity	Bid Price	Actual Quantity	Amount Paid
Soil excavation	10,000	20,000	8,000	16,000
Rock excavation	3,000	75,000	3,000	75,000
6" pipe	600	10,800	600	10,800
Crushed stone fill	4,000	80,000	4,000	80,000
Fill materia	16,000	120,000	7,000	140,000
Topsoil 4" deep	400	2,400	400	2,400
Total		$308,200		$324,200

Assume Bidder 2, in Figure 4.8, knew that the soil excavation quantity provided was high and the fill material quantity provided was low. By providing a low unit price for soil excavation and a high unit price for fill material, Bidder 2 earns an additional $16,000.

FIGURE 4.9   Unbalanced bid (Bidder 2)

In sum, heavy engineering projects such as earth dams, dredging operations, and underground utility work are often accomplished with a unit price contract since the quality of the work can be defined but the actual quantities are difficult to determine in advance. The owner risks not knowing the actual price until the work nears completion, but this disadvantage can be minimized by good design support. For example, good subsurface exploratory work can help predict actual quantities in advance. An owner presence in the field is necessary to verify quantities and authorize payments. However, with a good estimate of actual quantities and with adequate funding, work can begin before final design is complete, thus saving project time.

Cost Plus a Fee

In a cost plus a fee contract arrangement (also called a reimbursable or a time and materials contract), the contractor (and usually the designer) is reimbursed by the owner for his or her work costs and receives an additional agreed-upon fee or a fee that is a percentage of costs. It is important for the owner to spell out clearly in advance what costs will be reimbursed and which costs will be covered by the fee.

This contract makes sense when the scope of the project is difficult to define or when it is important to fast-track the project. The contractor can start work without a clearly defined project scope since all costs will be reimbursed and a profit guaranteed. This type of contract also allows the contractor, designer, and owner to work collaboratively early in the design/build process, encouraging value engineering and good estimating and scheduling support.

A variation of this type of contract is called a guaranteed maximum price (GMP). Here the contractor is reimbursed at cost with an agreed-upon fee up to the GMP (essentially a cap). After this point the contractor is responsible for any additional costs. The contract commonly includes an incentive clause, which specifies that the contractor will receive additional profit for bringing the project in under the GMP.

The risk to the owner is that, even with a GMP, the project begins with considerable unknowns. Project costs may be capped, but quality and scope may be sacrificed at the expense of the GMP. Without a GMP, scope and quality may be solid, but cost and schedule may increase. This type of contract requires a reputable contractor or construction manager whom the owner can trust implicitly.

In sum, a cost plus a fee contract makes sense when the owner needs to complete a project quickly or when the project is difficult to accurately define up front. The project needs a qualified and reputable designer and builder and an active owner organization. The risks to the owner are clear: because the project often begins before it is completely defined, costs may well exceed what were defined at the beginning. A GMP can provide a cap, but the cap may be protected by the contractor at the expense of quality and scope. This type of contract is used with both the construction project management and design/build delivery methods.

Figure 4.10 compares the three contract types we have discussed.

FIGURE 4.10 Cost versus price with the three contract types (in thousands of dollars)

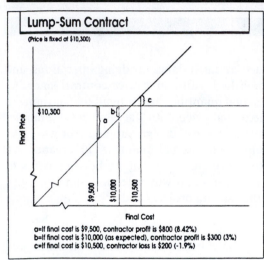

Assume that the contractor believes your project will wind up costing just about $10 million to build. These three graphs show the price to you and the profit or loss to the contractor for three different kinds of contracts at three different actual final cost levels. At point *a* in each diagram, the contractor has shaved $500,000 from the anticipated cost. At *b*, costs have run as expected. At *c*, there has been a cost overrun of $500,000. Basically, with a *lump-sum*, the contractor gets all the savings and takes all the risk. With *time-and-materials*, the owner gets the savings and takes the risk. And with *guaranteed-maximum-price*, the owner gets the savings, the builder takes the risk.

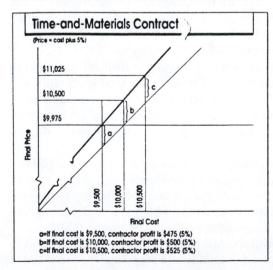

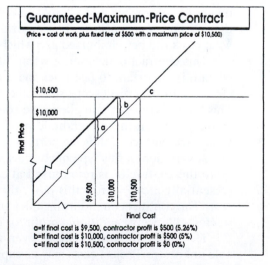

Source: Courtesy of John D. Macomber, George B. H. Macomber Company, Boston.

CONTRACT CHANGES

In each of the contracts we have discussed, an agreement is established between the owner and the contractor stating that a certain service or good will be provided for a stipulated fee or service. The contract is entered into after the work to be performed has been estimated and scheduled and a work plan established. Depending on the contract type, a bid may be submitted, or negotiations may occur between the owner and the contractor. The bid or negotiations are based upon the design to date and the best knowledge available about the project. If conditions change, however, the contract may have to change.

Contract changes occur for three main reasons:

- Because of a change in owner requirements, the scope of the project increases or decreases.
- Because of conditions unforeseen when the contract was agreed to, the work must be performed differently.
- Because of omissions in the documents or design features that cannot be built as specified, the design must be adjusted.

The impact of the change on the contract depends on which type of contract is in place and the reasons for the change. A cost plus fee contract can absorb all of the reasons we have cited without a change, except possibly in the case of a GMP. A GMP may have to be increased, depending on the terms of the GMP clause between owner and contractor. All three reasons would probably lead to a change in a fixed price contract because all may create increased costs and time that need to be fairly adjusted. In a unit price contract, the reasons may or may not lead to a contract change. In the case of an excavation project, an increase in rock would be covered by the unit price submitted, whereas the decision to now prohibit blasting would require a change in the contract.

Contract changes are a reality in construction projects, although most parties see them as disruptive and try to avoid them. In general, fixed price contracts require the greatest number of changes, cost plus a fee the least. Owners need to recognize that changes cost the project money; when negotiating a change with a contractor, they will generally not get as good a price as they would have if they had included the change item in the original project when the work was competitively bid.

Conclusion

Because no two projects are exactly alike, an owner looks at each one and chooses the delivery method and contract type to match the project. Each method—design/bid/build, design/build, and construction project management—has advantages and disadvantages. It is the owner's task to decide which method, given the project, maximizes the advantages and minimizes the disadvantages. The best way to do this is to examine the project risks. The owner should also look at his or her own organization and realistically assess what type of expertise exists there and what time commitment can be given to managing the project. Figure 4.11 shows what is gained and lost by each method.

Once the project is matched with a delivery method, the owner can choose a contract type. The goal here is to minimize risk while minimizing the costs to the organization.

Types of Contracts	Design/Bid/Build	Design/Build	Construction Project Management
Single fixed price or lump sum	✓	✓	✓
Unit price	✓		
Cost plus a fee	✓	✓	✓
Advantages			
Legal and contractual precedent	✓		
Cost determined before contract commitment	✓		
Fast-tracked construction allowed		✓	✓
Minimum owner involvement	✓	✓	
Cost benefit from competition	✓		✓
Negotiation with quality contractor for unique expertise		✓	✓
Allows adjustment to new conditions without changing agreement		✓	✓
Single firm control of design/construct process		✓	
Construction expertise can be incorporated into design		✓	✓
Value engineering opportunities		✓	✓
Disadvantages			
Design does not benefit from construction expertise	✓		
Design construction time is the longest	✓		
Adversarial relationship owner/designer vs contractor	✓		
Contract agreement affected by changes	✓		
Few checks and balances		✓	
Cost control occurs late in project		✓	
Contract amount may be complicated by continual contractor negotiations	✓		
Contract agreement affected by unforeseen conditions	✓		
Quality may be sacrificed for cost containment		✓	
Fixed price may not stand up	✓	✓	✓

FIGURE 4.11 Advantages and disadvantages of the three delivery methods

Again, different contract types match up better with specific project types than others. The owner must weigh the risks against the price and come up with a type that best protects his or her organization.

Chapter Review Questions

1. An owner chooses a delivery method in response to the amount and type of risk that he or she sees in a project. True or false?
2. The greater the risk that an owner sees in a project, the smaller the contingency fund that needs to be applied. True or false?
3. A delivery method is a type of contracting method. True or false?
4. A joint venture is the legal binding of two companies for the purpose of providing a competitive advantage that would be difficult to provide alone. True or false?
5. Contract changes are more likely to occur on a single fixed price contract than on a cost plus a fee contract. True or false?
6. What are the advantages of a design/bid/build delivery method?
   a. Reduced project time
   b. Nonadversarial relationships among participants
   c. Known project cost before construction
   d. All of the above
   e. None of the above
7. The developer of a 40-story high-rise office building desires the shortest possible construction time. What delivery method would be best?
   a. Design/bid/build
   b. Design/build
   c. Construction project management
   d. All of the above
   e. Choices *b* and *c* only
8. Which of the following reasons will *not* cause a contract change?
   a. A change in owner requirements
   b. Unforeseen conditions
   c. Designer omissions or errors
   d. Poor job-site productivity
   e. None of the above
9. Which of the following would be a source of owner risk?
   a. Project complexity
   b. Environmental regulations
   c. A short design/build time frame
   d. A complicated owner organization
   e. All of the above
10. Which type of contractual arrangement could be used when the quantities of work are difficult to determine in advance yet still provide price competition?
    a. Single fixed price
    b. Unit price
    c. Cost plus a fixed fee
    d. Cost plus a percent fee
    e. None of the above

Exercises

1. Investigate how the chosen delivery method affects both the order in which tasks are accomplished and the people who complete them.
   a. List 20–30 major steps that must be accomplished to bring a project from conception through completion.
   b. Create three separate studies (one for each delivery method) correctly ordering the steps. Use color to identify which principal player accomplishes each task.
2. Research a local project and report on the following:
   a. The delivery method employed
   b. The type of contract employed and between which parties (diagram the organizational relationships and types of contracts in *a* and *b*)
   c. When the concept phase for the project began and on what dates the designer and constructor were hired
   d. The number of subcontractors used and under what type of contract they were hired
   e. Project risk and how the delivery method and contract types were able to shift it.

CHAPTER

5 | PROJECT CHRONOLOGY

Chapter Outline

Introduction
Initiation of the Project
Feasibility Analysis
Financing
Design of the Project
     Programming
     Schematic Design
     Design Development
     Construction Documents
Procurement
Construction
Turnover and Startup
Operation of the Facility
Disposal of the Facility
Conclusion

Student Learning Objectives

In this chapter you will learn the following:

1. The principal tasks in the life cycle of a project
2. What information must be gathered and investigated to successfully initiate a project
3. The principal phases in project design
4. What must be done to move from construction to operation

INTRODUCTION

The life of a facility goes through many phases. It starts out as an idea. The idea is combined with money, and a project is born. The project is developed as drawings and specifications. It is then built. When it is complete, it is turned over to the owner as a finished facility and is occupied, maintained, and repaired as it ages and eventually dies. A facility can last for hundreds of years, but the period in which it is actually designed and built is very small. Figure 5.1 illustrates a design/build/use/dispose scenario for a shopping mall.

At some point in its lifetime a facility is likely to be renovated, either to renew obsolete systems or change its use. For example, during the late 1800s many New England mill buildings were constructed to house a growing manufacturing industry. As the economy changed from manufacturing to service, these buildings outlived their usefulness. Many were bought by developers for reuse as housing. Because of the span of the structural elements required for a mill operation, they made attractive residential units; and since often they were located along a river (a transportation advantage for moving materials), the site was also desirable. To be used as housing, however, the interior of the buildings had to be entirely gutted. New systems had to be installed, the facade had to be repaired and windows replaced, and the roofing system had to be renewed. Although it was not new construction, the facility now began a new life span.

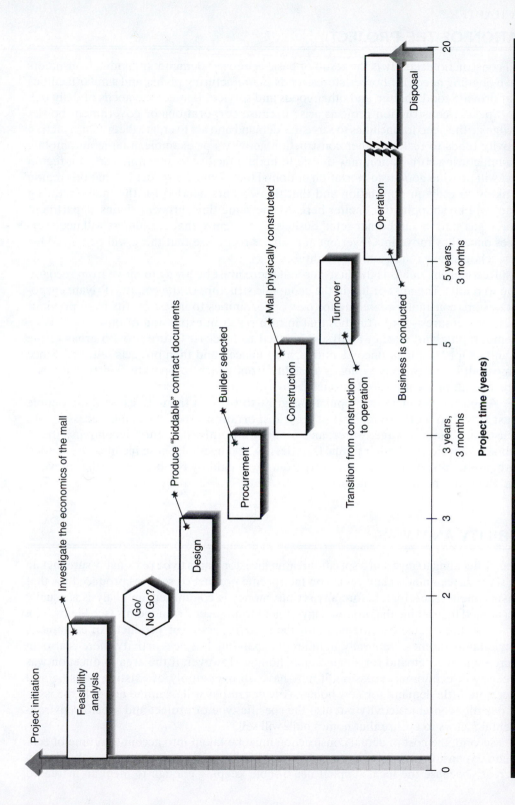

FIGURE 5.1 Life cycle of a shopping mall

INITIATION OF THE PROJECT

All construction activity is the result of basic economic demand. Individual consumers have ongoing needs for homes, stores, roads, manufacturing plants, and similar facilities that provide food, shelter, and other goods and services to meet the needs of daily life.

Specific construction projects arise because corporations or government bodies recognize the need for facilities to serve this demand and act to create them. Construction activity tends to foster further construction activity. For example, a large automobile manufacturing corporation may decide to build a facility to assemble cars in a region that will provide good transportation options. Home builders recognize that this region is likely to grow in population and that the workers needed for the manufacturing plant will be shopping for shelter here. At the same time, grocery chains, department stores, gas stations, and other retail businesses recognize that consumers will need services once they move in. Government agencies recognize that there will be a need for new schools, new roads, and new utilities.

Recognizing needs is the first step, but there must be a way to move from recognition to reality. The answer lies in the economic structure of the country. Private corporations are constantly searching for new opportunities to invest profits from previous business ventures—opportunities that in turn result in expansion of business activity. Demographic and market analyses are used to forecast future growth areas in the country. Opportunities, once identified, are financed and then projects initiated. Since almost all business activity needs a facility from which to operate, construction is a direct result of the increased business activity.

As businesses increase, populations grow to work in them. Because these people must travel to work, roads and other transportation modes become necessary. As houses are built, sewage, water, and other utility infrastructure accompany them. Schools, libraries, and other public facilities are also needed. These facilities are funded with public money that comes mostly from taxes paid by the businesses that move in and the workers who built homes.

FEASIBILITY ANALYSIS

Before deciding to invest in a specific area, an investor wants to be reasonably sure that he or she will see an adequate return on the specific product or services produced for that environment. Therefore, before any serious money is committed, an analysis is usually performed to examine the proposed investment from several standpoints (see Figure 5.2).

First, there must be a demand for the specific service or product. An example is single-family homes. Generally, in times of expanding business activity, there is also an increase in the demand for single-family homes. However, if the area in question was recently in economic recession, it may have an oversupply of existing housing and therefore little demand for new homes. Any developer will examine not only the issue of overall economic activity but also the specific type of project and specific environmental factors to ensure that homes built will sell.

Second, the cost of actual construction must be taken into account. In time of economic expansion, costs also increase. The price of materials such as lumber or brick may increase because the local supplier has trouble keeping enough to meet an increased

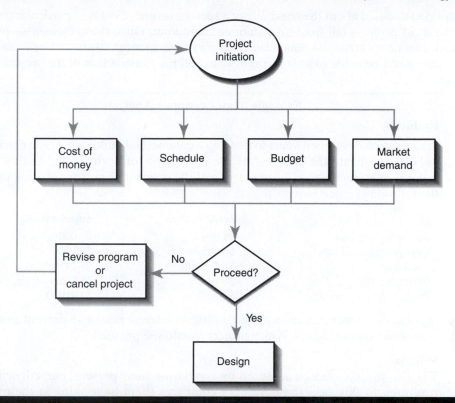

FIGURE 5.2   The decision about whether or not to move a project into design depends on cost of money, schedule, budget, and market demand. If the economics look favorable, the project proceeds

demand. The supplier may have to buy from other geographic areas where prices are higher. This cost is passed on to the builder. There may also be a shortage of skilled labor, which means importing labor or using less-skilled labor. Either way, both costs and risks to the project increase. Such factors could make it too costly to construct a facility and still realize a reasonable return on investment.

Third, the cost of money itself can be a key factor. Most construction projects use borrowed money. If interest rates are high, then the cost of servicing the investor's debt may make the return on investment too low. The investors may elect to put their money into another type of investment.

Finally, the timing of the project can be very important. Construction projects often involve long periods of time between conception and completion. During this interim period, which can sometimes be several years, the anticipated markets can change radically. Sometimes, if the investor is lucky, this change can be for the better; but just as likely it can be for the worse.

During the early analysis stage, the owner often consults with architects and construction professionals. Architects provide early design advice, and construction professionals offer cost and constructability advice. Their advice helps an owner make a more informed decision about the feasibility of a specific project. Cost is of particular concern since most projects fail from an economic standpoint. Once these elements—market need, cost of construction, financing costs, and time to market—have been analyzed, a decision will be made to go forward or to cancel the construction of the project.

Example of an Economic Analysis

Problem

A real estate developer wants to develop a commercial building lot. The marketing people investigate the area and determine a need for both a retail facility and a supermarket. A construction manager and the operations personnel come up with the following projections:

	Retail Facility	Supermarket
Size in square feet	95,000	20,000
Cost per square foot	$64.45	$62.20
Total cost	$6.12 million	$1.24 million
Economic life	20 years	15 years
Projected yearly income	$1 million	$320,000

The developer evaluates projects using an interest rate of 15 percent as a measure of the cost of capital. Which project should she pursue?

Solution

The two projects can be analyzed by comparing their present, annual, or future revenues. In this case, the developer compares them by looking at the present value of the two revenues: a net present value (NPV) analysis. The retail facility will have a negative income of $6.12 million in the first year but a positive income of $1 million per year for twenty years. Using a compound interest table (i=15 percent), the developer learns that this annual $1 million per year equals $6.25 million today. Thus, the NPV for this project is a positive $130,000.

The supermarket will have a negative income of $1.24 million in the first year but a positive income of $320,000 per year for fifteen years. The NPV of this revenue stream is $1.87 million, with the NPV for the project a positive $630,000.

As a result of this study, the developer decides to pursue the supermarket project.

Until construction actually begins, a project may have many go/no go decision points. The decision on feasibility is one of the first major ones—the time when many, if not most, projects do not go forward. Many are analyzed and found to fall short when the rate of return is calculated. Investors simply move on to more lucrative projects.

FINANCING

If the project gets past the first hurdle of profitability for the investor, the owner must next line up financial backing for some of the work. Although investors walk into projects with some money, most are unable to fund 100 percent of the work. Commonly, the initial investor acquires outside funds to supplement his or her own. A developer might borrow from banks or an insurance company or invite outside investors to share in future profits. A corporation wishing to build a factory could borrow from a bank or sell additional stocks or bonds. Whatever the source of additional funds, other individuals or firms decide to lend or invest funds based on their own expectation of return on investment. They, too, must be satisfied that the project will return their initial investment plus support a reasonable rate of return on their money. What might look like a significant opportunity to a developer may seem too risky in the eyes of a banker. If the developer and the lender are not of like mind, then the project is in danger of being canceled.

DESIGN OF THE PROJECT

If the owner decides to proceed at this point, he or she typically hires a design professional. If the owner elects to proceed using a construction management mode, then he or she now chooses a construction professional as well. The construction professional provides cost, schedule, and construction advice throughout the design process.

Design is usually divided into distinct stages so that the owner can review the progress at milestone points along the way (see Figure 5.3). For convenience, the discussion of the design stages will be based on building construction.

Programming

A *program* is a written statement of the requirements of the building. It is the basis of the design. The program describes the spaces needed, the services required in those spaces, and the relationships of the functions to be performed in the building. It can be written by the owner or user of the building, by the architect, or by a professional hired

FIGURE 5.3 The four phases of project design

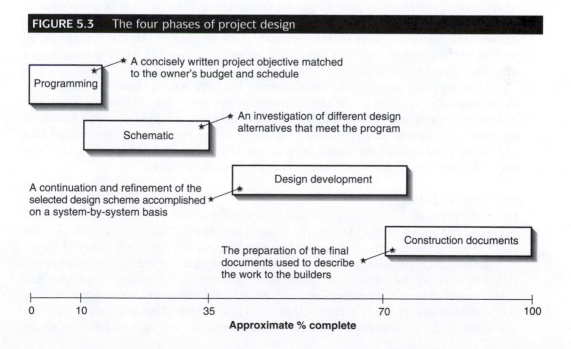

Programming — A concisely written project objective matched to the owner's budget and schedule

Schematic — An investigation of different design alternatives that meet the program

A continuation and refinement of the selected design scheme accomplished on a system-by-system basis — Design development

The preparation of the final documents used to describe the work to the builders — Construction documents

0   10   35   70   100

Approximate % complete

especially for his or her expertise in programming. Whatever the means, the key to the program is extensive involvement of the user because this is where unique and specific requirements are written down.

The nature of the programming process depends on two things: the sophistication of the owner and the complexity of the proposed facility. Owners vary considerably in their degree of understanding about the building process. Those who rarely build are not very knowledgeable and need a great deal of assistance as the program is developed. The professional hired for this task needs to educate the owner about the importance of certain information and must ensure that all that information is gathered and incorporated into the program.

Owners more knowledgeable about the building process do not need as much outside consulting support during this phase. They may even have personnel in house who can accomplish the task. Since much programming information is unique to specific user requirements and in-house personnel often know the nature of their facilities best, programs done in house can be well tailored to specific users.

Regardless of the owner's level of sophistication, however, the complexity of the project itself can determine how the programming needs to be accomplished. With very complex projects, it is necessary to devote more time and resources to programming to ensure that an accurate depiction of the needs and functions of the facility are incorporated. In such cases, a professional who specializes in that particular type of facility may be hired to complete the program.

If a construction professional has been engaged, he or she is providing early cost estimates, early schedules, and advice on constructability. At this stage the owner uses order of magnitude or square foot estimates to further check the financial feasibility of the project.

Costs are also considered at this stage in relationship to the schedule. Since borrowed money is frequently used to pay for construction, interest costs become a factor throughout the process. Participants are aware of the daily cost of interest that accumulates relentlessly. Delays of any sort add to the burden of this cost, requiring all project participants to expedite their work as much as possible while maintaining a necessary level of design quality.

When programming is complete, the owner has information about the needed size of the project in relation to the requirements of the users; the mechanical, electrical, and plumbing systems; vertical and horizontal circulation; and public areas. Usually, an estimate and schedule are produced to give the owner preliminary information that can be checked against the initial projections. Using the information gained at this stage, the owner may choose to proceed or to cancel the project.

Schematic Design

Once the program is complete and the owner has decided to proceed, the designer begins actual design of the project. The process begins with the *schematic design*—the stage in which the designer defines the building's characteristics in a number of ways.

Before schematic design begins, the owner selects a site for the building. Site investigations done by the owner give the designer information about soil conditions and makeup that in large part determine the type of foundation and structure possible for the particular site. The architect develops preliminary floor plans that reflect the relationships of the various functional areas to one another. Siting and location of the building are determined as well as its visual form. Preliminary decisions regarding structural, environmental, and other systems are made and outline specifications developed.

During this stage several options are often pursued. Sometimes the owner does not see all of these options. The architect's design team generates many alternatives and rejects many before they are developed into materials presented to the owner. This typical part of the design process helps the architect find the best design solution among many possible alternatives. Usually, two or three alternatives survive the process, which are presented to the owner for consideration.

If the construction professionals continue their involvement during this stage, they may develop early conceptual estimates for the owner. Their advice regarding construction feasibility of the proposed design options helps identify materials that may be difficult to obtain in the current marketplace and items that will need to be purchased early because of the lead time needed for fabrication and delivery.

When the schematic design is complete, the owner is again faced with the decision to proceed further or to cancel the project. At this time, all information developed to date—market information, financing costs, construction costs, and design—are factored into the decision. If all elements still indicate a favorable project from an investment standpoint and if the architect's design meets the owner's program and aesthetic criteria, then the project proceeds to the next stage of design.

Design Development

When the project team enters *design development*, it pursues a single design concept. The purpose of this stage is to refine the design and obtain detailed information from the users about their requirements. During this phase, the owner, the architect, and (if applicable) the construction professional finalize the design of the major building systems—for example, structural, plumbing, elevator, roofing, mechanical, exterior facade, electrical. Specialty consultants are often asked to design these systems and are usually coordinated by the architect, who ensures that their work is consistent with the intent of the design. Location of mechanical ductwork, the type of heating and cooling systems, the size and type of elevator systems, shaft space through the building: all must be carefully coordinated with how the occupants expect to use the space and what the architect visually intends. Conversations with users during this phase center around how many electrical outlets are required, what type of sinks are needed in the laboratory, what type of computer workstations are needed in the offices, what special services are needed for specific equipment, and so on.

As in all the other phases of project development, cost estimates are refigured. The estimates done at this point are probably the most important of the job because there is now sufficient information to generate real numbers from real subcontractors. These estimates are the first market test of the design. As a result, they give the owner a greater degree of certainty about the final cost of the project. Once again, he or she is faced with deciding whether to go forward or to abandon the project. The likelihood that it will be canceled diminishes as the process goes forward. If the early phases were sufficiently thorough, the gross costs and scope of the project should be known. Barring a significant change in the owner's needs or changes in the conditions of the job, information should build upon itself and become increasingly refined. There should be no surprises big enough to cause the project to be abandoned.

Construction Documents

At this last stage of design, the architect creates the final working *construction documents* used to bid the job for construction and to build the job in the field. These documents are particularly important because they represent the work as it will be actually constructed. They should meet the program criteria determined during the programming stage, reflect the design as agreed upon at the schematic phase, and refine all the detailed work that went into the design development phase. If the documents waver from any of these agreed-upon criteria, problems may ensue during construction that could cost the owner money and time.

PROCUREMENT

Procurement is defined as the overall process of finding and purchasing the materials called for in the contract and hiring the best subcontractors to build the project. The construction documents, both specifications and drawings, must be accurate and must clearly communicate to the bidders the scope of work as programmed by the owner.

The first task is to hire the many subcontractors who will actually erect and assemble the project. This can be done in several ways, depending on the contractual arrangement chosen. In the traditional contracting mode, the owner, with the architect's assistance, requests bids from a list of qualified contractors. Contractors and their subcontractors prepare their best estimate of what they believe the project will cost them to complete. This cost is submitted to the owner and the architect within a specified amount of time. After evaluating competing bids, the owner enters into a contract for construction. In the construction management mode, the project documents are divided into bid packages, which are logical subdivisions of work based on typical contractor specializations; for example, the structural, mechanical, electrical, and plumbing work are each bid on separately. Both the architect and the construction manager help the owner evaluate these bids. In either case, the owner's task is to find the best and least costly contracting firm to do the work in the field.

Sometimes the owner must purchase equipment or materials before a contractor is hired to do the work. Such materials are known as *long-lead items* and are usually purchased early because they take a longer time to be fabricated than the construction schedule allows for. During design development, these items are often identified. The owner can either purchase them directly or use the services of a construction manager who is skilled in procuring such items. When a contractor is hired, long-lead items are usually assigned to him or her for coordination and installation.

CONSTRUCTION

Once the procurement process has been completed, construction of the project can begin. The main element involved in construction is the task of managing and coordinating the field operations. This means scheduling the crews in the proper sequence, choosing the most efficient and safe construction techniques and methods, and directing the production process for the building activities. To accomplish this task, the construction professional must order the correct materials; ensure an adequate supply of the necessary tools and equipment; and monitor schedule, cost, and quality.

A parallel task is the contract administration. This job—the paperwork of the project—requires more than simple record keeping. It involves controlling changes to the scope of the project, accounting for payments and other costs to ensure adequate financial control, maintaining work schedules, keeping track of all contract documentation, and monitoring quality-control tasks. Contract administration is a team effort, involving the construction manager, the designer, and the owner; and it often requires meetings and other forms of communication to deal with problems quickly and effectively so that the project can remain on schedule.

BOX 5.1

LEADERSHIP IN ENERGY AND ENVIRONMENTAL DESIGN

Construction projects and their operation significantly affect the environment in many ways. Construction projects consume energy to build and operate, release atmospheric emissions, consume raw materials, generate waste, and occupy land. As the world's population grows, consuming more energy and raw materials and the planet becomes increasingly sensitive to gas emissions, a more integrated approach to building needs to occur. Owners and builders need to move away from the "lowest, first cost" approach to building and look at the project over its entire life—construction, operation, and decommissioning. Projects need to attain the optimal balance among cost, environmental, societal, and human benefits while at the same time meeting their operational needs.

Leadership in Energy and Environmental Design (LEED) represents a holistic approach to the design, construction, and operation of building structures. LEED has established a road map that can be used by design/build teams to construct more sustainable (green) building projects. In following the LEED approach, building teams take into consideration five key areas: sustainable site development, water savings, energy efficiency, materials selection, and indoor environmental quality. Projects are "scored" in the above five areas—platinum represents the highest level of certification followed by gold then silver. A LEED-certified building has reduced operating costs, provides a healthier work environment, and conserves natural resources.

For a builder, understanding sustainability and the impact of construction on the environment is both good business and a factor in short-term project success. By law, builders must meet the hard requirements set out in environmental law. Most of these laws are obvious, such as containing hazardous chemicals or controling runoff and site erosion. Ignoring these laws can lead to fines and the shutdown of the job. The scoring system set up for LEED certification, however, is for the most part voluntary. The exception to this is where LEED-certified buildings are required such as in New York where in October 2005 Mayor Bloomberg signed Local Law 86, which required many of New York's new municiple buildings, additions, and renovations to achieve rigorous standards of sustainabilty. Increasingly, owners are requiring LEED awareness as a pre-requisite for bidding, and builders

(*continued*)

BOX 5.1   Continued

who understand the LEED scoring system and how to implement sustainable construction are more likely to be engaged. As energy costs continue to climb, sustainable construction will become even more popular. Lastly, being defined as a "green builder" is also good public relations. Construction needs to improve its public image, and being viewed as positive, environmental stewards can only help.

So what does builder need to do to become "branded" as green? One of the better first steps is to incorporate LEED certification training for existing key staff members. Educating key project staff on the LEED scoring system will increase construction sustainability awareness through-

out the company and allow the constructor to provide more value to the client. Constructors should also begin to establish green practices as a way of constructing such as managing waste, controlling air and water pollution, and minimizing the impact of construction operations on the site and community. These practices should be published and made as part of all public relations and sales campaigns. Effort should be made to hire subcontractors with similar work habits and/or educate subcontractors and suppliers on sustainable practices. Lastly, constructors should support education and research efforts on new sustainable practices. Make an effort to place your company on the "cutting edge."

TURNOVER AND STARTUP

After actual construction is complete, the project must be turned over to the owner for use during the rest of its economic life. Often this turnover involves complicated technical issues and problems. For example, the startup of a building's mechanical and other environmental systems can involve much testing of piping, ductwork, machinery, and other components, both individually and as a total system. This process is never without complications and can often be one of the more intense stages of creating a project. It must also be done in conjunction with the owner's employees, who will be the ultimate operators of the facility. Commonly, the installing contractor trains the user's personnel in the operation and maintenance of the more complex systems. Arrangements for such training must be coordinated during this period. In the case of unique equipment, it may be necessary to order spare parts that then must be tagged, logged in, and stored in a known location—ideally in the new facility. Equipment such as elevators and systems such as roofs will be warranted by manufacturers or installers. These certificates of warranty must be recorded so that the employees can use them when the need arises. Finally, changes during construction must be documented. These final documents, which reflect the actual project, are called *as-builts*. They must be submitted in complete and usable form to the end user.

Turnover is also a legal process during which the building becomes the legal property and responsibility of the owner. This involves obtaining various legal certifications, such as the certificate of occupancy and the certificate of substantial completion, both of which represent legal and practical milestones that are spelled out in the original contracts for construction. The process is often long and tedious as many documents pass back and forth among the parties. Examples of such documents include insurance certificates, inspection reports, completed change orders, and various types of waivers that protect all the parties after the contractual relationship is severed at the end of the project.

OPERATION OF THE FACILITY

This phase is the responsibility of the owner and/or the tenant of the building and usually does not involve either the architect or the construction professional. It is the period in which the building is put to the use for which it was intended. The period can last for many years before a major renovation is necessary, kicking the building back into the design/build cycle.

This phase is also the period of greatest expenditure on the project since the total operating costs for a building are significantly greater than the construction costs. Knowing these operating costs is important in the planning of future facilities. It may often be more economical to buy more efficient mechanical equipment, easier-to-maintain flooring systems, and a better curtain-wall system. More money will be invested up front, but the payback can be realized in the operating costs of the facility. This is an economic analysis that compares the life expectancy of the facility, the design/build costs, the operating costs, and the cost of capital. Facility owners and managers usually need advice about the best model to use in making decisions during the planning stages of the project.

DISPOSAL OF THE FACILITY

At the end of its useful life, a project or facility may meet any one of a number of fates. It may be closed down or simply abandoned. It may be disassembled or removed. It may also be renovated or overhauled and thereby brought back to peak operating condition or may be remodeled and converted to another use.

For a project to undergo renovation or remodeling, the owner must perform an economic and financial analysis to determine if the new investment is viable. Thus, the facility and the owner begin a new life cycle.

Conclusion

Many people are involved in the life cycle of a building. First are those who analyze the need for the facility and decide whether it is economically and programmatically feasible. Then the project enters the design/build phase. Architects are hired to design it. Construction professionals are hired to carry out the actual assembly and erection process. All parties, no matter what the contractual arrangement, need to work in harmony to fulfill the many functions that must be performed. The following chapters explore in greater detail the various phases of the construction project.

Chapter Review Questions

1. The procurement phase precedes the design phase since it involves the bidding and award of architect services. True or false?

2. The feasibility stage of a project requires heavy owner involvement. True or false?

3. It is imperative for project success that the feasibility, design, procurement, construction, turnover, and operation stages described in this chapter occur in linear fashion. That is, no stage should proceed without the prior stage being completed. True or false?

4. Project design typically proceeds as follows: programming, design development, schematic, and construction documents. True or false?

5. As interest rates increase, income in future years becomes more valuable in offsetting up-front construction costs. True or false?

6. Advertising for subcontractors, review of subcontractors' bids, and awarding of contracts occurs during which project phase?
   a. Procurement
   b. Construction
   c. Design
   d. Turnover
   e. Feasibility

7. As-built drawings, warranties, guarantees, and operation manuals are all provided to the owner during which project phase?
   a. Feasibility analysis
   b. Design
   c. Construction
   d. Turnover
   e. Procurement

8. The production of drawings and specifications occurs in which project phase?
   a. Feasibility analysis
   b. Design
   c. Construction
   d. Turnover
   e. Procurement

9. Which of the following are considered in determining the feasibility of a project?
   a. Cost of money
   b. Estimated cost
   c. Market demand
   d. Project timing
   e. All of the above

10. The design of project systems occurs during which of the following design phases?
    a. Programming
    b. Schematic
    c. Design development
    d. Construction documents
    e. None of the above

Exercises

1. Analyze an actual project recently built in your area. Identify the major activities that occurred in each of the project phases and who accomplished them. Develop a flowchart or network diagram and present it to your class.
2. Class members should each examine a different local project and determine the following:

    The scope of the project (work included and work not included)
    Project cost per square foot
    Economic life
    Design–construction time
    Income in dollars per square foot
    Compare the viability of different project types at different interest rates.
3. Meet with an architect and an engineer and look at the level of the design effort at the end of the programming, schematic design, design development, and contract documents phases. What level of estimating and scheduling accompanies the design work?

CHAPTER

6

CONSTRUCTION SERVICES DURING DESIGN

Chapter Outline

Student Learning Objectives

In this chapter you will learn the following:

1. The roles and responsibilities of the construction professional during the design phase
2. The information that must be learned about the local work area and the site before design and preconstruction planning
3. A working understanding of value engineering
4. The specific estimating, scheduling, and procurement activities that occur during design

INTRODUCTION

Good design is a result of collaboration among many different people. Although there is always a lead designer, the product is a combination of the collaborative process and consultation with other experts. There is a continual interaction that produces ideas and tests concepts and finally results in a refined plan. Traditionally, construction professionals were not part of this team. Projects were completely designed by architects and engineers, often with the assistance of construction consultants, and then offered for bidding to a group of builders. Many projects are still produced this way. However, as projects become more complex and the need for early completion more accelerated, construction professionals may be brought in during the design process to provide preconstruction services. In such cases, their expertise has some effect on the ultimate design.

Preconstruction services can run from simple cost and scheduling services to integral involvement in the design effort. As an estimator or a scheduler, the constructor is an advisor to the team on cost issues and scheduling issues. As an integral part of the design effort, the constructor examines, recommends, and researches alternatives for various materials as well as details and reviews the constructability of the project components.

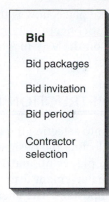

Design

Scope definition

Conceptual design

Design approval

Construction documentation

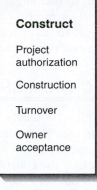

Bid

Bid packages

Bid invitation

Bid period

Contractor selection

Construct

Project authorization

Construction

Turnover

Owner acceptance

He or she may do value engineering studies to produce life-cycle cost analyses (discussed later in this chapter). Later in the design process, the constructor may help put the work packages together, prequalify bidders, and begin planning construction logistics.

Construction management as a profession is a relatively new entry into the field of design and construction. Traditionally, the designer produced a set of design documents and assisted the owner in hiring a builder to implement the design. Preconstruction services were performed by the designer. Many times the designer hired a construction consultant to assist in this task. However, as projects have gotten bigger, schedules shortened, technologies changed, and regulations increased, many owners prefer to separate construction and design expertise early in the project.

The ability to influence the course of a design is much greater at the beginning of a project, when the amount of money being spent is low. As the design becomes more detailed, however, the amount of money already invested increases; and any change has the potential to be costly. Once the project is in construction, any changes can be extremely costly both in time and in actual costs (see Figure 6.1).

As Figure 6.1 shows, there is much value to the owner in getting as much good advice as possible early in the project. Relatively small amounts of money are being

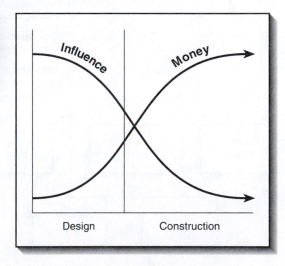

FIGURE 6.1 As time moves on in the life cycle of a project, influence decreases while costs committed increase

spent; so if changes must take place, now is the time. Also, construction methods and materials can be worked out conceptually much earlier and be incorporated early enough to make an impact on the way in which the documents are assembled. This gives everyone more options.

FINDING THE RIGHT CONSTRUCTION MANAGER

The effort and care that go into selecting the construction manager for a job is similar to the care that goes into selecting the designers and other consultants. The construction manager is a key team player no matter when his or her involvement begins. Matching the construction management firm with the type of job, its size, and the proposed delivery method is important. The chemistry among the architects, the owner, and the construction manager is also a key element but one that is a bit more difficult to gauge. When deciding whether a firm can handle the type and size of project, an owner can easily find the answer in the materials that the construction professional submits. However, the fit among team members can be fully understood only after the team is assembled and has been working together. Still, it is in everyone's best interest to investigate this aspect as thoroughly as possible beforehand. Speaking with people who have worked in the past with the firm—and specifically with the project members—will give some insight into how well they work in varying situations. Visiting the sites of their past work with them will indicate their individual pride and ownership toward the projects. Speaking in general about the industry and its recent and future changes will show how knowledgeable they are and how forward-thinking.

When the owner, sometimes with assistance of the designer, begins to search for the construction manager, he or she should consider several points (see Figure 6.2). To begin with, the owner should discover whether the firm has experience that is broad-based

FIGURE 6.2   Many factors should be taken into account in the selection of a construction manager

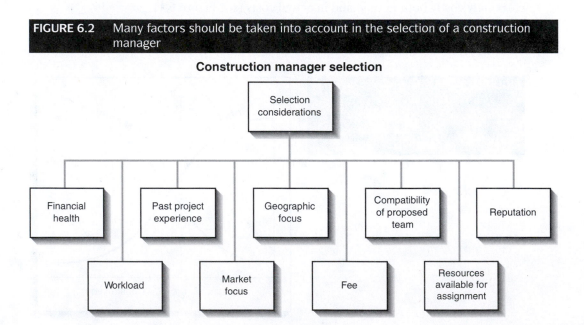

enough for the type of project and whether the scope of preconstruction work fits the talents of the firm. For example, if the owner wants only estimating and scheduling services, then the process of finding the right construction professional should concentrate on those attributes. However, construction management means different things to different people. Some general contractors call themselves construction managers but have little experience or knowledge about what this task actually entails. Sometimes the owner believes the services should encompass what traditionally are considered owner-provided services (such as relocation coordination) or architect-provided services (such as conceptual cost estimates). To avoid conflicts, the owner needs to be very specific about his or her expectations.

For most projects, the owner wants to hire a builder who has considerable construction experience; this is especially true for a large, complex project. Expertise should be demonstrated in preconstruction activities such as value engineering, estimating, scheduling, project control, and planning. The financial state of the company is also important: both its overall financial health and its bonding capacity. Research into prior successes on projects and overall customer satisfaction will give a sense of how well the firm will perform over time. A look at the organization, including employees' average years of experience, its retention record, its safety record, current projects, and the availability of specific staff members, will flesh out the specific characteristics of the firm. It is important to identify the specific people available for assignment. Every firm has an "A" team. The trick for the owner is to make sure he or she has this team assigned to this project. By networking with like owners, he or she can find out who performed best on their projects. Another indicator is the makeup of the proposed team that presents itself to the owner. Ideally, there should be a good cross-section of experience levels. If most team members are young, they do not have much collective experience to cull from. If most of the team is older, they may have too much old-school thinking. Ideally, the team members will have some experience working together as a team. The owner is also going to be interested in fees. If he or she is looking for preconstruction services only, the constructor can give a lump sum fee based on a specified scope of work. If the owner is also looking for construction services, the constructor will have to understand the delivery method that is intended, the cost of the work, and the schedule before giving a fee.

Request for Proposal

Many owners start with a preconstruction proposal so that they can keep their options open as they approach the time of construction. This gives the owner a way out if the makeup of the team is not effective. It also allows the owner the choice of putting the project out for a hard lump sum bid if that seems more appropriate. The preconstruction proposal that the owner puts together will come to the prospective construction managers in the form of a *request for proposal* (RFP). When responding to an RFP, the construction professional should expect to include some of the following in his or her response:

- Description of the project, schedule, and costs as understood from the RFP
- Comments on the sample contract provided with the RFP
- Description of services offered
- Identification of how fee would be configured

- Project participants with résumés
- Description of company safety plan
- Description of the range of company's services beyond the RFP
- Management plan

The owner, perhaps with the help of the designer, examines the responses from prospective candidates in light of the amount of effort that they put into them. Putting together a response is not a trivial task. To do a good job, many people are brought together. The marketing department includes standard pieces of material, but otherwise the response is crafted by the proposed team. Research into any specifics about the project will add strength to the proposal. Analyzing what the owner is asking for and responding exactly to that request will also help. Many firms, in their anxiety to look their best, include information not requested. This puts a burden on the owner and probably does not win any points for the candidate.

When the list has been pared down to two or three candidates, the owner usually sets up interviews. Because this is where the issue of personal chemistry among project members comes into play, the firm should bring the people who will work on the project to the interview. Generally, these interviews are set up in two parts: a formal presentation and an informal dialogue with questions and answers. Some owners send along questions ahead of time. The more the firm can find out about the owner's concerns in advance, the more prepared it can be in the interview. The best interviews are those in which people feel they have just attended the first project meeting. In other words, the discussion focuses on the project, and dialogue flows freely among all members of the team. A firm that keeps the discussion focused on itself is not going to be as successful as the firm that shows interest and knowledge about the project.

Team Introductions

When the construction professionals are hired, one of their first tasks is to learn the specific objectives and needs of the owner. These include the proposed schedule, budget, and operating objectives. Early discussions regarding the division of work among owner, designer, and construction professional will minimize future confusion. A construction manager must understand the owner's key staff members and their capabilities. These staff members will be able to help the construction manager find out specific information as it is required. Review and comment and incorporation of the owner's requirements for bidding, bonding, and any other procedures that are standard for the owner's organization will guide how the work packages are put together. Meetings with the designer should include discussions regarding design criteria, design to date (if any), areas of responsibilities for each party, and identification of personnel. This sets the stage for good working relationships among all parties. [In addition to these introductory meetings, there is a more formal kickoff meeting initiated by the owner and covering administrative issues such as the reporting and communication structure, format and content of meeting notes, and protocols for their distribution.] This meeting also reiterates expectations about roles and responsibilities of all parties.

TASKS AND RESPONSIBILITIES OF THE CONSTRUCTION MANAGER

Feasibility Studies

Before a commitment is made to a specific scope of work and a budget, the owner often does a feasibility study to look at several options (see Chapter 5). These studies are usually prepared with the assistance of professional consultants whose skills depend on the scope of study and when it is done. If the purpose of the study is simply to evaluate the market, identify the lending rates, and find the owner's financial fit, the owner will likely do the study with a financial advisor. If the study is programmatic (perhaps an investigation of what can fit on a particular lot), then an architect is best suited for the task. If the study economically evaluates different design solutions (such as renovating an existing facility or removing it and building a new one), then a construction professional might supply services to either the architect or the owner. This study would examine several options in light of the owner's objectives, reviewing town zoning laws, community sentiment, life cycle costing, available funds, schedule, and aesthetic value. A designer and a construction consultant together would provide the owner with the right information.

Before an owner's organization makes a formal commitment to a project, the owner needs justification for the requested level of funding. An organization usually has many competing needs for funds. To put together a good information packet, the owner might hire a designer or a construction professional to formulate budget numbers. Because most complex projects run for several years, developing a schedule gives the funding agency a sense of how much money will have to be committed on a yearly basis. The feasibility study can address all these concerns.

In most cases, neither the designer nor the construction manager is hired for a project during a feasibility study. For that reason, most architectural, engineering, and construction firms will act as consultants during this early stage. Sometimes they will continue on with the project, but often the owner opts to use consultants who will not be part of the project if it goes forward. First, the owner is sure of getting an unbiased opinion. The fear is that a consultant who hopes to get the job will, consciously or unconsciously, weight the data so that he or she is the logical candidate to continue with the project. Second, the owner may not be ready to commit to the project in the near future. The feasibility study may be one of many that he or she is conducting to test the fiscal waters for the next five to ten years.

Site Investigations

Before design can begin, the team must learn about conditions at the site. Site investigations include analysis of the soil composition in relation to types of foundations and the need for fill, clearing, and grubbing. They influence early estimates of the project and alert the design team if special instructions must be included in the documents. Access to the site, amount of laydown area available, railroad locations, utility availability, and routes into the site are all factors that will affect how the design team formulates the documents.

To begin this investigation, the construction manager first obtains a copy of the plot plan of the area. This includes information about the size of the site, existing structures, existing roads or rights-of-way, easements, and the compass points. These plot plans are public records and can be picked up at local town offices. Once the structural engineer has recommended a foundation type, the construction manager can study the soils report, visit the site, and note any surface conditions. For instance, existing ledge outcropping may have to be removed to accommodate the specific foundation design. The construction manager can make recommendations about methods of removal and associated costs. The structural engineer may opt to alter the design if the construction manager identifies less costly methods.

Site Visit

Maps, surveys, and soils reports all provide good information; but unshown conditions may exist, or information may be outdated. Surveys and maps only record the conditions of the moment, and that moment could have been years before. For instance, a structure shown on the survey may have been removed. The elevations may be different due to added fill. New roads may have been cut, or old roads may have disappeared. Trees and bushes may be gone. The construction manager must make sure that all site information is current, perhaps by using a detailed site analysis form (see Figure 6.3).

In addition to the conditions at the site itself, the project team is interested in the areas and conditions around the site that could affect the work. In an urban site, businesses in the area will be affected by the work. By having such information early in the process, the construction professional can work out a strategy that will minimize disruption to area businesses while allowing the project to proceed normally. Site visits also consider the availability of utilities. In an urban environment, it is usually fairly easy to tap into the main utilities that run in the street—gas, water, electricity, telephone, sewer, storm drainage. In a suburban or rural setting, such services may be more remote. They may have to be brought in from farther distances over property owned by others. By identifying the most economical method of getting utilities to the site, the team has good information to use when negotiating for rights-of-way. Equally important is the method of getting materials to the site. A site visit locates railroad lines, highways, local roads, waterways, and airports. Then the team can figure the most economical way of bringing deliveries to the site. This also could involve negotiations with local officials and neighbors and should be done early enough so that the construction schedule will not be affected. In larger projects, especially ones affecting a broad base of people and businesses (for example, the Central Artery/Tunnel Project in Boston; see "Construction, Not Disruption"), people are hired to focus exclusively on the areas around the site of the construction. Their job is to minimize disruptions while keeping the project moving forward efficiently.

Local Practices

In addition to examining the physical conditions at the site, the construction manager must gather information about local customs and practices—labor practices, regulations, market rates for labor and material, and availability of certain subcontractors. Understanding these customs and practices can make a big difference in how the work is divided up among the trades, which materials are used, and which methods are employed when installing products. Areas of investigation include the following:

- *Labor breakdowns.*   How the trades normally do business depends on customs built up over time. In some areas carpenters typically do work that in other areas laborers do. Sheetmetal contractors may install specific items that in

**JOB SITE
ANALYSIS**

SHEET NO.

PROJECT		BID DATE
LOCATION		NEAREST TOWN
ARCHITECT	ENGINEER	OWNER

Access, Highway	Surface	Capacity
Railroad Siding	Freight Station	Bus Station
Airport	Motels/Hotels	Hospital
Post Office	Communications	Police
Distance & Travel Time to Site		Dock Facilities

Water Source	Amount Available	Quality
Distance from Site	Pipe/Pump Required?	Tanks Required?
Owner	Price (MG)	Treatment Necessary?
Natural Water Availability		Amount

Power Availability	Location	Transformer
Distance	Amount Available	
Voltage	Phase	Cycle	KWH or HP Rate

Temporary Roads	Lengths & Widths
Bridges/Culverts	Number & Size
Drainage Problems	
Clearing Problems	
Grading Problems	
Fill Availability	Distance
Mobilization Time	Cost
Camps or Housing	Size of Work Force
Sewage Treatment	
Material Storage Area	Office & Shed Area

Labor Source	Union Affiliation
Common Labor Supply	Skilled Labor Supply
Local Wage Rates	Fringe Benefits
Travel Time	Per Diem

Taxes, Sales	Facilities	Equipment
Hauling	Transportation	Property
Other		

Material Availability: Aggregates		Cement
Ready Mix Concrete		
Reinforcing Steel	Structural Steel	
Brick & Block	Lumber & Plywood	
Building Supplies	Equipment Repair & Parts	

Demolition: Type	Number	
Size	Equip. Required	
Dump Site	Distance	Dump fees
Permits		

FIGURE 6.3   This form identifies most of the area and site conditions that should be determined before preconstruction planning

Source: From *Means Form Book.* © R. S. Means Co., Inc., Kingston, MA, 781-585-7880, all rights reserved.

Clearing: Area		Timber	Diameter	Species
Brush Area		Burn on Site		Disposal Area
Saleable Timber		Useable Timber		Haul
Equipment Required				

Weather: Mean Temperatures

Highs		Lows	
Working Season Duration		Bad Weather Allowance	
Winter Construction			
Average Rainfall	Wet Season		Dry Season
Stream or Tide Conditions			
Haul Road Problems			
Long Range Weather			

Soils: Job Borings Adequate? Test Pits

Additional Borings Needed	Location		Extent
Visible Rock			
U.S. Soil & Agriculture Maps			
Bureau of Mines Geological Data			
County/State Agriculture Agent			
Tests Required			
Ground Water			

Construction Plant Required

Alternate Method

Equipment Available

Rental Equipment   Location

Miscellaneous: Contractor Interest

Subcontractor Interest
Material Fabricator Availability
Possible Job Delays
Political Situation
Construction Money Availability
Unusual Conditions

Summary

FIGURE 6.3   continued

BOX 6.1

CONSTRUCTION, NOT DISRUPTION

by M. Ilyas Bhatti, P.E., President, The Bhatti Group, Former Associate Project Director, Central Artery/Tunnel Project; and Barry Friswold, Wallace, Floyd Associates; Mitigation Planner, Central Artery/Tunnel Project

Replacing the elevated interstate highway that ran through the center of Boston's historic and vibrant downtown was no small feat. The $14.7 billion highway, often referred to as the "Big Dig" is the largest highway project in American history, providing relief for a city center choked with congestion and associated environmental and safety hazards. The elevated highway was constructed in the 1950s for 75,000 vehicles per day but carried nearly 200,000. The new highway consists of eight to ten underground travel lanes and a landmark cable-stayed bridge that connects Boston's Interstate 93 downtown tunnels across the Charles River to the northern reaches of New England. The project also completed the nation's east-west Interstate 90 highway, with the addition of a crossharbor tunnel that doubles the existing four-land capacity to the airport and north shore.

Constructing a project of this magnitude required an extensive program to mitigate its impact on city residents, businesses, and visitors (see Figure A). It has been said that the 14 year central artery/tunnel (CA/T) project was like doing open-heart surgery on a patient who continued to work and play tennis every day. The project's central commitment to the people of Boston was to keep the city fully open for business and traffic moving during construction. In such a dense urban area, there were no feasible alternatives; sustaining the economic and civic life of Boston throughout construction was essential for obtaining and maintaining project support.

A comprehensive mitigation program was developed in concert with the requirements of federal and state environmental review process. This environmental review process began in the mid-1980s and was completed in 1991 when the actual construction of the project started.

Here we briefly describe four specific examples of construction mititgation.

FIGURE A

Mitigation Categories (partial listing):

- Noise Prevention and Monitoring
- Work Hour Limitations/ Construction Scheduling
- Incorporation of Arts and Design Features
- Development of Parks and Open Spaces
- Air Quality Maintenance
- Preservation of Joint Development Opportunities
- Historic Preservation and Archaeological Discovery
- Beneficial Re-use of Clay/Fill
- Maintaining Pedestrian and Business Access
- Pest Control
- Parking Replacement
- Maintenance of Traffic Flow and Transit Operations
- Expansion of Transit Alternatives
- Vibration Prevention and Monitoring
- Environmental Regulatory Reporting
- Preservation of Flora, Fauna, and Waterways

(continued)

BOX 6.1   Continued

NOISE MITIGATION

The CA/T committed to minimizing noise impact during construction. This goal was especially difficult because of Boston's unique neighborhoods, which integrate residential, commercial, and industrial activities. With this mix, daytime businesses often prefer work to be done at night in contrast to residents, who prefer noisy activity to be done during the day. To find an achievable balance, the CA/T project staff worked closely with all abutters to develop appropriate construction schedules, work hour limitations on jack hammering, restriction on the use of backup alarms, and ongoing noise monitoring (see Figure B). In some cases, the CA/T had to construct noise walls and noise curtains. In the historic North End, many houses had to be retrofitted with acoustical windows to dampen the effect of construction noise. This approach to

FIGURE B

BOX 6.1   Continued

construction resulted in the most comprehensive noise specifications in the country, and they have been used as a model for other public works projects.

TRAFFIC FLOW

The elevated highway was finally dismantled in 2005 when the project was substantially complete, making way for businesses housing, and parkland development. During construction, however, the project maintained all six lanes of the elevated Interstate 93 roadway (see Figure C). To accomplish this goal, the project had to phase in the underground tunnel construction located directly below the exiting elevated structure with great engineering precision and coordination. The first phase

of construction included construction of the new tunnel walls on either side of the current roadway system. Over time, the weight of the existing elevated structure was transferred to the new walls clearing the way for underartery tunnel excavation.

PEDESTRIAN AND BUSINESS ACCESS

In addition to keeping traffic moving, the CA/T Project constantly undertook mitigation measures to lessen the impact to pedestrian and business access. It incorporated standardize pedestrian walkway amenities into all contracts to ensure safe and efficient pedestrian flow. Contract specifications required the use of jersey barriers, standardized blue and gold plywood panels,

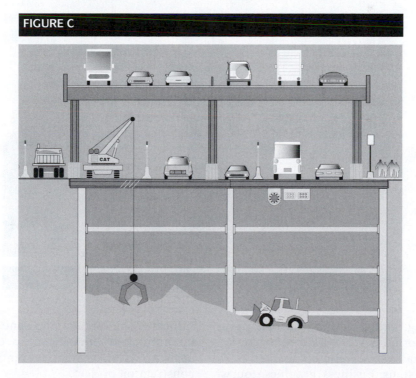

FIGURE C

(continued)

BOX 6.1   Continued

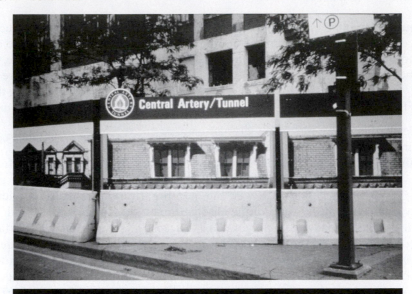

FIGURE D

FIGURE E

lighting, and temporary surface pavement for all CA/T work (see Figure D). The walkways were augmented with street signs, business graphics, tourist information, landscaping, and art to maintain and enhance the pedestrian environment throughout an ever-changing construction project.

BOX 6.1   Continued

AIR QUALITY

Air quality impact was mitigated with an array of dust control measures, such as the use of truck covers and designated truck routes. CA/T contract specifications also called for contractors to suppress dust on the worksites, sweep the streets, and wash truck wheels to minimize potential impact (see Figure E).

other areas another trade installs. Because the bid packages must be assigned before bid time, designers will want to designate specific scopes of work to each trade.

- *Codes and regulations.*   Since there is still no national standard for building codes and regulations, an understanding of local rules can go a long way to saving headaches on the job. Local officials can cause delays and cost the job money if the project goes forward without meeting certain criteria.
- *Labor availability.*   In some areas labor is at a premium; in others it is abundantly available. If there is a specific shortage in one area, the designers could call for a different material. For instance, perhaps there is a shortage of masons. Instead of using masonry units on the buildings, designers can call out a curtain-wall system, or the budget can reflect the increased labor costs for importing masons from a distance. Collective bargaining agreements should be reviewed along with agreement expiration dates. If certain trades have an expiration date during the construction period, the construction manager must watch negotiations closely. Not only will a strike disrupt the schedule, but new agreements usually lead to wage increases. Information about expiration dates can be accounted for in the design documents, the budget, and the schedule for the project.
- *Material and equipment availability.*   The local availability of certain materials, equipment suppliers, or fabrication facilities can influence how a designer specifies materials. The construction manager can help by investigating the ready availability of desired materials. If the materials are available locally, the labor force is probably familiar with their installation. For materials that are not locally produced, the construction manager must ascertain if there is local expertise in handling them. Including locally available materials and familiar installation methods in non–design-critical areas can make the job more economical. The designer may not want to give up using certain materials or critical detailing in highly visible areas but may be amenable to considering alternates in less significant spaces.

The building department, utility companies, and the chamber of commerce are all good sources of information about area methods of doing business, local regulations, informal business behaviors, the history of infrastructure development, and projected business development in the future. Information about material prices and availability can be obtained by talking with area building suppliers and specialty vendors. A visit to the union hall and a discussion with the business agent will give information about the availability of specific types of workers.

Understanding the site conditions and local customs and practices needs to be done very early in the design process because they affect decisions about the basic design. If the construction manager is not yet part of the design team, these investigations will fall to the designer. To gather this information, the designer will likely call on contractors that he or she has worked with in the past.

Value Engineering

Value engineering and cost reduction are often confused, which has given value engineering a bad name among designers. The distinction, however, is important. *Value engineering* is a process that considers cost in the context of other factors: life-cycle cost, quality, durability, and maintainability. *Cost reduction*, on the other hand, considers only first cost. While both are reactive in the sense that they respond to a given set of criteria, one considers the criteria in a broader context while the other reacts solely to budget problems. Project teams need to be very clear about which process they are involved in. Although tight budgets make cost reductions a fact of life, the owner needs to know exactly what he or she is buying. In a value engineering process the owner should be buying an item or system of equal value to another proposed system. In cost reductions he or she is accepting something of less value or less scope to save money.

Value engineering should be an active part of all design projects. Cost reductions become necessary when value engineering is not enough. Value engineering gives a "better bang for the buck," while cost reductions can reduce the quality or quantity of the project to save money.

Value engineering is not limited to the construction industry but is used throughout the business world to help analyze processes and products with the object of getting the best value for the least cost. Best value is not an inherent property. For each project, it takes on different meaning and is often a function of comparisons among other similar products. In construction this comparison is multiplied by many products, which can make for a complex exercise. Therefore, value engineering works best as a collaborative team effort. One reason why value engineering has taken on negative connotations is that designers sometimes feel that the construction professional is judging their work and making recommendations that compromise the aesthetic qualities of the project. If the designer is an equal partner in the process, this feeling is minimized. At the same time, the owner needs to understand fully the rationale for certain design choices so that, when the time comes for acceptance or rejection of a specific proposal, that rationale is weighed appropriately.

To bring a framework to the value engineering discussions, the owner sets the criteria with the help of the designer and the construction professional. Generally, these criteria fall into a few categories: best cost, best function, and best aesthetic value. Determining the best cost can be done effectively with a life-cycle cost analysis. Best function is defined by the use of the building. Best aesthetic value is a bit harder to define but can be as important as the other criteria. In the case of an emergency generator, the team looks at cost and function but does not focus on aesthetic value because the generator will be hidden from view. The cost will consider first cost, durability, maintenance, and dependability. The function will be determined by life safety requirements and the needs of the occupants in the building. In the case of a curtain-wall system, however, the owner looks at cost, function, and aesthetic value. Because the system will be the prime image of the building, aesthetic value may weigh more heavily than cost or even function. These are decisions only the owner can ultimately make.

Including value engineering in all projects may seem redundant. After all, isn't the design team putting together the best package that it feels will meet the owner's cost, function, and aesthetic criteria? Of course, a good design team does exactly that. However, every design firm has an established culture that may have standard practices that need to be challenged. The value engineering process can do this. In addition, circumstances that arise during the design may cause the team to treat something expeditiously. For instance, the owner wants to accelerate a work package to get the project started. The intent is to go back after the fact and revisit the decisions—which it is very easy not to do. Value engineering ensures that such an oversight does not happen. Another possibility is that the owner has a vision but does not explain it sufficiently to the designer. The designer responds with much more complexity than is necessary to satisfy the owner. During value engineering, this complexity will be questioned and clarified.

Construction professionals have access to many design firms in their professional lives. They bring to the table information about other products and processes that the specific design firm may be unaware of. During value engineering, these ideas can be examined and, if appropriate, incorporated. In addition, construction professionals can easily get information regarding the availability of certain products. If a product needs to be shipped over great distances, this can add to its cost. There may be a local product that can meet the same criteria.

Although value engineering takes place throughout a project, even during construction, the most value is gained early in the process: change from one system to another will have little impact on the schedule, and the amount of redesign and redraw is minimized. However, any savings generated during the early phases of design are the most difficult to document since there are often no formalized drawings or plans. The most discernable impact comes at the end of schematics and early in the design development phase. Here there is enough information generated to reasonably make judgments about the big system ideas. This is, of course, where the bulk of the savings can be realized. During the working drawings, the big ideas are already in place, and most ideas generated are in the details of the documents.

During construction, value engineering efforts continue. As changes are made to the project, the development of the design should follow the procedure set up during the design phase to evaluate the changes. The contractor can also apply value engineering principles in the field procedures, saving money on methods, equipment, or sequence of operations. Who realizes these field-generated savings depends on the form of the contract.

Some value engineering exercises are informal, with the team members agreeing on a format and a procedure. Others follow more formal lines that have been developed by others. Either way, the following are the main components of a good value engineering program:

1. **Identification of areas for review.** This can be done individually, with each team member critically examining the design drawings and specifications. The ideas formulated during this time focus on areas of the design that could take advantage of new products or processes, different use of materials, simplified systems, or reworked details (see Figure 6.4).

Labor, material, and equipment cost distribution chart

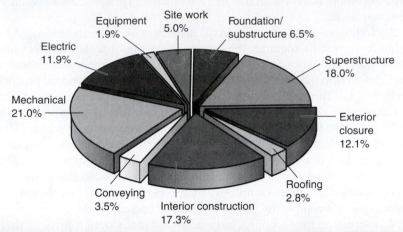

2. **Brainstorming session.**   Team members sit down together with lists of ideas and toss up ideas and thoughts for others to catch. The idea is to put as many ideas as possible on the table. Members should be inspired by others' thoughts and may come up with unique ideas because of the context of the discussion.

3. **Analysis of each recommendation.**   The group sets up criteria by which to evaluate each idea. The alternatives discussed in the brainstorming session are tested here against that criteria. In the brainstorming session, costs usually are not the first consideration. Once a proposal has merit based on functional requirements, then the costing exercise takes place. This is partly because the costing exercise can involve a fair amount of time and effort. It is also a result of keeping the brainstorming focus on function and off cost reduction.

4. **Report to management.**   Here the team puts together all the ideas into a package. Some may be carried forward for further analysis in other phases of the project when more information is available. Some have been rejected by the team for stated reasons, and some are recommended for immediate implementation. All topics discussed, whether rejected or approved, should stay part of the package for later reference.

When the costing exercise is initiated, the team can look at simple first cost, or it can view the proposal in terms of life-cycle costing. If the proposal is sound based on first cost, life-cycle costing may not be done. However, the danger here is that first cost may not translate into overall savings during the operating life of the structure. Therefore, it is better to look at the life-cycle aspects of any costs considered. Figure 6.5 illustrates the differences between first cost and life-cycle cost.

Cost	Repair	New
First cost	$ 15,000.00	
Mockups		$ 45,000.000
Remove lead paint, full prime, one finish coat	$ 366,400.00	
Wet seal	$ 111,450.00	
Weatherstrip	$ 37,000.00	
Aluminum cap	$ 75,000.00	
New curtain wall		$ 1,234,800.00
Subtotal	**$ 604,850.00**	**$ 1,279,800.00**
General conditions and fee (15%)	$ 90,728.00	$ 191,970.00
Subtotal	**$ 695,578.00**	**$ 1,471,770.00**
Soft costs (35% and 20%)[1]	$ 243,254.00	$ 294,354.00
Total project cost	**$ 938,832.00**	**$ 1,766,124.00**
Alternate[2]		
Patch/paint	$ (345,975.00)[3]	
Maintenance over 30 years (in current dollars)		
Repaint in 15 years	$ 316,000.00	
Reseal in 15 years	$ 111,450.00	
Weatherstrip in 15 years	$ 37,000.00	
Markups in 15 years (25%)	$ 116,213.00	
Spot seat in 5 years ($50,000)	$ 200,000.00	$ 250,000.00
Total maintenance	**$ 780,663.00**	**$ 250,000.00**
Energy savings over 30 years (in current dollars)		
$0.60/square feet × 29,500 square feet × 30 years		$ (531,000.00)
Life cycle over 30 years		
Net present value discounted at 8% annually	**$ 1,423,463.00**	**$ 1,634,827.00**

[1] Soft costs include design fees, consultants' fees, permitting costs, testing expenses, and other owner-direct costs.
[2] Alternate is a deduction from the $604,850 to patch and paint the curtain wall instead of the large scope of work.
[3] Figures in parenthesis are negative numbers, denoting savings.

FIGURE 6.5 Cost comparison between a new and a repaired curtain-wall system. The figure shows the difference between first cost (more than $800,000) and life-cycle cost (more than $200,000). The analysis brings the cost of a new system more in line with the cost of keeping the old one

Life-Cycle Costing

Increasingly, owners are considering more than first cost when looking at the design and construction of their building. Trends toward sustainable design call for an integrated approach that considers all phases of a facility from construction to operating and eventually to renovation, reuse, or demolition. Increases in energy costs, depletion of raw materials, and a growing awareness toward conservation and environmental stewardship are putting the spotlight on life-cycle costing. Programs such as LEED (see Box "LEED" in Chapter 5) and organizations such as the Green Building Council are promoting sustainable design and encouraging the use of life cycle in considering design and construction choices.

Life-cycle costing examines initial, operating, and maintenance costs as well as future benefits over the life of a building or systems in the building. Before this analysis can be applied, assumptions are made about the desired levels of quality in the building, the program constraints, and future projections of the cost of money. Life-cycle costing helps the design team decide on design options, site locations, material used in the building, and money invested in systems. It can be used in new construction or renovation projects. In renovation projects, the first issue to resolve is whether the building should be torn down or retained. If the decision has been made to keep the building, the next question is how extensive the renovation needs to be to meet expectations. These analyses can be accomplished through a life-cycle cost analysis.

The goal is to discover, given several alternatives that meet the client's needs, which one will cost the least over the life of the building. For instance, a specific nonconventional heating system could have a high first cost. First costs include costs directly related to the design, purchase, and installation of a system. But such a system may have a longer projected life than a conventional system, may burn fuel more efficiently, may not need as much maintenance, and may use a cheaper fuel source. Once all these costs are weighed, the actual long-term cost of the system may turn out to be less than other systems. If analyzed only on first cost, however, the unconventional system would have been rejected.

Because costs are spread over a number of years, the value of money needs to be leveled to make the comparison accurate. The assumption is usually that the purchasing power of money is worth more today than tomorrow. The trick is predicting just how much more. Tracking future inflation rates over 30 or 40 years is difficult because costs for labor, material, and energy will escalate at different rates. Similarly, estimating the initial cost of building components is not difficult compared with determining future costs. The direct costs of maintenance, for instance, may be easy to predict, but the indirect costs (such as loss of productivity during shutdowns) are not. External factors can come into play—for example, unexpected increases in energy prices. Estimating the life expectancy of building components is also full of variables and depends heavily on how well maintenance and repairs are performed over the life of the product or system. Even with these limitations, however, life-cycle costs give more broad-based information to the owner and the project team about the relative worth of building components.

Constructability Analysis

Although examining project components according to how complex they are to build is part of value engineering, the analysis can be accomplished in a more proactive way. Designers have traditionally left methods of installing building components to construction professionals. In a design–bid–build delivery method, this can lead to project components that are difficult to install, adding costs to the project as the constructor struggles to work out the details, affecting the overall schedule, and possibly creating unsafe working conditions. If the constructor is part of the discussions during design, however, these complexities can be identified and simpler solutions developed. This puts the constructor into a more proactive role in which issues of safety, schedule, and ease of construction are part of discussions before the design is developed. Thus, the team can establish procedures and use materials that will accomplish the owner's goals and be assembled in the field rationally and efficiently.

BOX 6.2

UP/DOWN CONSTRUCTION IN BOSTON: AN EXAMPLE OF CONSTRUCTION INNOVATION

by Dr. James M. Becker, President, Beacon Skanska Construction Company, Boston

How often have you heard the expression "It's a great idea, but where has it been done before?" Decision makers in the building industry have one goal: deliver a project on time and on budget. They go to great lengths to avoid any uncertainty that might threaten this objective. Their aversion to risk can stifle innovation in the delivery process. But barriers to innovation may be barriers to good business. Sometimes the parameters of a project cross the bounds of experience, where traditional methods are known to be at their limits. In these cases, innovation, with its inherent uncertainty, may offer a solution with more promise and less risk.

Such was the case in Boston on three recent projects, in which the introduction of up/down construction minimized risk and accelerated the delivery time on Rowes' Wharf, 75 State Street, and Post Office Square.

WHAT IS UP/DOWN CONSTRUCTION?

In up/down construction, a building's substructure is built at the same time as the superstructure. Up/down construction evolved from the Milan method for subway construction, which has been described as "cover, then cut"—that is, install parallel slurry walls, bridge between the slurry walls with a deck for traffic, and then mine underneath. The use of up/down construction at the Olympia Center project in Chicago in the early 1980s was a stimulus to the introduction of the concept at the Rowes' Wharf project.

Up/down construction requires no radical changes in technique but involves a creative sequencing of construction activities. It is best understood by dividing the process into four distinct but interconnected subsystems:

- ***Wall system:*** a concrete diaphragm wall constructed by the slurry trench method
- ***Column/foundation system:*** individual high-capacity units designed to support the column loads by end bearing, side friction, or a combination of both
- ***Floor system:*** floors that are commonly cast-in-place flat or framed slabs
- ***Excavation system:*** typically a horizontal mining operation with careful consideration given to sequencing, ventilation, and the method and point of soil removal

(continued)

BOX 6.2   Continued

EXAMPLE PROJECTS

Rowes' Wharf is a mixed-use building containing 330,000 square feet of office space; 100 residential condominiums; a 230-unit hotel; a 700-car, five-level, below-grade garage; a ferry terminal; and a marina. The project was constructed on the edge of Boston Harbor, and environmental considerations made it imperative that the harbor be minimally affected by construction.

Early during the preconstruction stage, team members decided to use up/down construction. This method minimized certain construction risks, and the additional direct construction costs of more than $2 million were offset by the projected time savings of more than four months. The up/down method also addressed the risks of wall leakage because tieback penetrations were eliminated. The risk of delays was minimized because structural steel work could occur independent of the subsurface excavation. The major risk that the developer-owner faced was the choice of a system that had not been used locally. Since there was no local contractor with experience in this type of construction, the owner risked delays from poor planning, unforeseen technical problems, and lack of coordination. However, once the concept was adopted, the design continued to evolve to the point where it became virtually impossible to build the final project conventionally. Before making a final commitment, a testing program was conducted to ensure that caissons could be augered and belled at the site. As it turned out, they could; but if this method had proved to be unworkable, the design team would have lost time and would have had to go back to the beginning.

75 State Street is a thirty-one-story office tower that includes six levels of below-grade space used primarily for parking. The 1.37-acre site is located near the original shoreline of colonial Boston. The project contains 745,000 square feet of above-grade space and 350,000 square feet of below-grade space.

Early investigation noted the proximity of the development to adjacent shallow-foundation structures and the Massachusetts Bay Transit Authority's Blue Line subway tunnel. It also noted that stable foundation material (bedrock) was 70–100 feet below grade.

The design team prepared several conceptual schemes and showed that the time saved using up/down construction was one to two months with a cost premium of about $1 million. This cost was equivalent to the money that would be saved on the reduction of carrying cost for the shorter construction schedule. Therefore, the decision for or against up/down construction became a technical one. Since the use of a diaphragm wall would prevent the need for tiebacks and better protect the foundations of existing buildings and structures than would conventional construction, the team chose up/down construction.

A major lesson learned on this project was the critical coordination necessary between the slab construction and the excavation. In some instances, excavation along the slurry wall alignment resulted in excessive inward movements of the wall before the floor systems could be placed. Since slab placement provides wall bracing, earlier placement would have prevented wall movement.

Post Office Square is an entirely below-grade, seven-level, 525,000-square-

BOX 6.2   Continued

foot parking garage. The project is located in the financial district and contains spaces for 1,400 vehicles. It is covered with a 1.5-acre park.

The constructability analysis indicated that up/down construction was the desired, if not the only, technical approach that would minimize risk and maximize ground stability with regard to adjacency. Cost and schedule analysis indicated that at this depth the up/down method would be no more costly or time-consuming than conventional open-cut construction. Another advantage emerged when traffic management planning was carried out with the city's transportation department. Truck traffic could be staged on the surface slab without the queuing normally required on city streets.

CONCLUSION

Up/down construction in Boston, from Rowes' Wharf to Post Office Square, became increasingly technically refined because the design and construction community openly shared its experiences. Although each project had many unique features, up/down construction was among the most unusual. Without the teams' willingness to accept the risks of innovation, many aspects of these projects would not have been feasible.

The innovation lay in the process, which was incrementally constructed of known subprocesses. The challenge was associated with management as much as with construction technology. The early introduction of the innovation concept into the project allowed for specialized structuring. In particular, it required the introduction of a separate "down" management team that focused exclusively on the problems of "down" construction. Innovation requires openness within the project team. But in the end, up/down construction in Boston was not just innovation but also good business.

Design Review

One of the major methods of obtaining information and generating feedback about design intent is to review the drawings and specifications as they become available. These documents lay out in increasing detail the scope of the project. There are traditional points of review. At each of these points, the constructor produces a schedule, an estimate, and review comments that look specifically at construction-related and contractual issues. Value engineering exercises also take place at these points.

Programming documents the plan in narrative form with some diagrams. At this stage alternate project configuration schemes (such as high-rise versus low-rise, steel versus concrete, rectangular versus square floor plate) are discussed along with alternatives for mechanical, electrical, and plumbing systems. Schematic design documents begin to graphically show the intent, and outline specifications describe more details of the systems. This is the time to discuss how the bid packages should be assembled. In design development, the project, which has been approved at the end of schematic design, is detailed. At this stage, long-lead items are identified, and those that must be prepurchased to arrive on site in time are developed on an accelerated schedule.

During the construction documents phase, bid packages are assembled, and all required state, local, and federal permits are identified.

Owner approval points occur at the end of programming, schematic design, design development, and just before bidding at the end of construction documents. For the owner to have good information to decide about moving forward, budgets need to be assembled, schedules analyzed, and construction issues discussed. Often the design team moves forward with instructions to make certain changes to get the project back within budget or to include scope not sufficiently covered.

Estimating

One of the first objectives that an owner develops is the amount of money that can be spent on the project. The project team uses this as a guide through early design discussion and, by preparing estimates, tests it at specific points in the development of the project. If the project is not staying within the budget, the owner can opt to increase the amount of money committed to the project or can direct the team to redesign until it meets the budget objectives. Estimating is normally part of the designer's scope of work. He or she will either employ a consultant who is familiar with the designer's work or, in larger firms, use in-house talent.

The design community and professional cost analysts do not necessarily have good information about the labor and material marketplace. Nor do they understand construction logistics and methods. On the other hand, construction professionals are not particularly adept at making design assumptions about the designer's intent. The estimating exercises can be set up so that both design and construction considerations are covered. Ideally, the best method is to engage two cost consultants: one familiar with the designer's work, one familiar with the construction marketplace. If this is too costly for the owner, then the construction professional can comment on the estimates produced by the designers. Early in the design process, this is a reasonable strategy since the costs are more conceptual. At the end of schematic design, however, it is important to employ a construction professional to develop costs. Once there is enough documented information regarding the scope of work, he or she can bring in material suppliers, subcontractors, and building trades representatives to advise on the costs of specific materials and fabrication methods.

All through the design process, there will be costing of several alternatives. Early on, these alternatives are system-level, exploring different options for roofing, cladding, foundation systems, and so on. Later these alternatives are more detailed-oriented, looking closely at one window product versus another or one brand of generator versus another. (Estimating is discussed in more detail in Chapter 9.)

Scheduling

Another early criterion established by the owner is the required completion date. Sometimes such dates are fixed firmly because of commitments or financing. One of the first activities for the construction manager is to confirm that this date can be met given the desired scope of work. If it cannot, the owner has the choice of paying a premium for accelerating the schedule or backing off on the desired scope of the project, perhaps completing it in phases. The constructor also looks at different delivery methods that may affect how quickly the project can be completed within the desired budget. This analysis will lead to a recommendation to the owner about the best project delivery method.

Once these alternatives are explored and a schedule is developed and agreed to, the project team must ensure that it is met. Early in the project, the construction team along with the designer and the owner should establish overall project milestones. Early schedules will be in bar chart formats that show very simple relationships. Later, as more specific information is generated, these schedules will be network-based, with more complex relationships among the activities. (Scheduling is discussed in detail in Chapter 10.)

Long-Lead Item Procurement

During the scheduling exercise, items are identified that have to be bought early to arrive at the site in time for installation. Often these are large items or systems such as air-handler units, steel assemblies, or curtain-wall systems. They require identification as early as possible since the designer must accelerate this portion of the design and isolate the bid package to separate it from the rest of the work that is proceeding at a specific pace. This can be more expensive for the designer since the work will be out of sequence within the production structure. The earlier he or she knows about the need for a long-lead item, the easier it will be to adjust the team to accommodate the need for a separate package.

Upon receipt of the required documents from the designers, the construction manager, in the owner's name, puts the package out to bid to a selected list of manufacturers. When the full design documents are complete and put out to bid, the specific items that were procured early are assigned to the appropriate subcontractor for delivery, storage, installation, and coordination. This assignment minimizes risk to the owner, who could, in other arrangements, be liable for any defects or responsible for delivery coordination.

Work Packages

Once the project delivery method is chosen, the desired scheduled completion identified and confirmed, and local practices regarding how work is accomplished understood, the project team starts to assemble the work packages (see Figure 6.6). This is a breakdown of how the work will be accomplished as it relates to availability of labor

FIGURE 6.6 The work package breakout guides the design and procurement efforts of the project team

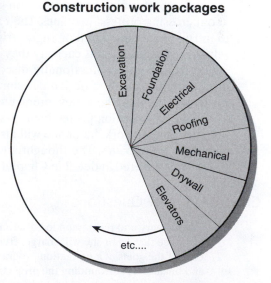

Construction work packages

and materials. The skill in assembling these packages is to identify the right amount and combination of work activities so that there is maximum competitive interest but minimum layering of subcontractors and vendors. Layering creates coordination complexities and can slow down the work. When assembling the work packages, the construction professional also considers skills needed to perform the work, trades involved, equipment needed, administrative activities such as permits, approvals such as shop drawings, deliveries and the logic of when things arrive on site, and any special procedures required to complete the activities.

One of the major pitfalls in defining work packages is the potential of assigning the same responsibility to more than one subcontractor or not assigning them to anyone at all. This occurs in areas such as cleanup or the furnishing of scaffolding or patching, coring holes, and other supporting activities that can be handled in a number of ways. Some constructors minimize this by carrying these activities in the general conditions. (Chapter 7 will discuss these issues at length.)

Conclusion

During the design period, a series of tasks falls outside the design activities themselves. These include investigations of local conditions, construction practices, labor markets, and the site with its surrounding conditions. The designer needs the information generated from these studies. In addition, he or she requires ongoing checks on costs, schedule, and constructability. These tasks are best handled by construction professionals. If the owner elects to wait until the bidding period to hire the builder, the designer will likely hire a construction consultant to assist with construction-related issues. Using the same firm during preconstruction and construction means that the understanding gained during the design period can be carried over into construction. However, it potentially limits the owner from putting the project out as a lump sum bid to general contractors. Unless the preconstruction professional is eliminated from bidding the project, other potential bidders will feel that they are at a disadvantage. This may result in prices that are not as competitive as they could be.

When performing preconstruction services, construction managers must be careful about crossing professional lines. Their responsibility is to advise the design team, not to intrude on architectural or engineering decisions. Their expertise is in construction-related issues, and in this capacity they affect design decisions but do not make them. Aside from being professionally discourteous and creating real liability concerns, interfering too much in design decisions can create mistrust among the project team members and affect how they interact with each other.

If the construction professional has been hired for the construction as well as the preconstruction work, he or she will also, in this same time frame, be planning for the construction activities. The thought and planning that needs to go into this phase of the work is covered in detail in Chapter 7.

Chapter Review Questions

1. The primary and recommended discriminator in the selection of the construction manager is the fee that he or she will charge. True or false?
2. One of the goals of a mitigation program is to maintain positive relations with the people and businesses surrounding the project. True or false?

3. A good value engineering program should lead to the lowest possible initial project cost. True or false?
4. As the estimate evolves through the design phase, the accuracy of the estimate should increase and the time required to conduct the estimate decrease. True or false?
5. Good work package definition is critical to successful price and schedule control. True or false?
6. Which is the best opportunity for the implementation of a cost-savings idea?
   a. Late, when influence is high and cost expenditures are high
   b. Early, when influence is high and cost expenditures are low
   c. Late, when influence is low and cost expenditures are high
   d. Early, when influence is low and cost expenditures are high
7. Which of the following is *not* a local condition necessary to investigate before the beginning of a project?
   a. Subsurface site conditions
   b. Site access
   c. Availability of skilled labor
   d. Codes and regulations
   e. Project drawings and specifications
8. Which of the following terms best describes the process of examining the project to discover the best way of assembling its component parts?
   a. Design review
   b. Value engineering
   c. Constructability analysis
   d. Estimating
   e. Scheduling
9. During which design phase is the final detailing of the project accomplished?
   a. Design development
   b. Construction documents
   c. Schematic design
   d. Programming
   e. None of the above
10. What is the term used to describe a material or component that requires significant time to acquire and bring to the job site?
    a. Long-lead item
    b. Milestone activity
    c. Critical activity
    d. Procurement item
    e. Mitigation item

Exercises

1. The design team has narrowed its mechanical system options to the following two choices. Both meet the technical and performance requirements necessary for the project, making the final decision one of economics. Given the following data, which option would you recommend?

	Option 1	**Option 2**
Initial purchase price	$200,000	$250,000
Annual maintenance and operating cost	$25,000	$20,000
Salvage value (after fifteen years)	$25,000	$30,000
Cost of money	8%	8%

2. Interview a general contractor or a construction management firm that has constructed a project that you are familiar with. Investigate the following:

    a. How many work packages was the project broken into? Give a brief scope of work for each package.

    b. Did the construction professional participate in any constructability analyses during design? If so, what were the details of the study?

    c. Did any value engineering occur on the project? Report on these studies.

CHAPTER

7

BIDDING AND PROCUREMENT

Chapter Outline

Student Learning Objectives

In this chapter you will learn the following:

1. The process involved in breaking down a project into work packages
2. The issues involved in prequalifying and inviting contractors to bid
3. The specific parts that make up a construction work package
4. The issues involved in analyzing bids and alternates and awarding a contract

INTRODUCTION

Deciding to bid on a project is not a trivial matter for a construction company since significant time and costs are incurred in preparing a bid. Motivation to bid varies depending on a number of factors. In a strong economic market, contractors are more able to choose which projects to bid on. In a slower economic market, the contractor may have to bid on less desirable work. The company's main motivation is to receive a good return on its investment. For a firm to grow and prosper, it must have profit to invest in itself. If a project has the ingredients necessary to return a good profit, the motivation to bid is high. The ingredients are different for different firms, however. Depending on the expertise in the company, one firm can turn a good profit on a project

Design

Scope definition

Conceptual design

Design approval

Construction documentation

Bid

Bid packages

Bid invitation

Bid period

Contractor selection

Construct

Project authorization

Construction

Turnover

Owner acceptance

while another may only get by. [The factors that make one company succeed over another include their relationships with key subcontractors, their knowledge of and experience with the specific type of project, their ability to buy out the job, their estimating capability, their project team setup, their safety record, how efficiently they conduct their business, overhead costs, and so on.]

Aside from the profit motive, companies may bid on projects for other reasons. If it wants to establish a relationship with a new client or maintain one with an established client, a company may bid on a less profitable project. A project that is unusual and can add variety to the company's portfolio will spark interest even if the profit margins look low. If the project has a high publicity quotient or benefits the community, the company may view it as a marketing strategy. In these cases, long-term goals concerning client relationships or community recognition outweigh the short-term goal of profits.

Once a company decides to bid on a project, no matter what its motivation, it enters into a process common to all construction companies. Estimators solicit prices from a number of subcontractors. The subcontractors do material takeoffs from the drawings and specifications that result in the quantities required on the job. These quantities are then multiplied by the unit cost. The unit cost is established by talking with vendors and suppliers—for example, determining the board-foot price of lumber or the cost for a fan coil unit. This total cost is the cost for material. A similar exercise is done for labor and equipment. The total of the costs of materials plus labor plus equipment is the direct cost of the work. The estimator then must add administrative costs for running the job at the job site. These are the field indirect costs of the work. Layered on are the overhead and the profit. Overhead is what it costs the company to run its business, and a portion is factored into each project. Finally, the company determines how much profit is reasonable for the job. This is done by analyzing the market, the motivations for doing the work, how busy the company is at the time of the bid, and so on. Final price, then, combines actual estimates for the cost of the work coupled with an analysis of the competition and the current marketplace.

Direct costs + Indirect costs = Cost of the work
Cost of the work + % for overhead and profit = Total cost to the owner

QUALIFICATION OF BIDDERS

Before a company is awarded a job, even if it is the low bidder, it will likely be put through a qualification process. There are two methods of qualifying bidders: pre-bid and post-bid qualification. Pre-bid qualification requires the interested contractor to submit information about the firm before the bid documents are released. This is usually done while contract documents are being finalized so that time is not spent during the bid period with pre-bid qualifications. However, it should be done close enough to the bid dates so that the information is applicable, especially information regarding current projects. Post-bid qualifications are submitted with the bid and reviewed by the owner during the bid opening and analysis. In either case, qualification is determined by evidence of capability from previous jobs, financial strength and stability, previous commitments, personnel availability, and safety record.

The advantage of prequalifying bidders is that, when the bids are received, the lowest bidder can usually be selected. This saves time and potential disputes with bidders disqualified after the bid on the basis of financial or technical ability. Even with the pre-qualification process, however, bidders can still be disqualified. Usually, the disqualification is based on the perception that the bidder did not follow the terms of the contract documents. Sometimes a bidder will submit a bid with material or method substitutes as the basis for its price. The owner has the option of allowing this but usually asks the other bidders in contention to rebid based on the substitution. The owner can also reject the bid. This sometimes can lead to a dispute and can slow the start of construction.

Construction managers usually keep a current list of qualified contractors and subcontractors on file so that they can quickly produce a bidder's list for the owner. The manager has only to update the qualifications for the final list of bidders after review with the owner. The number of bidders varies but generally is between five and seven for each major trade. With specialty trades it may not be possible to get this many bidders, but a minimum of three is necessary to judge the bids fairly. The goal is to keep the number small enough to generate interest and give each contractor a fair shot at the job while providing enough competition so that the owner feels he or she got the best price available.

WORK PACKAGES

One of the advantages of the construction management delivery method is that it is possible to package the work to the best advantage of the project in terms of both price and efficiency. It also allows for fast-tracking the work so that parts of the project (the foundation, for instance) can be bid and started before the entire design package is assembled. This, of course, can save time on the project. There are a number of drawbacks to fast-tracking a project, the biggest of which is the potential for changes as other related parts of the design are fully developed. But if the schedule is paramount, fast tracking can be of great benefit.

Even when the project is fully designed before it is bid, there are a number of advantages to breaking the project into various work packages. First, it allows for the incorporation of local practices. For instance, if the local market has small, reputable mill houses but not one large entity, the construction manager can break the work down so that the local firms can share the work. This saves the price of having to get material and labor from a distance. Conversely, if large subcontractors are available for the job, the construction manager might package pieces together to make the job more attractive and get better prices.

Second, packaging the work reduces overhead: the more packages, the fewer markups. Subcontractors typically mark up their work 20 percent. A general contractor typically marks up the subcontractors' work 10 percent. The same is true if subcontractors have to hire others to do part of their work. A heating, ventilating, and air conditioning (HVAC) subcontractor, for instance, may hire a sheetmetal subcontractor to fabricate and install the ductwork on the job. The HVAC subcontractor marks up his or her own work 20 percent, the sheetmetal subcontractor marks up his or her own work 20 percent, and the mechanical subcontractor puts 10 percent on top of that number to cover the cost of coordinating and guiding the work of the HVAC subcontractor. If there is a general contractor as well, the work gets marked up another 10 percent (see Figure 7.1). However, the

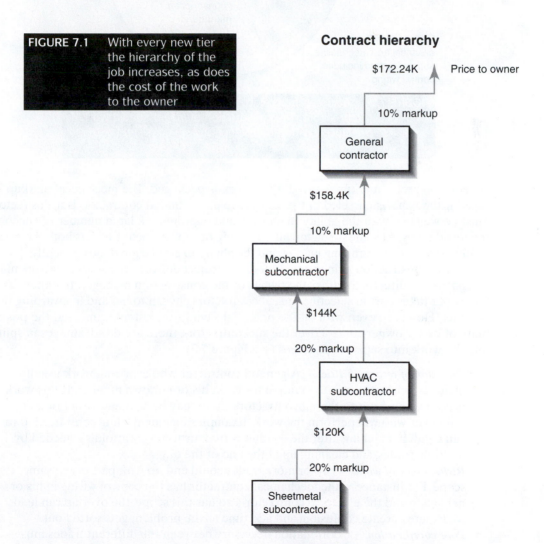

FIGURE 7.1 With every new tier the hierarchy of the job increases, as does the cost of the work to the owner

Contract hierarchy

$172.24K — Price to owner

10% markup

General contractor

$158.4K

10% markup

Mechanical subcontractor

$144K

20% markup

HVAC subcontractor

$120K

20% markup

Sheetmetal subcontractor

Direct cost of sheetmetal work = $100K

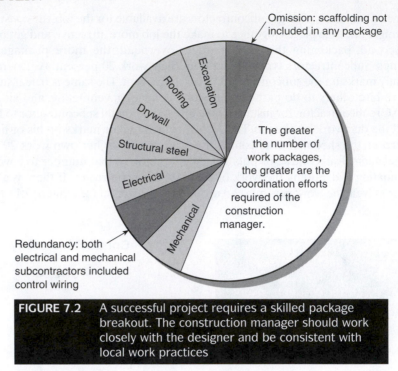

Omission: scaffolding not included in any package

Excavation

Roofing

Drywall

Structural steel

Electrical

Mechanical

The greater the number of work packages, the greater are the coordination efforts required of the construction manager.

Redundancy: both electrical and mechanical subcontractors included control wiring

FIGURE 7.2 A successful project requires a skilled package breakout. The construction manager should work closely with the designer and be consistent with local work practices

general contractor markup is saved if the work is packaged. The mechanical markup is saved if the work is parceled out separately to a sheetmetal contractor. But this factor must be weighed with the ability to manage and coordinate a large number of subcontractors directly. At some point, too little layering of subcontractors affects both the price received from the contracting market and the ability to get the job done efficiently.

In the construction management mode of project delivery, the subcontractors may be contracted directly to either the owner or the construction manager. In either case, the owner takes part in selecting the subcontractors chosen to bid and in awarding the contract. However, even with all the potential savings in cost and time and the possibility of better owner control over the subcontractors, there are disadvantages in splitting the work into separate packages (see Figure 7.2):

- *Omission of responsibilities.* A general contractor who is pricing work usually includes work common to multiple trades in his or her own number. If this work is not parceled out to the subcontractors, there may be a change order or a dispute over who will perform the work. Examples include drilling cores needed to run conduit, patching after the conduit is run, furnishing scaffolding needed by multiple trades, and cleaning up at the end of the day.
- *Redundancy of work.* Two or more trades could end up with part of the same scope. For instance, if the mechanical contractor has the control wiring in his or her scope and the electrical contractor also has this scope, the overlap can lead to disputes, create confusion, and add time as the problem gets sorted out.
- *Poor coordination.* Coordination necessary between the different trades must be incorporated into the project. Otherwise, there is a risk of disputes and time

spent sorting out who is doing what and when. A construction manager can provide such coordination and the leadership necessary to produce the work.

* ***Improper packaging of the work.***   Much of the success of packaging relies on the skills of the construction manager. If the work is put together incorrectly, there may be little interest in bidding, or the bids will come in high.

Breaking work into individual bid packages is best done using the services of a construction manager. By providing the traditional aspects of the work that a general contractor usually covers, the manager can minimize the risk associated with packaging while maximizing the savings in cost and perhaps time (that is, fast tracking) for the owner. How the packages are assembled is very important and depends on the local conditions in both the marketplace and the work force.

CONSTRUCTION DOCUMENTS

The construction documents translate the owner's needs so that the contractor can execute them correctly. They are the communication link among all parties in the project. The standardization of construction documents has evolved over time. Current practice is to bind all the narrative pieces into one document that accompanies the drawings to form the complete package. The package is divided into three general sections—bidding, contractual, and technical—each of which is made up of many subsections. The bid requirements, the agreement, technical specifications, drawings, addenda, and contract modifications all form part of the construction documents. Figure 7.3 illustrates the relationship of the many components.

FIGURE 7.3   Construction documents, as identified by the Construction Specifications Institute (CSI), are broken down into these components

Breakdown of documents used for construction

Construction documents		✓	Bid forms	✓	Bid documents
		✓	Instruction to bidders	✓	
Contract documents	✓	✓	Contract forms	✓	
	✓	✓	General conditions	✓	
	✓	✓	Supplementary conditions	✓	
	✓	✓	Technical specifications	✓	
	✓	✓	Drawings	✓	
	✓	✓	Addenda	✓	
	✓	✓	Change orders		

BIDDING INFORMATION

The bid documents are sent out with the drawings and specifications and are often bound in the specification book. They do not, however, form a part of the contract. Therefore, if legal provisions are stated here, they need to be repeated in the contract documents. This section of the documents contains the invitation to bid, the instructions to the bidder, and the bid form itself.

Invitation to Bid

The invitation to bid is a request for pricing. The owner usually prepares it with the assistance of the designer or construction manager. Although not officially part of the specifications, it includes information that is relevant to the project:

- *The type of project.* Different types of projects attract different contractors. For example, a road project may be attractive to a highway contractor but probably not to a contractor who specializes in industrial plants.
- *The size of the project.* Small contractors can only handle a certain workload, and large contractors might find it unprofitable to bid on a project under a specific size.
- *The location of the project.* Many contractors are local or regional in their ability to staff a job. If the staff has to travel any distance, there will be additional costs.
- *Bid due date.* This helps the contractor staff the bid correctly so that all prices can be gathered in the allotted time.
- *Start and completion dates.* Contractors use these dates to gauge whether or not the applicable staff is available for the duration. This could affect their price if they have to get labor from a distance.
- *Bonds.* If these are required, the owner needs to let the contractor know. Some will elect not to bid with this requirement.
- *Document location.* Bid documents can usually be picked up at the architect's or construction manager's office, but there may be a centrally located plan room as well.
- *Legal requirements.* Several items might be addressed here. The owner may want to describe the circumstances under which the bid would be disqualified or explain under what circumstances the contractor could withdraw the bid.

If the project is being let out as individual work packages, the construction manager may, as part of the invitation to bid, include a date to meet with contractors, subcontractors, material suppliers, and manufacturers before the bid date to ensure that each understands the components of the documents. A pre-bid conference held early can be valuable to the owner. It focuses potential bidders on the project and gives the designer a forum to explain the intent of the project and any nonstandard provisions. It may uncover holes in the documents or ambiguous wording, which can be dealt with during the bid period while allowing the owner to get competitive pricing. A pre-bid conference also allows contractors to ask questions, which will be followed up with a written response. Even a simple question answered at the time of the conference should be documented and sent out to all bidders, whether they were present at the conference or not.

Instruction to the Bidders

The instructions to bidders are usually bound in the specifications. Although they may repeat some of the information in the invitation to bid or on the bid form, the instructions are mostly concerned with the following:

- Bid due date
- Instructions about filling out the form
- Places to indicate fees for additional work
- Unit prices
- Location to deliver the bid
- Method of awarding contracts
- Expected dates of award and start of project

Bid Form

The bid form is the document on which the bidder submits the price. The form is usually prepared by the designer, with blanks left to be filled out by the bidder. This makes the bids more easily comparable. Items may include some or all of the following:

- Name of contractor
- Price both in numbers and in words, which minimizes decimal-point mistakes
- Price breakdown for the major trades, which can guide progress payments and assist the review of the bid's accuracy
- Amount of the bond
- Alternates: that is, the price of other materials or altered scope of work
- Fees for additional work so the owner can set parameters for any fees allowed within change orders
- Unit prices if quantities are unclear and cannot be figured accurately until construction: for example, the excavation of rock, which can be priced by the cubic yard; or asbestos removal, which may require a price for items encountered once walls are opened up, such as elbow wraps, duct penetrations, and gaskets
- Time required for the job so the contractor can decide the most efficient way to do the work and set his or her bid accordingly
- Space for the contractor to acknowledge receipt of all addenda issued after the bids have gone out
- Key subcontractors
- Legal status: for example, if the company bidding is a corporation, a partnership, or an individual
- Signature, title, and date

Alternates

In certain situations an owner wants to explore the cost for supplying an alternate material or method of construction. An *alternate* is a request for a price for substituting one material for another, for adding to the scope of work, or for deducting from the scope. Some bid documents contain many alternates to be priced by the contractor.

There are two ways to present alternates: as either an additive price or a deductive price. The additive alternate is usually the best method for the owner since it is priced as a new item; the deduct alternate may leave some of the cost in the price.

Designers like the deduct better because they can produce a complete set of documents that can then be deducted from more easily. The owner usually prefers the additive alternate because it brings in the best price. Either way, however, alternates should be used sparingly. Their addition means much more work for the contractor and may diminish interest in the project. Including a large number of alternates creates the impression that the owner and architect do not know what they want and will continue to waffle throughout the project. They can also make it difficult to keep track of costs.

Not all alternates exist alone; some are tied to other parts of the project. Thus, acceptance of one can mean a change down the road if team members do not understand all implications. Alternates can test the team's ability to analyze their worth and understand the consequences. It may be difficult to keep track of each consequence if there are too many.

Addenda

After the documents are issued but before the bids are due, changes often need to be made. The most common reason is the need to correct simple mistakes in the bidding documents. Contractors dig deeply into the documents and can spot things missed by the drafter or specification writer. Often the contractor may propose a better method or product to fit the character of the project. Also, the owner is often making a final review of the documents during the bid period. This may generate additional requests that need to be included in the bid documents. Sometimes addenda simply complete documents that had to get on the street before totally complete. There may also be additional general instructions or a change in the bid date.

Addenda are competitively priced by the contractors who are bidding the job and are acknowledged on the bid form in the space provided. If an addendum comes late in the bidding period, the bid time might be extended. Between the time of the bid opening and the signing of an agreement, there should be no changes to the scope of work. This clears the way for straightforward negotiations between the owner and the contractor concerning terms of the agreement. If changes are needed, they will be treated as changes to the contract after the initial negotiations are complete.

CONTRACTUAL INFORMATION

Many contracts are issued during the course of a project. One of the first is to the architect and the construction manager for preconstruction design and technical services. The contract issued with the construction documents goes to the firm (whether it is a construction manager or a general contractor) that will perform the work. This contract includes an agreement, general conditions, special conditions, sample of bond (if required), insurance requirements, and a sample insurance form. The construction manager and the general contractor, in turn, issue subcontractor contracts for the work to be done by the specialty trades after the project is awarded. These often tie the subcontractors to the conditions of the contract as laid out in the bid documents.

Agreement

There are several forms of contracts, as discussed in Chapter 3, but general provisions are common to most agreements:

- *Identification of the parties.*   Owner and contractor are fully described here. By signing the contract, both parties accept its obligations. The owner may be a tenant but is still liable for payment to the contractor. The contractor may be a specialty trade but is obligated to perform the services as outlined in the contract.

- *Description of the project and the work.*   The contract with the prime contractor may include just the construction work on the project or may be more inclusive, such as covering services typically assigned to the owner. To establish a baseline in the scope of work, the description must be clear. One method is to refer to the drawings and specifications with all addenda as the basis of the scope. However, if the extent of the work is more far-reaching, then a detailed and clear narrative description should be included. If changes are requested in the future, this description will form the basis of negotiations.

- *Date of start.*   The date that the contractor is expected to start is important. He or she usually can hold the quoted price for a certain time period (for example, 30 days); but if the commencement date is farther away than indicated in the bid, the price must be reevaluated. There are a number of reasons why the date can vary. The owner may need to obtain permits or community approval to develop the site, or there may be delays caused by the discovery of hazardous materials. Conversely, the owner may want to start immediately, before the terms of the contract are settled. In this case, a letter of intent will be issued to bridge the time.

- *Date of substantial completion.*   This is the date that the contractor needs to figure into his or her schedule. Probably some work will continue after this date (punch-list items, for instance), but the owner expects to be able to use the facility in its entirety by this date.

- *Liquidated damages.*   An owner may elect to include this clause if late completion of the work will cause hardships. The clause denotes a specific sum not related to the scope of work to be completed that covers damages incurred by the owner as a result of the contractor's failure to complete the work in the time specified. Although this has obvious advantages for the owner, it may cause the contractor to include an amount in the bid to cover part of this sum, thereby increasing the price; or it may create an adversarial relationship between the owner and the contractor.

- *The contract sum.*   This is the amount of money that the owner has agreed to pay the contractor for the scope of work as outlined in the construction documents. It includes the base bid with any accepted alternates.

- *Progress payments.*   Unless the scope of work is minor and short, the contractor usually receives interim payments (most often monthly) during the progress of the work. Typically the designer reviews the work accomplished during that month and approves or adjusts the sum submitted by the contractor.

- *Interest rates.*   If the contractor is not paid within a specified time (usually 30 or 45 days), agreed-upon interest rates will be charged to the owner.

- *Retainage.*   A percentage of the money due for work in place is retained by the owner as protection against work that is not done correctly or sufficiently. It ensures that the contractor will finish the project, particularly as the project nears completion. Typical retainage is 10 percent. It is often reduced to 5 percent when the work is half completed or can be eliminated entirely at this point. Retained monies are released at the time of substantial completion.
- *Final payment.*   This is a significant event for both the owner and the contractor. The owner is essentially waiving all claims against the contractor and proclaiming satisfaction with the job. The contractor, by accepting final payment, is waiving all claims against the owner except those enumerated in writing as outstanding.
- *Enumeration of contract drawings.*   This list constitutes the entire agreement between owner and contractor. It includes the agreement, conditions of the contract, drawings, specifications, and any addenda and accepted alternates.

General Conditions

The purpose of the general conditions is to establish the legal responsibilities, obligations, authority, and rights of all parties involved in the project. As their name implies, these conditions are general in nature and apply to any construction project. Although the owner can devise his or her own general conditions, most prefer to use a standard version—often called the boilerplate. This version is understood by all parties, includes tested language that has stood up over time, and has been revised as needed. There are many versions of this standard language—for example, those of the Associated General Contractors, the American Society of Civil Engineers, the U.S. government, and the Engineers Joint Contract Documents Committee, to name a few. On projects designed by architects, the most popular general conditions are those developed by the American Institute of Architects (AIA).

Special Conditions

The special conditions are sometimes called *supplementary conditions* or special provisions of the contract. They are intended to supplement the general conditions and are project-specific. Special conditions include additional owner requirements such as provisions for prevailing wages and additional insurance requirements. Sometimes owner requirements on the job, such as parking, use of toilet facilities, and working in occupied spaces, appear in supplementary conditions. However, because these are not contractual in nature, they are properly part of general conditions.

Bonds

If the contractor fails to perform in accordance with the contract, a bond will protect the owner. Sometimes an owner requires a bond from the contractor. The owner will pay for this bond but wants to know before entering into an agreement the amount of money required. If a contractor has an agreement with an owner to perform a certain scope of work for a specific price and does not complete the work, the bonding company will either pay for work to be completed or find someone to complete the work. However, the bonding company is responsible only up to the amount of the contract.

There are three types of bonds commonly required in construction:

1. **Bid bonds.** These are furnished with the bids and basically guarantee that the contractor will enter into a contract with the owner for the price of the bid. If the contractor withdraws, he or she agrees to pay a percentage of the bid cost as stipulated in the bid documents—usually 5–10 percent of the bid itself. There are certain situations in which the owner might not enforce this—for example, in the case of a clerical error that made the bid price many times lower than the prices of other bidders. The purpose of the bid bond is to ensure that a bidder does not withdraw his or her bid after becoming the successful candidate. If the bidder does withdraw, the owner will be compensated for the time it costs to get another bidder. Bid bonds are returned to all bidders upon acceptance of the lowest bid and to the lowest bidder after the contract is signed.

2. **Performance bonds.** These guarantee that a contractor will perform the contract in accordance with the terms of the agreement. If the contractor goes bankrupt or otherwise cannot complete the work, the bonding company becomes liable for it. However, liability is only for the cost of the contract and does not cover all the delays and indirect costs that usually result when a contractor pulls out in the middle of a job.

3. **Payment bond.** Also called labor and material bonds, these assure that the contractor will pay all bills, thus leaving the owner unharmed by claims and liens. When a contractor goes bankrupt, he or she usually leaves unpaid bills. The owner does not want to be left responsible, particularly for bills for materials, labor, and equipment that the defaulting contractor has already invoiced and been paid for. The payment bond is usually purchased at the same time as the performance bond from the same company and will cover the cost of unpaid bills in a default situation.

Because performance and payment bonds cost the owner money, they may not always be desirable. If the owner feels confident of the financial strength of the company or if the job is simple or short, a bond may not be necessary. However, with a complex, long-term project, it is sensible to require a bond. If one is required, it will be identified in the contract documents.

Insurance

There are many forms of insurance that a contractor can purchase to protect against risks during a construction project. Three are obligated by contract and law for the life of the project. Workers' compensation is a state law that compensates employees who are injured on the job. Comprehensive liability protects the contractor against third-party claims, and builder's risk protects against property damage during construction. A fourth type of insurance often carried by the contractor is umbrella liability. This works as excess coverage for the other three in case of a catastrophic incident and also boosts the coverage on all.

It is in the contractor's best interests to seek the advice of an insurance agent before deciding on coverage. The agent can review the construction documents for risks inherent in the type of project and the complexity. Because the contract only sets minimums, the contractor must assess the risk and make sure that he or she is covered.

1. **Workers' compensation.** This insurance covers disability and medical treatments for injuries resulting from accidents that occur during employment. Individual states set the

rules for this coverage, so it varies. However, they have the same basic provisions in common, covering medical expenses, hospitalization, and disability. Usually, workers are eligible after a specific number of lost workdays and are compensated at a percentage of their salaries. If an injury is permanent, they may be paid a fixed sum. Premiums for this coverage are based on payroll. Each state has established a rate for individual crafts based on the number of losses per craft. The rate is higher for crafts that experience more injuries and varies from company to company, depending on their individual history of claims. Just as classification premium rates are set by regulators based on aggregate losses by craft workplace exposure, individual risk rates are highly sensitive to the insured's particular corporate losses, subsequently reflected through individual debit or credit.

2.   **Comprehensive liability.** This provides protection from third-party claims. It covers injury to nonworkers at the site, damage caused by construction vehicles, damage occurring after completion but as a direct result of the contractor's work, damage caused by subcontractors, and sometimes injury to workers beyond and distinct from workers' compensation claims.

3.   **Builder's risk.** This is essentially property insurance for the building while it is under the control of the contractor. It covers losses resulting from fire, smoke, water, explosions, vandalism, and theft. The general contractor can obtain this insurance, but the owner may elect to carry it. If so, the contractor should examine the policy to make sure he or she is covered sufficiently. For instance, the contractor should determine the amount of deductible provided for within the policy (generally a large value) and understand who pays the deductible's value in the event of a loss.

Usually an owner requires a certificate of insurance to make sure of the contractor's full compliance. If the owner wants the contractor to use a specific form, a sample will be bound in the specification book.

BOX 7.1

RISK MANAGEMENT TRENDS

by Kevin Hines, CEO, Richard White and Sons, Newton, Mass.; President, Massachusetts Chapter of the Associated General Contractors

Over the past 25 years, the construction industry has significantly reengineered the way in which it does business. Materials, equipment, personnel, project delivery systems, cost, and management information systems have been dramatically altered and improved, all in the interest of enhanced competitive advantage in the marketplace and with the goal of increased profit margins.

Consistent with this retooling, contractors are more aggressively analyzing and proactively addressing the multiple risks inherent in construction operations.

(continued)

BOX 7.1 Continued

Risk management focuses on identifying and evaluating loss exposures and determining how to manage them through direct loss reduction and various risk financing techniques. In addition, careful contractual risk transfer—intentionally placing the ultimate risk of loss with the party who has the greatest ability to control that loss—is widely practiced throughout the industry.

Procedurally, the process of risk management should commence pre-bid, with a careful review of the contract documents from the perspectives of owner, architect, general contractor/construction manager, and subcontractor. This review should detail the various risks inherent in execution of the contract that could affect both the project itself and the multiple parties to the prime and/or subcontracts for the work. Risk and loss retention analysis determines specifically the critical relationship between the business entity's financial condition and the potential impact of significant unanticipated loss on that position. Generally, the work product of the process seeks to identify a sensible balance between some level of informed risk retention by individual stakeholders and the use of appropriate insurance products and/or reinsuring agreements. Clearly, the ultimate goal is to form a safety net of sorts that both limits the risks assumed by the business entity and protects the financial stability of the venture.

Here are the more notable recent trends:

1. Partnering between owners and contractors in project insurance is reflected in the growth of owner-controlled (OCP) or contractor-controlled (CCP) programs. In this model, all lines of insurance necessary for the protection of all parties to the project are purchased and controlled by one entity. Such programs may consolidate general liability, workers' compensation, and builder's risk coverage for the general contractor and for all subcontractors into one policy written by a single carrier for the specific project. Perceived advantages include the following:

- Economies of scale in premium-generated, underwriting, and administrative expenses
- Expanded coverage and higher policy limits based on underwriting experience
- Centralized safety programs
- Improved cash flow opportunity as a function of larger premium level
- Reduction in litigation as a function of the single carrier/single insured policy concept
- Improved opportunities for disadvantaged business enterprise participation in the project due to greater coverage availability

2. Significant risk management issues/changes are reflected within the widely used American Institute of Architects' General Conditions of the Contract for Construction, AIA Document A-201 (1997 edition). These include the following:

- A mutual waiver of consequential damages between owner and contractor
- Clear assignment of responsibility for preexisting environmental conditions encountered at the site
- Clarification of the indemnity agreement's intent between owner and contractor
- Mediation as a required precedent to arbitration, which positively influences potential litigation costs
- Clarification of the subcontractor's role in job site safety

(continued)

BOX 7.1   Continued

- Provision for the purchase of project-specific project management protective liability (PMPL) insurance to cover the owner's, architect's, and contractor's various liabilities during completion of the project

3. Careful consideration by the project owner of the contractor's insurance and safety programs and of the firm's actual loss or litigation history is a condition of both eligibility to propose or bid and an absolute determinant in final contractor selection.

4. With the explosion of design/build and build/operate/transfer project delivery systems, significant new exposures, opportunities, and systemic changes to traditional products and underwriting criteria in both the insurance and surety industries are being carefully evaluated and developed. Note that many of these changes are being implemented at the request of the construction community, which has clearly recognized the potential inadequacy of traditional products to meet the risk management issues of tomorrow's marketplace.

5. The distribution of insurance programs for contractors will continue to evolve into various safety groups, captive insurance organizations, self-insurance programs, and large deductible programs. Additionally, mergers and acquisitions within the insurance and surety industries, including the participation of global insurers in the marketplace, should continue to produce both aggressive underwriting and streamlined administrative and handling costs, resulting in a continued buyer's market.

Clearly, for the contractor the intended goal of these considerations is to reinforce a cornerstone of proper risk allocation: the risk assumed by the contractor must bear a reasonable relationship to his or her ability to profit on the project.

TECHNICAL INFORMATION

The technical information is presented in two formats: drawings and specifications. These two different formats (one graphic, one narrative) do not exist independently but as a unit. Information is usually only shown in one of the two places; however, both deal with the same components. For instance, a valve is shown in the drawing and includes its location in the system, how it interacts with other components, and how many are required. However, information is also needed about acceptable manufacturers, operational and maintenance criteria, requirements for submittals, warranties, and spare parts, which is better addressed in a narrative form.

Because different parties are assembling the plans and specifications, inconsistencies are possible. The contract usually spells out how they should be handled. Normally, the specifications will govern. However, the contract may call for the designer to resolve the conflict. When an item shows up in one place but not the other, the contractor is usually asked to assume that it exists. If the contractor identifies such an item, he or she should ask for clarification from the designer or call it out as a qualification in the bid form itself.

Drawings

Many professionals are involved in developing the drawings. For building projects, the architect coordinates and guides the efforts of all the other professionals. For highway projects or more complicated industrial efforts, the engineer plays that role. No matter who leads the effort, there are general guidelines that everyone follows so that coordination is simpler and translation in the field more predictable. For instance, the drawings normally follow general order of construction from site work to finish work. There is a similar numbering sequence: A-1 is architectural, P-1 plumbing, and so forth. Each section has typical symbols and abbreviations listed. Drawings are generally drawn to a marked scale; if not to scale, this will be noted.

There are often many standard details used on projects, but the aggregate of the building makes it a unique product. Therefore, firms usually have standards that they follow for numbering drawings. Not every firm follows the same standard. The contents of a typical package are shown in Figure 7.4.

FIGURE 7.4 Contents of a typical drawings package

Section designation	Title	Description
T	Titles, legends	These drawings are prepared by the architect and include the cover sheet, which gives the name of the project and the major consultants; a plot map that locates the project; abbreviations; table of contents; and legends.
D	Demolition drawings	These drawings are prepared by the architect. Sometimes demolition drawings for the trades are distinguished by DA for architectural demolition versus DH for heating, air conditioning, and ventilation demolition. The specialty demolition packages may be prepared by the specific engineering trade if there is some degree of complexity.
	Site drawings	These comprise a series of drawings that shows the location of the project, the property lines, survey information, any existing conditions to be maintained, roadways, and utilities. They are prepared by a civil engineer, a geotechnical engineer, a surveyor, and a landscape architect and include the site work on the job as well as the finished landscaping.
TS	Topographic survey	
SB	Soil borings data	
SD	Site demolition	
C	Civil	
L	Landscape	

(continued)

Section designation	Title	Description
A	Architectural drawings	These drawings are directly prepared by the architect and are the basis for all the other drawings done on the job. Normally they are organized from the more general information to more specific. The floor plans are first in the series. They proceed to reflected ceiling plan, elevations, sections, and finally details of the job.
S	Structural drawings	These drawings are prepared by the structural engineer. They include all the work necessary to support the structure.
P	Plumbing	These drawings are prepared by the plumbing engineer. They include specialty systems such as lab grade water or process piping.
FP	Fire protection	These drawings are also prepared by the plumbing engineer. They show the piping needed for a sprinkler system as well as a fire pump if necessary.
H	HVAC	These drawings are prepared by the mechanical engineer. They include the heating, ventilating, and air conditioning system for the building.
E	Electrical	These drawings are prepared by the electrical engineer. They include the power and lighting for the project but can also include telecommunication systems, security, and audiovisual support systems.

FIGURE 7.4   continued

Specifications

The technical specifications are written descriptions of the quality of the project. They detail the materials, equipment, and workmanship to be incorporated into the project. The specifications may be written by an in-house group or by a consultant whose primary business is specification writing. Engineers usually write the engineering sections; but no matter how the specifications are written, the designer provides direction and overall coordination.

Types of Specifications

How the specification is written determines how the contractor will use it. There are many types of specifications, depending on how specific the owner wants to be in instructing the contractor. Here are some of the more common:

- *Design specifications.*   These are also known as descriptive specifications. They are detailed descriptions of materials, workmanship, installation, and erection procedures. The contractor's obligation is to follow the instructions as laid out in the specifications. The owner takes responsibility for the results. This puts a huge burden on the designer to understand and specify how the building is put together and can lead to a good product as long as the system being described is a proven assembly.

- *Performance specifications.* These lay out the expected results of the work and leave the methods to the contractor. Performance may be expressed in a number of ways, depending on the item—for example, in terms of operational capacity, functional qualities, appearance, finish, color, texture, structural tolerances, mechanical parameters, and so on. Performance specifications give an incentive to the contractor to devise innovative approaches to the work. If these are identified before the bid, he or she is in a better position to win the project. If they are identified after the bid, it could mean an increased profit margin. Either way, as long as the owner gets the desired result, the project is successful.
- *Proprietary specifications.* These state exactly the product or method to be used. Sometimes they may allow for one specific alternate or have an "or equal" clause. The purpose is to ensure that the owner gets a preferred product or method. In large facilities, it is often important to maintain a specific valve or type of ceiling tile so that maintenance is easier.
- *Open specifications.* These are nonrestrictive and allow many different choices within set criteria. A number of different manufacturers may be listed, giving contractors great leeway in getting the best price.

Organization of the Specifications

The most widely used format for specifications is one developed by the Construction Specifications Institute (CSI), a trade association made up of constructors, designers, construction product manufacturers, and specifiers. CSI's primary focus is the commercial and institutional building market. Given the large number of project participants typically involved in a building project, CSI was formed to create standards and a format to improve communication among participants. In 1962 CSI developed the concept of divisions and sections within divisions to standardize construction project information. This was launched one year later and eventually trademarked as MasterFormat with 16 divisions. Prior to this publication each architectural, engineering, construction, and government agency had its own organizational system for project information resulting in confusion and miscommunication, delays, errors, and omissions.

MasterFormat 2004 was developed to address changes in the industry. New and changing materials, developing areas of technology, increased use of databases, and life cycle considerations are all incorporated in this new, expanded format. The expanded format contains 50 sections, 34 of which are active and the other 16 held in reserve. Although not fully adopted in the industry, project participants are making the transition to the new format (see Figure 7.5).

During the bidding period, the contractor uses all the documents to put together the pricing for the project. If standard formats are used, the contractor is able to focus the most attention on those things that are different from the norm. The designer should make every effort to organize the information so that the unique aspects of the job are easily recognizable. Otherwise, the contractor may miss important details that would change the pricing structure that he or she sets up for the project. Omissions or misunderstandings only do a disservice to the project. The assertion that the contractor should have picked up a detail rings hollow if the information about it is buried in the documents. Legally, the contractor is bound to provide the scope as expressed in the documents. The owner and the designer should make every effort to ensure that the contractor has covered all the peculiarities of the project. An unhappy contractor is not going to make a good team player.

00 Procurement and
contracting requirements

General requirements
01 General requirements

Facility construction
02 Existing conditions
03 Concrete
04 Masonry
05 Metals
06 Wood, plastics, and composites
07 Thermal and moisture protections
08 Openings
09 Finishes
10 Specialties
11 Equipment

12 Furnishings

14 Special construction

14 Conveying equipment
15–19 Reserved

Facility services
20 Reserved
21 Fire suppression
22 Plumbing
23 Heating, ventilation, and air
conditioning
24 Reserved
25 Integrated automation
26 Electrical
27 Communications
28 Electronic safety and security
29 Reserved

Specifications

Site and Infrastructure
30 Reserved
31 Earthwork
32 Exterior improvements
33 Utilities
34 Transportation
35 Waterway and marine construction

36–39 Reserved

Process equipment
40 Process integration
41 Material processing and handling
equipment
42 Process heating, cooling, and drying
equipment
43 Process gas and liquid handling,
purification and storage equipment
44 Pollution control equipment
45 Industry-specific manufacturing
equipment
46–47 Reserved
48 Electrical power generation
49 Reserved

FIGURE 7.5   CSI MasterFormat 2004

In addition to producing documents that are clear and well organized and conducting a pre-bid meeting, the designer and the owner should sit with the low bidder to review the pricing and discuss any unique aspects of the job. In this way, they work to make sure the contractor is entering into the project with enough money to complete it as designed and specified.

ANALYSIS OF BIDS

Once all the bids have been received, the construction manager tabulates them in a spreadsheet. Figure 7.6 shows how a spreadsheet can arrange the numbers so that comparisons can be quickly made. Such comparisons may consist of the base bid, alternates, addenda, unit prices, exclusions, qualifications, and value engineering suggestions.

	CGS Contracting, Inc.	Zone Free, Inc.	ABC Environmental	ASB & Company	Total Control, Inc.
Base	$524,400.00	$560,000.00	$629,000.00	$719,000.00	$760,500.00
Bond	$15,000.00	$11,200.00	$173,000.00	$21,800.00	$15,000.00
Total base bid	**$539,400.00**	**$571,200.00**	**$646,300.00**	**$740,800.00**	**$775,500.00**
Schedule	N/A	70	65	100	110
Shift (hrs)	N/A	8	8	8	8
Unit prices					
Transite panels (sf)	$5.50	$5.00	$2.90	$5.00	$5.00
Pipe insulation (lf)	$35.00	$15.00	$9.75	$18.00	$15.00
Fitting insulation (ea)	$55.00	$25.00	$25.00	$22.00	$17.50
Duct insulation (sf)	$9.50	$25.00	$12.00	$10.00	$12.00
Electrical wrap (lf)	$30.00	$20.00	$3.00	$20.00	$15.00
Penetration gaskets (ea)	$30.00	$150.00	$19.00	$20.00	$60.00
Labor rates (per hour)					
Laborer	$28.00	$31.00	$49.00	$47.00	$57.50
Foreperson		$35.00	$62.00		
Supervisor	$38.00	$40.00	$75.00	$50.00	$70.00
Project manager		$50.00			
Other					
Equipment rates (per day)	$72.00	$62.00	$50.00	$75.00	$87.00
HEPAs					
Disposable material					
Costs (cy)		$28.00			
PCB disposal	N/A	$8.00	$7.90	$10.00	$7.50
Alternate					
Deductions (less)					
Equipment removal	($12,000.00)	($5,000.00)	($6,800.00)	($17,500.00)	($30,000.00)
Total (deductions included)	**$527,400.00**	**$566,200.00**	**$639,500.00**	**$723,300.00**	**$745,500.00**

Key sf = square feet; lf = linear feet; ea = each; cy = cubic yard

FIGURE 7.6   Bid spreadsheet for an asbestos project

At first look, the numbers in Figure 7.6 point to CGS as the low bidder, even with the deduct alternate. However, before awarding the bid to that company, the owner and the construction manager should carefully examine CGS's assumptions made in the base bid about the quantity of material. The unit prices are higher than they are for the other contractors, and the labor rates are not much lower. A review of the scope will help determine if the company made an error. If, in fact, it did carry the right scope, the owner and the manager should still have a concern: if changes are expected on the job based on unseen conditions (that is, asbestos buried in walls), then how many changes need to occur before the next lowest bidder's number compares favorably with the low bidder's? The owner and manager should examine their expectations about unforeseen conditions and evaluate the bids based on a reasonable assumption about changes to the base scope.

If bidders provide pricing that is outside the plans and specifications, the project team needs to decide how to handle this. Generally, the following guidelines are used:

1. If the bidder who is low, even without an alternate, suggests an equal to or better alternate that makes him or her even lower, the owner has the option of accepting this bid.
2. If the bidder who is not low provides an unequal but acceptable alternate that then makes him or her low, the owner has the option of giving the other bidders in contention the opportunity to bid this alternate as well.
3. If the bidder who is not low and won't ever be low suggests an acceptable alternate, the owner has the option of having the low bidder price this alternate.

AWARD OF THE CONTRACT

Award of the contract can be as simple as accepting the lowest bidder, and in the end it often *is* this simple. However, many factors come into play when bids are received. The apparent low bidder can turn out not to be the lowest after the de-scoping session takes place. The low bidder may be too far from the other bidders, raising the suspicion that he or she has missed something. By law the bidder is required to honor the price, no matter what; but nobody wants a contractor on the job who is not going to do well. Bids often come in with information missing: for example, receipt and acknowledgment of addenda, signatures, exclusions that mean they haven't addressed all the conditions. In all cases, the owner has the right to reject or accept the bids. Minor clerical errors are usually okayed for correction; but in general, if a bidder has not met the requirements of the bid, the bid will be rejected.

The bidding period is a time of anxiety for the owner and the designer. Until this time, numerous estimates have predicted the price of the project. In most cases, the project does not get bid if these estimates come in higher than the money available to complete the job. The normal procedure is to redesign or reduce scope until the project's budget is on target. However, these are only estimates of the work, not the real pricing. The owner may elect to test the market with the higher estimate, hoping that competitive pressure will drive the price down. Even with an estimate on target, however, the project may be priced higher than any estimate shows for reasons that are not always apparent. There may be a sudden glut of projects on the market. The project may not fit the profile of available work force in the region. Whatever the reason, if the project comes in higher, the owner has options. The contract with the designer often has a redesign clause that requires him or her to design a project that fits the owner's budget. Redesigning is time-consuming, however, so the owner may elect to work with the low bidder to bring down the price through value engineering, cost cutting, or scope reduction.

Once the bid is accepted, contract negotiations begin. Since the contractor has already had the opportunity to review the contract, this is normally a straightforward process. However, even the simplest negotiations can take time. If the owner wants to save time, he or she might opt to send the contractor a letter of intent. This usually states a specific time period, methods of payment, and conditions of termination if the negotiations fall through. The contractor can start mobilizing for the job but should not commit anything outside the scope of the letter of intent. Once the owner and the contractor sign the contract, the construction phase begins. Chapter 8 explores that phase.

Conclusion

During the bidding period the design work is launched into the construction arena. The method of assembling the bidding documents is normally determined early in the design process with the help of the construction professional. Sometimes the project is bid out to one prime contractor; sometimes it is broken into smaller bid packages. How it is handled is determined by the delivery method chosen by the owner. In addition, these bid packages are either fast-tracked or released simultaneously. A fast-track approach leaves the option of holding back pieces of the project. This reduces the number of bids that must be processed at once. Pieces such as roofing, which occur later in the construction process, can be bid on later. The disadvantage to the owner is that all the costs are not known when the contract is signed.

Bidding can be an intense period in the project. Anxiety levels are high for all parties. Owners are concerned about getting the best contractor for the best price. Designers are concerned that their design meet the budget, and contractors are concerned about submitting a bid too high and losing the job or submitting too low and losing money on the job. But if the bidding process is handled well, the probability of a successful project is good.

Suggested Reading

Ayers, Chesley. *Specifications for Architecture, Engineering, and Construction.* New York: McGraw-Hill, 1984.

Rosen, Harold J. *Construction Specification Writing.* New York: Wiley, 1981.

Chapter Review Questions

1. To ensure maximum competitive advantage and the best subcontractor price for an owner, a construction manager should seek 12 or more bidders per work package. True or false?
2. A bid breakdown submitted by the bidder can be useful in guiding contractor progress payments. True or false?
3. Builder's risk insurance insures the property while it is under construction for damage resulting from fire, smoke, water, explosion, and vandalism. True or false?
4. A bidder who submits the low bid using an alternate not equal to the original specifications but now acceptable to the owner should win the contract. True or false?
5. Bid alternates priced by the contractor and accepted by the owner lead to an increase in the contract sum. True or false?
6. Which of the following terms indicates a change or clarification issued to all bidders before the receipt of bids?
   a. Contractor agreement
   b. Bid alternates
   c. Addenda
   d. Change order
   e. None of the above

7. Which of the following bonds guarantees that if a contractor's proposal is accepted, he or she will enter into a contract?
   a. Bid bond
   b. Performance bond
   c. Payment bond
   d. Lien bond
   e. None of the above

8. Which specification establishes an expected level of performance that must be met, leaving the means and methods to the construction team?
   a. Design specification
   b. Performance specification
   c. Proprietary specification
   d. Open specification
   e. All of the above

9. According to the CSI format, where would information about insulation requirements be found?
   a. Division 2
   b. Division 5
   c. Division 7
   d. Division 9
   e. Division 12

10. Which of the following is *not* a potential disadvantage associated with breaking down a project into additional bid packages?
    a. Increased need for project coordination
    b. Increased probability of trades being assigned the same work
    c. An increase in owner/construction manager overhead
    d. Increased probability of omitting work
    e. All of the above are potential disadvantages

Exercises

1. Investigate a project you are familiar with and report on how the project was broken into work packages. Address the following issues:
   a. Graphically describe the work breakdown structure for the project, identifying the sub-contracts by first tier, second tier, third tier, and so on.
   b. Briefly write up the scope of work for each work package.
   c. What was the approximate dollar value of each package and the percent of the total cost of the project?
   d. Develop a bar chart for the project, using one bar for each work package. Graphically show the design, bid and award, and construction phase for each work package.

2. Examine in detail one of the bid packages considered in exercise 1:
   a. What were the bonding requirements?
   b. When and where were the bids due?
   c. When could the work begin? When did it have to end? Was there a liquidated damage clause? Was there a bonus for early completion?
   d. Describe the information required on the bid form.
   e. Review and report on the information included in the general conditions.
   f. Were performance specifications included? Provide an example.
   g. Were there any bid alternates? Provide an example.

Chapter Outline

Student Learning Objectives

In this chapter you will learn the following:

1. The activities necessary to properly organize and prepare a project for construction

2. How construction sites are staffed and the relationship between the field and the home offices

3. The physical and administrative work necessary to properly close out and turn over a construction project

INTRODUCTION

Once a project enters the construction phase, the builder's work is pretty much the same no matter what contract form or delivery method was chosen. The same activities are necessary to get the project built: the subcontractor's contracts must be negotiated, the project staffed, a detailed schedule of values and work schedules developed, and the job site assembled. To simplify our discussion in this chapter, we assume here that the builder is a construction manager at risk. This means that the subcontractors work directly for the builder with no direct contractual relationship with the owner.

Construction is show time. After all the time they have spent planning and designing, the project members are going to test out their assumptions. The project, which until now has been real only on paper, is now entering a new phase. It will be transformed from two dimensions to three dimensions: from a computer graphic image to a full-scale object. Any inconsistencies not apparent in the two-dimensional image will become glaringly apparent when the builder starts to assemble the pieces. His or her skill is to identify these inconsistencies early enough so that they have minimal impact on the project.

Design	Bid	Construct
Scope definition	Bid packages	Project authorization
Conceptual design	Bid invitation	Construction
Design approval	Bid period	Turnover
Construction documentation	Contractor selection	Owner acceptance

After the drawings and the design are complete, the need for planning, anticipation, and even design does not end. Rather, the need shifts into the field. Every day that work is installed, the conditions at the site change, and the construction manager must remain constantly aware of these shifting circumstances. Staying ahead of the day, the week, and the month gives him or her time to plan, meet problems, and solve them before they affect the pace of the job. This is the manager's main job in the field. Even during the bestplanned design phase, there are plenty of opportunities to test the skill of the construction manager. Unforeseen conditions, changes in the scope, changing regulatory rules, and community sentiment may all affect the schedule and costs on the job. The manager's real skill is to solve the problem before it *is* a problem. This can only be done through anticipation and contingency planning and by putting together a well-organized team of people.

A large part of organizing for construction is creating the best possible relationship among the work that needs to be accomplished, the people who are accomplishing it, and the conditions under which they are working. The work that needs to be accomplished is largely outside the control of the contractor. The designer and the owner determine the scope of the project, and the design has usually been completed—at least until changes occur. The amount of money to be spent has been determined, and the amount of time in which to do the work has been set. The means and methods of producing the work, however, are very much under the control of the contractor. It is his or her job, then, to set up the other two components—the personnel and the working conditions—so that the work can be done most efficiently.

SUBCONTRACTS

Once the owner has accepted the project bids, the construction manager enters into final negotiations with the subcontractors. At this time both parties discuss obligations to the owner, closeout requirements, and the assumptions that formed the basis of the bid, especially in areas where assumptions could vary. A final price is agreed to after these discussions, and the subcontractor signs a contract with the construction manager. These contracts are between the contractor and the subcontractor. There is no direct contractual relationship with the owner.

Subcontracts can be signed by the contractor with either a trade contractor or a supplier. The difference is that a trade contractor has a specific construction skill such as carpentry or plumbing whereas a supplier furnishes a product to the job such as a refrigeration unit or an electrical generator. Either a trade contractor or a supplier can sometimes be contracted to another subcontractor, making him or her a second-tier subcontractor. A mechanical subcontractor, for instance, may hire a sheetmetal subcontractor to fabricate and install the ductwork.

Although there is no direct contract between the owner and the subcontractor, there are provisions in the owner–contractor general conditions that pass on the same owner obligations to the subcontractor and subcontractor obligations to the owner as exist between the owner and the prime contractor. If the prime contractor defaults, provisions in the general conditions assign the subcontract to the owner, as long as the owner is willing to accept it. This provision attempts to offset the disruption caused by the default of the prime contractor.

Subcontractors do a large percentage of the work on most projects, and they are at considerable risk. They are bound by the terms of the contract between the owner and the prime contractor but have no part in negotiating them. Unless a specific time frame for payment such as "upon completion" of a trade is in the contract, subcontractors are not paid until the owner pays the prime contractor. When a change order needs to be negotiated, payment can occur many months after the work is complete. Thus, the subcontractor must carefully consider the terms and conditions of the contract to minimize his or her risk.

After signing an agreement with a subcontractor, the construction manager works with him or her to develop a detailed schedule for all work activities. This schedule is prepared before construction begins. Once the construction manager knows in detail when certain activities will be performed on the job, he or she will concentrate on providing the staffing to accomplish them.

With the subcontractors on board, the construction manager has the majority of the work force assigned since the subcontractors will do most of the work. What is left are the home office support, the field supervisory personnel, and any laborers who are carried as part of the construction manager's general conditions.

STAFFING

On any construction project, there is a split in how the project is managed between the home office and the field office. Where certain tasks get done depends in large part on the size and the location of the job. Some parts of the project always get managed from the home office, no matter what the size of the job (see Figure 8.1). These usually concern communications with the owner. For instance, reports assembled for the owner and presented to upper administration are usually done through a project executive. Also, information regarding impending problems and suggested solutions are usually delivered by home office personnel. On the other hand, some tasks can only be performed in the field, such as supervision of subcontractors and management of the safety program.

Although project organizations are temporary, they must still interact with the corporate structure of the company. Home office staffs tend to grow and shrink with the

Home office	Field office
Prepare bid document	Assist in bidder prequalification
Prequalify bidder	Assist in bid evaluations
Evaluate bids	Set up project field office
Prepare fair cost estimates	Manage and coordinate work
Schedule job	Administer testing/surveying services
Report to the owner on the management level	Keep job diaries and other necessary records
Establish and maintain project control systems	Maintain record drawings
Provide technical and administrative assistance and supervise the field as required	Provide input for progress control systems
	Initiate contracts and review and recommend progress payments
	Maintain job safety
	Maintain liaison with the designer, obtaining technical assistance as required
	Prepare weekly reports on contract status and work force and evaluate change orders as necessary
	Obtain progress and record photos

FIGURE 8.1   These are typical responsibilities of the home office and field office

ups and downs of the market. This means that some functions may take place at the home office during good times but shift to the field during slow times. Such functions include scheduling, procurement, estimating, and accounting. They may also start in the home office and shift to the field during construction if the project is particularly long or complicated. Thus, it is helpful if a similar structure exists in both the field and the home office for handling these operations.

When a contractor is gearing up for construction, he or she may find it difficult to hire the right number of people at the start of the project. A manager's ability to easily staff the job correctly is also affected by market conditions. If times are good, it is difficult to get staff at the beginning of the job. If times are bad, the home office tries to move people from overhead into a job payroll position. A project manager must be careful about when he or she staffs a project. If there is insufficient work, the money lost to the project can never be recovered. However, understaffing can cost time on the project that may never be recovered.

At the end of a project, it can be difficult to get people off the job if there is no pressure for staff members on other jobs. Ideally, a job will have a gradual buildup, a level production period, and a gradual decrease. The project manager should analyze this pattern and try to mimic it as closely as possible. Understanding this pattern also helps the manager organize the job site to safely handle the amount of workers there at a given time. However, a job slowdown because of an owner situation can be difficult to accommodate. Slowing down or stopping work means finding other places for the workers. Once they are gone from the site, it is difficult to get them back. Thus, a slowdown must be carefully discussed with the owner so that both team members understand and make provisions for the consequences.

Although each project requires a different staffing scheme, Figure 8.2 shows a typical one. If the job is large there may be more task breakdown; if it is small, less breakdown.

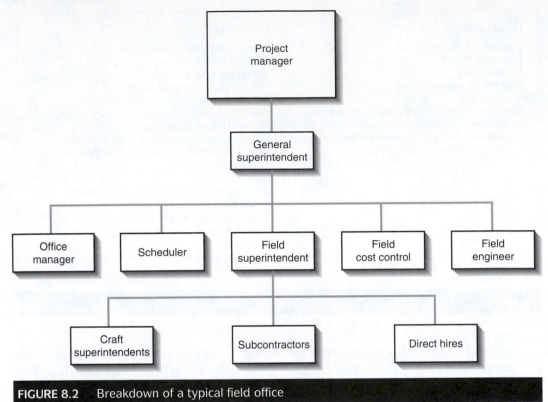

FIGURE 8.2 Breakdown of a typical field office

JOB START

Before actual construction starts, the owner, the architect, and the contractor usually hold a preconstruction meeting, which is often called and chaired by the owner. Here the focus shifts to the logistics of getting the project built. Agreement about communication protocol is established, site rules are reviewed, and certificates of insurance are submitted. The contractor establishes when the work is to begin. Team members discuss means and methods. They review general and special conditions of the contract to ensure that the contractor understands his or her obligations. Administrative details such as change order procedures, shop drawing procedures, and application for payments are worked out. Other site-specific issues such as traffic regulations, use of the owner's facilities, and construction of the site office and facilities are also reviewed.

One important issue is communication protocol. Discussions clarify the specific roles of each project participant; establish lines of communication; and set procedures for submittals, questions and answers about design, emergencies, community relations, and dispute resolution. Often a project runs into trouble when communication protocols are either poorly worked out or ignored by project participants. To ensure that the right information gets to the right people at the right time, these protocols must be observed.

CONSTRUCTION PRODUCTIVITY

Organizing the operations of a job site is primarily about maximizing the productivity of the workforce and equipment. Increased productivity leads to reduced labor and equipment cost and a shorter overall project duration, which in turn lowers the direct cost of project operations as well as project overhead. Early completion may also lead to a more satisfied client and an early completion bonus if offered.

Productivity can best be visualized as the amount of output per hour worked. This could be the amount of cubic yards excavated per hour of equipment operation or the square foot of drywall installed by a carpentry crew. Good productivity is attained by utilizing the best equipment and mobilizing the best people, laying out the job site efficiently, scheduling the work correctly, and providing good management support and oversight.

Equipment selection is a factor of the equipment available, cost, and the constraints imposed by the accessibility of the site as well as the workplan and order of planned operations. For instance, a number of relatively inexpensive mobile cranes could be used on a job site that allows vehicular movement around the site whereas a single permanent and more expensive tower crane would be used on a job sited in a dense urban environment. The tower crane is more expensive but provides an extended reach over the entire site. With each equipment selection comes productivity and cost standards—meeting or exceeding these standards is a factor of the workplan, operator skill, and job-site management. Selecting the wrong equipment, however, may lead to poor productivity throughout the project.

It is the desire of every project manager to employ a cadre of highly skilled and motivated workers. Good workers are more productive and do work of high quality requiring less rework. They are better able to work around other trades, need less instruction and guidance, display initiative and sound judgment, and work safer. Workers who do not display these traits need to be trained or replaced. Hiring and retaining good workers is every constructor's goal. Part of retaining good workers is providing good working conditions, and one of the most important factors of good conditions is the site itself.

A well-organized site is organized to minimize worker movement and conflicts between concurrent operations. Materials are delivered directly to where they will be installed or if they need to be stored, a secure and protected location is utilized. Worker and equipment movements are "choreographed" to minimize crossover points which lead to work slowdown and collisions. A wellorganized site will have many of the following characteristics:

- Activities scheduled to minimize conflicts between trades and to allow each operation to run in an efficient manner.
- Deliveries of stock and equipment, temporary structures and enclosures, scaffolding and required power and water placed and ready to go the day the work is scheduled to begin.
- Crew size planned with consideration for the size of the work space.
- Productive crews kept together working activities in a repeated fashion to build up a rhythm—crews will "learn" the job and get better and more productive

with time. This concept of a "learning curve" should be considered when a schedule is created.

- When conflicts do occur, priority given to critical activities, since by definition, a delay in a critical activity leads to a delay in project completion (see Chapter 10).

Productive jobs begin with the proper equipment selected, good crews, a well-organized job site, and a good schedule, but all of the above does not deliver a productive job without good leadership. This is because every project is subject to circumstances beyond the control of the project planners. Workers get sick, equipment breaks down, design changes occur, and bad weather just happens. Strong project leaders take these impacts in stride and make correct and timely adjustments to the workplan. These adjustments are all part of the project control process discussed in Chapter 11. Project leaders need to provide continual oversight to the project cognizant of work quality and, with an eye, to the adjustments needed in crew and equipment composition necessary to maintain quality. Construction is a people business and project leaders need to maintain a high level of crew morale and camaraderie.

PROCUREMENT

During the latter stages of design, the owner or the construction manager purchases critical items needed on the job earlier than normal bidding processes allow for. These may be large equipment items such as air handlers built specifically for the job or materials such as structural steel that are needed early in the construction process. Once the contractor starts buying out the subcontracts, more items will be identified that need to be purchased out of sequence. For instance, special materials such as exotic woods may come from far away, and common materials such as steel may be in short supply at the time of construction. In such cases, both are candidates for early buyout. An understanding of global economic conditions and local construction activities will help identify which items should be bought early.

In a simple world, purchasing would involve ordering a specific item for a specific amount of money to be delivered at a specific time. In the more complex world of construction, the project manager has to consider many factors, especially when the purchase involves much money or is large. Before committing to a specific item, the construction manager should consider the following:

- Evaluate the difference in the handling cost versus the worth of the item.
- Discuss custom items with the designer; a standard product may do the same job.
- Order in bulk to bring down the unit cost.
- If the owner organization has agreements with vendors, use leveraging power to reduce costs.
- Understand production schedules and stay within normal ranges to keep costs at a minimum.
- Consider shipping costs to choose the best method of getting the material to the site.
- Evaluate the cost and risk to the job of storing materials before they are installed. In addition to the risk involved in double handling, stored materials

can be damaged or buried behind other materials. Theft or misplacement can occur. The time spent shuffling materials around the site can add up.
- Conversely, consider the cost of not having the material on site when needed—direct costs of rush shipping and indirect costs of interrupted work.

Procurement deals with the entire cycle of material handling—from purchasing, shop drawing approval, fabrication, delivery, installation, testing, and then turning over the completed project to the owner. If procurement is treated only as a purchasing function, the construction manager may have problems down the road. Vendors do not voluntarily share information about production problems, and sometimes conditions change on the job, accelerating the schedule of delivery. Both issues must be anticipated, understood, and planned for. A routine trip to a vendor's facilities, periodic phone calls to check on progress, and understanding production schedules and routine plant shutdowns are all pieces of information that become important if problems or changes arise on the job. If the construction manager is aware of such information, he or she can take corrective action quickly, preventing schedule problems.

The control of material purchasing, delivery, and storage on the site can have a large effect on overall production on the job. A missing widget can delay a major installation, and the early arrival of ductwork can cause storage problems at the site.

JOB SITE

A construction site is like a factory. Both transform raw materials into a finished, permanent product that is more than the sum of its parts. The difference between a site and a factory, of course, is that the construction site is set up from scratch for each project. A factory exists in one place, and materials come to it to be processed with an established set of tools. Typically, each new product requires only minor retooling at the plant. The construction site, on the other hand, deals with one unique product. When the product is complete, the site is disbanded and its parts sent off to new sites. The advantage is that the site can be set up specifically to manage a particular project most efficiently. The disadvantage is that lessons learned during the project are often not transferrable to the next project, where site conditions will dictate new lessons. This is the unique challenge of construction.

Before the contractor sets up the job site, he or she should plan it on paper. A scaled version of the site, with dimensions, access road, utility locations, elevations, and existing structures, should be noted. The layout should be drawn with an eye to how material will arrive and be processed and how people will move into and around the site. For instance, the main office trailer should be located close to the site entrance. Construction sites are messy, confusing, and ever changing. Visitors can be easily disoriented, which may contribute to safety problems. By locating the office near the entrance with clear signage, visitors can sign in and be escorted to wherever they need to go. This location will also provide a security point for unauthorized visits. If large equipment is to be warehoused on the site, an area near the entrance can also facilitate these deliveries. The goal of the site is to make the sorting, processing, and movement of materials from storage to laydown areas to installation areas as short as possible. Figure 8.3 illustrates a typical job-site layout.

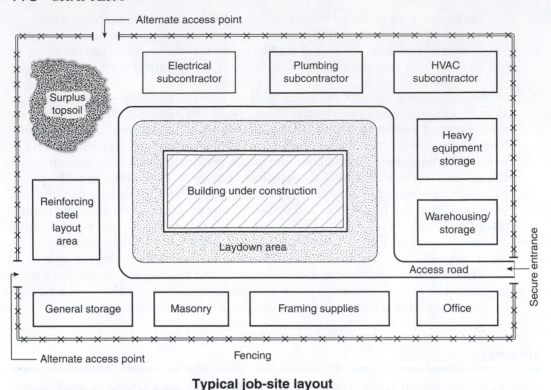

Typical job-site layout

FIGURE 8.3   Job sites should be designed to expedite the movement of people, equipment, and material

BOX 8.1

ORGANIZING FOR EFFICIENCY: THE CONSTRUCTION OF THE EMPIRE STATE BUILDING

The Empire State Building, which at the time of its construction was the tallest building in the world, was designed and built at a speed that even today would be considered impossible.[1] The 85-story, 1,252-foot-tall office tower was opened to the public less than two years after the owner obtained title to the property. In that time the existing four-building Waldorf-Astoria complex was demolished and the new building designed and constructed.

The Empire State Building was designed by the architects Shreve, Lamb, and Harmon, who worked closely with the contractor, subcontractors, and manufacturers. It was imperative to the owners that the project be completed by May 1, 1931, the date when new leases would take effect (a standard real estate practice

---

[1]This vignette is based on an in-house notebook found in the records of Starrett Brothers and Eken, the builders of the Empire State Building. The author is unknown.

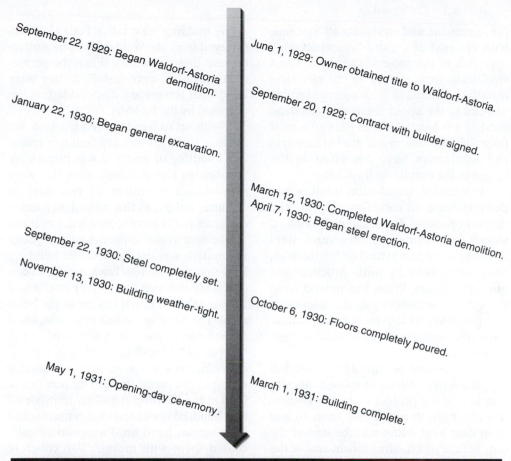

September 22, 1929: Began Waldorf-Astoria demolition.

January 22, 1930: Began general excavation.

September 22, 1930: Steel completely set.

November 13, 1930: Building weather-tight.

May 1, 1931: Opening-day ceremony.

June 1, 1929: Owner obtained title to Waldorf-Astoria.

September 20, 1929: Contract with builder signed.

March 12, 1930: Completed Waldorf-Astoria demolition.

April 7, 1930: Began steel erection.

October 6, 1930: Floors completely poured.

March 1, 1931: Building complete.

FIGURE A   The 85-story, 1,252-foot-tall Empire State Building was constructed and opened to the public less than two years after the owner received title to the building site

of the day). The project was finished on March 1, 1931, two months early. Figure A notes some of the significant project milestones.

The project team's success in meeting the owners' ambitious deadline was due to the builder's early involvement in planning and design. It was also due to the thoughtful organization of the job site and the manner in which the workers and materials were orchestrated.

Fast tracking was still an innovation in 1930, but its use was readily apparent in the construction of the Empire State Building. As Figure A shows, the demolition of the Waldorf-Astoria and the construction of the building's foundations were already underway before the structural steel was detailed and the mechanical and electrical systems designed. The builder, key subcontractors, and manufacturers were all consulted in the design of

(*continued*)

BOX 8.1   Continued

the electrical and curtain-wall systems, with the goal of a more "constructable" approach to the project. The result was a significant time savings in the electrical installation because high-voltage service was run to the upper floors and electrical conduit was located within each structural floor slab. Aluminum and marble suppliers and fabricators were consulted in the design of the curtain-wall system.

Fabrication, installation, jointing, and delivery were all considered during the decision process. By designing standard shapes and using the structural steel frame as a support structure for the wall, time was saved in both procurement and installation. Work has moved from the exterior scaffolding to the interior of the building, which increased productivity and soon provided a weather-tight enclosure.

The efficient organization of the job site, which streamlined all movements, was also key to the project's success. Usually workers need to travel four times to and from their workstations: at the start of the day, before lunch, after lunch, and at the end of the day. At the project's peak, 3,439 workers were involved, some working up to 80 floors in the air. Their movement would strain the elevator system and waste time. The constructors addressed this problem in a number of ways. First, they contracted with a reputable restaurant to manage a series of high-quality, low-priced lunch counters within the building. At peak construction the restaurant ran five counters, all constructed and paid for by the contractor. Second, the constructors addressed the elevator problem. Each work area was zoned with specific express elevators. Starting times were staggered to reduce the pressure on the elevator system. Two mine cage lifts were used and adjusted

as the building grew taller. Four elevators salvaged from the Waldorf-Astoria supplemented these elevators. When the permanent elevators were installed, they were lined with temporary, disposable finishes and used by the builders.

With up to five hundred trucks a day arriving at the job site, efficient movement and handling of material was imperative for success. Hoists (there were six) were scheduled a minimum of two days in advance, and trucks that missed their delivery times might have to wait a day or more for the next available time. A narrow-gauge rail system was used within the building. Raw materials such as brick, sand, and cinders were dumped from street level into a hopper that fed into a rail car in the basement. The car was pushed to a hoist, lifted to the appropriate floor, and moved by rail to a particular location. In this way, tremendous efficiency was possible in handling, for example, the more than 10 million bricks used in the building. A rail car transported four hundred bricks at a time, none touched by a human hand until a mason actually coated them with mortar. Two concrete batch plants were constructed at the basement level. Thus, concrete delivery trucks were not necessary.

The 22-month project was a huge accomplishment for the project team, and from its perspective the project was a success. Unfortunately for the owners, the project was completed when there was an oversupply of available office space and a depression economy. The building was also located somewhat far from public transportation. So the project was initially a financial failure.

Reference
Willis, Carol, ed. *Building the Empire State.* New York: Norton, 1998.

For the site to operate efficiently over time, many organizational and procedural decisions and policies need to be made:

- Contractor's designated area for storage
- Designated locations for lunch and breaks
- Use of toilet facilities
- Start and finish times for work; regular and overtime rules
- Security access after hours
- Everyday access to and from the site
- Safety rules and first-aid stations
- Emergency evacuation and accident procedures

The superintendent must ensure that each new employee is aware of these rules and that all employees, including supervisory and management, abide by them.

PROJECT COMPLETION

Construction Closeout and Turnover

The completion of the project is actually more complex than it seems. One common miscalculation is underestimating this complexity. A poorly planned, understaffed project closeout can have an adverse effect on a company's reputation.

By the end of the job everyone is tired. Huge efforts have been expended to get a job physically complete and occupants moved in. The job does not end there, however. Instead, the last phase of the project begins. This is when it moves from being physical and tangible to administrative, involving closeout, commissioning of systems, and turning over the project to the owner. This is also startup time for the owner.

It is often difficult for the contractor to switch gears to organize the effort at the end of the job, a problem that unfortunately can lead to bad feelings with the owner. Closeout usually takes place while the owner is occupying the facility. The punch list items that are left over can be a source of annoyance for the owner, with people complaining when they move in that the facility is not complete. Pressures for staffing on other jobs and dwindling general conditions funding often mean there are not enough construction people left on the job at the end. Subcontractors have left the site with their trailers and work force, so every piece of work that needs to be completed or changed is difficult to schedule. There is a major difference between the importance that the contractor places on last-minute items and their importance for the owner. After getting major systems built and operating, it is difficult for the contractor to put the same effort into the small details that must be accomplished at the end of the job. Because the end of the job is near, his or her focus is on the next job. The owner, on the other hand, is gearing up to take over the facility. People are moving, and the owner's representatives are under pressure to ensure that the facility is functioning as promised.

Commissioning

Commissioning is an emerging practice that is increasingly being utilized in the construction industry, especially in special-use buildings. It is proving to be beneficial in improved system performance by ensuring that the building systems are designed initially to meet the stated objectives, that they are installed according to the drawings and specifications, and that they function as the design intended. To accomplish this, commissioning agents are most effective if part of the team early in the design process.

Although construction or engineering firms on a project can offer commissioning services as part of additional services, the most common form of commissioning is by independent agents. This independence ensures that the focus is on the stated objectives of the owner. Early in the process of design, the scope of the commissioning work is determined, and a budget and schedule are established. The scope is dependent on the type of building, the perceived vulnerabilities, and a cost-benefit analysis on the most important functioning systems.

Commissioning services traditionally focus on HVAC, electrical, and fire alarm systems, but any building system is a candidate for commissioning. Depending on the building use and the perception of critical systems, other systems such as plumbing, roofing, exterior wall enclosures, security, and communication are increasingly being included in the scope of commissioning. The risk of something not working is different for each organization. An evaluation of these risks will help define the scope of commissioning.

The development of the scope will identify the performance criteria for each system, and spell out specific requirements for each subcontractor for testing and inspection, for documentation, and for training. The identification of the expected training level will also help operations personnel determine the staffing levels and qualifications required to run the new systems.

During construction, the commissioning agents will review relevant submittals, ensuring that the performance criteria are being maintained. They will especially pay attention to alternate products proposed for use.

All the planning and review of design and submittals cumulates in the inspection and testing. This can take place initially in the factory before the equipment or system is even on site but the bulk of the effort is on site when the systems are near completion and especially after they are completed. At this time, the commissioning team will confirm that the equipment or system meets the performance criteria laid out in the specifications. The team will test and sometime stress the systems in a variety of operating modes and will model a variety of environmental conditions. This team also oversees the training of the operations personnel and ensures that all relevant information—i.e., warranties, operations and maintenance (O&M) manuals are turned over to the owner.

Planning

Project closeout officially begins when the contractor turns over the certificate of substantial completion to the owner. Planning for the end of the project, however, actually happens at the beginning. During design, the designer puts together the closeout requirements, which become part of the specifications. At the start of the construction project, the contractor meets with the owner to review all these requirements. Important points include the following:

- Responsibilities for each participant: owner, contractor, designer
- Clarification of what constitutes substantial completion and final completion
- Verification of government regulations

- Schedule of owner-furnished equipment and furniture
- Confirmation of warranty start and duration
- Review of turnover procedures

At this time, a second meeting should be established, to be held a few months before the end of the project. At this meeting, agreed-upon procedures and responsibilities should be reviewed to refresh everyone's mind.

During preconstruction, a second series of meetings should be held with the trade contractors to clarify expectations for the end of the project. Although these expectations are spelled out as part of their contract, reviewing them means that everyone is clear about specifics. At the time of contract negotiations, these requirements are included as part of the contract.

Administratively, closeout includes organizing and turning over documents to the owner. Before turning them over, the contractor must make sure that they are complete according to the requirements of the specifications. A list of some of these documents follows:

- Guarantees and warranties
- Certificates of completion
- Operations manuals and instructions for equipment
- Keying schedule
- Maintenance materials, spare parts, special tools
- As-built drawings
- Certificates of code compliance
- Lien waivers
- Consent of surety for final payment

The field office also has to be decommissioned, including the equipment. How the equipment was purchased determines how it is decommissioned. Often the owner purchased it for this specific project. In this situation, the contractor usually negotiates a buyout with the owner, who generally will have no use for the equipment in his or her own operations. The builder, on the other hand, can move it to another site, perhaps offsetting the need to purchase new for that job.

Several other activities are also involved in decommissioning the field office:

- Inventorying equipment, office supplies, and furniture
- Changing the field office address
- Terminating phone, radio, and pager accounts
- Terminating office equipment, rentals, and leases
- Demobilizing the office and taking it off site
- Reassigning field office staff

Perhaps the most important and the most visible aspect of closeout is closeout of the construction and the subcontracts, which involves the following:

- Preparing the closeout schedule
- Terminating temporary utilities

- Issuing contractors' certificate of completion
- Conducting a pre-punch list inspection
- Preparing a punch list with the architect
- Completing a punch list
- Performing the final inspection
- Receiving a certificate of completion or substantial completion
- Requesting final payment
- Issuing a lien waiver and consent of surety of payment
- Receiving final payment

There can be a long time between occupancy and receipt of final payment. Minor issues can drag on. However, it is in everyone's best interest to resolve any lingering issues and complete this phase.

Owner Startup

Like closeout, planning for startup begins early in the project. People who are going to ultimately run the facility should be involved in the design so that they understand the rationale behind design decisions and have time to get familiar with new technologies as they are incorporated. If these same people can stay with the project through design and into construction, they will have a thorough understanding of not only design parameters but also installation conditions.

During design, team members should hold reviews that focus on operations and maintenance issues, including the following:

- Size and layout of working space around equipment
- Suitability of equipment models in relation to existing inventory
- Proposed control systems and their effect on energy costs and staffing requirements
- Life-cycle costs of equipment and building systems
- Environmental considerations: airflow, noise, odors, safety, accessibility for people with disabilities
- Personnel and budget planning for operations and maintenance staff, including training requirements (with the goal of having trained staff on opening day)

If these reviews take place during design, the startup period will flow much more smoothly. This phase begins when equipment starts coming on line. If a formal commissioning process is required, this phase is merged with that one for equipment testing.

These are the main components of a startup program:

1. Scheduling activities, determining construction completion, and putting together an action plan that outlines who will oversee testing
2. Determining that each component of the project is in working order and can be operated as planned
3. Providing a training program for O&M personnel
4. Confirming O&M manuals

This program is developed and carried out by the contractor and the manufacturers working in conjunction with the owner's operating staff and the contractor's construction forces.

OPERATING PHASE

During the operating phase, the facility is staffed entirely by the owner's employees. During the first year, many elements of the project fall under warranties. The contractor, therefore, continues to have some involvement to intervene, enforce warranties, and address operating concerns. The owner's staff members serve as the first contact for any problems; but they in turn call the contractor, the subcontractor, or the supplier directly depending on the nature of the problem. It is in the contractor's best interest to be responsive during this phase. It is often a frustrating time for the owner as the bugs of new equipment are worked out. If it is difficult to get the attention of the installer or the manufacturer, that frustration can exceed the actual bounds of the problem.

Conclusion

The construction period can be the most exciting part of the design/build cycle. Every day the conditions of the job change. There will always be problems to solve, logistical challenges to meet, new people to work with, daily satisfactions in getting specific tasks accomplished. It also can be the worst part of the design/build cycle. If the project gets out of control from a cost, schedule, or logistical standpoint, it is very difficult to get it back on track. Tempers get short; motivation to cooperate is lessened; efforts to blame increase. The only way to avoid this negative cycle is to ensure that the job is planned well and that contingencies are built in. These contingencies can be money, time, or alternate methods of accomplishing the work. In any case, the construction project manager must be quick to recognize when the project is going off track and be prepared to act decisively to get it back on track, often before anyone else notices that it has strayed. This is especially true toward the end of a job, when money and time are tight and there is little room to maneuver. Here is where the true worth of a construction professional is tested. Last-minute details, pressures from the owner to finish, loss of staff and subcontractors as the project winds down all play against getting the project 100 percent complete. However, that is the goal and the expectation. It takes specific planning and vigilance to ensure that this happens.

How the job is staffed, relationships between the home and field offices, and the specific form of the company will all contribute to the success of the construction phase.

Chapter Review Questions

1. Which type of organizational structure can be described as a two-boss system?
   a. Generalist
   b. Departmental
   c. Matrix
   d. Design/build
   e. None of the above
2. Which of the following is *not a* typical support staff responsibility?
   a. Accounting
   b. Marketing
   c. Legal
   d. Superintending construction operations
   e. None of the above

3. One advantage of a corporation is that stockholders are only liable for corporate debts up to the amount of their investment. True or false?

4. Which of the following might be a benefit of a strong and effective partnering program?
   a. A decrease in litigation costs
   b. Better communication across disciplines
   c. An increase in employee job satisfaction
   d. More collaborative problem solving
   e. All of the above

5. Setting up a construction job can be equated to organizing a factory. For a project to be effective, the handling of all materials must be efficiently managed. True or false?

6. Total Quality Management (TQM), developed by the Corps of Engineers in the 1980s, is a structured approach that encourages project teams to look beyond traditional adversarial roles toward cooperation and open communication. True or false?

7. Of the following activities, which is (a) an administrative closeout item, (b) a field office decommissioning item, or (c) an item involved in the physical completion of the project?

   Completion of punch list
   Reassignment of the field office staff
   Request and receipt of final payment
   Submission of as-built drawings

Exercises

1. Visit a job site and sketch the manner in which the site has been organized. Note the following on your drawing:
   a. Site entrance(s)
   b. Physical facility under construction
   c. Contractor trailers (label with specific trade)
   d. Material laydown areas (label with specific materials)
   e. Service utilities and phones
   f. Signs
   g. Sanitary facilities
   h. Parking
   i. Other key features as appropriate

2. Review the technical requirements (drawings and specifications) for a project and write a detailed narrative describing its physical construction. If the size and scope of the project is substantial, focus the narrative on a specific portion. The narrative should clearly identify the trades involved, the order in which the work occurs, and the preparation necessary to accomplish the work.

CHAPTER

9

ESTIMATING PROJECT COSTS

187

Chapter Outline

Student Learning Objectives

In this chapter you will learn the following:

1. How an estimate evolves over the life of the project
2. The common characteristics of every estimate
3. The three basic estimate types used during project design
4. How to organize, structure, and complete a unit price estimate

INTRODUCTION

There are many costs associated with construction projects. Some are not directly associated with the construction itself but are important to quantify because they can be a significant factor in whether or not the project goes forward. These include costs incurred through financial agreements, real estate transactions, consultant services, public relations, marketing, government regulations, maintenance, and operations. None is a direct cost of construction, but all put financial pressure on the project.

Early on, the owner wants to understand the nature of these costs as well as have some indication of what the construction itself will cost. To address this need, an estimate is put together. At this point in the project, little specific information is available, especially about construction costs; so the estimate is based on past similar projects and some judgment calls on the part of the estimator.

Estimating is a dynamic process that begins in the very early stages of a project and ends when the project is turned over to the owner. As a project moves along in time, the amount of information generated increases. This information improves an estimate's accuracy but also costs more to develop and takes more time. Estimating is critical in the development of the project because it informs the owner of costs, which in turn guide design decisions.

Estimators consider past projects while anticipating new factors. Some of these factors include current technologies, marketplace demands on material and labor, quantities of materials, timeline of collective bargaining agreements, level of quality, and the requirements for completion.

A good data base of actual costs from past project experiences facilitates the preparation of a quick and accurate estimate. Professional estimators spend considerable time and resources developing and protecting this data base. Each new project provides a clearer picture of the actual cost of construction and adds to the value of the data. Larger design and construction companies maintain their own data bases. Smaller companies may rely on the data developed from independent cost consultants and cost data suppliers such as R. S. Means. These groups sell construction cost information to owners, designers, and constructors.

COMMON ESTIMATING TRAITS

As estimators begin to develop their estimates, the specific format they use varies with the type of estimate, type of project, and company procedures. However, as experienced estimators know, all estimates share common traits such as the following:

- As projects develop, there is continual competition among issues of quality, size, performance, and cost. Owners want the biggest building with the best finishes and systems that will perform over time for the least amount of money. With these criteria, conflicts are bound to arise. The design and construction team uses estimates to ensure that good cost information is developed and a feedback loop established so that these conflicts can be addressed as quickly as possible. As project information becomes available, it is passed through a costing exercise. The owner can decide to proceed based on this information or ask for some alteration in the design. The designer can then devise ways to meet the cost targets. Through this feedback loop, conflicting demands of cost versus performance can be resolved.
- Estimating combines science and art. Estimates are a product of information supplied by the designer, the owner, and the suppliers. Experienced estimators use much judgment in interpreting and configuring this information.
- Estimates are not guarantees of costs. Used properly, however, they can be important tools in bringing a project under or at budget with the appropriate features for the owner. Nor are they guarantees of project satisfaction. The costs developed during design and even at the bidding stage are almost never the final and complete costs of the project.
- An estimate can only be as accurate as the information upon which it is based (see Figure 9.1). Estimates depend on many factors. Document completeness, data base currency, and the skill and judgment of the estimator all affect the accuracy of the estimate.
- An estimate's accuracy increases as the design becomes more precisely defined (see Figure 9.2). A normal feature of the design process is that earlier stages of design are less precise than later stages. Estimates provided at schematic design will, by their nature, be less accurate than the ones provided at design development.

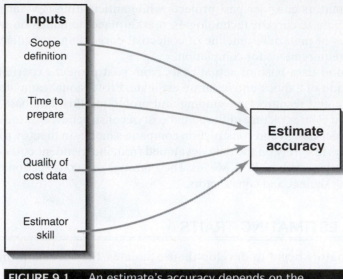

FIGURE 9.1   An estimate's accuracy depends on the quality of key inputs

- Methodology and procedure are important for accurate estimating. Otherwise, the ability to process all the information that makes up an estimate will suffer. As the design process proceeds, the level of detail increases. Estimates, as a consequence, become more complex, reflecting the many different factors that go

FIGURE 9.2   As a project moves on in time, the time required to complete the estimate and the accuracy provided both increase

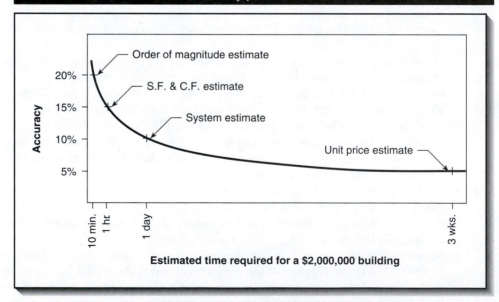

into each unit of work. Calculations increase in number, and the potential to leave something out becomes greater. Only through adherence to strict methods and procedures can mistakes be minimized.

- Each estimate is based on previous estimates. A good, accurate estimate does not stand alone. It is the product of lessons learned from previous estimates.

THE FUNCTION OF THE ESTIMATE

From an owner's perspective an early estimate helps define the affordability of the project, how big the project can be for the money available, and what level of quality is possible. The estimate can also guide the decision among two or three possible options. Identifying costs early facilitates sound decision making, but such estimates will have little hard design information.

Estimates offer guidelines to the designer, who selects materials and sizes the project to fall within the owner's budget. As the project proceeds, the design must be continually compared to this budget. If it begins to exceed the budget, the designer must determine the best alternatives for cost reduction. Estimating and designing are intimately related. A change in one forces a change in the other. As computers become more sophisticated project management tools, designers are increasingly able to specify a material item and instantly review the impact of this decision in the computerized estimate.

At the end of the design process, estimates must also be prepared by individual trade contractors to figure their bid price. These are done with design documents complete or nearly complete and are the most time-consuming and most accurate of the estimates. The project management team often prepares a detailed estimate at this point to verify the accuracy of the bid prices and to negotiate with the trade contractors.

In addition to offering objective information about design costs, an estimate can be used by the project manager to define the scope of work for each subcontractor as well as determine fair pricing. Because each estimate is broken down by units of work, the project manager can extract information regarding quantity and cost for a particular situation. An estimate can also be used as a planning tool. Procurement specialists use it to define how much of a given item will need to be purchased. In the field, superintendents consult the estimate to determine the total quantity of work to be built in a particular location, the total number of hours needed to do the work, and the materials required.

ESTIMATE CONSIDERATIONS

Every estimate, whether prepared in the conceptual phase or at bid time, considers the same basic issues. Project price is affected by the size of the project, the quality of the project, the location, construction start and duration, and other general market conditions. The accuracy of an estimate is directly affected by the ability of the estimator to properly analyze these basic issues.

Project Size
The size of the project is a factor of the owner's needs. In an estimate, size is handled differently depending on which stage the project is at. At the conceptual stage, size is an issue of basic capacity, such as apartment units for a real estate developer or miles of

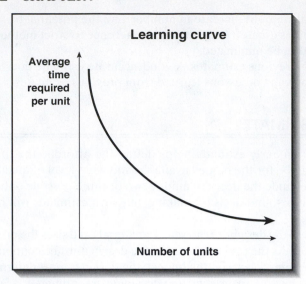

FIGURE 9.3 As operations continue, crews "learn" so that the time required to complete the next similar unit is less

roadway for a highway engineer. As the project becomes better defined, its size begins to be quantified more accurately.

The principle of economy of scale is an important factor when addressing project size. Essentially, as projects get bigger, they get more expensive but at a less rapid rate. This occurs because the larger the project, the more efficiently people and equipment can be used. Also, as people repeat a task, they get better and faster, reducing the cost of labor. On large commercial building and heavy engineering projects, worker productivity is plotted into learning curves (see Figure 9.3). Estimators treat project size by establishing tables that recognize the typical size of a project and a respective price and then adjust up or down from this norm (see Figure 9.4).

Project Quality

An owner may require a high-quality project to create a specific image; for example, the boardroom of a corporation may require high-end finishes to create an atmosphere of prosperity. Or the owner may need a facility for a specific use. In the case of a nuclear power plant or a missile launch site, concerns about public safety will push the design team to specify a higher level of quality. Whatever the reason, the consequences are always the same: an increase in costs. Early in the project, an estimator must discuss expectations of quality with the users, the designers, and applicable government agencies.

As the expected quality of a project increases, the cost of providing this quality increases as well but at a progressively greater rate. Similarly, as the quality of a project increases, the user experiences increased project satisfaction but at a lesser rate. Figure 9.5 shows the importance of arriving at the optimum level of quality for the project since to specify a level of quality higher than what is required can increase the project's cost substantially while not providing the same corresponding value to the client.

An example is the specification of a crane system for an assembly plant. The owner needs a two hundred–ton lifting capacity and the ability to maneuver the load to within one-half inch. The plant foreman notes that the floor operations will be speeded up if

Square Foot Project Size Modifier

One factor that affects the S.F. cost of a particular building is the size. In general, for buildings built to the same specifications in the same locality, the larger building will have the lower S.F. cost. This is due mainly to the decreasing contribution of the exterior walls plus the economy of scale usually achievable in larger buildings. The Area Conversion Scale shown below will give a factor to convert costs for the typical size building to an adjusted cost for the particular project.

The Square Foot Base Size lists the median costs, most typical project size our accumulated data, and the range in size of the projects.

The Size Factor for your project is determined by dividing your project area in S.F. by the typical project size for the particular Building Type. With this factor, enter the Area Conversion Scale at the appropriate Size Factor and determine the appropriate cost multiplier for your building size.

Example: Determine the cost per S.F. for a 100,000 S.F. Mid-rise apartment building.

$$\frac{\text{Proposed building area} = 100,000 \text{ S.F.}}{\text{Typical size from below} = 50,000 \text{ S.F.}} = 2.00$$

Enter Area Conversion scale at 2.0, intersect curve, read horizontally the appropriate cost multiplier of .94. Size adjusted cost becomes .94 × $96.00 = $90.25 based on national average costs.

Note: For Size Factors less than .50, the Cost Multiplier is 1.1
For Size Factors greater than 3.5, the Cost Multiplier is .90

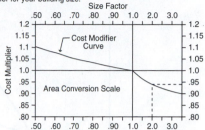

Building Type	Median Cost per S.F.	Typical Size Gross S.F.	Typical Range Gross S.F.		Building Type	Median Cost per S.F.	Typical Size Gross S.F.	Typical Range Gross S.F.	
Apartments, Low Rise	$75.50	21,000	9,700 -	37,200	Jails	$230.00	40,000	5,500 -	145,000
Apartments, Mid Rise	96.00	50,000	32,000 -	100,000	Libraries	141.00	12,000	7,000 -	31,000
Apartments, High Rise	109.00	145,000	95,000 -	600,000	Living, Assisted	123.00	32,300	23,500 -	50,3
Auditoriums	126.00	25,000	7,600 -	39,000	Medical Clinics	131.00	7,200	4,200 -	15,7
Auto Sales	94.00	20,000	10,800 -	28,600	Medical Offices	123.00	6,000	4,000 -	15,0
Banks	169.00	4,200	2,500 -	7,500	Motels	91.00	40,000	15,800 -	120,0
Churches	116.00	17,000	2,000 -	42,000	Nursing Homes	127.00	23,000	15,000 -	37,0
Clubs, Country	118.00	6,500	4,500 -	15,000	Offices, Low Rise	107.00	20,000	5,000 -	80,0
Clubs, Social	113.00	10,000	6,000 -	13,500	Offices, Mid Rise	107.00	120,000	20,000 -	300,0
Clubs, YMCA	133.00	28,300	12,800 -	39,400	Offices, High Rise	136.00	260,000	120,000 -	800,0
Colleges (Class)	144.00	50,000	15,000 -	150,000	Police Stations	166.00	10,500	4,000 -	19,0
Colleges (Science Lab)	216.00	45,600	16,600 -	80,000	Post Offices	126.00	12,400	6,800 -	30,0
College (Student Union)	165.00	33,400	16,000 -	85,000	Power Plants	940.00	7,500	1,000 -	20,0
Community Center	120.00	9,400	5,300 -	16,700	Religious Education	108.00	9,000	6,000 -	12,0
Court Houses	161.00	32,400	17,800 -	106,000	Research	177.00	19,000	6,300 -	45,0
Dept Stores	70.50	90,000	44,000 -	122,000	Restaurants	153.00	4,400	2,800 -	6,0
Dormitories, Low Rise	125.00	25,000	10,000 -	95,000	Retail Stores	75.00	7,200	4,000 -	17,6
Dormitories, Mid Rise	158.00	85,000	20,000 -	200,000	Schools, Elementary	111.00	41,000	24,500 -	55,0
Factories	68.00	26,400	12,900 -	50,000	Schools, Jr. High	115.00	92,000	52,000 -	119,0
Fire Stations	124.00	5,800	4,000 -	8,700	Schools, Sr. High	118.00	101,000	50,500 -	175,0
Fraternity Houses	117.00	12,500	8,200 -	14,800	Schools, Vocational	112.00	37,000	20,500 -	82,0
Funeral Homes	131.00	10,000	4,000 -	20,000	Sports Arenas	92.50	15,000	5,000 -	40,0
Garages, Commercial	84.00	9,300	5,000 -	13,600	Supermarkets	74.00	44,000	12,000 -	60,0
Garages, Municipal	106.00	8,300	4,500 -	12,600	Swimming Pools	173.00	20,000	10,000 -	32,0
Garages, Parking	45.50	163,000	76,400 -	225,300	Telephone Exchange	201.00	4,500	1,200 -	106,0
Gymnasiums	115.00	19,200	11,600 -	41,000	Theaters	107.00	10,500	8,800 -	175,0
Hospitals	203.00	55,000	27,200 -	125,000	Town Halls	127.00	10,800	4,800 -	23,4
House (Elderly)	103.00	37,000	21,000 -	66,000	Warehouses	54.00	25,000	8,000 -	72,0
Housing (Pubic)	95.00	36,000	14,400 -	74,400	Warehouse & Office	59.00	25,000	8,000 -	72,0
Ice Rinks	137.00	29,000	27,200 -	33,600					

FIGURE 9.4   This figure illustrates both typical project sizes and method for modifying for economy of scale

the crane's precision of movement is halved to one-quarter inch. The value to the owner of providing more precise movement must be compared to the cost of providing it. In this case the quarter-inch precision is only provided by one crane manufacturer, increasing the cost tremendously.

The tools that the estimator uses to estimate quality get more refined as the design of the project becomes clearer. In the early stages the estimator must compare the

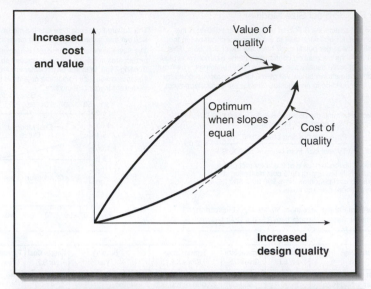

FIGURE 9.5 The optimum level of design quality is the point at which the slope of the two curves is equal. Beyond that point the cost of providing one more unit of the value exceeds its corresponding value to the owner

project to other past projects broken down into quality levels. As the example in Figure 9.6 shows, a three-quarter project cost signifies a project quality level with 75 percent of projects of lesser quality and 25 percent more expensive. The estimator must now quantify the work required and the corresponding prices.

As the estimator moves to the bidding stage, quality must be precisely quantified per individual unit. This is one reason why a detailed estimate takes longer to prepare and requires more clearly defined contract documents.

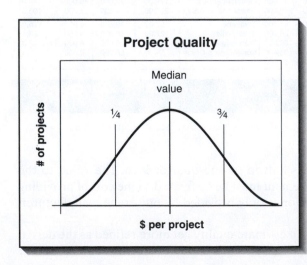

FIGURE 9.6 Past projects can be broadly categorized into quality levels such as one-quarter, median, and three-quarter, which are considered when using Means's square foot costs

Source: From *Means Square Foot Seminar Workbook*, published annually. © R. S. Means Co., Inc., Kingston, MA, 781-585-7880, all rights reserved.

Location

Constructing a facility in Peru is very different from constructing one in California. The differences are in the labor costs, the availability of materials and equipment, delivery logistics, local regulations, and climate conditions. Material costs are a factor of availability, competition, and access to efficient methods of transportation. Labor costs, particularly unionized labor, are a factor of the strength of the local bargaining unit. The cost of labor is also a factor of the degree of sophistication and level of training found at the project location. On some projects (the Alaskan Pipeline, for example), the numbers and the skill levels of workers required are not available locally and must be imported. Understanding the need for such importation adds significantly to the accuracy of an estimate.

Local conditions can influence the costs of the project. The need for citizen involvement, local taxes or fees, and government requirements all can cost the project money. Extreme climate conditions, political instability, and earthquake zones all add to the cost in ways that may not be entirely obvious without some investigation.

The cost of labor and material in different locations can be predicted by establishing location indices for different cities and parts of the country. An index is created for a particular city by comparing the cost of labor, equipment, and material for that city to the national average. This allows an estimator using national average costs to adjust the estimate to a particular location. Most major design and construction companies have developed an accurate record of location indices, which they use for their pricing, or they buy this cost data from national pricing suppliers. To predict the costs of other local factors, such as political instability, a company either uses its own experience in the locale or teams up with a local partner who knows how the local atmosphere can affect project costs.

Time

A project is estimated at a given point in time, but usually the actual procurement and field construction occur at some point in the future. Sometimes this future can be years away, especially in the case of a very large or phased project. The estimate, then, must take into consideration when the actual project will be built. Labor and material costs usually escalate in time; so by examining past and current trends, the estimator can predict where these costs will be at the time of actual construction.

In addition, the estimator takes past actual costs and adjusts them to today's costs. R. S. Means and *Engineering News Record*, for example, track actual project costs by using historical indices, which allow adjustment for time. This adjustment combined with location adjustments allow one to estimate the cost of a new project in Boston by looking at a similar project built 10 years ago in Phoenix.

Time/Location Adjustment

Problem

You have been asked to prepare an estimate for a 40,000 square-foot office building to be located in Canton, Ohio, with construction to start in the spring of 2007. Your company constructed a similar building in San Antonio, Texas, in 1980 for $1.5 million.

Solution

Refer to the 2007 *Means Square Foot Data Book*. Use historical and location indices to make necessary adjustments.

According to *Means*, the estimated time and location index for Canton is 154.1; whereas the combined time and location index for San Antonio in 1980 is 55.0.

Calculation

The Canton building cost can be calculated as follows:

$$\frac{\text{San Antonio building cost}}{\text{San Antonio index}} = \frac{\text{Canton building cost}}{\text{Canton index}}$$

$$\frac{\$1{,}500{,}000}{55.0} = \frac{\text{Canton building cost}}{154.1}$$

Crossmultiply:

$$\frac{\$1{,}500{,}000 \times 154.1}{55.0} = \text{Canton building cost}$$

$$= \$4{,}202{,}727$$

Thus, the estimated building cost in Canton is $4,202,727.

Others

An estimator who accurately incorporates project size, project quality, location, and time has an estimate that reflects the fair value for the project. In a normal market without any unusual circumstances, this estimate should reflect the price that is paid.

Market conditions, however, shift; and owners, designers, and contractors all look at a given project from different perspectives. In a market without much work, contractors may bid a project at cost or with little profit to cover their overhead and keep their staff employed. On complicated projects, contractors may bid the work low in hopes of making significant profit on future changes. Conversely, they may bid the work high to cover the increased risks of a complex project. It is not unusual for contractors to offer very competitive prices when they hope to enter a new market or establish a relationship with a new owner. Some owners and designers are viewed as difficult to work with and may not receive good prices, particularly if the market is strong. Such issues are difficult to quantify but should be considered in the preparation of the estimate. They are usually treated as a percentage applied at the end of the estimate, included in either overhead or profit or in a final contingency.

TYPES OF ESTIMATES

An estimate can be prepared at any point in the life of a project. Estimates are developed early in the design process so that the owner and designer have cost information to guide the design. They are also developed during later stages of design to ensure that costs are within a given budget. During bidding, the owner uses estimates to check that the bids are a fair cost for the work. At bid time, the most extensive estimate is done by the contractor. This bid represents the actual costs as the project goes forward into construction. Estimates continue to be used during construction in case there are changes on the job or to help organize a specific set of activities.

A series of estimate types has been developed that serves each of these situations. The differences among these estimates are a function of the information available at the time of the estimate. Generally, estimates done in the later stages of design and during the bidding period are more accurate than ones done early.

Estimating during Design

Design estimates are important tools for the owner and the project management team as they develop the project's scope of work. The discipline of providing cost information throughout the design phase makes cost a significant driver for the project team. Designers, in their zeal to provide exciting solutions to the program, sometimes lose sight of the budget parameters. Owners can also get caught up in the excitement of desirable design features that in reality could compromise the budget or mean cutting the project in other areas. By providing cost information early and updating it throughout the project, cost professionals can keep the project team well grounded in the realities of cost.

Rough Order of Magnitude Estimates

In the conceptual stages of a project, very little is known about specifics. Design information may only contain sketches or concepts. Descriptions are generally in terms of capacity, such as the number of hotel rooms, hospital beds, or parking spaces. *Rough order of magnitude (ROM)* estimates typically establish a cost per unit of capacity (see Figure 9.7). These units are developed mainly from past projects. Examples are cost per bed for a hospital, cost per apartment, cost per pupil for a school, or cost per mile for a highway. By multiplying this cost times the number of units proposed for the project, a preliminary number can be established. If the costs are developed according to a national average, they must be adjusted using the appropriate city cost index. Costs taken from past projects must be adjusted to current or future dollars. If the project is smaller or larger than normal, the cost is adjusted for size. An appropriate contingency should also be applied to allow for scope adjustments and economic or market conditions.

As with all estimates, the accuracy of a ROM estimate depends on the quality of data used. If the company doing the estimate has a good historic data base of similar projects, that is the best source for that information. If these data are not available, there are nationally published data bases that can be consulted.

One advantage of a ROM estimate is that it can be calculated quickly, often in a few hours, and is typically assumed to have an accuracy of plus or minus 20 percent. This quick turnaround can enable an owner to look at several options without having to invest too heavily in any one. These estimates are often the first costs that an owner sees. Although they are normally accomplished with little information, the number put forward at this time tends to be the number that the owner remembers; and consequently all estimates that follow are compared to this. It is therefore important for the estimate to be qualified. All assumptions should be listed and all information considered identified. In the early stages of project development, this type of estimate is an important tool, but its limitations must be fully understood and articulated.

		K1010 | Square Foot Costs								
				UNIT COSTS			**% of TOTAL**			
		K1010 | S.F. Costs	UNIT	1/4	MEDIAN	3/4	1/4	MEDIAN	3/4	
74	0010	**SCHOOLS Elementary**	S.F.	90	111	137				74
	0020	Total project costs	C.F.	5.95	7.65	9.85				
	0500	Masonry	S.F.	8.15	13.50	20.50	5.80%	10.65%	14.95%	
	1800	Equipment		2.65	4.41	8.30	1.90%	3.38%	4.98%	
	2720	Plumbing		5.25	7.40	9.90	5.70%	7.15%	9.35%	
	2730	Heating, ventilating, air conditioning		7.85	12.50	17.45	8.15%	10.80%	14.90%	
	2900	Electrical		8.50	11.15	14	8.40%	10%	11.70%	
	3100	Total: Mechanical & Electrical	↓	30	38	45.50	24.50%	27.50%	30%	
	9000	Per pupil, total cost	Ea.	10,500	15,600	46,200				
	9500	Total: Mechanical & Electrical		2,950	3,750	13,400				
76	0010	**SCHOOLS Junior High 4 Middle**	S.F.	92.50	115	137				76
	0020	Total project costs	C.F.	5.95.	7.70	8.65				
	0500	Masonry	S.F.	11.70	15.10	17.65	8%	11.60%	14.30%	
	1800	Equipment		3	4.84	7.45	1.81%	3.26%	4.96%	
	2720	Plumbing		5.95	6.75	8.75	5.40%	6.80%	7.25%	
	2770	Heating, ventilating, air conditioning		10.95	13.30	23.50	9%	11.80%	17.45%	
	2900	Electrical		9.20	11.10	14.25	7.90%	9.30%	10.60%	
	3100	Total: Mechanical & Electrical	↓	28.50	38	47.50	23%	26.50%	29.50%	
	9000	Per pupil, total cost	Ea.	11,900	15,600	21,000				
78	0010	**SCHOOLS Senior High**	S.F.	96	118	149				78
	0020	Total project costs	C.F.	6.10	870	14.40				
	1800	Equipment	S.F.	2.57	6.25	8.95	1.86%	3.22%	4.80%	
	2720	Plumbing		5.60	8.30	15.35	5.70%	7%	8.35%	
	2770	Heating, ventilating, air conditioning		11.20	12.85	24.50	8.95%	11.60%	15%	
	2900	Electrical		9.80	12.50	19.30	8.45%	10.05%	11.95%	
	3100	Total Mechanical & Electrical	↓	32.50	37.50	64	23%	26.50%	28.50%	
	9000	Per pupil total cost	Ea.	9,225	18,800	23,500				
80	0010	**SCHOOLS Vocational**	S.F.	79	112	140				80
	0020	Total project costs	C.F.	4.92	7.05	9.75				
	0500	Masonry	S.F.	4.65	11.50	17.55	3.53%	4.61%	10.95%	
	1800	Equipment	"	2.37	3.26	8.50	1.24%	3.73%	4.68%	
	2720	Plumbing	S.F.	5.05	7.55	11.10	5.40%	6.90%	8.55%	
	2770	Heating, ventilating, air conditioning		7.10	13.20	22	8.60%	11.90%	14.65%	
	2900	Electrical		8.25	10.80	15.40	8.45%	10.95%	13.20%	
	3100	Total: Mechanical & Electrical	↓	28.50	31.50	54.50	23.50%	29.50%	31%	
	9000	Per pupil total cost	Ea.	11,000	29,500	44,000				
83	0010	**SPORTS ARENAS**	S.F.	69	92.50	142				83
	0020	Total project costs	C.F.	3.56	6.75	8.70				
	2720	Plumbing	S.F.	4.01	6.10	12.85	4.35%	6.35%	9.40%	
	2770	Heating, ventilating, air conditioning		8.65	10.20	14.20	8.80%	10.20%	13.55%	
	2900	Electrical		7.20	9.80	12.65	8.60%	9.90%	12.25%	
	3100	Total: Mechanical 4 Electrical	↓	17.95	32	42	21.50%	25%	27.50%	
85	0010	**SUPERMARKETS**	S.F.	64	74	87				85
	0020	Total project costs	C.F.	3.56	4.30	6.50				
	2720	Plumbing	S.F.	3.57	4.50	5.25	5.40%	6%	7.45%	
	2770	Heating, ventilating, air conditioning		5.25	7	8.50	8.60%	8.65%	9.60%	
	2900	Electrical		8	9.20	10.90	10.40%	12.45%	13.60%	
	3100	Total: Mechanical & Electrical	↓	20.50	22.50	31	20.50%	26.50%	31%	
86	0010	**SWIMMING POOLS**	S.F.	103	173	370				86
	0020	Total project costs	C.F.	8.30	10.35	11.30				
	2720	Plumbing	S.F.	9.55	10.95	15	4.80%	9.70%	20.50%	
	2900	Electrical		7.80	12.60	18.35	6.50%	7.25%	7.60%	
	3100	Total: Mechanical & Electrical	↓	18.95	48	66	11.15%	14.10%	23.50%	
87	0010	**TELEPHONE EXCHANGES**	S.F.	137	201	255				87
	0020	Total project costs	C.F.	8.55	13.75	18.85				
	2720	Plumbing	S.F.	5.80	9.20	13.10	4.52%	5.80%	6.90%	
	2770	Heating, ventilating, air conditioning	↓	13.45	27	33.50	11.80%	16.05%	18.40%	

FIGURE 9.7 Note the highlighted cost. A median-quality senior high school cost $18,800 per student in 2007

Source: From *R. S. Means Assemblies Cost Data*, 2007. © R. S. Means Co., Inc., all rights reserved.

Square Foot/Cubic Foot Estimates

Once a design has reached the early schematic stage, it will start to produce floor plans, elevations, and building sections. This information makes possible the calculation of floor areas or building volumes, which can then be multiplied by appropriate unit costs to produce a *square foot* or *cubic foot estimate*. The appropriate unit costs are derived from either in-house sources that track past similar projects or outside data sources. This base cost is adjusted to reflect more project-specific factors. Any actual project data that can be folded into the historic data will improve the accuracy of the estimate. Information regarding structural systems, building height, exterior closure, and overall footprint of the building are all factors that will be assumed by the estimator if real data are not available.

A square foot or cubic foot estimate, while more complete than a ROM estimate, is still quite schematic in detail. It is, however, easy to prepare, taking only a couple of hours. The general assumption for accuracy is plus or minus 15 percent—better than the ROM estimate because it is based on more project-specific information.

Square Foot Estimate Example

Problem

Estimate the cost to construct a 55,000 square-foot motel. The motel will be a two-story building. The exterior wall will be made of decorative concrete block, and the building will use a precast concrete floor system. Other features include 150 ceiling smoke detectors, 10 nickel-cadmium emergency lights, and a 500-square-foot gunite pool.

Solution

Refer to the 2007 *Means Square Foot Cost Data Book*, pp. 168 and 169 (see Figures A and B). This two-page model is one of seventy different types of commercial, industrial, and institutional models included in the *Means* data book. Examples include a factory, a jail, and a warehouse.

The first page of the model displays a pricing breakout by size and exterior wall and structure. At the bottom of the first page are the prices of some common building additives. The second page provides a detailed breakout of one of the building models (notice the highlighted $148.70 on the first page): a 49,000-square-foot, three-story motel. This page provides a good overview of what is included in the $148.70 per square foot price. Notice that the general contractor's overhead and profit and a 6 percent design fee are included in this price. Also notice that any site work beyond the excavation and backfill for the foundation is not included.

Calculation

1. Interpolate a base price between $148.70 (49,000 square feet) and $147.30 (61,000 square feet). The interpolation can be set up as follows:

$147.30   61,000
?   55,000
$148.70   49,000

$$148.70 - \frac{6,000 \times 1.40}{12,000} = \$148.00$$

The base cost for the building = $148.00/square foot $\times$ 55,000 square feet = $8,140,000.

Commercial/Industrial/Institutional	M.430	Motel, 2-3 Story

Costs per square foot of floor area

Exterior Wall	S.F. Area	25000	37000	49000	61000	73000	81000	88000	96000	104000
	L.F. Perimeter	433	593	606	720	835	911	978	1054	1074
Decorative Concrete Block	Wood Joists	147.75	143.75	138.55	137.15	136.15	135.70	135.45	135.10	134.20
	Precast Conc.	157.90	153.85	**148.70**	147.30	146.35	145.85	145.55	145.20	144.35
Stucco on Concrete Block	Wood Joists	147.20	143.20	138.05	136.60	135.60	135.20	134.85	134.50	133.65
	Precast Conc.	158.00	153.95	148.80	147.40	146.35	145.95	145.60	145.25	144.40
Wood Siding	Wood Frame	145.25	141.40	136.65	135.25	134.30	133.90	133.60	133.25	132.45
Brick Veneer	Wood Frame	150.45	146.15	140.35	138.80	137.75	137.25	136.90	136.55	135.55
Perimeter Adj., Add or Deduct	Per 100 L.F.	4.10	2.75	2.10	1.70	1.50	1.30	1.10	1.05	1.00
Story Hgt. Adj., Add or Deduct	Per 1 Ft.	1.45	1.30	1.00	1.00	1.00	1.00	.90	.90	.85
For Basement, add $ 25.15 per square foot of basement area										

The above costs were calculated using the basic specifications shown on the lacing page. These costs should be adjusted where necessary for design alternatives and owner's requirements. Reported completed project costs, for this type of structure, range from $52.95 to $272.35 per S.F.

Common additives

Description	Unit	$ Cost	Description	Unit	$ Cost
Closed Circuit Surveillance, One station			Sauna, Prefabricated, complete		
Camera and monitor	Each	1675	6' x 4'	Each	4950
For additional camera station, odd	Each	910	6' x 6'	Each	5925
Elevators, Hydraulic passenger, 2 stops			6' x 9'	Each	7300
1500# capacity	Each	53,600	8' x 8'	Each	8600
2500# capacity	Each	56,200	8' x 10'	Each	9600
3500# capacity	Each	60,400	10' x 12'	Each	11,900
Additional stop, add	Each	8750	Smoke Defectors		
Emergency Lighting, 25 watt, battery operated			Celling type	Each	171
Lead battery	Each	265	Duct type	Each	440
Nickel cadmium	Each	770	Swimming Pools, Complete, gunite	S.F.	60.74
Loundry Equipment			TV Antenna, Master system, 12 outlet	Outlet	288
Dryer, gas, 16 lb. capacity	Each	820	30 outlet	Outlet	185
30 lb. capacity	Each	3525	100 outlet	Outlet	173
Washer, 4 cycle	Each	995			
Commercial	Each	1400			

FIGURE A	Model of costs for constructing a motel: Pricing breakout by size and exterior wall and structure; detailed breakout for a 49,000-square-foot, three-story motel

Models costs calculated for a 3 story building with 9' story height and 49,000 square feet of floor area			Motel, 2-3 Story			
			Unit	Unit cost	Cost per S.F	% Of Sub-Total
A. SUBSTRUCTURE						
1010	Standard Foundations	Poured concrete; strip and spread footings	S.F. Ground	1.26	42	
1030	Slab on Grade	4″ reinforced concrete with vapor barrier and granular base	S.F. Slab	4 45	1.48	
2010	Basement Excavation	Site preparation for slob and trench for foundation wall and footing	S.F. Ground	.14	.05	3.3%
2020	Basement Walls	4″ foundation wall	L.F. Wall	69	1.70	
B. SHELL						
B10 Super structure						
1010	Floor Construction	Precast concrete plank	S.F. Floor	9 59	6.39	8.5%
1020	Roof Construction	Precast concrete plank	S.F. Roof	9.51	3.17	
B20 Exterior Enclosure						
2010	Exterior Walls	Decorative concrete block — 85% of wall	S.F. Wall	14.83	4.21	
2020	Exterior Windows	Aluminum sliding — 15% of wall	Each	503	1.68	9.7%
2030	Exterior Doors	Aluminum and glass doors and entrance with transom	Each	1531	5.05	
B30 Roofing						
3010	Roof Coverings	Built-up for and grovel with flashing; petlite/EPS composite insulation	S.F. Roof	5.31	1.77	1.6%
3020	Roof Openings	Roof hatches	S.F. Roof	.12	.04	
C. INTERIORS						
1010	Partitions	Concrete block — 7 S.F Floor/L.F. Partition	S.F. Partition	15.79	18.05	
1020	Interior Doors	Wood hollow core — 70 S.F. floor/Door	Each	4.57	6.53	
1030	Fittings	N/A	-	-	-	
2010	Stair Construction	Concrete filled metal pan	Flight	11,550	2.83	37.4%
3010	Wall Finishes	90% paint, 10% ceramic tile	S.F. Surface	1.26	2.89	
3020	Floor Finishes	85% carpet, 5% vinyl composition tile, 10% ceramic tile	S.F. Floor	8.37	8.37	
3030	Ceiling Finishes	Textured finish	S.F. Ceiling	3.28	3.28	
D. SERVICES						
D10 Conveying						
1010	Elevators & Lifts	Two hydraulic passenger elevators	Each	87,220	3.56	3.2%
1020	Escalators & Moving Walks	N/A	-	-	-	
D20 Plumbing						
2010	Plumbing Fixtures	Toilet and service fixtures, supply and drainage — 1 Fixture/180 S.F. Floor	Each	4095	22.75	
2020	Domestic Water Distribution	Gas fired water heater	S.F. Floor	.78	.78	21.4%
2040	Rain Water Drainage	Roof drains	S.F. Roof	1.35	.45	
D30 HVAC						
3010	Energy Supply	N/A	-	-	-	
3020	Heal Generating Systems	Included in D3050	-	-	-	
3030	Cooling Generating Systems	N/A	-	-	-	5.2%
3050	Terminal & Package Units	Through the wall electric heating and cooling units	S.F. Floor	5.88	5.88	
3090	Other HVAC Sys & Equipment	N/A	-	-	-	
D40 Fire Protection						
4010	Sprinkle's	Sprinklers, light hazard	S.f. Floor	1.71	1.71	1.5%
4020	Standpipes	N/A	-	-	-	
D50 Electrical						
5010	Electrical Service/Distribution	800 ampere service, panel board and leaders	S.F. Floor	1.85	1.85	
5020	lighting & Branch Wiring	Fluorescent fixtures, receptacles, switches and misc. power	S.F. Floor	6.68	6.68	8.2%
5030	Communications & Security	Alarm systems and emergency lighting	S.F. Floor	.56	.56	
5090	Other Electrical Systems	Emergency generator, 7.5 kW	S.F. Floor	.10	.10	
E. EQUIPMENT & FURNISHINGS						
1010	Commercial Equipment	N/A	-	-	-	
1020	Institutional Equipment	N/A	-	-	-	0.0%
1030	Vehicular Equipment	N/A	-	-	-	
1090	Other Equipment	N/A	-	-	-	
F. SPECIAL CONSTRUCTION						
1020	Integrated Construction	N/A	-	-	-	0.0%
1040	Special Facilities	N/A	-	-	-	
G. BUILDING SITE WORK	**N/A**					
			Sub - Total		112.23	100%
CONTRACTOR FEES lGeneral Requirements: 10%, Overhead: 5%, Profit: 10%l				25%	28.05	
ARCHITECT FEES				6%	8.42	
			Total Building Cost		148.70	

FIGURE B

Source: From *Means Square Foot Data Book*, 2007, pp. 168, 169. © R. S. Means Co., Inc., all rights reserved.

2. Add the costs of the pool, smoke detectors, and emergency lights.

150 smoke detectors × $171/each = $25,650
10 emergency lights × $770/each = $7,770
500-square-foot gunite pool × $60.74/square foot = $30,370

Total additive cost = $63,790

Total project cost (with additives) = $8,203,790

This cost assumes a construction start in early 2007 in a national average location. The price does not include the cost of land purchase or any substantial site work.

Assemblies Estimates

In the later stages of design, when more information is available, it is possible to configure estimates into a series of systems. This method, called *assemblies estimating*, uses system or assembly units of a project. In a ROM estimate, the unit is the number of beds or miles of road. In a square foot estimate, the unit is the square foot area of the project or gross areas of the project. In an assemblies estimate, the unit is the foundation, the roofing, the electrical system, and so on. Since the units are smaller, the estimate becomes more flexible but also requires more designer input, takes longer, and costs more money to prepare. However, its accuracy is in the 10 percent range.

The information needed for an assemblies estimate must be in a form that can be quickly itemized system by system. Most companies use a breakdown called the *uniformat system* (see Figure 9.8). This allows estimators to work with smaller and smaller subsystems within the bigger system. For instance, interior construction may have as one of its subsystems drywall partitions. This subsystem includes the cost of the metal studs, drywall installation, taping, and finishing. It is listed by different fire ratings, whether or not it is insulated, and whether or not it is finished on both sides. Both in-house data bases and off-the-shelf systems include these options. The smaller the system, the more flexibility there is in the use of the estimate. Figure 9.9 illustrates a partition assembly.

Uniformat
1. Foundation
2. Substructure
3. Superstructure
4. Exterior closure
5. Roofing
6. Interior construction
7. Conveying
8. Mechanical
9. Electrical
10. General conditions
11. Specialties
12. Site work

FIGURE 9.8   Projects may be organized according to the CSI 50-division master format or the 12-division uniformat. The uniformat reflects how the project is built, the master format how the trades are organized

C10 Interior Construction

C1010 Partitions

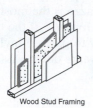

Wood Stud Framing

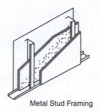

Metal Stud Framing

The Drywall Partitions/Stud Framing Systems are defined by type of drywall and number of layers, type and spacing of stud framing, and treatment on the opposite face. Components include taping and finishing.

Cost differences between regular and fire resistant drywall are negligible, and terminology is interchangeable. In some cases fiberglass insulation is included for additional sound deadening.

System Components	QUANTITY	UNIT	COST PER S.F.		
			MAT.	INST.	TOTAL
SYSTEM C1010 124 1250					
DRYWALL PARTITION, 5/8" F.R.I SIDE, 5/8" REG.1 SIDE, 2"×4" STUDS,16" O.C.					
Gypsum plasterboard, nailed/screwed to studs, 5/8"; F.R. fire resistant	1.000	S.F.	.42	.46	.88
Gypsum plasterboard, nailed/screwed to studs, 5/8"; regular	1.000	S.F.	.43	.46	.89
Taping and finishing joints	2.000	S.F.	.08	.92	1
Framing, 2 × 4 studs @ 16" O.C., 10" high	1.000	S.F.	.43	.92	1.35
TOTAL			1.36	2.76	4.12

C1010 124		Drywall Partitions/Wood Stud Framing						
	FACE LAYER	BASE LAYER	FRAMING	OPPOSITE FACE	INSULATION	COST PER S.F		
						MAT.	INST.	TOTAL
1200	5/8 FR drywall	none	2×4, @ 16"O.C.	same	0	1.35	2.76	4.11
1250				5/8" reg. drywall	0	1.36	2.76	4.12
1300				nothing	0	.89	1.84	2.73
1400		1/4" SD gypsum	2×4 @ 16" O.C.	same	1-1/2" fiberglass	2.90	4.24	7.14
1450				5/8" FR drywall	1-1/2" fiberglass	2.56	3.73	6.26
1500				nothing	1-1/2" fiberglass	2.10	2.81	4.91
1600		resil. channels	2×4 @ 16" O.C.	same	1-1/2" fiberglass	2.58	5.35	7.93
1650				5/8" FR drywall	1-1/2" fiberglass	2.40	1.29	6.69
1700				nothing	1-1/2" fiberglass	1.94	3.37	5.31
1800		5/8" FR drywall	2×4 @ 24" O.C.	same	0	2.09	3.49	5.58
1850				5/8" FR drywall	0	1.67	3.03	4.70
1900				nothing	0	1.21	2.11	3.32
1950		5/8" FR drywall	2×4, 16" O.C.	same	0	2.19	3.68	5.87
1955				5/8" FR drywall	0	1.77	3.22	4.99
2000				nothing	0	1.31	2.30	3.61
2010		5/8" FR drywall	Staggered, 6" plate	same	0	2.63	4.61	7.24
2015				5/8" FR drywall	0	2.21	4.15	6.36
2020				nothing	0	1.75	3.23	4.98
2200		5/8" FR drywall	2 rows 2 × 4	same	2" fiberglass	3.37	5.05	8.42
2250			16" O.C.	5/8" FR drywall	2" fiberglass	2.95	4.59	7.54
2300				nothing	2" fiberglass	2.49	3.67	6.16
2400	5/8 WR drywall	none	2×4, @ 16" O.C.	same	0	1.37	2.76	4.13
2450				5/8" FR drywall	0	1.36	2.76	4.12
2500				nothing	0	.90	1.84	2.74
2600		5/8" FR drywall	2×4, @ 24" O.C.	same	0	2.11	3.49	5.60
2650				5/8" FR drywall	0	1.68	3.03	4.71
2700				nothing	0	1.22	2.11	3.33

FIGURE 9.9 The partition assemblies listed are differentiated by the type of framing, thickness, type of drywall, and whether or not insulation is used

Source: From *Means Square Foot Data Book*, 2007. © R. S. Means Co., Inc., all rights reserved.

As the project design develops, the systems estimate is updated to inform the project team of design decision impacts. As long as good data are available, the designer should be able to look at the costs of different alternatives and make a selection based on cost as well as durability over time. Take, for instance, choices for flooring: vinyl tile, carpet, terrazzo, quarry tile, ceramic tile, and many more. By comparing cost, intended use, and maintenance issues, the choices become clarified. Terrazzo is the most expensive of the options but will last the longest and keep its finish. However, if the terrazzo is laid in an area where there will be renovations, it is not easy to patch. Vinyl tile, on the other hand, usually has the least first cost but over time wears down. Assemblies estimating allows a project team to prepare this sort of analysis.

Estimating during Construction

Once the design documents are complete, companies interested in actually performing the work price the project. Estimators working on this type of bid hope to win the job with the most competitive number while maintaining a reasonable profit for the company. This estimate is the most detailed of all estimate types and is also the most important. It carries with it legal implications. If its bid is accepted, a construction company is legally bound to a specific price for a specific scope of work. During the actual construction, however, there is give and take over the individual prices of each piece of the construction. The contractor must continually negotiate with suppliers and subcontractors over these prices throughout the procurement stage. If the contractor is a good negotiator and has priced the project with an adequate contingency, then the final outcome should give the company a fair profit.

Especially on large complex projects, the scope of work is a continual focus of discussion between the contractor and the designer. No matter what type of contract is signed, someone is always at risk. Wherever that risk exists is where team members hotly debate about what is reasonable to include and what should be accepted as a change. The contractor can help this situation by listing any qualifications when the bid is submitted. Thus, discussions about the real scope of work can happen before there is any legal commitment regarding costs.

Many factors affecting costs lie outside the scope of work. There are owner-requested changes, unforeseen conditions, and new regulatory requirements. These also must be priced as they emerge. Because the pricing established at bid time is done on a unit basis, it can help the contractor give information quickly to the owner about the cost impact of each change.

Detailed estimates take weeks to prepare and involve people from many different disciplines. A general contractor who is preparing a bid requests proposals from subcontractors and quantifies (takes off) and prices work that will be done by his or her own work force. Quotes from material suppliers (also called vendors) are used where possible to get precise material prices. When quotes cannot be obtained, contractors use company records and published cost data. Current wage rates and perceived worker productivity are figured into these costs. The estimator must, in essence, build the project on paper. Hypothetical methods of construction; logistics of the site, with its constraints for storage and maneuverability; delivery strategies; and the schedule of activities all must be understood before a realistic price can be assembled.

Organization of the Estimate

Good organization is key to preparing reliable estimates and avoiding mistakes. Preparing a detailed estimate is a complex organizational task. Many people, both inside and outside the company, are involved. Information comes from a variety of sources and must be carefully catalogued. The estimating team's goal is to minimize the number of company hours involved while preparing a competitive estimate.

To begin, adequate space is set up, the right mixture of senior and junior team members are assigned, and procedures and forms are assembled. A notebook or file system is set up to track all activities. Much of this tracking is done with computer estimating software.

The most important information for the estimating team comes from the contract documents, which explain the scope of the work, the quality of the work, the conditions the contractor is expected to meet, the legal requirements of the job, and the schedule of completion. Of all sources of information received during the bid period, these require the most careful consideration and handling. Drawings and specifications, which make up the contract documents, are usually available from the owner or architect for a refundable deposit. By setting up a plan room in the office or some other central location, the contractor makes these documents available to subcontractors. When the contractor receives the set of documents, the first task is to verify that a full set has actually been received. The drawings are numbered by discipline and the specifications separated by trade. Addenda, which are issued during the bid period, need to be carefully tracked and the information made available to the subcontractors.

Quantity Takeoff

Once the estimating tasks are identified, categorized, and organized, the team begins the quantity takeoff. This is the foundation of the estimate. Its purpose is to accurately determine the quantity of work that needs to be performed on the project. Every work item is measured and quantified, separating the work into units of labor, material, and equipment. Most estimators use the CSI's 50 divisions. The goal of the quantity takeoff process is to calculate every item of the project—no more and no less. To effectively accomplish this, the takeoff must use the correct units. The process requires a thorough understanding of the work involved in each of the different disciplines of the project. Often the best approach is to build the project item by item on the takeoff form and then quantify each item. Preprinted takeoff forms, which identify all estimate items, can serve as checklists.

Unit Pricing

The next task is to determine how much each unit will cost to produce, deliver to the site, accept and store at the site, install in the correct position, and maintain until the project is turned over to the owner. Production of the product and delivery to the site are included in the material unit price. The cost of installing the product is part of the labor unit price. The equipment necessary to move the unit into place and install it is included in the equipment unit price. Project overhead covers the costs of accepting the material, storing it at the job site, and protecting it until the project is accepted. Company overhead includes the cost of preparing the estimate, marketing the company, and providing broadbased technical and administrative support for the project.

Material Costs

Of all the prices that need to be identified, the material prices are usually the most straightforward to determine. The most reliable source is the supplier. However, the estimator must ensure that the price quoted actually covers all the specification requirements and the estimator's assumptions. The following points must be verified:

- The material quoted is the correct model number, color, and finish.
- The price is valid until the scheduled delivery time.
- The price includes delivery to the job site.
- Adequate warranties and guarantees are provided.
- The lead time fits into the scheduled need on site.
- There is adequate stock available.
- Payment terms, discounts, and credits are well documented.

Labor Costs

The price of labor is the most difficult factor to determine because both the hourly wage rate and crew productivity must be considered. The wage rate is a factor of the rates paid to a specific trade. Union rates are available from the union locals and employer bargaining groups. Nonunion labor rates are determined by each company and depend on the geographic area. In either case, wage escalation must be factored in, particularly on long-term projects. Union rates are generally negotiated for one to three years by each trade, so these agreements need to be researched. Factors to consider include the following:

- Expiration dates of the union agreements
- Amount of overtime anticipated
- Availability of skilled labor in the area
- Amount and nature of any hazardous conditions

The expiration of a union agreement probably means increases in labor rates and could, with disputes, mean interruption in the project. For projects with an aggressive schedule, overtime is likely; and if the project is in a remote area, there will be increased costs in bringing in labor. If the conditions have any special hazards, the rates will also be higher to compensate for the increased risk.

Once the quantity of work is known and the hourly wage determined, the last step in determining labor cost is to estimate how long the activity will take. Determining crew durations or productivity requires experience and the ability to visualize how the work will be done in the field. An estimator needs to know the following:

- Expected efficiency rate
- Other work occurring at the same time that could interfere with this activity
- Expected weather conditions
- Specific conditions of the work: that is, working on ladders or scaffolding versus working on the ground
- Duration and frequency of overtime

Past project experience is essential in determining these factors. Thus, in most offices the quantity takeoff may be assigned to a junior estimator, but senior members almost always determine the unit prices.

Equipment Costs

Equipment, which includes small tools needed to complete specific tasks, are covered item by item. However, large, mechanically driven machinery such as cranes, lift trucks, and the like are usually covered on a project basis since they often are used throughout the project for different activities. Equipment costs fall into two general categories: the equipment itself and the cost of operating it. The first category covers ownership, lease or rental, interest, storage, insurance taxes, and license. If the company owns the equipment, these costs are determined in-house. If not, the equipment supplier provides a quote. The second category includes gasoline, oil, periodic maintenance, transportation, and mobilization. The cost of the operator is normally covered under the labor line item.

Subcontract Work

The contractors bidding on the project break down the job into work packages and request bids from prequalified subcontractors for each package. Most general contractors do some of the work with their own work force and therefore do not request bids in these areas. It is important for the estimator to be in contact with the subcontractors during the bid period. This communication can minimize misunderstandings about the scope of work assumed by the subcontractor. It also encourages the subcontractor to put in a fair bid. When the bids arrive from the subcontractors, a debriefing session should take place to ensure that commonly missed items have been picked up. When the estimator is starting to apply overhead and profit to the base costs, it is important to be able to separate subcontractors' work from the contractor's. Because subcontract prices include tax, insurance, and overhead and profit, the adjustment on this price will be different from the adjustment done for the work of the contractor's own forces.

Overhead

In the CSI format, Division 1 is general requirements. This line item is also called *project overhead*. It picks up the costs associated with operating the job site and some home office expenses. Job site costs include the field office people, safety, security, photography, and cleanup. These costs are typically itemized, with quantities and unit prices figured exactly. Figure 9.10 lists typical general requirements. One of the line items on this summary is for main office expense. This is usually carried as a percentage and includes costs such as office rent or real estate costs, vehicles, engineering support, clerical staff, top management salaries, marketing, legal, and accounting fees.

The equipment overhead accounts for the costs of managing the purchase or rental, storage, and handling of materials and equipment. Labor overhead is the greatest of the cost categories. The base labor cost includes the worker's take-home pay plus any fringe benefits, including vacation time and paid sick days. Added are the costs associated with workers' compensation insurance, unemployment, social security taxes, builders' risk insurance, and public liability costs. Subcontractors'

PROJECT OVERHEAD SUMMARY

SHEET NO.

PROJECT

ESTIMATE NO.

LOCATION   ARCHITECT   DATE

QUANTITIES BY: PRICES BY: EXTENSIONS BY: CHECKED BY:

DESCRIPTION							
Job Organization: Superintendent							
Project Manager							
Timekeeper & Material Clerk							
Clerical							
Safety, Watchman & First Aid							
Travel Expense: Superintendent							
Project Manager							
Engineering: Layout							
Inspection/Quantities							
Drawings							
CPM Schedule							
Testing: Soil							
Materials							
Structural							
Equipment: Cranes							
Concrete Pump, Conveyor, Etc.							
Elevators, Hoists							
Freight & Hauling							
Loading, Unloading, Erecting, Etc.							
Maintenance							
Pumping							
Scaffolding							
Small Power Equipment/Tools							
Field Offices: Job Office							
Architect/Owner's Office							
Temporary Telephones							
Utilities							
Temporary Toilets							
Storage Areas & Sheds							
Temporary Utilities: Heat							
Light & Power							
Water							
PAGE TOTALS							

FIGURE 9.10 A checklist of common overhead items

DESCRIPTION						
Totals Brought Forward						
Winter Protection: Temp. Heat/Protection						
Snow Plowing						
Thawing Materials						
Temporary Roads						
Signs & Barricades: Site Sign						
Temporary Fences						
Temporary Stairs, Ladders & Floors						
Photographs						
Clean Up						
Dumpster						
Final Clean Up						
Punch List						
Permits: Building						
Misc.						
Insurance: Builders Risk						
Owner's Protective Liability						
Umbrella						
Unemployment Ins. & Social Security						
Taxes						
City Sales Tax						
State Sales Tax						
Bonds						
Performance						
Material & Equipment						
Main Office Expense						
Special Items						
TOTALS:						

FIGURE 9.10 continued

costs also are adjusted for overhead as a percentage. Although the subcontractors include overhead for most of these categories in their own prices, the contractor's price covers the costs associated with organizing the bid packages, prequalifying subcontractors, reviewing the bids, and managing the subcontractors' work in the field.

Profit

A company grows and maintains its corporate health through its ability to make a profit. The investment of time and energy and the acceptance of risk inherent in a construction project make the inclusion of profit even more critical. Profit is added after the contractor has priced the labor and equipment involved. Overhead has covered the costs associated with managing the job in the field and the costs of supporting the project in the home office. If no profit were added, the business might stay afloat for some time but would not grow. The company would also have no financial tolerance for mistakes or unforeseen conditions. Eventually, a company without adequate profit would not survive.

Companies must add a profit margin into each project. The amount of profit added is a factor of the type of project, its size, the amount of competition anticipated, the desire to get the job, and the extent of the risks. If the company needs work, is faced with substantial competition, or has a strong desire to move into a new relationship with a client, the profit charged might be small. However, the company should not have too many small-margin jobs on the books at the same time so that it has sufficient coverage if something occurs on one job. A project with a high risk or one with little competition allows a company to add a higher profit.

Conclusion

This chapter has discussed why estimates are prepared and how and by whom they are used. An estimate is not static but evolves with the project. When used properly, it provides the owner with a better product. Estimates are first used in the conceptual stage. Because little information is available at this stage, they are only able to provide a rough idea about the project's cost. As the design evolves and more is understood about the project, the estimate becomes progressively more accurate. During design, the estimate can be used to evaluate systems and products and is an integral part of the value engineering process. With the design complete, the estimator is now able to provide a complete and accurate estimate that reflects the true value of the project. This detailed estimate uses unit prices; and when used by the contractor, it is called a *bid estimate*. The bid estimate is the most important estimate done on a project. This is the cost that the owner agrees to pay for the work and what the contractor agrees is the amount it will cost to do the work. It creates a legal bond between owner and contractor.

Every estimate must consider certain basic factors: project size, project quality, location, time, and other market issues. Project size determines the quantities of material, labor, and equipment required for the project. Project quality determines the unit prices used. Location can be treated either by researching local prices or by using specific area cost indices. Project time and market considerations are more difficult to quantify since both depend on economic and local issues and must predict future trends. Projecting past trends to the future is often the best way to handle these factors.

Whenever money is a significant factor in a building project, estimates are essential. A good estimate prepared at the right time gives the owner the information needed to make informed decisions. A bad estimate can cause a project to have serious cost overruns and, if it is a bid estimate, can bankrupt a contractor. Companies invest significant money in preparing good estimates and building data bases of costs. That investment contributes to the long-term health of the company.

Chapter Review Questions

1. A project that is built significantly under budget is good and indicates a competent designer. True or false?
2. An estimate prepared by the design firm at the end of design development guarantees the project completion cost to the owner. True or false?
3. As a project moves on in time, the accuracy of an estimate improves and the cost and time to complete it lessen. True or false?
4. Cost data provided by national firms (such as R. S. Means) must be adjusted to the specific project location. True or false?
5. Quality construction is good, and every designer should specify the highest-quality project components. True or false?
6. Which of the following will *not* increase the cost of a project?
   a. Increased square footage
   b. Increased inflation
   c. Increased availability of labor
   d. Increased demand (faster schedule) for the finished project
   e. Increased quality expectations
7. As the square footage of a project increases, what happens to the cost per square foot?
   a. It decreases at a decreasing rate.
   b. It decreases at an increasing rate.
   c. It increases at a decreasing rate.
   d. It increases at an increasing rate.
   e. It stays the same.
8. How long should an estimate for a $2,000,000 building project, prepared at the end of design development, take?
   a. One day
   b. One to two weeks
   c. Two to three weeks
   d. One month
   e. Two to three months
9. When considering project quality, which of the following is true?
   a. As quality expenditures increase, the cost of providing the quality increases at a decreasing rate.
   b. As quality expenditures increase, the value of the increased quality to the owner increases at a decreasing rate.
   c. As quality expenditures increase, the cost of providing the quality decreases at an increasing rate.
   d. As quality expenditures increase, the value of the quality to the owner increases at an increasing rate.
   e. None of the above takes place.

10. Which of the following is *not* a reason for construction cost variation among different geographic locations?
    a. Local union bargaining agreements
    b. Physical project size
    c. Rail/roadway/harbor capability
    d. Local construction activity
    e. None of the above

Exercises

1. Using published cost data, compute the cost to construct a two-hundred-bed dormitory. Use rough order of magnitude (cost per bed) data.
   a. What is the cost of this dormitory in Chicago, Atlanta, and Dallas?
   b. What would the same project have cost in 1960, 1970, and 1980? Today?
2. Using unit price data, construct an assembly for the following:
   a. A roofing system
   b. A typical partition wall
   c. A pavement system
   Then explain why an assembly can be useful to an estimator.
3. Examine an estimate for a project that was recently constructed in your area, addressing the following:
   a. How was the estimate divided up? Did it follow the CSI format or another?
   b. How were general conditions and home office overhead handled?
   c. Were material supplier and subcontractor prices used? If so, how were they treated?

10 PROJECT PLANNING AND SCHEDULING

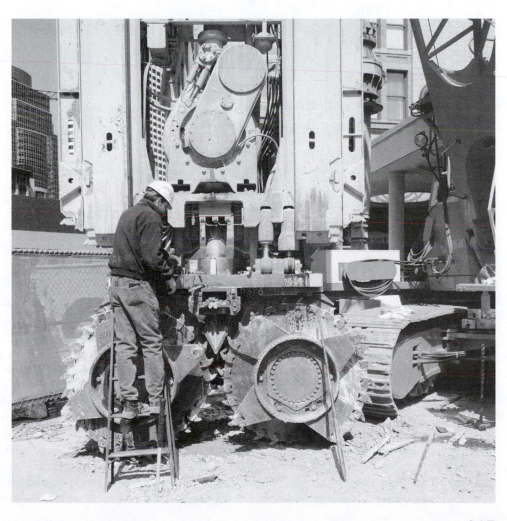

Chapter Outline

Student Learning Objectives

In this chapter you will learn the following:

1. Uses of schedules and types of scheduling methods
2. How and why schedules are used in the preconstruction and construction stages of a project
3. How to construct a network diagram
4. How to determine the duration of an activity
5. How to perform the basic network calculations

INTRODUCTION

In project management, a schedule is the tool most commonly used to plan the project step by step. By systematically analyzing each activity and its relationship to the ones that come before and after it, the project manager can build the project on paper before committing resources to it. Schedules in their simplest form are timetables that identify at which point in time each action will occur on a project. In their more complex form they establish relationships, identify resources needed to complete each task, and highlight the activities that, if late, could jeopardize the overall completion date. They are powerful tools.

Schedules are essential to the successful execution of any complex project. They are not unique to construction but are found in many industries, including business, manufacturing, and publishing. Whenever people, equipment, materials, and organizations are brought together and directed toward a common goal, they need a common tool that will identify how resources are going to be committed. Schedules are particularly useful when companies undertake multiple projects that use common resources. Tradespeople, work space, equipment, and management personnel are not available in unlimited quantities, so they must be allocated properly for efficiency.

Schedules have been formally used in construction since the 1950s. In 1956, the E. I. du Pont de Nemours Company, using a UNIVAC computer, developed a critical path method (CPM) schedule for a $10 million chemical plant in Louisville, Kentucky. At about the same time, the U.S. Navy used a performance evaluation and review technique (PERT) network schedule to manage the development of the Polaris missile. PERT and CPM, both network-based scheduling systems, were also used throughout the 1960s by the Army Corps of Engineers, NASA, the Atomic Energy Commission, RCA, General Electric, the Apollo Program, the Veterans Administration, and the General Services Administration.

Once formalized schedules were used on only the largest of projects and were developed by people with sophisticated engineering principles using early computer technology. These schedules were run on large mainframe computers, which by today's standards were difficult to operate. Today, with the help of personal computers and their simplified operating hardware, more owners, designers, and construction professionals use network schedules at many levels. Not only are they commonly used in the planning stage, but they have also become a basic part of the control system of most construction projects.

Construction schedules are considered acceptable in court when arguments occur over project completion or delivery dates or in the formal coordination of project participants. Conflicts can occur over many issues during the course of a construction project. Design changes, poor weather conditions, labor actions, miscommunication of deliveries: all are a common basis for conflicts. If the parties involved are unable to work out their differences through negotiation or arbitration, the alternative is to use the court system. At the court level, judgments that involve time and project coordination are made using a network schedule.

Schedules establish the start, duration, and completion dates of a project or a task. They let people and organizations know in advance when to expect a certain action to take place. Contractors, and suppliers, to stay profitable, have many jobs that must be organized and planned. The start and completion date of a particular job is essential information because it allows them to determine whether or not the job can be accomplished in the context of their other work. Knowing precisely how long an activity will take also has substantial cost implications. For instance, a large crane can rent at more than $10,000 per week (see Figure 10.1). If the duration of that activity is not figured closely, a contractor can quickly consume any planned profit. A contractor's overhead also depends on how long a project is expected to take. Examples include site fencing rental, job superintendent salary, and the maintenance of a field office.

Scheduled start dates determine when goods and services need to be brought to the job site, when a work force needs to be mobilized, and when equipment rentals begin. This date is critical to the accurate pricing of the project. A delay in the start of the project could significantly affect the cost of a material and the rate at which labor can be bought. Both are significant parts of a contractor's estimate and are priced to be bought during a specific time frame. If there is a delay, the price may increase. Early arrival of materials can also be problematic. Materials brought to the job site early can

01 54 | Construction Aids

01 54 33 Equipment Rental

			UNIT	HOURLY OPER. COST	RENT PER DAY	RENT PER WEEK	RENT PER MONTH	CREW EQUIPMENT COST/DAY	
50	7005	Electric, 10 ton	Ea.	21.95	640	1,915	5,750	558.60	50
	7010	Muck cars, 1/2 C.Y. capacity		1.65	21.50	64	192	26	
	7020	1 C.Y. capacity		1.85	30	90	270	32.80	
	7030	2 C.Y. capacity		1.95	35	105	315	36.60	
	7040	Side dump, 2 C.Y. capacity		2.15	41.50	125	375	42.20	
	7050	3 C.Y. capacity		2.90	48.50	145	435	52.20	
	7060	5 C.Y. capacity		4.10	61.50	185	555	69.80	
	7100	Ventilating blower for tunnel, 7-1/2 H.P.		1.29	50	150	450	40.30	
	7110	10 H.P.		1.49	51.50	155	465	42.90	
	7120	20 H.P.		2.44	67.50	202	605	59.90	
	7140	40 H.P.		4.29	95	285	855	91.30	
	7160	60 H.P.		6.49	147	440	1,325	139.90	
	7175	75 H.P.		8.30	196	587	1,750	183.80	
	7180	200 H.P.		18.70	293	880	2,650	325.60	
	7800	Windrow loader, elevating		39.00	930	2,785	8,350	869	
60	0010	LIFTING & HOISTING EQUIPMENT RENTAL, without operators R015433							60
	0120	Aerial lift truck, 2 person, to 80' -10	Ea.	22.35	615	1,840	5,525	546.80	
	0140	Boom work platform, 40' snorkel R015433		13.25	223	670	2,000	240	
	0150	Crane, flatbed mntd, 3 ton cap. -15		17.70	217	650	1,950	271.60	
	0200	Crane, climbing, 106' jib, 6000 lb. capacity, 410 FPM R312316		68.15	1,400	4,230	12,700	1,391	
	0300	101' jib, 10,250 lb. capacity, 270 FPM -45		73.80	1,775	5,360	16,100	1,662	
	0400	Tower, static, 130' high, 106' jib,		71.45	1,625	4,890	14,700	1,550	
	0500	6200 lb. capacity at 400 FPM	Ea.						
	0600	Crawler mounted, lattice boom, 1/2 C.Y., 15 tons at 12' radius		26.58	605	1,820	5,450	576.65	
	0700	3/4 C.Y., 20 tons at 12' radius		35.44	755	2,270	6,800	737.50	
	0800	1 C.Y., 25 tons at 12' radius		47.25	1,000	3,025	9,075	983	
	0900	1-1/2 C.Y., 40 tons at 12' radius		51.20	975	2,925	8,775	994.60	
	1000	2 C.Y., 50 tons at 12' radius		54.00	1,175	3,495	10,500	1,131	
	1100	3 C.Y., 75 tons at 12' radius		66.25	1,425	4,270	12,800	1,384	
	1200	100 ton capacity, 60' boom		76.70	1,850	5,515	16,500	1,717	
	1300	165 ton capacity, 60' boom		102.30	2,300	6,890	20,700	2,196	
	1400	200 ton capacity, 70' boom.		130.85	2,675	8,030	24,100	2,653	
	1500	350 ton capacity, 80' boom		182.90	3,500	10,530	31,600	3,569	
	1600	Truck mounted, lattice boom, 6 x 4, 20 tons at 10' radius		33.59	1,175	3,540	10,600	976.70	
	1700	25 tons at 10' radius		36.28	1,275	3,840	11,500	1,058	
	1800	8 x 4, 30 tons at 10' radius		49.47	1,375	4,130	12,400	1,222	
	1900	40 tons at 12' radius		50.73	1,425	4,310	12,900	1,268	
	2000	8 x 4, 60 tons at 15' radius		52.34	1,525	4,540	13,600	1,327	
	2050	82 tons at 15'		54.44	1,625	4,840	14,500	1,404	
	2100	90 tons at 15'		60.67	1,775	5,310	15,900	1,547	
	2200	115 tons at 15'		74.05	1,975	5,900	17,700	1.772	
	2300	150 tons at 18'		74.51	2,100	6,280	18,800	1,852	
	2350	165 tons at 18'		87.35	2,200	6,615	19,800	2,022	
	2400	Truck mounted, hydraulic, 12 ton capacity		45.25	605	1,810	5,425	724	
	2500	25 ton capacity		45.45	625	1,880	5,650	739.60	
	2550	33 ton capacity		46.30	660	1,975	5,925	765.40	
	2560	40 ton capacity		44.70	630	1,895	5,675	736.60	
	2600	55 ton capacity		66.40	880	2,645	7,925	1,060	
	2700	80 ton capacity		78.75	975	2,920	8,750	1,214	
	2720	100 ton capacity		95.75	2,500	7,525	22,600	2,271	
	2740	120 ton capacity		93.21	2,750	8,280	24,800	2,402	
	2760	150 ton capacity		114.91	3,525	10,540	31,600	3,027	
	2800	Self-propelled, 4 x 4, with telescoping boom, 5 ton		19.10	290	870	2,600	326.80	
	2900	12-1/2 ton capacity		32.75	520	1,565	4,700	575	
	3000	15 ton capacity		35.00	615	1,850	5,550	650	
	3050	20 ton capacity		35.85	640	1,920	5,750	670.80	
	3100	25 ton capacity		47.95	820	2,460	7,375	875.60	

FIGURE 10.1 Expensive equipment, such as large crawler cranes, rent for $31,000 per month and therefore must be used efficiently

Source: From *Building Construction Cost Data Book.* © 2007 by R. S. Means Co., Inc., all rights reserved.

FIGURE 10.2   At congested job sites, deliveries must be precisely scheduled because of limited space

Source: Photo by Margot Balboni, Geoscapes.

be lost, stolen, or vandalized. At a job site where setup and storage space are restricted, such as a downtown site, early deliveries can cause space problems (see Figure 10.2).

There are times, however, when contractors want key materials delivered early to eliminate the risk of holding up the project because of delays in either fabrication or delivery. Even then they must accurately budget storage costs and therefore need to know how long the material must be stored before it will be installed.

SCHEDULING THROUGHOUT THE PROJECT

Preconstruction Planning

Scheduling is a key activity during the preconstruction stage. Project financing, commitment to tenants, and market projections all depend on understanding the scheduled start and completion. A retail operation that misses the Christmas shopping season will experience heavy losses. International athletes were seriously affected when Montreal's Olympic stadium was not finished for the 1976 Olympics. A delayed highway connector can seriously disrupt the businesses that depend on the connection. The only way to accurately predict whether or not the required completion dates can be met is by using a schedule. The earlier the dates are projected, the earlier the owner can make choices based on those dates.

During preconstruction, the first schedule is assembled with little information. As the project evolves, the managers will continually refine the schedule to optimize the project activity duration, creating efficiencies in time and money. Forces in the marketplace, such as availability of key subcontractors, also affect how the schedule is assembled. It may make sense for the project manager to reschedule some portion of the work to a more opportune time to accommodate the use of this work force. So that the overall schedule is not affected, he or she may be forced to move certain activities to a different time. Otherwise, either the project will be delayed or additional hiring costs will be incurred to substitute another work force. Another example of refinement is combining certain operations during a particular week. Key project resources such as a crane, a backhoe, or a management team may be on site already for another activity but be underused. By scheduling these operations concurrently, the manager may gain more efficiency. The initial schedule is a tool for the project team to begin to make intelligent management decisions.

The scheduling process during preconstruction should be viewed as an opportunity to design and build the project on paper before actual construction. This allows all project parties to visualize the process and make all the necessary provisions to properly coordinate it. The team may now decide to order key long-lead purchase items such as structural steel, elevators, compressors, or electrical switchgear. It may determine that it will be necessary to fast-track the project to shorten its delivery time.

In summary, scheduling during preconstruction provides the project team with the necessary information to properly plan and coordinate the entire design/build process. Knowing when all the key events are going to occur is critical to the overall success of the project. Most construction projects must be coordinated around public commerce and the existing operations of surrounding buildings, roads, and pedestrian paths. Most involve many design professionals, regulatory agencies, financial institutions, and ultimately the end users. All of these entities are keenly interested in how the project will affect them, whether in inconvenience or in actual involvement of time and effort. The answers can only be provided through a schedule.

Construction Scheduling

Project schedules are essential to the successful coordination of a project's day-to-day activities. Material deliveries, equipment, and people are all orchestrated through the schedule. As a project progresses, delays inevitably occur. The project manager's job is to effectively deal with these delays and to anticipate them as much as possible. If problems never occurred on a project, the project manager's role would be less critical. It is the intelligent response to bad weather, equipment failures, strikes, design errors, and omissions that separates the well-managed project from the disaster.

During construction, a CPM schedule may record the actual daily activities at the site. The schedule often is placed on the wall of the job-site trailer, where it is clearly visible to all the tradespeople. The project manager can graphically record progress, often with colored markers and symbols. Not only does the schedule record issues for the day, but it can also help the manager anticipate future problems. This information may also be essential to successfully negotiating a future change order or a delay claim. Remember that tomorrow's lawsuit may be occurring today. Written documentation in a court of law has much more weight than does someone's memory.

Postconstruction Scheduling

As a project nears completion, the ultimate user becomes more involved in the construction process. In many projects the owner begins to occupy the facility during construction. This partial occupancy must be closely scheduled, requiring weekly meetings to coordinate the construction work with the tenant improvement work necessary to allow occupancy.

Most projects require testing and acceptance of equipment, and training of people who will ultimately use and maintain the equipment. At the same time, deficiencies need to be corrected and incomplete work closed out. All need to be coordinated and controlled to occur smoothly.

An important function for the project team is to close the books on the project. If the people and companies involved are to learn from the project experience, they must record its actual events. Unplanned events such as coordination difficulties, production rate differences, or delivery delays should all be recorded. These actual data should be stored so that, in the future, better planning and scheduling can occur. Record keeping is also important in case of future claims or disputes.

THE PLANNING AND SCHEDULING PROCESS

The planning and scheduling process, which begins in the preconstruction stage, can be divided into seven steps:

1. **Establish objective.** Scheduling begins with a plan. The first step is to establish an *objective* that can be defined as a specific, measurable project goal. The objective can be as small as replacing a door lock or as large as the construction of a major facility. The key is that the objective should be attainable and fit within corporate goals.

2. **Identify project activities.** The second step is to break down the project into definable work activities that, when completed, reach the objective. The level of detail used is important because activities must be appropriate for the way in which the construction manager will manage the project. An activity should be action-oriented, visible, and measurable. For example:
   - Survey and layout site.
   - Procure structural steel.
   - Form footings.
   - Install elevator cab.

   Activities should be sortable by area, discipline, and phase. For example, a manager should be able to create a report that shows only the electrical work or another that shows just the finish work in the office suite. Because most schedules are computer-generated, managers must consider the report's level of detail as the activities are defined and coded. Highly detailed reports require more activities of a smaller detail and are more expensive to create and manage. Less detailed reports are easier to produce but provide less control.

3. **Determine activity sequence.** The next step is to sequence the project activities. Construction managers must determine in what order activities occur. The best way is to examine each activity independently and ask the following questions:
   - What activity must precede this activity?
   - What activity must succeed this activity?

The more activities that can occur concurrently, the faster the job will be completed. However, concurrent work requires more resources, greater work space, and a higher level of control.

4.   **Determine activity durations.** At this point the duration of each activity must be determined. If an estimate has already been prepared, each activity should be examined in light of what duration assumptions were made at the time of the estimate. At this stage it is best to calculate the normal duration for each activity: that is, the duration that will complete this activity in the most effective manner. Undoubtedly, some activities may have to be expedited to meet time constraints; but it is best to complete the scheduling process first, determine the critical path, and then expedite only those activities that are deemed critical. Likewise, it is best to assume that a normal level of resources is available. After the schedule is completed and compared with other company projects, the manager can analyze the resources being assumed for each project.

5.   **Perform schedule calculations.** Once the activity durations are determined, it is possible to add up the durations of the different activity sequences or paths. The longest path through the network is called the *critical path* and determines the duration for the project. Paths that have a shorter duration have extra time, also called float or slack. The result is a list of the specific start and finish times for each activity. Activities along shorter paths will have flexibility, while those along the longest path(s) will have no flexibility and are labeled critical.

6.   **Revise and adjust.** Scheduling is an iterative process; the result of Step 5 is only the beginning. As we have mentioned, up to this point normal levels of resources and optimum crew sizes have been assumed. In other words, the first schedule is the most efficient with the least direct cost. However, it may show overcommitted resources or an unacceptable completion date. If this is the case, the scheduler has many tools to work with. He or she can defer work, increase crew sizes, or plan overtime work to meet project goals. As adjustments are made and the project's duration shortened, direct costs increase; but because the job is shortened, indirect costs go down. In some cases substantial incentives/bonuses may be provided for delivering the project early and should be considered. This process of accelerating work to shorten the duration of a project is called *crashing*. It is an important step in determining the optimum duration for a project.

7.   **Monitor and control.** The optimum schedule is the baseline or target schedule for the project and defines when the work begins. As the work proceeds, changes may occur due to scope revisions, unforeseen conditions, or mistakes. The project manager's goal is to make the appropriate adjustments to keep the forecasted completion date. The target/baseline schedule is kept secure, and revisions are sequentially labeled and notes made as to who or what drove the schedule change. This information may be important in the event of a future dispute.

SCHEDULING METHODS

A schedule can be used to manage, coordinate, control, and report. Depending on the user's sophistication, the schedule can take different forms. For instance, the owner/developer of a $500 million high-rise does not need to get involved in coordinating the drywall finish work. He or she would, however, be interested in when the project is due for completion as well as the progress of the project as compared to overall schedule and budget. This type of information can be best provided with a bar chart. A bar chart can be developed quickly and inexpensively and is simple enough for an untrained reader.

The field superintendent, on the other hand, is concerned about the delivery of key materials as well as the coordination of the many subcontractors on the project. His or her job is to ensure that the job proceeds and that no one particular event disrupts the flow of the project. Thus, it is essential that a schedule be prepared that accurately reflects the detail of the actual project. A CPM schedule that is network-based provides the necessary detail to accomplish what the superintendent needs. This schedule is expensive to produce and requires a fairly high degree of technical competence, but it also provides the degree of information necessary to adequately control the project.

One of the drawbacks of network-based schedules is that they require technical sophistication. To address this problem, other scheduling methods have evolved. An example is the matrix schedule, which combines the graphical characteristics of the bar chart with the technical detail of a network schedule.

Bar Chart Schedules

The bar chart is graphically the simplest of the scheduling methods. Most project people understand it, and it can be produced more quickly than any of the other methods. To quickly examine overall timing, owners, designers, and construction professionals frequently use it in the planning stage of a project. In its most elementary form it may break down a project into three bars reflecting design, bid and award, and construction. The bar chart in Figure 10.3 reveals several important facts about the project.

1. Its planned overall length
2. The planned duration of each project component (that is, design, bid and award, and construction)
3. The calendar start and finish dates for each project phase

Bar charts can also be used to report information to people who are concerned about a project but may not be involved in day-to-day management. Bar charts can provide a quick, visual overview of a project and can be color-coded and time-scaled, working well as a tool to compare actual progress to planned. However, because of their limits, they are best used in conjunction with network-based scheduling methods. Such methods are used by the scheduler and other management people to detail the workings of the project. The bar chart can then be extrapolated from the network schedule to communicate the results. It is important to remember that a bar chart does not communicate the interrelationships among project activities.

Because of the inherent graphic limitations of a bar chart, it cannot define individual activity dependencies. For instance, it is not clear from a bar chart whether the work defined by one bar depends on the completion of work defined by an earlier completed bar. Common sense and personal experience may tell us that it is dependent, but the bar chart does not define this dependency. Therefore, bar charts cannot be used to calculate specific project activity start dates, completion dates, and available float time.

A bar chart can report information calculated by a network-based schedule. Figure 10.4 illustrates a logic-based bar chart. Note how the critical path, early completion,

Description	Orig Dur	Early Start	Early Finish
ROTC			
Schematic Design	63d	03SEP96 *	29NOV96
Contract Documents	63d	02DEC96	28FEB97
Construction	97d	17MAR97	31JUL97
Move	11d	11AUG97 *	25AUG97
SEVT			
Contract Documents	35d	03SEP96 *	21OCT96
Construction	42d	22OCT96	19DEC96
Move	4d	24JUL97	29JUL97
Railroad (TMRC)			
Contract Documents	32d	02JAN97 *	14FEB97
Construction	43d	03MAR97	30APR97
Move	50d	01MAY97	11JUL97
MITERS			
Contract Documents	32d	02JAN97 *	14FEB97
Construction	43d	03MAR97	30APR97
Move	2d	23JUN97 A	25JUN97 A
Cambridge Partnership			
Schematic Design	10d	03NOV97 *	14NOV97
Contract Documents	20d	17NOV97	15DEC97
Construction	20d	16DEC97	14JAN98
Move	5d	15JAN98	21JAN98
Educational Opportunities Program			
Schematic Design	15d	21APR97 *	09MAY97
Contract Documents	30d	12MAY97	23JUN97
Construction	70d	30SEP97 *	08JAN98
Move	5d	09JAN98 *	15JAN98
Chairman of Corp.			
Schematic Design	1d	03SEP96 *	03SEP96
Contract Documents	1d	04SEP96	04SEP96
Construction	1d	05SEP96	05SEP96
Move	1d	06SEP96	06SEP96
Ling & Phil			
Schematic Design	52d	02JAN97 *	14MAR97
Contract Documents	44d	17MAR97	15MAY97
Construction	38d	04JUN97	28JUL97
Move	4d	31JUL97	05AUG97
EAPS-Flume/Rocks			
Schematic Design	20d	17FEB97 *	14MAR97
Contract Documents	30d	28APR97	09JUN97
Construction	55d	25JUN97	11SEP97
Move	10d	12SEP97	25SEP97
Music			
Schematic Design	53d	01APR97 *	13JUN97
Contract Documents	44d	16JUN97	15AUG97
Construction	31d	02JAN98	13FEB98
Move	10d	16FEB98	27FEB98
HST-E25			
Schematic Design	21d	02JUN97 *	30JUN97
Contract Documents	35d	01JUL97	19AUG97

Timeline columns: 1996 (SEP OCT NOV DEC), 1997 (JAN FEB MAR APR MAY JUN JUL AUG SEP OCT NOV DEC), 1998 (JAN FEB MAR APR MAY JUN JUL AUG SEP OCT NOV DEC), 1999 (JAN FEB MAR)

FIGURE 10.3 Bar charts are simple to read. They show the overall length of the project but do not show the interrelationships among activities

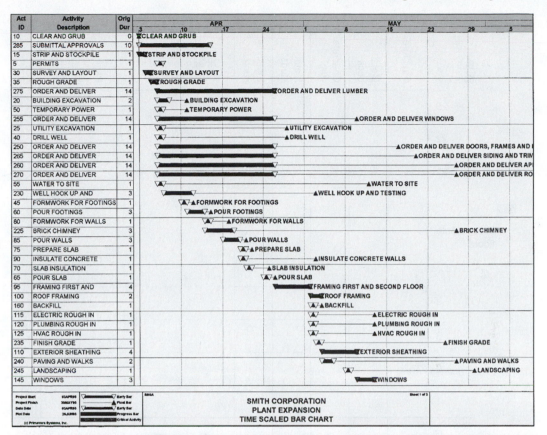

Act ID	Activity Description	Orig Dur	
10	CLEAR AND GRUB	0	CLEAR AND GRUB
285	SUBMITTAL APPROVALS	10	
15	STRIP AND STOCKPILE	1	STRIP AND STOCKPILE
5	PERMITS	1	
30	SURVEY AND LAYOUT	1	SURVEY AND LAYOUT
35	ROUGH GRADE	1	ROUGH GRADE
275	ORDER AND DELIVER	14	ORDER AND DELIVER LUMBER
20	BUILDING EXCAVATION	2	BUILDING EXCAVATION
50	TEMPORARY POWER	1	TEMPORARY POWER
255	ORDER AND DELIVER	14	ORDER AND DELIVER WINDOWS
25	UTILITY EXCAVATION	1	UTILITY EXCAVATION
40	DRILL WELL	1	DRILL WELL
250	ORDER AND DELIVER	14	ORDER AND DELIVER DOORS, FRAMES AND
265	ORDER AND DELIVER	14	ORDER AND DELIVER SIDING AND TRIM
260	ORDER AND DELIVER	14	ORDER AND DELIVER AP
270	ORDER AND DELIVER	14	ORDER AND DELIVER RO
55	WATER TO SITE	1	WATER TO SITE
230	WELL HOOK UP AND	3	WELL HOOK UP AND TESTING
45	FORMWORK FOR FOOTINGS	1	FORMWORK FOR FOOTINGS
60	POUR FOOTINGS	3	POUR FOOTINGS
80	FORMWORK FOR WALLS	1	FORMWORK FOR WALLS
225	BRICK CHIMNEY	3	BRICK CHIMNEY
85	POUR WALLS	3	POUR WALLS
75	PREPARE SLAB	1	PREPARE SLAB
90	INSULATE CONCRETE	1	INSULATE CONCRETE WALLS
70	SLAB INSULATION	1	SLAB INSULATION
65	POUR SLAB	1	POUR SLAB
95	FRAMING FIRST AND	4	FRAMING FIRST AND SECOND FLOOR
100	ROOF FRAMING	2	ROOF FRAMING
160	BACKFILL	1	BACKFILL
115	ELECTRIC ROUGH IN	1	ELECTRIC ROUGH IN
120	PLUMBING ROUGH IN	1	PLUMBING ROUGH IN
125	HVAC ROUGH IN	1	HVAC ROUGH IN
235	FINISH GRADE	1	FINISH GRADE
110	EXTERIOR SHEATHING	4	EXTERIOR SHEATHING
240	PAVING AND WALKS	2	PAVING AND WALKS
245	LANDSCAPING	1	LANDSCAPING
145	WINDOWS	3	WINDOWS

Project Start	03APR95		Early Bar
Project Finish	30MAY95		Float Bar
Data Date	03APR95		Early Bar
Plot Date	24JUN95		Progress Bar
(c) Primavera Systems, Inc.			Critical Activity

SMITH CORPORATION
PLANT EXPANSION
TIME SCALED BAR CHART

Sheet 1 of 3

FIGURE 10.4   This bar chart is network based. Critical, early start, and float information are identified

and float information are identified. Bar charts such as these can also be sorted by total float, trade, project phase, or location. When used in this manner, the bar chart presents complicated, network-generated scheduling information clearly and concisely. Notes, dates, or other pertinent information are often shown on this schedule.

In summary, bar charts are excellent communicators of time-related project information. They are quick and easy to develop and understood by most people. Their major limitation is that interdependencies among activities cannot be shown. Thus, complicated management decisions should be made using other, more thorough scheduling methods.

Matrix Schedules

Matrix schedules are typically used for repetitive work, as on a high-rise office building. A quick review of this schedule gives the management team an overall view of the project, including the interdependencies among listed activities. Subcontractors or project people responsible for a specific task need only look at their particular responsibilities and see what precedes and succeeds their work. For example, in the matrix

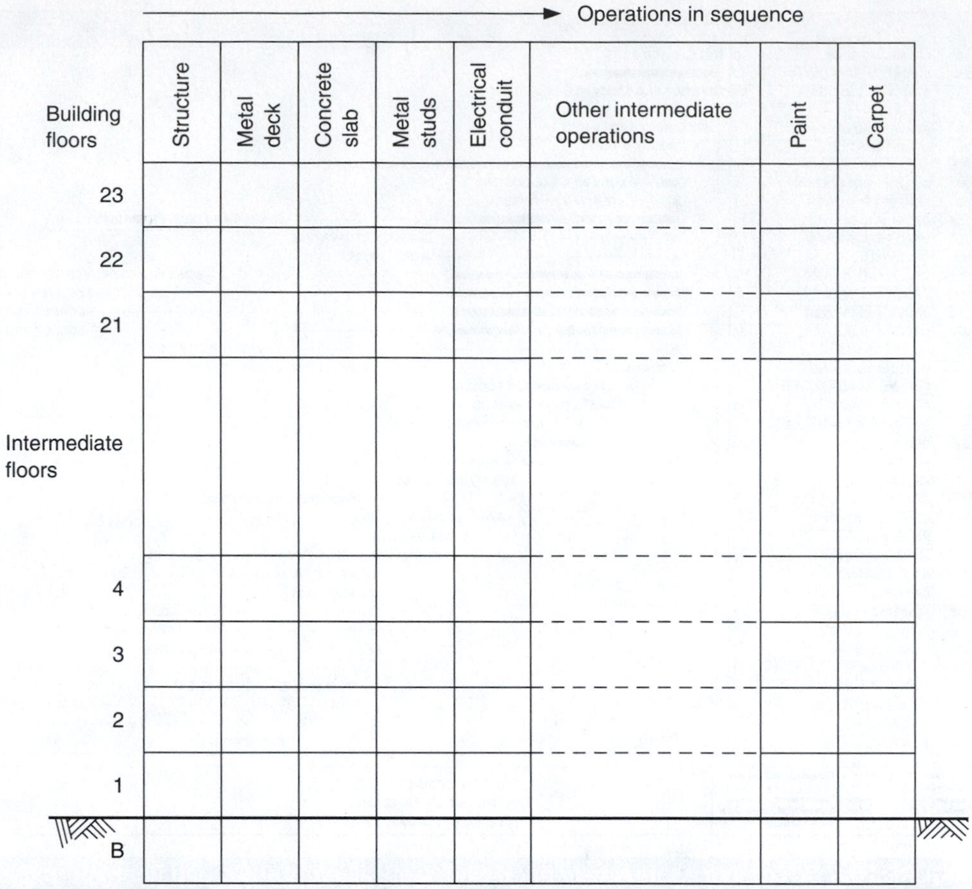

FIGURE 10.5   A matrix schedule is graphically simple, visually defining the interrelationships among major operations

schedule in Figure 10.5, the metal studs follow the concrete slab and precede the electrical conduit. The crew can also see that the work on the fifth floor occurs before the sixth. By examining the schedule more closely, the crew can also see when the work is scheduled to start and finish (see Figure 10.6).

A matrix schedule is a good tool for controlling field activities because it can be posted at the field office and updated as the work proceeds. Superintendents can easily color in the boxes as the work is accomplished to provide a more visual picture of the job's progress. Forepersons responsible for a specific trade are able to critique their own progress in relation to related work.

A matrix schedule generally does not consider all project activities but is best used as a coordination schedule to communicate with field or office personnel. It may be used for presentation purposes since it presents information in a way that can be easily understood by nontechnical people. It also presents information in a manner that allows for self-correction. Most project people can find a specific task on the schedule and see the due date and the activities that precede and succeed the task.

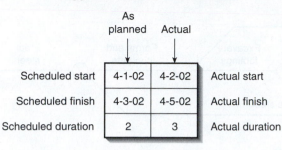

Typical cell matrix schedule

	As planned	Actual	
Scheduled start	4-1-02	4-2-02	Actual start
Scheduled finish	4-3-02	4-5-02	Actual finish
Scheduled duration	2	3	Actual duration

FIGURE 10.6 Planned start, finish, and durations are defined before the job begins. Actuals are noted as work proceeds

Network Schedules

The workhorse of the construction schedule is the network schedule, often called a *critical path method* (CPM) schedule. It is best prepared by a team of people who have complete knowledge of all aspects of the project. A complete network schedule requires that all the work to be completed on the project be defined and organized. In network scheduling each item of work is called an *activity*. These activities are each given a duration (in hours, days, weeks, and so on), and they are connected by network diagrams. The completed network thus defines activity interrelationships and durations, considers available resources, and assumes how the project will be pursued. A network schedule can be viewed as a road map that, if followed, will bring the project to its desired destination.

A project team that diligently prepares a network schedule has readied itself for the effective management of the project. Preparing a network schedule is like preparing an estimate. It forces a thorough review of all the contract documents as well as communication with all the participants. Questions such as what work can be scheduled concurrently or, more specifically, what task precedes placing floor tile are all answered by the network schedule.

As Figure 10.7 shows, network schedules can take two forms: activity on arrow notation or activity on node notation (also called precedence notation). In activity on arrow notation, the work or activity is shown on the arrows, which are connected by nodes. In precedence notation, the work occurs on the nodes, which are connected by arrows.

Both forms of network schedules are used in industry, with identical end results. In the network scheduling packages such as Primavera and Microsoft Project, activities are displayed as bars, with the beginning and end of each bar connected to its predecessors and successors.

Preparing a network schedule is like building the actual project on paper. The schedule preparer must identify all the necessary tasks and then logically arrange them in the order in which the work will be accomplished in the field. The process, if approached correctly, should force controversy because there is usually more than one way to build a project. Discussions usually focus on the order of the activities and the duration of a given task. These discussions are good because they require the project team to consider other options. Remember, it is better to argue about the planned approach to the project in the office on paper before the project begins rather than during the actual construction.

Network schedules

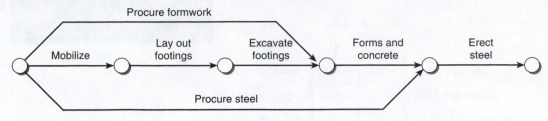

(a) Activity on arrow notation

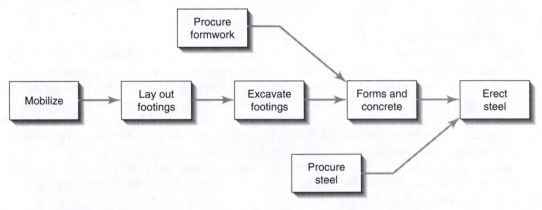

(b) Activity on node notation

FIGURE 10.7 Network logic can be shown in either (a) activity on arrow or (b) activity on node notation

When a network schedule is compared to the matrix and bar chart schedules, many differences appear. The network schedule is clearly the biggest undertaking. The thorough preparation of a network schedule for a large commercial project such as a high-rise office building can take several weeks and consume tremendous resources. Fairly detailed project information must be available; and to provide the opportunity for updates and revisions, computer hardware and software must be purchased. The preparation and interpretation of a network schedule requires technical training. Therefore, matrix and bar chart schedules are derived from the network schedules to communicate schedule information to both field personnel and nontechnical people such as the public and financial backers.

Owners, designers, construction managers, and other interested parties have come to understand the benefits provided by networks. Most project managers are now educated in scheduling theory and know how to use computers to produce network schedules. That is why many, if not most, major construction projects require that a network schedule be submitted before any construction can begin. This schedule may be developed independently by the contractor if the project is bid. Or in the case of a construction management or negotiated approach, the owner, the designer, and the construction professional may develop the schedule jointly. In any case, before the work begins, the schedule should be complete and on hand to monitor the progress of the work. The impact of any delays, changes, or natural disasters can now be compared to the baseline schedule. This provides the opportunity to prepare thorough reviews of the project status before making any adjustments to the project plan.

CREATING THE SCHEDULE

Activity Definition

Activities can be divided into three categories: production, procurement, and administration. Production activities include the on-site construction of the project. Examples are rough and finish electrical and plumbing work and carpentry, painting, flooring, and ceiling work. Procurement activities track the material from the supplier to the job site. This includes the preparation and approval of submittals and the manufacturing and shipping of the material to the site. Administration activities include inspections, permits, and other government or bureaucratic activities that must occur on a project. Schedules are generally created by first identifying all the activities in each of these categories, organizing the work by discipline, area, and/or project phase.

Network Diagram

The network diagram is the tool used to organize all of the project activities. It is like a road map for the project—starting on the left (where the project begins) and reading across to the right (where the project ends). Depending on the sophistication of the project, many paths may exist through the network. Creating accurate network diagrams is difficult since they involve all the organizations in a project, each with individual goals. Creating the network diagram should be viewed as a management exercise and an opportunity to bring together all the key players on the project to determine the best way to complete the project. It is far better to work out different approaches in a conference room than in the field. Post-It notes are a good way to work out the logic of a project (see Figure 10.8). By working as a group to create the initial sequence of activities, all the team members have some input very early in its development.

Activity Duration

Activity duration is the amount of time assigned to complete a particular activity. Schedules use only whole numbers. With new construction or renovation, workdays are typically used as the time unit. However, in fast-moving facilities, maintenance work hours or even minutes may be a more appropriate time unit. Durations can be figured in a number of ways:

1. Durations can be determined by examining past similar projects. Many projects use the same activities over and over, so by maintaining good records, managers can predict durations accurately.
2. Durations for work that will be subcontracted, deliveries and vendor items, and work that will be performed by other divisions can be best determined by talking

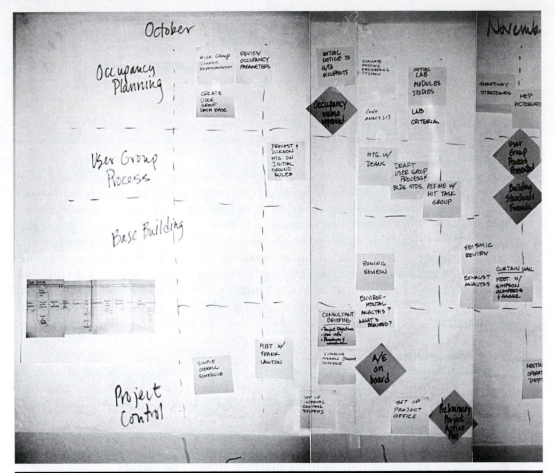

FIGURE 10.8   Post-It notes are often used to build a network's logic

to the appropriate people. Since this work is generally contracted, it is imperative that the contract defines the scheduled start, finish, and activity duration.

3. Cost data books such as those published by R. S. Means can be used as a source of duration information. Means defines standard crew size and crew productivity. It also defines a man-hour unit: the time it takes for one worker to complete one unit. This information can be used to establish durations, particularly when the scheduler has little past project experience.

Duration Calculation Example

Problem

What is the duration in days to install thirty-two, eighteen-gauge, 6′8″ by 3′0″, steel knockdown doorframes?

Source: *Means 1997 Building Construction Cost Data*, line 081-118-0025

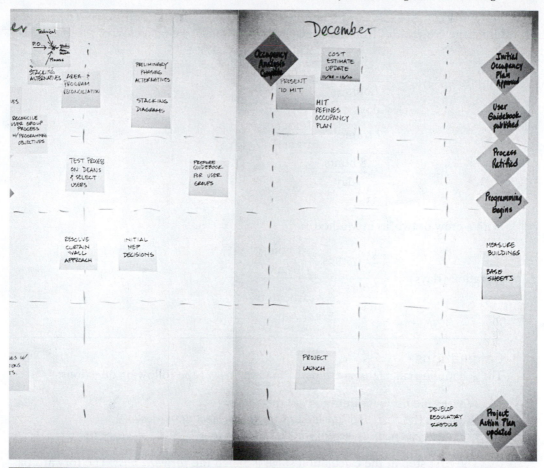

FIGURE 10.8 continued

Means crew: two carpenters
Means daily output: sixteen each
Means labor hours: one

Solution

Method 1
Use if the crew is the same as listed in the *Means* book (two carpenters):

$$\text{Duration (days)} = \frac{\text{Quantity}}{\text{Daily crew output}}$$

$$= \frac{32 \text{ frames}}{16 \text{ frames/day}}$$

$$= 2$$

Method 2

Use if the crew varies from the crew listed in *Means*. Assume a crew of three:

$$\text{Duration (days)} = \frac{\text{Quantity} \times \dfrac{\text{manhours}}{\text{frame}}}{\dfrac{8 \text{ hours}}{\text{days}} \times \text{Workers in crew}}$$

$$= \frac{32 \text{ frames} \times \dfrac{1 \text{ hour}}{\text{frame}}}{\dfrac{8 \text{ hours}}{\text{day}} \times 3}$$

$$= 1.33$$

With a crew of two, as in Method 1:

$$\text{Duration (days)} = \frac{32 \text{ frames} \times \dfrac{1 \text{ hour}}{\text{frame}}}{\dfrac{8 \text{ hours}}{\text{day}} \times 2 \text{ carpenters}}$$

$$= 2$$

Calculations

The scheduling calculations are performed to answer the following questions:

1. What is the project's duration?
2. What are the start and finish dates for the project activities?
3. Can a project activity be delayed? If so, how long?

The first step in the calculation stage is called the *forward pass*. The forward pass determines the early starts and finishes for each activity and the project duration. The forward pass is conducted by adding activity durations along the different paths, beginning at the start node and ending at the finish node. Many notations are used in network scheduling. For the purposes of this exercise, activity on arrow (*i–j* notation) and activity on node (precedent) will be used (see Figure 10.9).

The forward pass begins with the first node assigned "time 0"; the duration of each successive activity is added to this time. In activity on arrow notation, the *i* node time of an activity with only one precedent is equal to the *i* node time of its precedent plus its precedent's duration. In precedent notation the early start time of the activity with only one precedent equals the early finish time of that preceding activity (see Figure 10.10).

When a node has more than one predecessor, the early node time equals the largest time calculated from the converging paths (see Figure 10.11). In summary, the forward pass defines the project duration and the earliest possible start and finish time for each activity given the durations and logic assumed for the project.

The backward pass is the second step in the calculation process. It follows the forward pass since it requires that the overall project duration be known. The backward pass begins with the last node and is completed by working backward through the

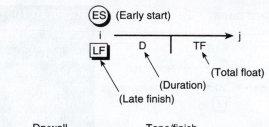

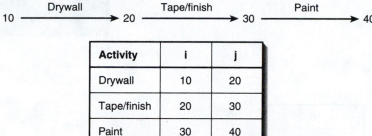

(a) i–j notation

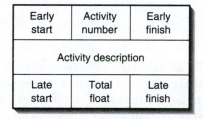

(b) precedent notation

FIGURE 10.9 (a) The *i* node defines the beginning of an activity, the *j* node the completion. The *i–j* notation provides a numerical address for each activity. (b) In precedent notation, each activity is identified by a unique activity number

Forward pass

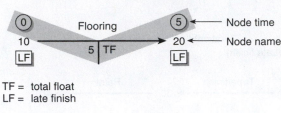

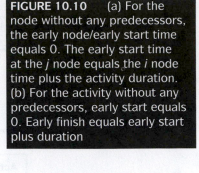

FIGURE 10.10   (a) For the node without any predecessors, the early node/early start time equals 0. The early start time at the *j* node equals the *i* node time plus the activity duration. (b) For the activity without any predecessors, early start equals 0. Early finish equals early start plus duration

TF = total float
LF = late finish

(a)

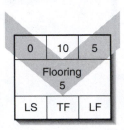

(b)

network, subtracting the activity's duration from the previous late time. In activity on arrow notation the late event time at the *j* node of an activity with only one successor is equal to the late event time at the *j* node of the successor minus the successor's duration. In precedent notation the late finish time of an activity with only one successor is equal to the late start time of the successor (see Figure 10.12).

In the case of multiple successors, the late event time for the node equals the smallest of the succeeding nodes' late times less the activity duration. In precedent notation the late finish time equals the smallest late start times of all the succeeding activities (see Figure 10.13). In summary, the backward pass determines the late start and finish time for a network. These times represent the latest time that an activity can start and finish and still complete the project on time.

The last calculation is to compute the float time (also called slack time) for each activity. Float represents extra time—flexibility for an activity. Float can be calculated as follows:

Float = Late start − Early start
Float = Late finish − Early finish
Float = Late finish − (Early start + duration)

Figure 10.14 illustrates these calculations.

It is important that a project manager knows before a project begins where float exists on the project. Projects that do not have float are defined as critical and must be monitored closely. If any are delayed, the project is delayed. Every project will have at least one path through the network where all activities are critical. This is called the

Forward pass

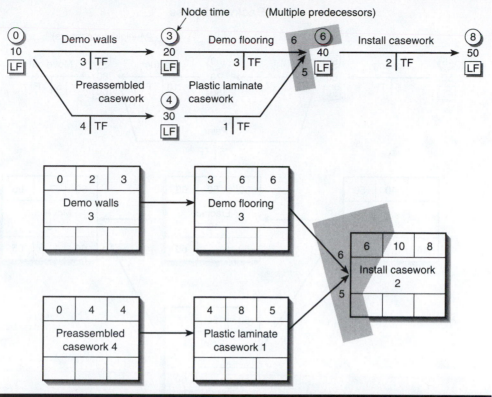

FIGURE 10.11 Where two or more paths converge, the larger time is carried forward

Backward pass

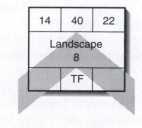

FIGURE 10.12 (a) For the node without any successors, the late start time equals the early finish time at the *j* node. The late start time at the *i* node equals the *j* node time minus the activity duration. (b) For the activity without any successors, late finish equals early finish plus the project duration. Late start equals late finish minus duration

Backward pass

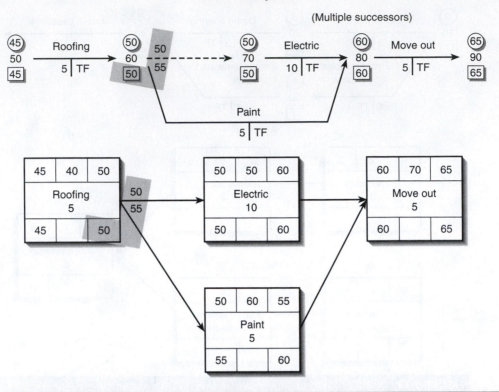

(Multiple successors)

FIGURE 10.13   Where two or more paths converge, the smaller time is carried. (*Note:* A dashed line signifies a dummy activity equals zero duration.)

critical path. This path, along with others that have small amounts of float, demand close management attention.

Refining

Once the calculations have been completed, the project team knows the planned project completion date as well as the start, finish, and float for each project activity. Rarely does the initial calculation yield a schedule acceptable to all parties. Normally, the completion date is unacceptable, certain activities cannot start when scheduled, or other activities cannot run at the same time due to limited equipment or space. The project team needs to make these adjustments and rerun the schedule. Modern computer-based scheduling software makes these recalculations easy.

Project managers should also investigate the benefits of completing the project early. Early completion allows the facility or service to generate revenue sooner as well as reduces the project's indirect cost. Accelerating the project, also called crashing, increases the direct cost to the project. This is because of the additional cost of overtime, congestion of people and equipment, and increased supervision. The goal is for project managers to find the optimum or minimum total cost duration (see Figure 10.15).

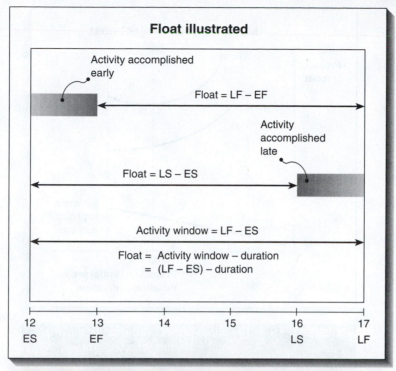

Float illustrated

Activity accomplished early

Float = LF − EF

Activity accomplished late

Float = LS − ES

Activity window = LF − ES

Float = Activity window − duration
 = (LF − ES) − duration

| 12 | 13 | 14 | 15 | 16 | 17 |
| ES | EF | | | LS | LF |

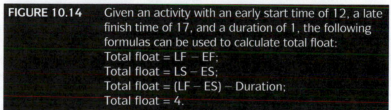

FIGURE 10.14 Given an activity with an early start time of 12, a late finish time of 17, and a duration of 1, the following formulas can be used to calculate total float:
Total float = LF − EF;
Total float = LS − ES;
Total float = (LF − ES) − Duration;
Total float = 4.

Refining the schedule may take many reruns and involve many people and organizations, but it is an important step in planning a project. It can be viewed as brainstorming, part of value engineering, or a constructability analysis. The process should involve the key people in an organization working together to find the best way to construct a facility. When the best schedule is complete, it should be distributed throughout the organization, and the project begins!

Monitoring

The planning process has now provided a schedule and a budget that will meet the project goal. They reflect the best information available at the time. The next step is for the project manager to implement the plan and complete the project on time. Suppliers, subcontractors, labor, weather, and even owners constantly create obstacles that the project team must overcome to get the job done as scheduled.

To get the job done, the manager must disseminate instructions clearly to the right people. A full CPM schedule is usually too detailed and complicated for the running of

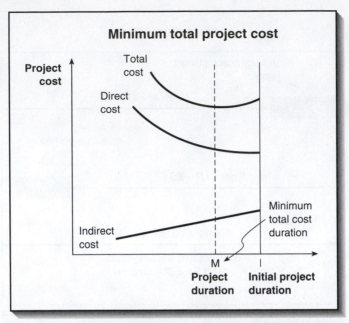

Minimum total project cost

FIGURE 10.15 The initial project duration is shown as point I. As the selected work is accelerated, the project is economized to point M

field operations, so weekly activity lists are generally provided to field supervisors. At the end of the week, actual progress is measured and compared to the weekly instructions, allowing productivity to be measured and adjustments made.

As the project is monitored, the manager may need to make adjustments to keep the job on track. Crew sizes, work schedules, equipment provided, or work planned may have to change as the work proceeds. Changes in contract may cause work to be added or deleted, with an appropriate adjustment in the contract completion date. Accurate records should be kept throughout the job in case a dispute arises. This project control cycle is the subject of Chapter 11.

Conclusion

Clearly, the schedule is a powerful management and communication tool. Because of the increased complexity in construction techniques and materials as well as diverse labor issues and the pressures of budgets, scheduling has increasingly been the standard control method. Otherwise, it is difficult, if not impossible, to coordinate the diverse activities in a construction project. An effectively managed project must closely coordinate the activities of the owner, the designer, the construction manager, and all the other people who come together at the job site. Questions from the owner about when the move can be scheduled, from the designer asking if a late change in a lobby detail will affect completion, or from the electrical subcontractor wanting to know if he or she can substitute a long-lead fixture can only be studied and answered using schedules. In a construction project, where time truly equals money, the management of time is critical, and the best way to manage time is through scheduling.

Schedules are created by first identifying the goal of the project and its activities. Activity detail should be adequate enough to organize and assign responsibility to specific project people. The logic of the project is next determined by identifying for each activity what work immediately precedes, succeeds, and runs concurrently. Once the duration of each activity is determined, the project's duration can be calculated and the start and finish time for each activity defined. The critical path for the project can also be determined. Before the project begins, the manager should examine the schedule to ensure that adequate resources are available and that each activity can be completed as planned. If adjustments must be made, they should be done on paper before the project begins. The last step in the scheduling process involves monitoring the planned schedule as the project is built. As changes and delays occur, adjustments must be made to complete the project on time.

Chapter Review Questions

1. What is the primary disadvantage of a bar chart schedule?
   a. Insufficient level of detail
   b. Inability to consider activity interrelationships
   c. High level of preparation time
   d. Ease of interpretation
   e. None of the above
2. In a network schedule, what is the fundamental unit of work?
   a. Node
   b. Activity
   c. Event
   d. Arrow
   e. None of the above
3. Activity on arrow and activity on node are both examples of which method of scheduling?
   a. Bar chart
   b. Horse blanket
   c. Matrix
   d. Network
   e. Linear balance
4. Which of the following is the first step in the planning and scheduling process?
   a. Identify project activities
   b. Establish the project's objective
   c. Determine the sequence of activities
   d. Perform schedule calculations
   e. Monitor and control
5. A matrix schedule provides the readability of a bar chart schedule while addressing project logic. True or false?

Questions 6 through 10 refer to Figure A.
6. What is the earliest that activity 5–15 can finish?
7. What is the project's duration?
8. What is the latest that Concrete 2 can finish and not delay the completion of the project?
9. What is the ES time for activity 25–45?
10. What is the total float for activity 45–60?

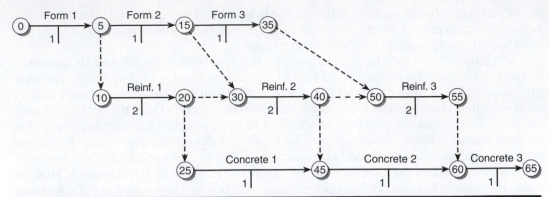

FIGURE A   Network for questions 6–10

Exercises

1. Talking with a scheduler, review a schedule for a construction project with which you are familiar. Find out the following:
   a. How long did it take to complete the schedule?
   b. When in the design/build process did the scheduling begin?
   c. Is the schedule broken down into phases? Areas?
   d. How is the schedule coded? By subcontract? By responsibility?
   e. What activities fall on the critical path?
   f. How often is the schedule updated?
   g. Is the schedule being used for any advanced project management activities such as resource leveling, cash flow projections, and so on?
2. Working in a small group, construct a schedule for a small project or focus on part of a larger project (with fewer than one hundred activities). Examples include a single-family house; tenant fitup work for a commercial building; or the work of a particular major trade for a large project such as mechanical, electrical, site, or concrete work. Use available scheduling software as appropriate.

11

CONTROLLING PROJECT COST, TIME, AND QUALITY

Chapter Outline

Student Learning Objectives

In this chapter you will learn the following:

1. The objectives of a project control system
2. The basics of how a project control system works
3. The process of preparing a project for construction and control
4. The models used to monitor and control cash inflows and outflows
5. How to properly measure and document cost and schedule performance

INTRODUCTION

Project control begins with the identification of the owner's objectives and ends when those objectives have been met. The owner, the designer, and the construction professional together design, estimate, and schedule the project to meet these objectives. This is the basis of the control system. On large or complicated projects, the control effort is a major undertaking with multiple organizations involved.

The purpose of project control is to guarantee that the project's design, budget, and schedule are met by the project team. If any objective begins to slip, the control system will identify this deviation early so that the appropriate correction can be made.

Project control begins with a plan that identifies the objectives of the project and specific checkpoints throughout the project cycle. The plan is a road map that allows the project team to constantly monitor and make corrections as necessary. It consists of design documents for quality checks, an estimate that establishes budget requirements, and a schedule for project milestone dates.

Project control is an action-based process that encourages continual monitoring of operations. To be successful, the actual work with its cost and duration must be completely and accurately documented. Comparisons should be made to project standards and variances noted. By creating such a feedback loop, adjustments can be made for upcoming activities. In addition, actual durations, costs, and important events should be recorded for use on future projects.

The project control process includes the following steps, which act as a feedback loop:

1. The control process documents progress and allows the project team to adjust to unexpected occurrences, such as change orders, strikes, or bad weather.
2. Costs and time of completion are continually updated.
3. A reporting system notifies all necessary parties of the project status. This allows the input of outside technical experts and senior managers, who can assist and plan adjustments as necessary.
4. The project control system is iterative: the process occurs over and over, encouraging continual adjustment of the project plan.

PROJECT CONTROL OBJECTIVES

Standards

A system of control is essential for the successful delivery of any construction project. To begin the process, managers first establish the standards that define success for the construction project. Cost, schedule, and quality are the basis of these standards and are configured so that they are measurable and can provide direction to the project. The project team will continually use these standards to check progress and provide direction. Just as transport aircraft, cargo ships, and truckers are tracked at specific checkpoints to monitor progress, construction projects must continually report in.

The standards used for control vary by project depending on the level of control necessary. Fast-paced projects with many parties and contractual obligations must be more tightly monitored than a single contractor's excavation project, for instance. Drawings and specifications define the standards for quality control. Drawings define the quantity of work required, locations, and widths and heights. Specifications provide performance standards that address alignment, compression strengths, finishes, and so on. The project estimate establishes the overall budget for the project and can be broken down to specify milestone costs for each component of work. The schedule defines when specific work items need to be accomplished as well as provides key milestone and delivery dates. Estimating data can be integrated with schedule information to provide additional project standards.

Measurement standards serve as the goals for the project participants. They are targets and, if well thought out, can organize a very complicated project. Each project participant can be given a task with a corresponding budget and time frame in which to accomplish the job. For example, a carpenter can be given the task of framing one hundred feet of interior partition, a budget of $1,500 for materials, and a duration of two days.

Actuals

The second component of the project control system is measurement of actual progress. This includes accurate cost, schedule, and quality information about the project. Actual performance compared to planned performance provides the management team with feedback about how well the project is proceeding. Also, actual cost and schedule performance information can be stored for reference when estimating and scheduling future projects.

Measuring actual performance is a complicated process since the necessary information resides in many different places. An on-site review of daily reports, a walk-through by trained schedulers, submitted quantity reports, or video reports can provide information about the percent complete for the project. If properly cost-coded, worker time sheets and equipment logs can define how many hours were spent working on a particular task. These documents also define the labor and equipment costs that can be charged to a particular project. Purchase orders, delivery tickets, and receipts provide actual costs for material, equipment, and vendor purchases. Weather conditions and unforeseen circumstances can be picked up from daily reports.

Such information provides the raw material for the project control reports necessary to monitor progress. These reports will then be properly processed, sorted, filtered, and delivered to the appropriate managers in a timely manner. Figure 11.1 illustrates a report showing actual performance compared to budgeted performance.

The feedback from the data can only be useful if put together in a combined form so that the correlation among cost, schedule, anticipated events, and unanticipated ones can be examined. In Figure 11.1, the hours expended are greater than the hours budgeted for the work. The inconsistency can be explained through an analysis of several possible options:

1. Poor worker performance
2. Incorrect reporting
3. Differing site conditions
4. Wrong equipment assigned
5. Bad weather
6. An error in the estimate

Once the project management team has this information, it then determines which reason or reasons explain the variance noted in the report. A check of past daily reports should verify the weather for the reporting period. A walk through the site with the superintendent and the estimator will give the team information about the approach being used, the actual site conditions, and the time and quantities assigned in the estimate. If the estimate, site conditions, and weather all appear to be normal, then worker performance should be examined. If a worker has little experience at a task, supervision is not adequate, work hours are too long, or the conditions of the job site are not conducive to productivity, the explanation for the variance probably resides in performance issues.

Key to the reporting process is that any inconsistency be identified quickly and the proper adjustment made in a timely manner. Good reports are accurate, show variances (differences) between budgeted amounts and actual amounts, forecast goals for future work periods, and suggest corrective actions. Timeliness is also important: if all the appropriate tasks have been accomplished but too late for any corrective action, the control effort has been wasted.

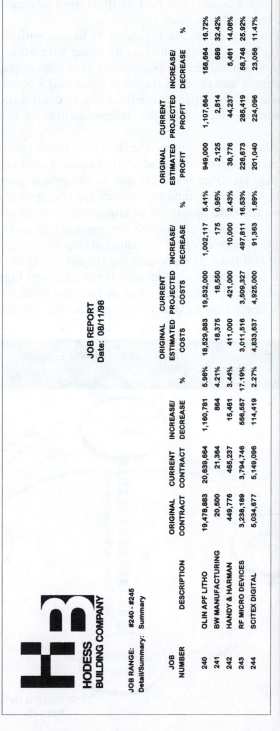

JOB REPORT
Date: 08/11/98

HODESS BUILDING COMPANY

JOB RANGE: #240 - #245
Detail/Summary: Summary

JOB NUMBER	DESCRIPTION	ORIGINAL CONTRACT	CURRENT CONTRACT	INCREASE/ DECREASE	%	ORIGINAL ESTIMATED COSTS	CURRENT PROJECTED COSTS	INCREASE/ DECREASE	%	ORIGINAL ESTIMATED PROFIT	CURRENT PROJECTED PROFIT	INCREASE/ DECREASE	%
240	OLIN APF LITHO	19,478,883	20,639,664	1,160,781	5.96%	18,529,883	19,532,000	1,002,117	5.41%	949,000	1,107,664	158,664	16.72%
241	BW MANUFACTURING	20,500	21,384	864	4.21%	18,375	18,550	175	0.95%	2,125	2,814	689	32.42%
242	HANDY & HARMAN	449,776	465,237	15,461	3.44%	411,000	421,000	10,000	2.43%	38,776	44,237	5,461	14.08%
243	RF MICRO DEVICES	3,238,189	3,794,746	556,557	17.19%	3,011,516	3,509,327	497,811	16.53%	226,873	285,419	58,746	25.92%
244	SCITEX DIGITAL	5,034,677	5,149,096	114,419	2.27%	4,833,637	4,925,000	91,363	1.89%	201,040	224,096	23,056	11.47%

FIGURE 11.1 Job report illustrating budgeted cost versus actual cost with variance

Source: Courtesy of Kenneth Leary.

BASIC CONTROL THEORY

The process of project control can best be illustrated as a control loop that repeats itself in a similar pattern (see Figure 11.2).

The control process (step 1 in Figure 11.2) begins with the initial project plan, which includes budget, schedule, and quality along with other planning information such as staffing and administrative procedures. This plan is the result of the work of many different people and requires technical input and a commitment from management. The estimate and the schedule are the primary control tools described here, but the level of quality as defined by the design documents is also managed during construction.

The project plan is used to initiate the field operations (step 2). The order in which the work is completed and the type and level of staffing are determined by the project plan. The initial plan identifies resources such as equipment, people, and materials that are needed at the job site. The field supervisors are responsible for the productive use of these resources. The field people are an important resource in determining the durations and resources needed to accomplish the construction activities. Ideally, they have been involved in the planning effort described in step 1.

The lightning bolt (step 3) represents the impact of external factors such as labor strikes, vandalism, bad weather, or other unanticipated events that affect the field operations. Estimates and schedules generally provide for some inefficiency, but excessive problems can severely disrupt the field activities and thus the schedule. The arrow between

FIGURE 11.2　Project control is an interactive process: actual performance is compared to planned performance with adjustment made, and the process is repeated as necessary

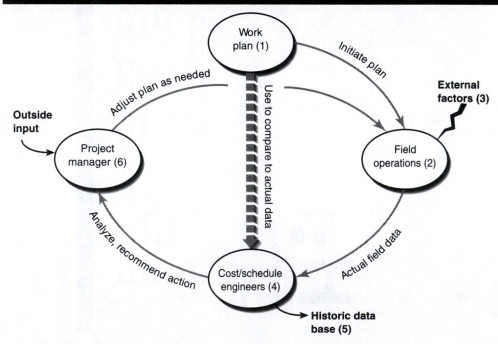

field operations and the cost/schedule block represents the processing of actual information from the field. Schedule information such as activities completed or partially complete, deliveries, or submittals received and approved or disapproved need to be recorded. Cost information such as equipment hours, labor hours, material purchases, or subcontracts signed also need to be recorded. Since the process involves many people in the organization, it also needs close coordination. Preprinted forms and a cost-coding system facilitate this effort. A good cost-coding system will ensure that the data are assigned correctly and thereby allow a true comparison of actual performance versus planned.

The cost/schedule engineers block (step 4) represents the processing of data from the field and the comparison with the initial plan. Any differences between the actual and planned performance should be noted at this point. The technical people who established the initial workplan recommend adjustments based on their analysis of actual field operations. There are many reasons why a plan needs to be adjusted, but the goal is to keep the budget and schedule on target. The best way to accomplish this is for the technical people to make timely and accurate recommendations to the project manager for a final decision.

Historical data (step 5) represent the permanent storage of information for use by the company in future job planning. The actual field information collected represents the type of performance that is being delivered and should be used to update the company data base. This is how a data base is built and maintained. The cost-coding system that the company establishes initially as well as the accuracy of the data captured and how they are processed dictate how useful the data base will prove to be.

The arrow between cost/schedule engineers (step 4) and project management (step 6) represents the dissemination of status reports to the project team. For the reporting process to be useful, it must deliver accurate information to the right people on time. The reports should be sorted so that managers only get information that is pertinent to their job. The reports should also be prioritized to focus on the most important activities with key variances noted.

Project management (step 6) represents the final decision point in the control process. The goal of a project control system is to deliver to the decision makers accurate and timely project status information so that intelligent decisions can be made. A plan has been set and actual progress measured. Management must now decide on the best course of action to take. Figure 11.2 indicates outside input support. This could come in the form of technical staff or consultant support. The reports that have originated in the cost/schedule engineering should highlight critical areas of concern as well as a recommended plan of action.

The arrow from project management (step 6) to field operations (step 2) represents the completion of the project control system. Management has made a decision, and final instructions are now being given to the field. Adjustments may be made in the project plan, or the instructions may be to continue as originally scheduled. For these instructions to be effective, they must be delivered soon enough to be smoothly implemented.

The project control cycle is a feedback loop providing each project participant with a measure of the success of his or her past decisions. An estimator can see the accuracy of an estimate just as a project superintendent can see if productivity was increased in the last reporting period. This loop allows learning to occur and adjustments to be made. Without a project control cycle, project people might continue to make the same mistakes and have little opportunity to measure the effect of specific decisions.

BOX 11.1

CONTROL IN ACTION

One of the major challenges to the implementation of an effective control system in companies today is communication between the home office and the field office. Timely, accurate instructions need to be provided to the field, and accurate, up-to-date status information on the project needs to be reported back to the home office.

The method of choice in most companies today is a turnaround document (TAD). A TAD is prepared by the home office and provides specific work instructions to the field manager: activities to be completed, start and finish dates, assigned employees, and subcontractors and vendors are all identified. On the same form is space for the field manager to fill in actual performance alongside the planned. The manager reports information such as percent complete, actual start date, factors causing delays, and other pertinent status information. This form is returned to the home office (hence the name *turnaround document*) at the end of the reporting period, with a new form issued for the next period after project statusing is complete. Daily and weekly meetings enhance this process, along with site visits by home office executives, schedulers, and estimators. Status photographs are taken regularly, which are logged into the job records. Cost information is provided to the home office by submitted time sheets, subcontractor and vendor invoices, and equipment use reports. With a good cost-coding system in place, accurate job records can be maintained, provided the forms are filled out and inputted correctly.

Technologies available today allow communication in real time and much more with visualization. With three-dimensional CAD systems and electronic links from the field office to all project participants (home office, owner, designers and key vendors), instructions and communication can be immediate and more thorough. Work instructions can be provided in videos that simulate today's work viewed by the field and explained by home office and/or key designers. The simulation can be seen from any angle and can be stopped, rotated, and discussed at any point. Constructability questions and concerns can be immediately resolved. Schedule, estimate, and TAD information can be provided electronically to the field; and communication can be opened up to all participants as necessary using a project web page. Digital cameras can provide electronic real-time information back to the home office. With inexpensive locator devices, key points can be identified on the project, allowing for accurate statusing. Most material and equipment will be bar coded; so with a quick swipe, material installed will be immediately recorded and equipment used properly charged. Equipment maintenance, material ordering and stocking, and project invoicing will all become more efficient and accurate.

Some of these concepts are already being used. What prevents full installation is the sophistication of software, data transmission speed, the adoption of a common symbol library, and the sophistication of the work force. As these problems are solved, all of these concepts will be employed, along with many more.

The project control cycle can be repeated as often as necessary to control a particular project—monthly, weekly, daily, or even hourly for tightly controlled maintenance operations. However, the more frequent the reporting process, the more cost is incurred by the company because of the additional time necessary to collect, process, and interpret results.

PREPARING A PROJECT FOR CONSTRUCTION

Preparing a project for construction means that the project must be broken down to a suitable level of detail so that it can be monitored and controlled. Establishing the scheduling activity as a common denominator often works because cost, time, and quality-control standards can be set up for each activity. Creating a baseline (also called a target or project forecast) is the first step in the control process. The baseline establishes the goals for the project and allows management to measure how well the project is proceeding and what the end result will be. The estimate serves as the cost baseline for a project, while the schedule serves as the time baseline.

Cost Baseline

The estimate is the tool used to establish the costs on a project. These costs are later refined as a project proceeds. The conceptual estimate—the first estimate performed—establishes the initial cost for the project. As design proceeds, square foot and assemblies estimates tighten up the budget. Once the design is complete, bids are solicited, with the accepted bid price establishing the construction budget for the project. This budget is based upon a detailed estimate prepared by the contractor using a complete design and including many subcontractor and vendor quotes.

From the contractor's perspective, the accepted bid price, which becomes the contract price, is the cost baseline for the project and the target by which the success of the project will be measured. Material quantities, labor unit prices, and assumed productivity rates used in this estimate become the baselines to measure the project's success. From the designer's and the owner's perspective, the agreed-upon contract price is the culmination of a series of pricing exercises that have been prepared since the first conceptual estimate. If the scope of the project has been well managed and the estimates done well, then the bids received should be close to the prior estimates. The quality of the contract documents, the bidding environment, and the location and type of project are all factors that affect the prices received.

Throughout the design/build process, the application of Pareto's Law plays an important part in the control of project costs. Vilfredo Pareto (1848–1923), an Italian economist, believed that 80 percent of the outcome of any project is determined by 20 percent of its included elements. Thus, any project control system needs to identify the major cost elements of the project early and develop a system of controls to monitor and manage them. Projects are broken down through the CSI format, a work breakdown structure (WBS), and bid or work packages. In some cases these may or may not be the same. Project managers focus on the elements that will have the greatest impact on the final project cost and/or the element with the greatest risk of escalation. Figure 11.3 illustrates a cost report.

PROJECTED COST REPORT & WORKSHEET

HODESS
BUILDING COMPANY

JOB NUMBER: 00239
JOB DESCRIPTION: UNIPHASE

L-LABOR
O-OVERHEAD
M-MATERIAL
S-SUB

If the Actual Costs to Date exceed the Current Estimate, the Actual Cost will be used for the Projected Project Cost.

Changes to the Current Estimate can be made here by the Project Manager and Management during review which would later be entered into the cost system.

COST CODE		DESCRIPTION	ORIGINAL ESTIMATE	ADJUSTMENTS	CURRENT ESTIMATE	ACTUAL COSTS TO DATE	% COMPL	COST TO COMPLETE	PROJECTED COST	CHANGE TOTAL	PROJECTED VARIANCE
008		DOORS & WINDOWS									
008100	L	DOORS & FRAMES	1,400	200	1,600	420	26.25%	1,180	1,600		0
008100	M	DOORS & FRAMES	7,149	(375)	6,774	1,712	25.27%	5,062	6,774		0
008100	O	DOORS & FRAMES	500	0	500	0	0.00%	500	500		0
008360	S	OVERHEAD DOORS	4,000	0	4,000	4,250	106.25%	0	4,250		250
008805	M	ALUMINUM & GLAZING	895	135	1,030	1,000	97.09%	30	1,030		0
009		FINISHES									
009100	S	METAL STUD & DRYWALL	24,190	0	24,190	20,790	85.94%	3,400	24,190		0
009510	S	ACOUSTICAL CEILINGS	13,600	400	14,000	12,750	91.07%	1,250	14,000		0
009705	S	EPOXY FLOORS	15,764	0	15,764	16,133	102.34%	0	16,133		369
009900	S	PAINTING	2,500	250	2,750	0	0.00%	2,750	2,750		0
009950	M	FRP PANELS	13,840	0	13,840	12,840	92.77%	1,000	13,840		0

FIGURE 11.3 Job cost report showing actual versus estimated cost, with variance and projected cost at completion

Source: Courtesy of Kenneth Leary.

248

The estimate is clearly the baseline for the control of project costs. As the project moves to the construction stage, the estimate becomes extremely detailed, with numerous items to control and monitor. The detailed estimate provides specific direct cost targets such as material quantities, labor rates, equipment rates, and hours as well as indirect cost elements such as field overhead, contingency, and home office overhead. At this stage the application of Pareto's Law becomes important. By using detailed and summary reports, project managers focus on the elements in need of tight control and only look at less critical elements at a summary level.

Time Baseline

Through the schedule the project team manages the time and related resources required to complete the project. When the schedule is combined with the estimate, the cash flow can be projected. To do this accurately, the schedule must be managed and continually updated to reflect the work that is occurring in the field. As with cost control, the schedule can be used either at a summary level or at the more detailed level, depending on the level of control required. Using bid packages, WBS, and the CSI can establish the necessary levels of control. Detailed control can be managed through network schedules, whereas summary control can be handled through bar charts or timetables.

Most projects are developed in full detail using a network-based CPM schedule with summary reports generated as necessary for reporting purposes. For example, on large projects detailed network schedules are developed for each of the major systems, which is necessary to coordinate and control the system work. However, when the project is examined in its entirety, the system work is shown only as a single bar (see Figure 11.4).

Control systems are most effective when the level of control is appropriate for the work and the people being controlled. As level of control and corresponding detail increase, the cost of the system also increases because of the need to gather, store, and process more information. A high level of control may be necessary on fast-paced, highly technical work or on a project in which many different parties interface. However, overcontrolled projects hamper the creativity of the supervisors and end up wasting time and money. Figure 11.5 compares varying the level of control with the benefits of early completion.

The baseline schedule identifies the key milestone dates of the projects as well as key material delivery dates. Subcontractor start and finish dates are also shown. These dates are all important control points because they affect the work of the people involved in negotiating contracts for materials and services. A delayed material delivery can have a domino effect on the following work of the project. Milestone dates, such as the delivery of the first floor for tenant occupancy, are important to monitor because they establish constraints for outside users.

Baseline Summary

The estimate and the schedule are the two primary tools used to control the cost and time elements of a project. The level of detail should be dictated by the degree of control necessary. As the control system is established, the project manager must determine the most time- and cost-sensitive parts of the project and design the system to focus on these areas. A proper and well thought-out breakdown of the work along with the correct level of summary and detail control will give him or her the control tools needed to manage

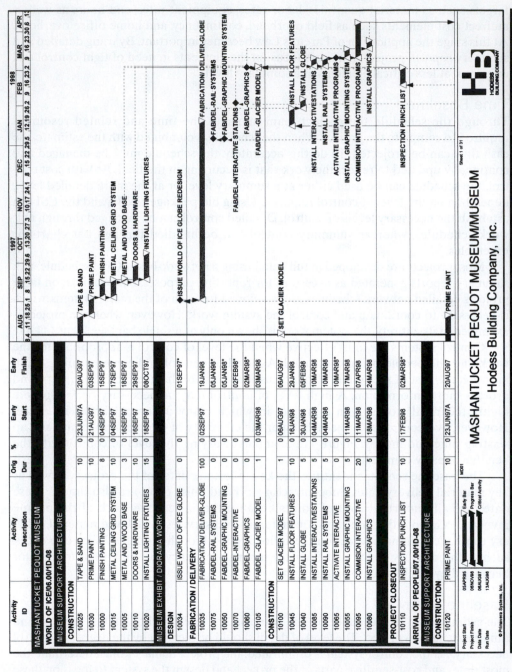

FIGURE 11.4 Schedule report sorted by work area and responsibility

Source: Courtesy of Kenneth Leary.

Choosing the level of project control			
	Ability to influence project duration		
Benefit of earlier completion	Low	Medium	High
$5,000/month	Critical path	Master project planning	Cash flow
$25,000/month	Master project planning	Cash flow	Resource loading
$50,000/month	Cash flow	Resource loading	Resource leveling
$100,000+/month	Resource loading	Resource leveling	Earned value and progress measurement

FIGURE 11.5 Fine tuning the project strategy

Source: Courtesy of Kenneth H. Stowe, P. E., George B. H. Macomber Company, Boston, MA.

the project cost effectively. The estimate and the schedule establish the baseline for the project. As the project proceeds, the actual cost and schedule for the project will change for many reasons. The baseline, however, will not change. It will always serve as a measure of how the project was planned at the beginning of the project.

MINIMUM COST SCHEDULING

It is usual for the estimating and scheduling departments to prepare baseline estimates and schedules for a project on the basis of normal work conditions, equipment, and crew sizes. However, as a management team prepares the final plan for construction, it also establishes the most efficient project duration. This process, called *minimum cost scheduling*, involves analyzing the critical path and shortening the project's duration as long as money can be saved. And costs often *can* be saved; as the duration of a project is reduced, indirect costs are also reduced.

If the daily indirect costs for a project are less than the costs required to shorten a project, then the total project's costs are reduced. Figure 11.6 plots minimum cost duration.

Crashing

Crashing a project means the process of accelerating an activity or multiple activities to shorten the overall duration of a project. By adding additional people, equipment, or work hours, a project manager can shorten an activity's duration. If the activity affected is critical, the project will be shortened as well. Activities are crashed for different reasons:

1. An activity may need to be completed by a specific date for contractual reasons.
2. Some activities can be accomplished more economically during a certain time of the year, encouraging managers to accelerate preceding activities.
3. The cost to accelerate an activity, which shortens the project's duration, may be less expensive than the cost of running the project for the same period.

When an activity is crashed, its direct costs increase. (As we have discussed, direct costs involve materials, labor, and equipment directly associated with the installation

BOX 11.2

DIRECT VERSUS INDIRECT COSTS

DIRECT COSTS

The costs involved in the construction of a project can be broken down into two major categories: direct and indirect. Direct costs are associated with the physical construction of the project and include such things as the purchasing of building materials, equipment operations, and all installation labor. The cost of roofing material, the purchase of asphalt, or the cost of landscape material are all considered direct costs. So are the rental of a paving machine and its operator, the daily wage of a carpenter, and the costs associated with finishing concrete. As long as work proceeds, direct costs continue to accrue. Once work is stopped, direct costs generally stop as well.

INDIRECT COSTS

Indirect costs are not as easy to visualize. They are generally broken down into two categories: home office overhead and general conditions.

Home Office Overhead

Home office overhead includes the corporate costs associated with keeping the company in business. The expenses involved in marketing the company, necessary legal and accounting expenses, and the costs associated with bidding work are all examples.

Home office overhead can be figured by comparing the volume of business that a company does in a given year with the annual costs of doing business. This home office cost, usually figured as a percentage, must be recouped by income from earned projects. A company reduces its project overhead by reducing the home office's cost or by increasing business volume.

PROJECT OVERHEAD (GENERAL CONDITIONS)

Indirect costs can also occur in the field. These costs are called general conditions, field office overhead, or project overhead. They are necessary to supervise and support the job site. Examples are the rental of the job-site trailer; the superintendent's salary; and the cost of security fencing, guard, and signs.

Whereas direct costs are a factor of the size and quality expected of a project, indirect costs are a factor of the project's duration and the degree of supervision required. If a project increases in length or requires a high level of coordination, the indirect costs will increase. By minimum cost scheduling, project managers can determine the optimum duration for the project, minimizing the project's total cost, which equals a project's direct cost plus its indirect cost.

or construction of the project.) These costs increase because of the inefficiencies caused by accelerating the work at a rate faster than normal. People may end up working in tighter quarters, or equipment may sit idle; but these cost increases may be justified if indirect costs are saved or if the owner provides a bonus for early completion.

A reduced project duration can earn additional bonus money, prevent the payment of fines or damages to the owner, or save the company additional indirect costs.

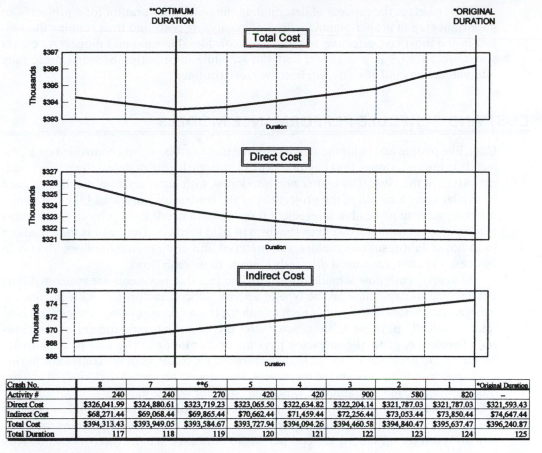

Crash No.	8	7	**6	5	4	3	2	1	*Original Duration
Activity #	240	240	270	420	420	900	580	820	–
Direct Cost	$326,041.99	$324,880.61	$323,719.23	$323,065.50	$322,634.82	$322,204.14	$321,787.03	$321,787.03	$321,593.43
Indirect Cost	$68,271.44	$69,068.44	$69,865.44	$70,662.44	$71,459.44	$72,256.44	$73,053.44	$73,850.44	$74,647.44
Total Cost	$394,313.43	$393,949.05	$393,584.67	$393,727.94	$394,094.26	$394,460.58	$394,840.47	$395,637.47	$396,240.87
Total Duration	117	118	119	120	121	122	123	124	125

Note: Indirect Cost Per Day $597.00
  Early Finish Bonus $200.00 Per Day = Total of $797.00 Per Day
  **6 = Optimum Duration

FIGURE 11.6 The optimum or minimum cost duration is found by comparing the cost to accelerate (crash) the project with the indirect cost of operation

Source: Courtesy of Kenneth Leary.

The amount of the bonus to be received or the fine to be paid should be described in the contract.

Although there is a clear benefit to optimizing a project's duration on the basis of cost, crashing is not a routine step in project planning. The integration of scheduling and estimating information cannot be easily linked since the activity units are often not the same. It is also unusual to calculate crash costs for each activity and then formally analyze and compare those costs with indirect costs. This process takes a considerable amount of time and is difficult to automate. Another real concern is that, as a project is crashed, multiple critical paths are created. As more critical paths appear, there is a greater risk of delaying completion of the project.

Nevertheless, the process of determining the optimum duration for a project is an important step in proper planning. Properly analyzing costs and then running the project in the most cost-effective way can save considerable time and money. As expert system technology improves and cost and schedule information becomes more fully integrated, this kind of study will become more routine.

COST AND SCHEDULE PERFORMANCE MODELS

Cash, like people and equipment, is a resource that must be tightly controlled on a project. It is the rare owner that begins a project with cash equivalent to the project budget sitting in the bank. The owner needs to know, with accuracy, how much cash must be available each month of the project to pay the contractor's invoices. Like the owner, the contractor must be able to predict his or her cash needs for a project. Contractors receive income from the owner in the form of paid invoices. That cash is then paid out to in-house labor, subcontractors, and material and equipment suppliers. To stay in business, the contractor must diligently manage these cash flows.

Managing cash flow is made difficult by the fact that payments are made in different increments depending on the type of activity. Subcontractors generally invoice the general contractors at the end of each month for the work completed. The general contractor typically pays the subcontractor after the owner has paid the general contractor's invoice. A general contractor pays his or her labor at the end of each week. Materials are generally provided to the contractor on credit, with the contractor paying the supplier in full at the end of the month. To properly project cash flow, each activity must be tracked in the manner in which the payment will be made.

The cost of each activity must first be identified from the estimate and assigned to the corresponding activity on the schedule. In Figure 11.7, each activity shows the duration and cost. By calculating the cost per day to fund each activity (activity cost/activity duration), also called the cost slope, the project manager can calculate the total cost per day to run the project. These costs can be added up weekly or monthly. The figure illustrates a cost-loaded schedule and is the basis for projecting both income and costs.

Income Projection

A schedule of values curve is the cost-loaded schedule that projects the value of work that is planned to be invoiced at the end of each payment period. This is prepared in advance of construction and submitted to the owner or owner's agent for approval. The income that the contractor receives is the amount of the invoice less owner retainage. Retainage is money held back by the owner until the contractor satisfactorily completes the contract. Retainage of 5–10 percent of the amount invoiced is normal. As Figure 11.8 shows, the values on the income curve equal the values on the schedule of values curve less retainage. The income curve is a step curve, reflecting the fact that the contractor submits an invoice at the end of each payment period equal to the schedule of values curve and will receive a payment three weeks later equal to that value less retainage. No income is received until the next invoice is paid one payment period later. All retainage is paid to the contractor at the end of the project. The final point on the schedule of values curve equals the income curve, which equals the contract amount.

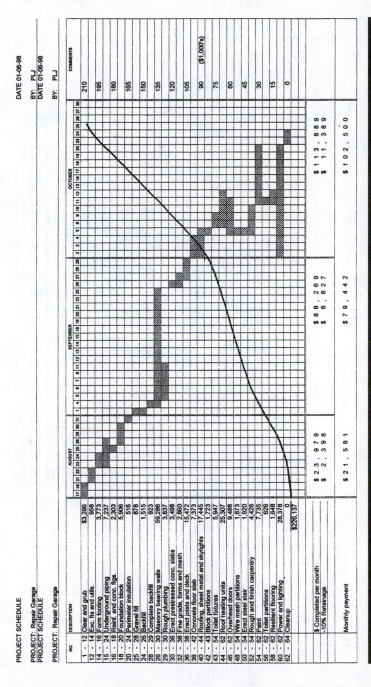

FIGURE 11.7 By integrating an estimate with a schedule, a manager can project costs by month and cumulatively

Source: From *Scheduling and Project Management Workbook*, published annually. © R. S. Means Co., Inc., Kingston, MA, 781-585-7880, all rights reserved.

255

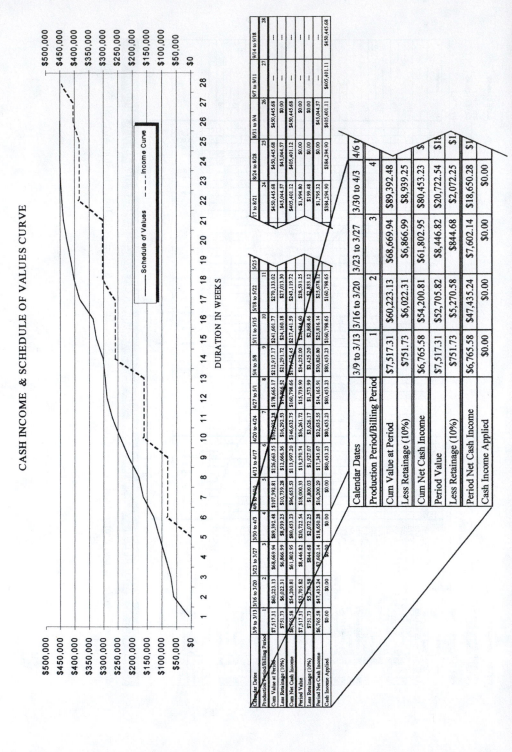

FIGURE 11.8 Illustrated cash income and schedule of values curve. Note that the contractor has earned $89,392.48 at period 4 but receives this amount less retainage ($80,453.23) at period 6

Source: Courtesy of Kenneth Leary.

256

The projected payment period totals are commonly negotiated between the contractor and the owner. It is in the contractor's best interest to shift as much value as possible to the front of the job, overvaluing early activities while undervaluing later items. This ploy is commonly called "front-end loading." Within reason, this is an accepted practice since in the early part of a project contractors often are faced with hidden costs not easily attached to specific work activities. This also helps offset owner retainage, which can severely affect a contractor's cash flow.

When assigning a cost to an individual activity, the contractor must be sure that the amount attached reflects his or her complete costs, including both direct and indirect costs and profit. Subcontractor costs must be marked up, and material and labor costs must also include appropriate markups. The costs assigned to each activity are what will be eventually billed to the owner; therefore, all costs and profit must be identified.

Payment Projection

Before construction the contractor should prepare a payment projection (also called a cash requirements curve), which projects the cash payables expected from the contractor to run the project. This curve is prepared similarly to the income curve except that now the contractor is forecasting the cash that is leaving the company to pay for labor, materials, subcontracts, and other commitments. Another difference is that the costs assigned to each activity are direct costs and do not include general contractor overhead or profit, which are not directly paid out. At the end of the project, the final point on the cash requirements curve indicates the total amount of money that the contractor has spent for labor, materials, equipment, and subcontracts, just as the income curve reflects the total amount of money paid to the contractor by the owner.

The basis for the cash requirements curve is the cost curve, which is a summary of all payment categories such as labor, materials, and subcontractors on a period basis, usually the month. The direct cost of each item is taken from the estimate, and the placement of each activity is taken from the schedule. In plotting the cost curve the contractor adds up the period costs and plots them in an S curve (see Figure 11.9).

The cost curve thus identifies the direct cost of the project at any point in time. This information can be used to project payroll requirements as well as material expenses for the project. The reason that the costs have been categorized as labor, material, or subcontractor is that the terms for payment of each is different. In-house labor is paid weekly, materials are paid at the end of the month, and subcontractors are paid after the general contractor receives payment from the owner. Therefore, to properly model the cash payables, the contractor must account for these payment scenarios. In Figure 11.10, the cost curve has been modified to account for the different cost categories. The labor category is drawn as a sloped line to denote that labor is paid weekly or throughout the payment period. The materials are shown being paid in full at the end of the month. Subcontractors are paid last, with the general contractor often holding back a 10 percent retainage.

The cash requirements curve is the contractor's attempt to model as precisely as possible his or her cash needs for a project. When this curve is compared to the cash income curve, we can visualize the contractor's cash flow (see Figure 11.11). The computation of both a cash requirements curve and an income curve allows the construction professional to, with accuracy, project his or her cash needs and excesses for the project.

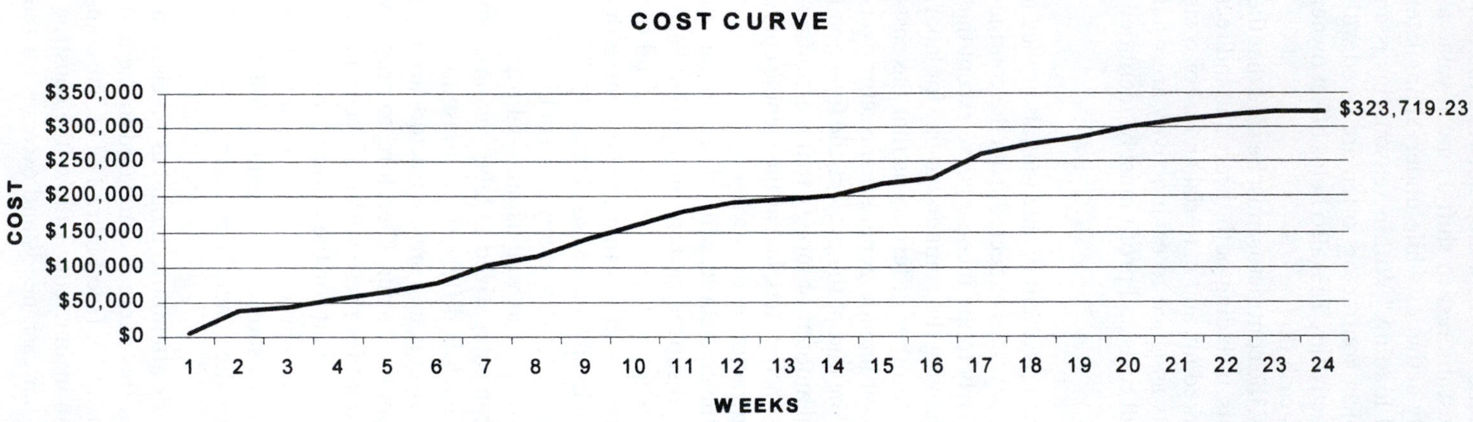

COST CURVE

Cost curve showing cumulative cost (y-axis, $0 to $350,000) over weeks 1 through 24, rising to $323,719.23.

Calendar Dates	3/9 to 3/13	3/16 to 3/20	3/23 to 3/27
Production Period	1	2	3
Labor	$4,151.92	$5,963.14	$4,399.07
Material	$350.00	$2,578.01	$659.51
Subcontractor		$23,023.00	
Suppliers			
Period Cost Totals	$4,501.92	$31,564.15	$5,058.58
Cummulative Totals	$4,501.92	$36,066.07	$41,124.65

FIGURE 11.9 Cost curve

Source: Courtesy of Kenneth Leary.

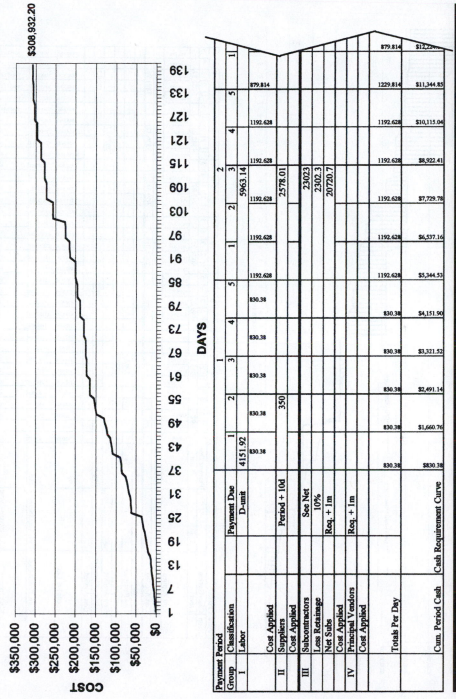

FIGURE 11.10 The cash requirements curve models the contractor's cash needs. This curve takes into account four different payment groups

Source: Courtesy of Kenneth Leary.

CASH INCOME V/S CASH REQUIREMENTS CURVE

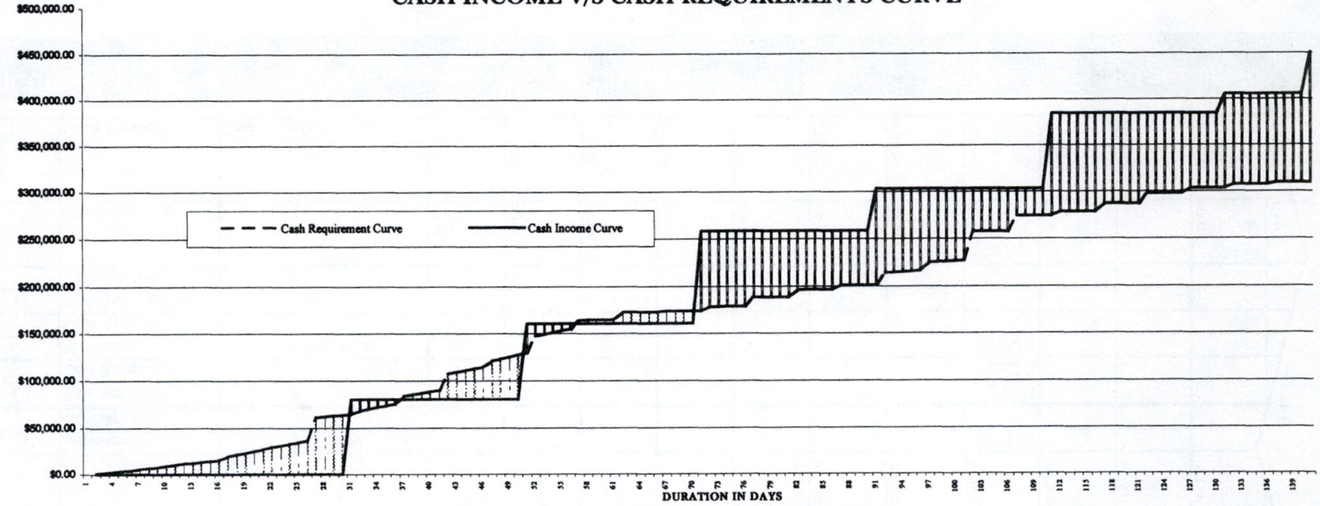

- - - Cash Requirement Curve

—— Cash Income Curve

DURATION IN DAYS

FIGURE 11.11 A contractor's cash flow can be forecasted by overlaying the cash income and cash requirements curves

Source: Courtesy of Kenneth Leary.

As Figure 11.11 shows, this project will need a source of additional financing for the beginning of the project; but as the project nears completion it will begin to produce the positive cash flow needed to cover the contractor's general requirements and provide a profit.

Early negative cash flow is typical for most projects and must be planned for. Owner retainage, as well as a lag between the receipt and payment of requisitions, is often the cause. Contractors can minimize this negative cash flow by front-loading the job, but the owner must agree to this method because the owner could be paying more than the work is worth and therefore be at risk. Since contractors do not pay their subcontractors until after they receive owner payment, cash flow can be improved by using more subcontractors early in the job. Negotiating a lower rate of owner retainage, freeing up retainage earlier, arranging additional credit from material suppliers, or prearranging a credit line from a bank can all help cover the early cash flow problems.

Float in the schedule can also be used to help manage cash flow. Early, high-cost activities that demand contractor investment such as in-house labor or material purchase items can be delayed if they have float. Subcontractor work or deliveries from material suppliers who are extending credit can be scheduled early to help boost contractor cash flow.

Cash requirement and income projections should be done for all company projects since most companies have projects running at different stages of completion. Projects requiring an influx of cash can be helped by other projects that are nearing completion and generating positive cash flow. Most of the newer scheduling software packages allow activities to be cash-loaded to produce these kinds of cash studies. Spreadsheets can also be used to summarize overall company cash flow.

CONTROL IN ACTION

A project begins with a workplan that includes a budget, a schedule, and an engineered approach designed to complete the project most effectively. Preparing a workplan involves the many project participants, whose goal is to most efficiently use the company's resources. The estimate and the schedule form the basis of an analysis of the project.

Projects begin with this plan, but the reality of construction is that events occur that force the plan to be altered. An owner adds or deletes work, forcing a change in the project's scope; bad weather interrupts the project; a labor strike occurs; or productivity in the field is less than planned. To manage these events, the project team must establish a system to capture the actual events of the project, analyze them, and make appropriate adjustments so that the project's budget, schedule, and level of quality are adequately maintained.

Cost Engineering

For the project team to effectively manage and control the construction process, data used to compare against the baseline system are first generated in the field. Developing an effective method of gathering and analyzing these data is key to maintaining control over the construction process.

People sometimes liken cost engineering to cost accounting, but the two disciplines should not be confused. Both are concerned with costs, but the accountant focuses on historical costs for tax purposes, bill paying, and invoicing of clients. The cost engineer, on the other hand, is concerned with forecasting and trending, using project information to measure how well a project is doing and what the outcome will be. The two disciplines must work together. The accountant needs project information to properly invoice customers and to pay bills. The project manager uses accounting information for estimating and budgeting purposes.

Cost coding is the framework through which information is gathered and stored on a project. The coding structure selected determines the level of detail that can be used to study the project and the time and energy required to manage the system. Several structures of accounts are normally used on a project. One is needed to separate costs and operations along the lines of the WBS. A second structure is necessary to analyze the cost and efficiency of different operations performed on the project. Contractor performance on wall framing, concrete placement, or site clearing is important to track both to measure performance and for future estimates. A third structure is needed to manage resources used in requisitioning and reporting. Actual people, equipment, and material costs must be tracked for payroll purposes as well as for invoicing and requisitions. The structure used in this area should be compatible with the company's accounting system. Here is an example of a project cost code:

Project Number	Area	Operation	Distribution	Cost
99BR02	02	096600	02	$3,500

1. **Project number.** The project number allows the costs to be stored and separated by project type, year, and particular project. In this case the first two fields indicate that this project began in 1999. The B indicates that it was won through a competitive bid, and the R indicates that the project is a renovation. The 02 indicates that this is the second project this year for the company.

2. **Area.** These two fields allow the stored cost information to be sorted and stored by the area of the particular project. In this case the 02 refers to the second floor on this project. Companies might separate project information by phase, wings, or other locations on the project.

3. **Operation.** Here the CSI format indicates that the work item being coded is resilient tile flooring. By storing information by operation, the company can begin to develop historic costs for different types of materials and operations.

4. **Distribution.** The 02 indicates that the assigned cost is for material. An 01 might indicate a labor cost, an 03 an equipment cost. This field allows the project manager to assign the cost to vendors or subcontractors or make other assignments.

5. **Cost.** The last entry is the actual cost of the work item. In this case, $3,500 was spent to purchase resilient floor tile on this renovation project.

The cost engineering function allows the project manager to input and retrieve information about a project in an organized fashion and quickly determine the status of a project as well as forecast its future. The development of good historical information for future estimates is also an important component of the cost engineering process.

Progress Evaluation and Control

The estimate and schedule prepared before the project begins establish the baseline for the construction project. Once the project begins, actual progress is periodically determined so that any necessary adjustments can be made quickly. Through the cost-coding system, actual cost information about the project is also collected. Actual progress when combined with actual cost to date allows the productivity on the project to be measured. Productivity information, cost to date, and schedule progress help management properly control a project.

The method used to measure work progress depends on the type of work. Following are several different approaches.

Units Completed

When an activity requires repeated installation or removal of a common piece of work, each repetition involves approximately the same level of effort. In this case, *units completed* is used as a straight line measurement. An example is the installation of floor tile. The job calls for the installation of 2,000 square feet of tile. An evaluation of the work to date shows that 1,500 square feet have been installed, which indicates that the activity is 75 percent complete.

Incremental Milestone

When an activity involves an operation that will be accomplished in a specific, known sequence, the approximate level of effort necessary to accomplish each milestone (usually based on the number of hours required) is measured. An example is the installation of a bridge crane in a factory. The milestone completion percentages for the on-site installation may be recorded as follows:

Received and inspected	20 percent
Crane installed	35 percent
Alignment completed	50 percent
Testing completed	90 percent
Owner accepted	100 percent

Cost Ratio

This method is used for tasks that occur over a long period of time and are continuous throughout. Project management and quality assurance programs are examples. These services are budgeted by dollars or work hours. Percent complete is measured as follows:

$$\text{Percent complete} = \frac{\text{Actual cost or work-hours to date}}{\text{Forecast cost or hours at completion}}$$

Other Methods

The previous methods are the most common, but other methods of measuring progress are sometimes used when activities are composed of specific work elements that are of very different cost or work effort. Here the work may need to be prorated to account for the disparity. In some cases (creative work is an example), it is very difficult to determine how long an activity will take and how much has been done. In this case the physical start of the activity can be assigned 50 percent complete and the completion 100 percent. In the end, the subjective opinion of the supervisor may be the only option, but this should only be resorted to when other more objective methods are impossible.

Determining the percent complete of an activity is an important step in the control process. Once the progress of an activity is determined, it is possible to compare the present status of a project with the baseline. This comparison is the best way to determine how the project is proceeding and if any remedial actions need to be taken.

Cost and Schedule Performance

The evaluation of actual performance to planned performance is a critical and recurring step in the control process. Actual is compared to planned on an activity-by-activity basis. The level of detail that can be evaluated depends on the level of detail established within the cost-coding system. The frequency of this evaluation depends on the type of project and the level of control required. The greater the level of detail established and the more frequent the reviews, the greater the cost of the control system.

The first step in evaluating status is to compute the earned value of the activities completed during the reporting period. The earned value of an activity, or an account, is computed as follows:

$$\text{Earned value} = (\text{Percent complete}) \times (\text{Budget for activity})$$

For example, a framing activity is budgeted to cost \$5,000 and consumes 40 work-hours. The activity is 40 percent complete as measured by one of the methods discussed in the previous section. Therefore the activity has earned \$2,000 and 16 hours.

This evaluation can be done for all the activities computed to date on the project. The dollars and hours earned can also be combined to look at the project as a whole and the overall percent complete for the project calculated as follows:

$$\text{Percent complete} = \frac{\text{Earned work-hours or dollars all accounts}}{\text{Budgeted work-hours or dollars all accounts}}$$

The earned value calculation computes the work that has been accomplished to date. Budgeted work-hours or dollars represent what work has been planned. Actual work-hours or dollars to date represent what work has been paid for.

Performance is checked like this:

Schedule performance: Compare budgeted work-hours to earned work-hours.
    If earned exceeds budgeted, more work has been done than planned.
Budget performance: Compare budgeted work dollars to actual work dollars.
    If actual exceeds budgeted, more work has been paid for than done.

Two other calculations can further analyze both schedule and cost performance on a project. The schedule or cost variance is calculated by subtracting the budgeted work-hours from the earned work-hours for the schedule variance or the actual dollars from the earned dollars for the cost variance. The performance index is calculated by dividing earned work-hours by budgeted work-hours for the schedule index or earned dollars by budgeted dollars for the cost index. A positive variance and an index of 1.0 or greater is favorable.

Consider the framing example discussed previously. The activity was budgeted to cost $5,000 and consume 40 work-hours. One carpenter was assigned to the task for five days. After three days the job was determined to be 40 percent complete. To date, $2,550 has been paid out on the activity. What are the schedule and cost variances and indices?

Schedule variance = Earned work-hours − Budgeted work-hours
−8 hours = 16 hours − 24 hours
Cost variance = Earned dollars − Actual dollars
−$550 = $2,000 − $2,550

$$\text{Schedule performance index} = \frac{\text{Earned work-hours}}{\text{Budgeted work-hours}}$$

$$= \frac{16}{24}$$

$$= 0.667$$

$$\text{Cost performance index} = \frac{\text{Earned dollars}}{\text{Actual dollars}}$$

$$= \frac{\$2,000}{\$2,550}$$

$$= 0.784$$

The framing example indicates a situation in which both cost and schedule performance are not meeting what was planned. The work is taking longer than planned and is costing more. If this type of performance is also occurring on the other project activities, the project might be in serious trouble.

What might explain the poor variance and performance indices indicated in the framing example?

1. The work being performed is different from the work that was budgeted for. Due to owner or designer changes or differing site conditions, the field crews are doing more work or work of a different type. In this case the schedule and cost budgets must be changed to reflect the actual fieldwork.
2. The productivity in the field is not as good as planned. This may be due to poor field supervision, use of the wrong equipment, or a poorly trained work force. Identifying this problem early in the project is essential so that the necessary corrections can be made.
3. The cost variance and cost performance index may be affected by the actual unit prices being paid for labor and materials. Due to local market factors, labor agreements, or a higher rate of inflation than planned for, material and labor prices may be greater than budgeted. Identifying this situation early will allow the project team to adjust the project budget and/or the project's scope.

To be an effective control tool, management should calculate the schedule and cost variances and indices for the project at the end of each reporting period. For the calculations to be useful, the baseline estimate and schedule and the actual cost and performance data must be accurate. Remember, garbage in equals garbage out! With good data, management should be able to quickly identify trouble areas to make timely, intelligent adjustments in the project. The result of this analysis should demonstrate any trends and provide an accurate forecast of the project's future.

Project Documentation

The last step in the project control process is composed of three actions:

1. All actions that occur in a control period need to be documented for administrative and historical reasons.
2. The status of the project and any recommended changes in schedule or budget need to be communicated to all project participants.
3. Through formalized reports, the forecasted completion date and cost as well as other critical information such as milestone dates, major purchases, or governmental or regulatory reports must be communicated.

Documentation

By thoroughly documenting project information, the team is able to develop a file of historical information that can be used in a variety of ways. Historical information is necessary in the event of a lawsuit from suppliers, subcontractors, the owner, or the public. A lawsuit may occur many years into the future, so it is critical that companies establish a formalized system of documenting project events for record purposes. Daily reports, manning reports, key deliveries, visitors, owner or designer field instructions, tests conducted, activities started or finished, and any unusual occurrences should all be documented for future reference. The original and revised CPM schedules should also be marked up and stored.

Accurate actual project information is also necessary for estimating and scheduling future projects. The selected system of coding and the effort that goes into inputting and verifying the accuracy of the collected data dictate their value. Field people must take the time to accurately enter project information as it occurs, and the home office must enter this information into the company data base. Good coordination between the home and the field will help guarantee an effective data base.

Project Coordination

The level of support from the field in providing data for the cost control system depends on the value of the information that is fed back to the field. An action-oriented system in which analysis is quickly followed up with a recommendation ensures that information will arrive in the field in time to be implemented. This is a good time for the project managers to applaud positive results or make the necessary changes to get the project back on track.

Instructions back to the field can occur daily, weekly, or monthly depending on the nature of the project. The field people need to know if any changes should occur in the schedule, the staffing of the project, or planned major purchases or deliveries and whether or not any overtime or second shifts will be required. Feedback on construction methods and equipment used for a given activity is essential if productivity improvements are going to be made. It is normal for some activities to be done faster than planned and others to be done slower. Some deliveries will arrive early, others

```
                                    PRIMAVERA PROJECT PLANNER

REPORT DATE 21AUG98  RUN NO.  26                              START DATE 12MAR98  FIN DATE 1SEP98
             15:30
TARGET V/S ACTUAL                                            DATA DATE 22MAY98  PAGE NO.   1
```

ACTIVITY ID	TAR DUR	CUR DUR	%	CODE	ACTIVITY DESCRIPTION	CURRENT START	FULL RNG FINISH	TARGET START	FULL RNG FINISH	VAR.
KKP100	0	0	0		START OF PROJECT	22MAY98		12MAR98		-51
KKP520	0	0	0		STRUCTURAL SYSTEM COMPLETE		9JUN98		3JUN98	-4
KKP610	0	0	0		ENVELOPE WEATHER TIGHT		3JUL98		29JUN98	-4
KKP760	0	0	0		SHEETROCK & TAPE COMP.		20JUL98		14JUL98	-4
KKP930	5	5	0		Punch List	25AUG98	31AUG98	19AUG98	25AUG98	-4
KKP940	1	1	0		Owners Acceptance	1SEP98	1SEP98	26AUG98	26AUG98	-4
KKP950	0	0	0		PROJECT FINISH		1SEP98		26AUG98	-4
General Conditions										
KKP10	1	1	100	01	Permits-Gen. Admin.	12MAR98A	12MAR98A	12MAR98	12MAR98	0
KKP130	1	1	100	01	Erosion Control	12MAR98A	12MAR98A	12MAR98	12MAR98	0
KKP150	0	0	100	01	Construction Survey	16MAR98A	13MAR98A	16MAR98	13MAR98	0
KKP110	1	1	100	01	Site Security-Office Trailer	16MAR98A	16MAR98A	16MAR98	26AUG98	117
KKP290	1	1	100	01	Crane-1st Floor	20APR98A	20APR98A	20APR98	20APR98	0
KKP320	1	1	100	01	Erect Staging 1st Floor	22APR98A	22APR98A	22APR98	22APR98	0
KKP380	1	1	100	01	Crane-2nd Floor	8MAY98A	8MAY98A	8MAY98	8MAY98	0
KKP400	1	1	100	01	Erect Staging 2nd Floor	11MAY98A	11MAY98A	11MAY98	11MAY98	0
KKP440	1	1	0	01	Crane-Roof Framing	28MAY98	28MAY98	22MAY98	22MAY98	-4
KKP700	1	1	0	01	Remove Staging	6JUL98	18AUG98	30JUN98	12AUG98	-4
Site Work										
KKP30	15	20	100	02	O&D Precast Conc. Curb, Coping, Frames	12MAR98A	8APR98A	12MAR98	22APR98	10
KKP140	1	1	100	02	Clear & Grub Site	13MAR98A	13MAR98A	13MAR98	13MAR98	0
KKP160	2	2	100	02	Excavate Trenches & Backfill	16MAR98A	17MAR98A	16MAR98	18MAR98	1
KKP180	2	2	100	02	Drive Sheet Piling	16MAR98A	17MAR98A	16MAR98	18MAR98	1
KKP200	3	3	100	02	Site Drainage	16MAR98A	18MAR98A	16MAR98	18MAR98	0
KKP190	5	5	100	02	Excavate-Earthwork	19MAR98A	25MAR98A	19MAR98	25MAR98	0
KKP310	1	1	100	02	Backfill-Rough Grade	21APR98A	21APR98A	21APR98	21APR98	0
KKP720	1	1	0	02	Install Precast Curbing	7JUL98	19JUL98	1JUL98	13JUL98	-4
KKP730	1	1	0	02	Asphalt Base & Binder Course	8JUL98	20AUG98	2JUL98	14AUG98	-4
KKP740	1	1	0	02	Fin. Gr. Topsoil & Landscaping	8JUL98	20AUG98	2JUL98	14AUG98	-4
KKP910	1	1	0	02	Asphalt Finish Coat	9JUL98	21AUG98	3JUL98	17AUG98	-4
KKP920	1	1	0	02	Line Parking Lot	10JUL98	24AUG98	6JUL98	18AUG98	-4
Concrete										
KKP210	2	2	100	03	Form Footings	26MAR98A	27MAR98A	26MAR98	27MAR98	0
KKP220	1	1	100	03	Place Steel Rein. Footings	30MAR98A	30MAR98A	30MAR98	30MAR98	0
KKP230	1	1	100	03	Pour & Strip Footings	31MAR98A	31MAR98A	31MAR98	31MAR98	0
KKP240	8	8	100	03	Form Foundation Walls	1APR98A	9APR98A	1APR98	10APR98	0
KKP250	1	1	100	03	Place Steel Rein. Found. Walls	13APR98A	13APR98A	13APR98	13APR98	0
KKP260	1	1	100	03	Pour & Strip Found. Walls	14APR98A	14APR98A	14APR98	14APR98	0
KKP280	1	1	100	03	1st Flr. Pre-stressed Slabs	20APR98A	20APR98A	20APR98	20APR98	0
KKP370	1	1	100	03	2nd Flr. Pre-stressed Slabs	18MAY98A	18MAY98A	8MAY98	8MAY98	-6
KKP570	4	4	0	03	Concrete Topper 2nd Floor	24JUN98	29JUN98	18JUN98	23JUN98	-4
KKP710	1	1	0	03	Conc. Walk & Entrance Walk	7JUL98	19JUL98	1JUL98	13JUL98	-4
Masonry										
KKP40	20	22	100	04	O&D Brick	12MAR98A	10APR98A	12MAR98	22APR98	8
KKP270	3	3	100	04	CMU Walls Basement	15APR98A	17APR98A	15APR98	17APR98	0
KKP330	11	17	100	04	CMU Walls 1st Floor	23APR98A	15MAY98A	23APR98	7MAY98	-6
KKP340	9	10	100	04	Brick Veneer 1st Floor	24APR98A	7MAY98A	23APR98	5MAY98	-2
KKP410	7	3	60	04	CMU Walls 2nd Floor	19MAY98A	27MAY98	12MAY98	21MAY98	-4
KKP420	8	4	50	04	Brick Veneer 2nd Floor	19MAY98A	27MAY98	12MAY98	21MAY98	-4
KKP500	4	0	100	04	Precast Concrete Coping		22MAY98		28MAY98	
Metals										
KKP50	10	10	100	05	O&D Stl. Reinforcing & App. Shop Dwgs.	12MAR98A	25MAR98A	12MAR98	27MAR98	2
KKP60	20	22	100	05	O&D Stl. Framing-App. Shop Dwgs.	12MAR98A	10APR98A	12MAR98	22APR98	8
KKP360	1	1	100	05	Set Stl. Col. & Channel 1st Flr.	23APR98A	23APR98A	23APR98	23APR98	0
KKP430	1	1	100	05	Set Stl. Col. & Channel 2nd Flr.	11MAY98A	11MAY98A	13MAY98	13MAY98	2
KKP390	2	5	100	05	Costruct Stairs	15MAY98A		11MAY98	11JUN98	
KKP450	1	1	0	05	Set Roof Steel	28MAY98	28MAY98	22MAY98	22MAY98	-4
KKP460	2	2	0	05	Set Steel Joists	29MAY98	1JUN98	25MAY98	26MAY98	-4
KKP470	1	1	0	05	Set Steel Roof Deck	2JUN98	2JUN98	27MAY98	27MAY98	-4
KKP490	1	1	0	05	Roof Hatch	3JUN98	3JUN98	28MAY98	28MAY98	-4
Carpentry										
KKP790	2	2	0	06	Install Counter Tops	22JUL98	23JUL98	16JUL98	17JUL98	-4
KKP780	3	3	0	06	Finish Carpentry	22JUL98	3AUG98	16JUL98	28JUL98	-4
Moisture & Thermal Protection										
KKP300	1	1	100	07	Damp Proof Foundation	1APR98A	1APR98A	1APR98	20APR98	13
KKP510	1	1	0	07	Roof Scuppers & Leaders	28MAY98	4JUN98	28MAY98	29MAY98	-4

FIGURE 11.12   Tabular updated schedule versus target report

Source: Courtesy of Kenneth Leary.

late. Work will be added and deleted. All of these occurrences necessitate that the network schedule be updated and recalculated (see Figure 11.12).

The field needs to know if the critical path has changed and what activities are now critical or near critical. Not every activity can be closely monitored, so it is important that the field knows exactly where to focus its attention.

Trending, Forecasting, and Reporting

Looking back at how the project has succeeded, failed, or proceeded is called *trending*. By isolating the different areas of the project over a period of time, project managers are better able to see what decisions have worked and not worked and what changes need to be made. By projecting current trends to the future, the project team is better able to forecast future costs and completion dates. The productivity of different trades, material unit prices, labor unit prices, or other indices or variances may be tracked over the project's duration. As each element is better understood, its impact can then be forecasted through the remainder of the project.

It is important for all participants—owner, designer, construction manager, and contractors—to know with some certainty the ultimate cost and completion date for the project. At the end of the project everyone will be moving on to other projects, so each person needs to predict how long his or her involvement will be. Each also must be able to predict his or her financial commitment, when money has to be expended, and when he or she can expect to have money come into the company. Both time and financial commitments are projected through forecast reports. Calculations such as cost to complete, cost at completion, and projected date of completion are all done by forecasting. In many ways the extension of trending as described previously is the method through which forecasts are made.

A good report should try to include in one format some analysis, trending, and forecasting. Questions answered by the report should include the following:

1. How is the project doing? (analysis)
2. Is the production improving? (trending)
3. What is the projected outcome? (forecasting)

Conclusion

Project control is a continuous cycle in which project managers identify a goal, measure results, analyze, make adjustments, and report results. It is an action-based process with a feedback loop that can cycle as often as necessary, depending on the nature of the project. The estimate and the schedule establish the cost and timing goals. As the project proceeds, the actual results are compared to the target dates and costs established by the estimate and schedule. Significant deviations from the plan should be analyzed so that corrections can be made either in the ongoing project or in the company's data base so that future estimates and schedules will not repeat mistakes. Project control should be viewed as a learning process in which team members exchange information, make adjustments, and record results.

In establishing the initial project plan, the team integrates the estimate and the schedule to arrive at the most optimum schedule and budget for the project. Estimates and schedules are usually prepared independently; but as the final preparations are made for the project, every effort should be made to integrate the two. When projects are shortened, indirect costs are saved while direct costs go up. The optimum duration is the duration at which the project can be constructed for the least cost. This is found by analyzing the project's critical path and crashing critical activities as long as the direct cost of shortening the project is less than the indirect cost of the project.

Field performance is periodically measured with the actual results compared to the set standards. The level of detail is determined by the cost-coding system adopted for the project. As the level of detail increases, the cost of managing the control process increases.

Performance is calculated by computing cost and schedule variances and performance indices. Productivity performance is also measured. Managers use these calculations to analyze the project's performance and make changes if necessary. Actual performance data and any other information about the project need to be documented and stored. Management decisions need to be communicated promptly to all key project participants. A timely response from management gives feedback to the field and provides ample opportunity for the field to implement any recommendations. The last control responsibility is for management to continually report on the progress of the project. Reports should be timely, should indicate key variances between budgets and actuals as well as project trends, and should forecast the project's completion cost and date.

Chapter Review Questions

1. An increase in indirect costs could be directly attributable to an increase in what aspect of a project?
   a. Quality
   b. Direct costs
   c. Duration
   d. All of the above
   e. None of the above
2. Which of the following is *not* a suggestion for making controlling successful?
   a. Managers should make sure that the mechanics of the control process are understood by organizational members involved with controlling.
   b. Managers should use control activities to achieve many different goals.
   c. Managers should ensure that control activities are supported by all organizational members.
   d. Managers should make sure that information used as the basis for taking corrective action is timely.
   e. All of the above are valid suggestions.
3. When estimates and schedules are initially prepared, unlimited resources are assumed. True or false?
4. Which of the following best models accounts payable for a general contractor?
   a. Cost curve
   b. Cash requirements curve
   c. Production curve
   d. Cash income curve
   e. Schedule of values curve
5. To create an accurate cash flow projection, estimate and schedule information must be accurately integrated. True or false?
6. The control cycle/control loop is designed to occur on a monthly basis. As the cycle is accelerated, the accuracy of the collected data decreases. True or false?
7. The standards established for the design of an effective financial accounting system are the same as those required to run a successful management control system. True or false?

8. Time card information recorded in the field is essential actual data for the accomplishment of which of the following task(s)?
   a. Payroll
   b. Job costing
   c. Measurement of job-site productivity
   d. Completion of invoices
   e. All of the above

9. Which is the term used for looking at the past successes, failures, and tendencies of a project?
   a. Trending
   b. Reporting
   c. Forecasting
   d. Variance
   e. All of the above

10. One important function of the documentation stage is storing project information for future estimates, schedules, and project plans. True or false?

Exercises

1. Gather from a local construction company some example forms used to report actual cost, schedule, and performance information from the field to the home office. Report on the cost-coding system used. Explain what value each bit of information provides to the following company departments:
   a. Estimating
   b. Scheduling
   c. Project management
   d. Accounting
   e. Contract administration
   f. Purchasing

2. Examine a new communication, computational, or software technology and explain what economic benefits it can provide to the construction project control process. Possible topics might be advances in three-dimensional CAD, estimating/scheduling/CAD integration, Internet communications, or digital photography.

12 | JOB-SITE ADMINISTRATION

Chapter Outline

Introduction
Communication
    Notice to Proceed
    Meeting Minutes
    Requests for Information
    Daily Reports
    Diaries
    Progress Photographs
    Monthly Reports
    Electronic Communication
Submittals
    Shop Drawings
    Product Data
    Samples
Application for Payment
    Schedule of Values
    Stored Material
    Lien Waivers
    Retainage
    Final Payment
Changes to the Work
    Change Orders
    Extension of Time
Claims and Disputes
Conclusion

Student Learning Objectives

In this chapter you will learn the following:

1. The administrative tools used to manage, control, and document the construction process
2. The administrative process used to review and approve shop drawings, product data, and samples
3. The process followed to review, control, and approve contractor progress payments
4. The steps followed to legally change a construction contract

INTRODUCTION

After a construction project has been completed, the team responsible for carrying out the work usually is split up and assigned to various other jobs. Individual memories of the project dim with time and are, at any rate, only one person's view. To ensure that the construction team leaves behind an independent and permanent record of the project, the owner makes record keeping part of the contract. (The AIA's "General Conditions of the Contract for Construction" [AIA Document A201] is commonly used by the owner and will be referred to throughout this chapter.) The general conditions of the contract spell out—sometimes specifically, sometimes generally—the requirements for this documentation. Not all documentation kept at the site is required by the contract. Some of the record keeping is worked out among the owner, the contractor, and the architect early in the job for ease of communication and to suit the particular needs of the project.

The documents, if assembled with diligence and care, contain the whole story of the project. If there is a need to refer to any issues related to the project, these documents become critical. For all parties involved, such documentation is essential, both during construction and after the project is turned over.

During construction, the documentation protects all parties by keeping track of all actions in the field. Procedures are set up and outlined either through the contract or by mutual agreement at the start of the project. Any deviations from the contract documents are recorded and approved before becoming part of the work. Before money is paid out, a record shows that the work was actually performed. Checks and balances for how items are approved are in effect. If there are disputes, either during or after construction, the documentation can help sort out the issues.

After construction is completed, this documentation serves the owner throughout the life of the building. Shop drawings, as-built drawings, and operation and maintenance (O&M) manuals all give the owner information about materials and methods used to construct the facility. Whenever the owner needs to repair or alter the building, this information will help him or her make decisions in keeping with the original intent of the project.

COMMUNICATION

Any successful relationship, either personal or professional, relies on good communication between the parties. A construction team is no different. There are many methods of communication—some formal, some informal. Informal communications are necessary to keep the job running smoothly; but if decisions are made or agreements reached, these communications need to be documented. Formal communication should have an organized method that is understood and agreed to by all parties. In this way, each person can feed into another's system, easily referencing documents as needed.

Notice to Proceed

This correspondence from the owner is the first formal communication under the construction contract. It forms the basis of a legal contract between the owner and the contractor. Because negotiation of the provisions of the contract usually takes a certain amount of time, this notice allows the work to begin before the actual contract is signed.

The letter is a legal document in itself and has two basic provisions: it accepts the bid proposal submitted by the contractor, and it establishes a start date and a completion date. Documenting the start date is particularly important if the length of the construction is a contract item.

Meeting Minutes

There are several types of meetings held by the contractor on the site. There is the weekly or biweekly job progress meeting to review the status of the job. In addition, he or she will meet with the subcontractor's foreperson to review job progress and plan the activities in the field until the time of the next meeting. There are safety meetings to deal with any special safety or environmental concerns. There are meetings held to discuss specific issues with subcontractors and suppliers, and there are schedule coordination meetings. All of these are formal meetings that should have an agenda, a structure, and a leader. The most common meeting held on a construction project is the job progress meeting. This meeting includes the designer and the owner.

Minutes should be kept for all meetings, but the ones for the job progress meeting have the most detailed format. Either the designer or the contractor keeps the minutes at each job meeting, depending on the provisions of the contract. In either case, standard items are included, although the actual format will vary. All progress meeting notes should have the following categories:

- Title of the meeting
- Project name
- Project number
- Date of the meeting
- People in attendance
- People to receive copies
- Date and location of the next meeting

The format of the body varies depending on the style of the company taking the notes. The intent is not to deliver a word-by-word depiction of the meeting but to highlight the issues. The minutes are meant to be action-oriented, bringing up critical issues and recording who is responsible for solving them, what action needs to be taken, and when an answer is expected. Generally, the agenda addresses global and administrative issues first and then moves to the technical issues. Technical discussions can consume quite a bit of time—conceivably the entire meeting. When administrative and technical issues flow from meeting to meeting, they are considered old business and are discussed as such. Once they are resolved, they are dropped from the meeting minutes. New business is what is brought up for the first time on the day of the meeting. Any new business items are handled after the old business items are discussed. They are recorded as new business but move to the old business category if they remain through the next set of meeting notes.

The notes should be distributed as soon as possible while the issues are fresh on everyone's mind. Disagreements about wording or content can be taken up at the next meeting. All parties need to take these notes very seriously. Specific wording can make the difference in how the issue is interpreted if there is ever a need to revisit it. Meeting minutes also can be the first place an issue appears that later results in a claim or a dispute.

Figure 12.1 shows an example of meeting minutes.

Requests for Information

In the field, conditions arise that need clarification. During demolition or excavation, for example, existing conditions can be different from those expected. The drawings may have omissions or errors or can be interpreted in more than one way. A superintendent may need some detail on the drawings explained. There are many reasons explaining the need for further information, and there is a standard procedure for addressing this need. The request for information (RFI) is a form, usually supplied by the contractor, that formalizes this request. It documents the question and the answer. Its purpose is to ensure that all parties are aware of the request and that all agree with the answer.

RFIs can pass through many hands before they are answered. For instance, a supplier may request information from the subcontractor, who in turn requests information

ACC Contracting Company

Job meeting #5
  10/8/01
Renovation of Hygenics Laboratories
Project # 8872

In attendance:
F. Foley (ACC)
T. Brown (ACC)
S. Black (RAB)
P. Bitters (RAB)
R. Clebbs (Hygenics)

cc:
M. Martin
D. McCauley
F. MacIntosh

Initiated	Item #	Issue Discussed	Responsible	Action Date
8/27/98	0001	ACC issued updated schedule on 10/8. Will issue a project status report on 11/5, including schedule update.	ACC	11/5/98
8/27/98	0002	Commissioning schedule—F. Foley to update status after next commissioning meeting on 10/9.	ACC	10/15/98
9/24/98	0003	A/V package awarded to Techno. Coordination meeting held on 9/22. Schedule, submittals, and coordination among trades were discussed.	Record	
9/24/98	0004	Ground floor meeting held on 9/17. ACC issued schedule to subcontractors. Framing 85% complete. Lecture hall framing to begin this week. Windows scheduled for 12/6/98.	Record	
10/8/98	0005	As-built drawings were updated as of 9/26/98. T. Brown to check status. Electrical progress as-builts needed by 10/20/98. T. Brown to check with electrical sub.	ACC	10/15/98
10/8/98	0006	Stem length for W1 fixture resolved. Issue regarding attachment of baffles is unresolved. Sample to be completed by 11/5/98. T. Brown to coordinate.	ACC	11/5/98
10/8/98	0007	P. Bitters to conduct preliminary punchlist of one finished room to serve as a model for all the subs by 10/18.	RAB	10/18/98

FIGURE 12.1 Meeting minutes record the actions and decisions that occur during a meeting. They organize and foster communication among participants

from the superintendent, who in turn requests information from the architect, who sends it along to the engineer or another consultant for the answer. This answer then makes the reverse trip: to the architect, to the superintendent, to the subcontractor, to the supplier. As you can imagine, often the time involved in moving the paper around does not work with the schedule. There are shortcuts, but all parties must be careful that no one is left out of the loop and that any discussions or decisions are formalized. For instance, the supplier could send the request directly to the consultant with copies to all parties in between. This will save many days. Sometimes a phone conversation with the architect or an on-site visit from the engineers produces the answers, and the whole team can keep going. However, there are dangers in taking these shortcuts, especially if there is no follow-up. Decisions made in the field could be made out of context and turn out to be incorrect. For instance, on a recent project, the electrical engineer was out of town on a day that an issue came up in the field. The electrical foreman on the job called the office of the engineer to get clarification on a design point and spoke to a junior assistant. Between the two of them they agreed on the intent of the drawings but never documented the conversation. Many weeks later, the owner was walking through the site and noticed that the network conduit had been run incorrectly. The problem was traced back to that undocumented conversation. The senior engineer, had he known, would have flagged the answer as incorrect. By the time it was discovered in the field, the change had cost $20,000. Such a communication breakdown can happen easily if the project is on a tight schedule. The intent of an RFI is to ensure that this type of situation does not occur. But like any good tool, it is only good if it is used correctly.

The form of the RFI and the numbering system are important. Since this is a contractor's form, it varies in how it appears. However, certain criteria should be met to make the form effective, both for on-site use and for future reference regarding decisions made in the field. Each request is sequentially numbered—as simple as 1, 2, 3, and so on. It should be clear who the request is from. This will give the architect a contact name in case of questions. Drawing references aid the architect and the engineer in getting right to the problem and help future audiences research a point if needed. Usually, the contractor asks for a response by a certain date. This needs to be a realistic request because, in many cases, the architect must research the request before responding. New drawings may be necessary as well. There are certain situations in which information is needed as soon as possible; but if all requests are given that priority, their sheer volume will quickly overwhelm the architect. A log of RFIs is kept by the contractor and the architect. Both will want to track the pathway of these requests and highlight any that may be outstanding. If it is logged in and coded appropriately, the RFI can also supply information to the project team about how many requests come from different areas. This will be helpful for the architectural team for future projects. By understanding common areas of questions, architects can concentrate on how they develop details on future documents.

RFIs are most often direct questions with direct answers that have no other impact on the project. However, they also can be the first step in what eventually becomes a change order or a dispute. If the answer to an RFI leads to a change in money or time, then the change order process will need to begin.

Figure 12.2 shows an example of an RFI.

Daily Reports

The daily report is kept by the superintendent as a record of the day-to-day activities and conditions on the job site. It is usually kept on a preprinted form that minimizes the amount of information that has to be filled in. Although this report is an internal document used to study patterns on the job, it may also be used in the event of a dispute. The report usually has the following components:

- Date and sequential numbering
- Project name and number
- Name of individual filling out the report
- Weather information (A call to the weather bureau means that accurate details can be included, such as the correct temperature. If work activities are disrupted

Contractor Name

Request for Information

Project : *Project Name*	RFI NUMBER:
To: *Architect name*	
From: *Contractor name*	Date: *Date of request*

	Drawing Reference:	Spec Reference:
	Drawing No.	*Spec section, paragraph*

Description of information required:

Example request for information:

Consistent with phase 1 of project, we plan to utilize flexible cable in drywall partitions and hung ceilings. The wiring method will be as follows:
- Hospital grade BX in lab areas
- MC cable in offices and places of assembly
- 3-wire hospital grade cable for special devices
- Emergency circuits to be installed in pipe

Subcontractor: *Electrical subcontractor*   Date required:_____

Requested by: *Name of the person*   Date:_____   Signed:_____

Response:

Example response: This is acceptable and is consistent with the standards set up in Phase 1.

Arch/Eng.: *electrical engineer in this   Date: Signed:
example*

FIGURE 12.2   A typical request for information (RFI) form, with a request from the electrical subcontractor to the electrical engineer. The form flows from the subcontractor to the contractor to the architect to the engineer. To save time, the subcontractor may send the form simultaneously to all parties

by weather conditions and there are subsequent problems in the schedule, this information can help to determine if a time extension is warranted. If a material fails that requires a certain temperature to set or bond, this information is crucial in determining why it failed.)

- Descriptions of activities on the site that day, including deliveries and important visitors (Recording deliveries can substantiate the conditions of a purchase order and, in the event of a schedule delay, determine if the timing of the delivery was a factor.)
- Records of subcontractors working on site (This can aid in deciding over a period of time whether the job is being staffed sufficiently, perhaps preventing a schedule delay or determining responsibility for one.)
- Large equipment on site (Substantial costs are associated with large equipment use. Thus, knowing when the equipment is on site and in use helps determine what payments are owed to the vendor. In the event of an accident, this information can be critical.)

Diaries

These are personal accounts of the day's activities and are useful if a dispute arises. They differ from the daily reports by offering an insight into the attitudes and opinions formed about occurrences on the job. Often diaries are kept by many different people on the site, but each should be in a person's own handwriting in a bound book with his or her signature and date directly under the last line of text, leaving no question about who wrote in the diary and when. Included in diaries are phone conversations, problems or special events, any personal conversations, and anything else the person feels is important. Diaries are, by nature, subjective accounts of what occurred during the day; but the person writing should keep in mind that a diary is a public record and can be used in a legal dispute.

Progress Photographs

Progress photos and other forms of visual recording (such as time-lapse photography or videos) can be taken periodically or when a specific event warrants it. Photos and videos record work progress in a way that narratives and other reports cannot. Videos and time-lapse photography capture methods, process, and progress.

Digital cameras are a way of sharing this information electronically. Details, conditions around the site, quality of installation, progress over time, and critical activity sequences all can be captured much more vividly in a visual format. The primary intent of progress photos is to disclose the quantity and kind of work that was completed since the last batch of photos was taken. The photos should be labeled with the date they were taken and some notation regarding location and subject matter. As with other types of records, photos should be stored so that they are readily retrievable.

Figure 12.3 shows a progress photo.

Monthly Reports

Monthly reports are intended to be read by members of the owner's organization as well as the project team. It is often presented to the owner when the monthly requisition is submitted and may be part of a special administrative meeting that includes a larger number of owner representatives—for example, the financial people. It serves as an executive document and is often distributed to the owner's upper management. The format is usually worked out between the owner and the contractor at the start of the job. It includes a narrative of the job progress to date, a list of subcontractors under contract, cash flow actuals

FIGURE 12.3   Progress photos visually record the status of a project at a specific point in time

Source: Courtesy of Beacon Skanska Construction Company, Boston. Photo by Abbott-Boyle, Inc., Photographers.

and projected, an updated schedule with critical path shown, equal opportunity goals and actuals, safety report, log of construction change requests, change orders, and shop drawing submittals. It is, in effect, a summary of the project on a monthly basis.

Figure 12.4 illustrates a sample table of contents for a typical construction status report to the owner.

Electronic Communication

Through electronic mail (e-mail), many of us have been introduced to the possibilities of communicating through the computer. More than a simple message center, however, computerized communication has extensive uses—from attaching documents to sharing information to using the Internet as a resource. Growing familiarity with computers and owners' expectations about Internet use have led construction companies to invest more heavily in this technology. As a result, Internet use has grown rapidly in the industry. Many companies advertise on the Internet in hopes of reaching a wider audience. Owners are increasingly using this source as a way of getting to know a company's expertise. Its potential as an advertising tool is growing as more owner companies integrate the use of the Internet into their own business practices. The ability to include

Monthly status report
Contents

1. Project overview
   a. Summary
   b. Photographs
2. Financial status
   a. Cost report
   b. Change event log
   c. Cash flow
3. Schedule
   a. Summary bar chart
   b. Project schedule
4. Safety
   a. Site inspection report
5. Document control
   a. Construction change request log
   b. Shop drawings/submittal log
   c. Request for information log
   d. Updated drawing list
6. Administration
   a. Staff organization
   b. EEO/affirmative action
   c. Project directory

FIGURE 12.4 Sample table of contents for a monthly report

video, up-to-date project information, educational information, and links to other sites means that companies can share not only information about their own firm but also have an educational platform. More people will interact with such a rich venue, which can only be good for business. The Internet also is a good in-house tool to involve employees in the development of material posted on the site. Newsletters, project information and photos, and awards and recognition can all be shared by employees and viewed by potential clients. Certainly, management issues need to be worked out about who controls the information that is posted, but companies are taking up the challenge; and as a result, there are thousands of sites to view on the Internet today.

The Internet also has many other valuable uses. It is becoming a common platform for electronic project management programs. Electronic project management systems have evolved over the last 10 years from stand alone software that organized information to web-based systems that encourage collaboration and communication. These systems have the potential to reduce cost and time, and to improve communication, and organization of documents and collaboration. Its full potential has not yet been realized although it is most effective in cutting time related to work flow processes such as contracts, change requests, submittals, and requests for information. Although the future looks assured for some form of web-based project management, there are challenges to realizing its full potential. The technologies needed to support these systems are still not prevalent in many construction site offices; the culture of project teams where information is guarded makes it difficult to readily share information in this way, and much of the software development is still relatively new.

Probably one of the fastest-growing areas for Internet use is research. Many organizations now have information posted on the website. By bookmarking favorite items, the student and the practitioner can have such information instantly. Up-to-date construction data are available through government sites and others such as *Engineering News Record*. Information about labor issues and legislative actions can be found on the Association of General Contractors' site. Site safety tips and news about safety initiatives can be found on OSHA's site. Information about current books, journals, and other publications can also be found through these groups, and most of these sites provide links to other sites, enhancing a user's ability to "surf the net." In the future, books such as this one may actually be online, with date-sensitive information automatically updated. Links could be added to the book, and a search for material would bring the user to specific references.

BOX 12.1

ADVANCED PROJECT COMMUNICATION

Leveraging the Internet and Computer-Aided Design to Achieve Project Goals

by Kenneth H. Stowe, P. E., George B. H. Macomber Company, Boston

To develop and achieve project goals often requires sophisticated computerized models and vast amounts of complex communications. Project management requires attention to lines of communication and the computerized information tools used for access, manipulation, and storage.

Project communications often take place among team members in different companies, separate professions, and isolated geographic areas. Many projects are extremely time-critical and are managed in changing environments, making communication accuracy and speed vital. Pressure to compress project timelines requires faster design, faster decisions, and concurrent design and construction. Project members must work more as a team and less as individuals with different agendas. The Internet is a vital tool serving these projects.

SHARING INFORMATION

Among the electronic vehicles used to share information are e-mail, file attachment, and disk exchange. Many project teams now elect to use a shared, secure website for vital data storage and advanced communications. The data include master schedules, computer-aided design (CAD) files, specifications, drawing and submittal logs, site photographs, meeting minutes, requests for information, change orders, daily field reports, and so on. Sharing eliminates duplication and inaccuracies. Immediate access speeds response. Elements of the project data that are related can even be threaded for better understanding of complex interactions.

Sharing project data has a positive influence on a team. It increases the sense of unity, accountability, and responsiveness

(continued)

BOX 12.1   Continued

when the entire team observes a request for information being submitted and when and how it is answered. The team can collaborate with pictures, CAD, even videos and animation with fewer time or geographical limits. Other members can comment or intervene if necessary, so decisions are made quickly with more participation and, accordingly, with more commitment. Faster, more informed decisions lead to faster time-to-market projects.

INTEGRATING THE MODELS

Creating one secure site for current and archived project information opens the door to computer-integrated construction modeling. Integrated models combine two or more sets of project data to provide powerful decision-making and communication vehicles. Examples include (1) cost and schedule integration to create cash-flow and resource projections; (2) CAD and estimating integration to facilitate quantity takeoff, graphic audit trail, and geographic cost reports; (3) CAD and scheduling integration to create geographic schedule output and storyboards.

EFFICIENCIES BY COMBINING CAD AND INTERNET

Sharing project data often results in more accurate models because more sharing means more input to the design effort. This may include constructability input, phasing requirements, and cost-saving ideas. Three-dimensional features of the CAD model derive greater value because they reach a greater audience earlier in the process. Nongraphical enhancements to CAD models (such as manufacturing data, links to specifications, and so on) generate efficiencies. The CAD model serves as the

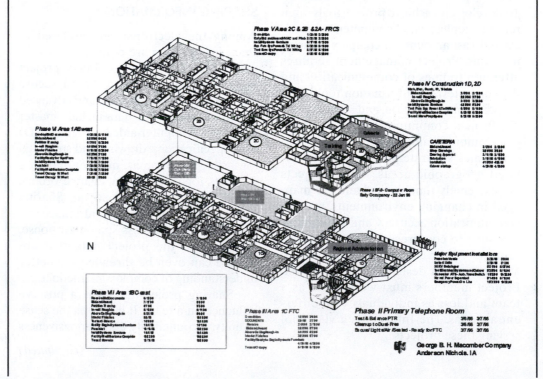

trade and vendor coordination vehicle, providing an electronic as-built.

The project website for one project team allowed CAD to provide efficiencies well beyond design. Centerbrook Architects, working from their Connecticut office on the $20 million phased renovation project at Dartmouth College in Hanover, New Hampshire, posted CAD files to a project website. The owner, consultants, and the construction manager, who lived in three different states, immediately had access to them. As the construction manager, the George B. H. Macomber Company quickly downloaded the CAD files, performed some cost and schedule analysis, and posted some very advanced products back to the project site. The team had collaborated and achieved five positive results:

- Faster distribution of the drawings and savings on printing, packing, and shipping

- Faster and more accurate development of the estimated quantities

- Three-dimensional color output (see the accompanying figure) for better understanding of the estimate and the construction manager's assumptions

- Faster distribution of the estimate and the schedule

- Graphical presentation of the phasing and essential dates

GREATER UNDERSTANDING LEADS TO COMMITMENT

At the conceptual stage, estimators calculated quantities directly from the CAD file and documented their cost estimate graphically, coloring more expensive areas with darker colors. Later, at the schematic

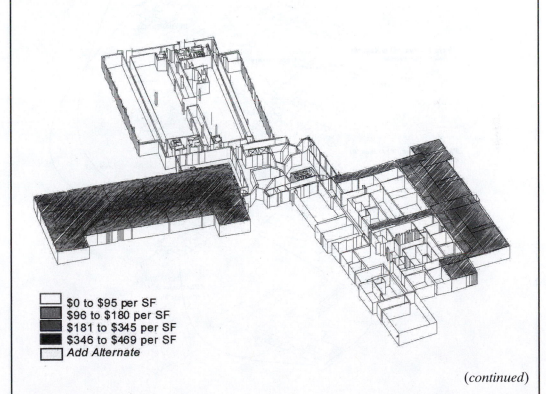

☐ $0 to $95 per SF
▨ $96 to $180 per SF
▨ $181 to $345 per SF
■ $346 to $469 per SF
☐ *Add Alternate*

(*continued*)

BOX 12.1   Continued

phase, they created isometric views of all floors affected on the project and showed the construction phase limits and dates, which departments were moving, and to where. Dates on the graphic were linked to the master CPM schedule, so they were automatically revised as the schedule was refined. These graphics were then posted to the website so the team could immediately view them and print them hundreds of miles away. This teamwork led directly to greater understanding of the scope of work by the project community, greater buy-in, and faster resolution of issues.

Sharing CAD, schedule, and cost models brings up the question of ownership. Who "owns" the data? Who governs the process of changes and enhancements to

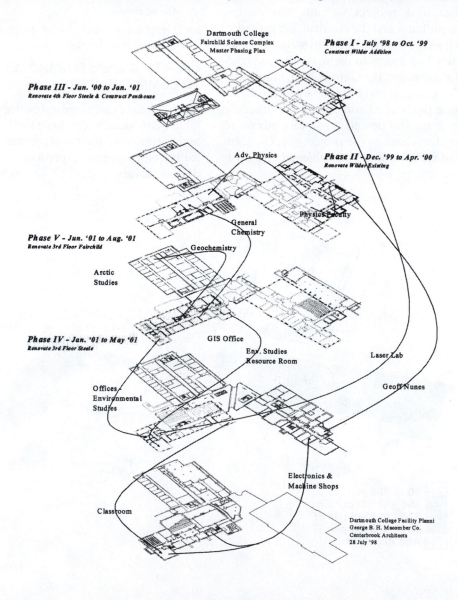

Dartmouth College
Fairchild Science Complex
Master Phasing Plan

Phase I - July '98 to Oct. '99
Construct Wilder Addition

Phase III - Jun. '00 to Jan. '01
Renovate 4th Floor Steele & Construct Penthouse

Adv. Physics

Phase II - Dec. '99 to Apr. '00
Renovate Wilder Existing

Physics Faculty

General
Chemistry

Phase V - Jun. '01 to Aug. '01
Renovate 3rd Floor Fairchild

Geochemistry

Arctic
Studies

Phase IV - Jan. '01 to May '01
Renovate 3rd Floor Steele

GIS Office

Env. Studies
Resource Room

Laser Lab

Offices
Environmental
Studies

Geoff Nunes

Electronics &
Machine Shops

Classroom

Dartmouth College Facility Planni
George B. H. Macomber Co.
Centerbrook Architects
28 July '98

the model? The team must decide the protocols for access and enhancements to the data. In charge of each model should be one skilled person who encourages participation and order and is responsible to the team for the integrity, accuracy, level of detail, and responsiveness of the model.

The potential for advanced project communications using the Internet is vast and offers no less than an opportunity for enhanced decision-making, understanding, acceptance, commitment, and execution resulting in lower costs, higher quality, and earlier completion.

SUBMITTALS

Many submittals are required during construction (see Figure 12.5). Developing an effective tracking system for them will prove invaluable because the number needing to be processed can be daunting. The project team has to agree about which ones will need to be processed immediately and which ones can be processed with more time allowed. Otherwise, the architect and the engineer will be overwhelmed with submittals, all potentially arriving in their offices at once. Submittals include shop drawings, product literature, samples, reports from independent testing agencies, O&M manuals, and warranties. The technical specifications detail what needs to be submitted, and the general conditions explain the procedure for submitting them. Submittals are sent to the designer for review and approval. Before they are submitted, the general contractor reviews each one to ensure that it meets the requirements of the drawings and specifications. By far, the most time-consuming and labor-intensive submittals are the shop drawings.

Shop Drawings

Shop drawings translate the intent of the design documents into a buildable system. To do this, they must be detailed and precise. Thus, review can be time-consuming. Because of the number of people involved in reviewing shop drawings, the process can lag.

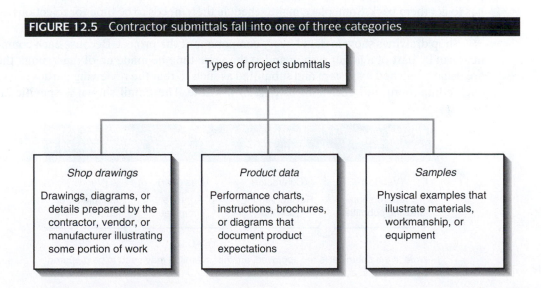

FIGURE 12.5 Contractor submittals fall into one of three categories

Types of project submittals

Shop drawings

Drawings, diagrams, or details prepared by the contractor, vendor, or manufacturer illustrating some portion of work

Product data

Performance charts, instructions, brochures, or diagrams that document product expectations

Samples

Physical examples that illustrate materials, workmanship, or equipment

The contractor must be aware of the areas with potential for delay in order to keep tight control of this flow.

Before construction begins, the contractor submits a preliminary schedule of shop drawings. This is usually worked out with consultation from the subcontractors and suppliers. A careful review of the dates and coordination with the overall schedule of the job can avoid delays later. Once the preliminary schedule is set, the design and construction team review it, highlighting critical items—those that, if delayed, will affect the overall schedule of the job. One example is door frames. If these are late, they will affect the completion of the wall system, which in turn will affect finish of the floor. Such items should be flagged and given special attention as they make their way through the shop drawing approval system.

The person designated to track the shop drawings will have to do the following:

- Make sure they are received on time from the subcontractor or the vendor
- Monitor the length of the review in the contractor's office
- Track the review in the architect's and engineer's office
- Facilitate the back-and-forth comments until an approved system is produced

Figure 12.6 illustrates the submittal process.

Materials cannot be ordered until the shop drawings are approved. Delays in approval are potential scheduling bottlenecks if not handled properly. Understanding factory schedules, plant shutdowns, material runs, supply and demand cycles, delivery times, and so on will help to reinforce the importance of timing on shop drawings. A delay of a week or two from the proscribed schedule can actually result in a much longer delay if other factors come into play (such as a plant shutdown). Turnaround time on shop drawings needs to be carefully coordinated and should be planned early in the project. Some shop drawing reviews take longer than others; those in which other consultants such as engineers are involved by necessity lengthen the time needed for review. Two to three weeks for review is a good rule for most shop drawings. There is usually a log established that shows when the drawings are needed from the subcontractor or supplier, when the contractor needs to issue them to the architect, and how long the architect has to get them back. Someplace in the schedule there needs to be time for rejections and revisions to cycle through the system, especially for custom assemblies.

Shop drawings show in detail every component of the project. Because each component can be part of a larger system and at the same time be made up of many units, they are usually batched by system and submitted as such so that the reviewing parties can see each component and each unit as part of a whole. The detail shown is specific and

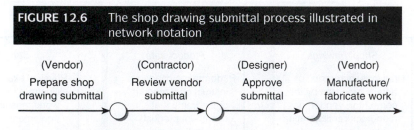

FIGURE 12.6   The shop drawing submittal process illustrated in network notation

(Vendor)	(Contractor)	(Designer)	(Vendor)
Prepare shop drawing submittal	Review vendor submittal	Approve submittal	Manufacture/ fabricate work

Note: If the submittal is not approved, another submittal may need to be prepared by the vendor, and the process repeated.

includes all information needed to assemble the system, down to the type of fasteners used. For instance, an elevator system, its cab, and controls are best designed by the elevator manufacturer. The details of the elevator system installation are developed by the elevator manufacturer and submitted to the architect for review. The review is necessary to ensure that the proposed design is compatible with the overall design program. By seeing the whole assembly, details about installation and fit of materials can be seen as well. This is where the contractor's expertise is heavily relied on. Sometimes the shop drawings will propose a particular method of assembly or use of materials not envisioned in the design documents. Approval of the shop drawing itself does not mean the method is approved. If the proposed method changes the intent of the drawings, the contractor has to specifically tell the architect this, and the architect has to approve the change in writing. If the change results in a change in cost or time on a project, a change order must be issued to document everyone's agreement. The shop drawing process serves as an

---

BOX 12.2

HYATT REGENCY WALKWAY COLLAPSE

On July 17, 1981, 113 people were killed and 186 injured when two suspended walkways collapsed in the Hyatt Regency Hotel in Kansas City. This was the most devastating structural collapse in U.S. history—an accident that could have been prevented if a better-coordinated engineering review had taken place in the shop drawing process.

The hotel's design called for three walkways to span the atrium at the second, third, and fourth floors. The original design specified six single forty-six-foot rods to run from the ceiling through the fourth-floor box beams and on through the second-floor box beams. The box beams were made up of a pair of eight-inch channels with the flanges welded toe to toe so that the weight of the platforms was carried on washers and nuts attached to the hanger rods. The third floor was offset and supported independently on its own set of hanger rods (see Figure A).

During the course of construction, shop drawings were prepared by the steel fabricator suggesting that a set of two hanger rods replace the single hanger rod on the second- and fourth-floor walkways. Thus, a rod would extend from the roof framing to the fourth floor, and a second rod would run from the fourth-floor walkway to the second floor (see Figure B). This change transferred all of the second-floor load to the fourth-floor box beam, doubling the load transmitted through the fourth-floor box beam to the upper hanger rod. This submittal was stamped by the architect, the structural engineer, and the contractor, indicating their review.

The collapse occurred when the washer and the nut on the upper hanger rod pulled through the fourth-floor box beam, sending both platforms to the lobby floor, with the fourth-floor platform landing on top of the second-floor platform. Even though a government investigation found that the original design was inadequate, investigators believed that if the change had not been made, the collapse would not have occurred. The judge held the structural engineering consultants liable for the accident, even though the engineers argued that the steel fabricators should be held responsible.

(continued)

BOX 12.2   Continued

FIGURE A   Schematic of walkways as viewed from the north wall of the atrium

Source: U.S. Department of Commerce/National Bureau of Standards.

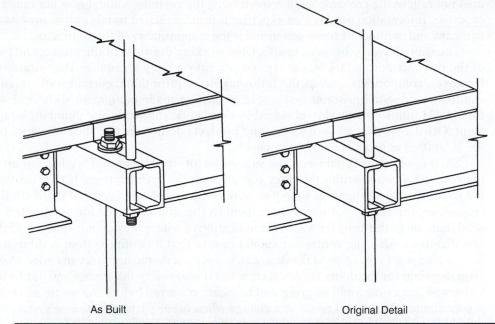

As Built   Original Detail

FIGURE B   Comparison of interrupted and continuous hanger rod details

Source: U.S. Department of Commerce/National Bureau of Standards.

The judge based his ruling on the fact that engineers, as licensed professionals, are responsible for assuring the structural safety of a building's design. He also stated that an engineer should not be allowed to abdicate his or her responsibility to another party, such as the steel fabricator. Further, the purpose of the shop drawing review process is to provide the opportunity for the engineering firm to verify the structural integrity of the design details.

This building failure illustrates the importance of good communication among the project participants since any engineer or architect who took the time to review the impact of this change could have seen the possibility of a structural problem. Unfortunately, it appears that each reviewer stamped the submittal but assumed that someone else would complete the review.

References

"Hyatt Hearing Traces Design Chain." *Engineering News Record,* July 26, 1984.

"Hyatt Ruling Rocks Engineers." *Engineering News Record,* November 28, 1985.

U.S. Department of Commerce, National Bureau of Standards. *Investigation of the Kansas City Hyatt Regency Walkway Collapse.* Washington, D.C.: U.S. Government Printing Office, 1982.

opportunity for the incorporation of cost-saving ideas from contractors, vendors, and manufacturers. These may be formally submitted as part of a formalized value-engineering submittal. However, changing any aspect of the design intent during the shop drawing process is fraught with danger, as in the case of the Hyatt Regency disaster.

Because the shop drawings often contain information that is outside the expertise of the architect or the engineer, they cannot approve them beyond stating that they conform to the intent of the design document. However, as the Hyatt example illustrates, this does not relieve the professional of responsibility for anything within his or her range of expertise. Information outside that expertise is usually related to fabrication process or to means and methods of construction and is the responsibility of the contractor.

The shop drawings become, in effect, the working drawings of the project and part of the contract documents. Not every component on the job requires shop drawings. However, components such as the following do require them: curtain-wall systems; window washing/fall restraint systems; large custom-made equipment such as elevators, HVAC units, structural steel assemblies; millwork; casework; and plumbing equipment. Off-the-shelf items such as flooring products do not require shop drawings but are submitted as product data or samples.

Shop drawings originate with the subcontractor or supplier and are handed up to the contractor, who verifies that they comply with the specifications. If they do, then the handoff to the designer is simply an administrative one. However, if there are discrepancies, the contractor may return them to the subcontractor for resubmittal or send them on to the designer with clear indication of where they do not conform to the specifications. Also, the contractor should ensure that an entire system is submitted before pieces get passed on to the designer. It does not do the architect any good to see shop drawings for the doors, for instance, without also seeing the frames and hardware. Otherwise, approval could be given and fabrication started before the whole assembly is coordinated. This could result in a change when other parts of the same system are detailed and found to be incompatible with the parts already approved.

When a designer reviews a shop drawing, he or she has the option of approving it, approving it with comments, approving it with corrections but requiring a final submittal, or rejecting it in total. The designer stamps this decision on the drawing itself (see Figure 12.7). If the drawing is rejected, the most sensible step for the contractor to take

CANNON	
NO EXCEPTIONS TAKEN	☐
MAKE CORRECTIONS NOTED	☐
REVISE AND RESUBMIT	☐
REJECTED	☐

REVIEW IS FOR CONFORMANCE WITH THE DESIGN CONCEPT OF THIS PROJECT. THIS SUBMITTAL HAS BEEN REVIEWED FOR GENERAL COMPLIANCE WITH CONTRACT DOCUMENTS. CONTRACTOR IS RESPONSIBLE
FOR QUANTITIES DIMENSIONS AND COMPLIANCE WITH CONTRACT DOCUMENTS AND FOR INFORMATION THAT PERTAINS TO FABRICATION PROCESSES, CONSTRUCTION TECHNIQUES AND COORDINATION OF THIS WORK WITH ALL TRADES WHICH WILL BE AFFECTED THEREBY THIS REVIEW IS NULL AND VOID IF SHOP DRAWINGS DEVIATE FROM CONTRACT DOCUMENTS AND DO NOT INDICATE OR NOTE DEVIATIONS.

_____ DATE _____

FIGURE 12.7 Each shop drawing submitted is typically stamped by the designer, who indicates the next course of action

Source: Courtesy of Cannon Design, Boston.

is to set up a face-to-face meeting with all involved parties to work out an acceptable approach. This will save potential repeat resubmittals.

When the shop drawing is accepted, fabrication can begin. The acceptance assumes that all coordination among trades has been accomplished.

Product Data

Product data are submitted as supplements to the shop drawings or to verify that a standard product will meet the specifications. Many things are included under product data: illustrations that show the product, information about the performance of the product, and brochures that describe the product. If the product is as specified by the contract, then product data submissions will be easily approved. However, if the product varies from the contract documents, discussions will take place regarding the relative merits of this product versus the one specified. Sometimes the change saves money for the contractor or the owner. Sometimes the specified product is not available within the time frame needed, and sometimes a new product is introduced onto the market after the specifications were issued. This new product might perform better and thus be an acceptable substitute.

Samples

Samples usually are submitted to show the actual characteristics of a specific material, such as paint colors or finishes, flooring, and wood types. The samples need to be large enough for the designer to understand the actual characteristics because the final finish plan is assembled by the architects using these samples. Sample submission is the first time during the project that team members see actual colors, textures, and finishes.

APPLICATION FOR PAYMENT

Most construction projects are long enough that contractors need to be paid regularly. Usually the contractor submits monthly requests for payment. These are prepared either on a contractor's own form or on AIA Document G702, "Application and Certificate for Payment." In either case, an owner will look for very specific information to be included. The AIA Document G702 is organized as follows:

Line number	Description	Example
	Contract Amount	
1	Original contract sum	90,000
2	Any changes that have been approved	+10,000
3	Total current contract sum (line 1 plus line 2)	100,000
	Total Earned	
4	Total of all work completed and all stored material that has been paid for by the owner	50,000
5	Amount of money retained from total in line 4 (usually 10%)	−5,000
6	Total earned less the money retained (line 4 minus line 5)	45,000
	Payment Already Received	
7	Less previous Certificate for Payment (taken from the prior certificate)	25,000
8	Current payment due (line 6 minus line 7)	20,000
9	Balance to finish, including retainage (line 3 minus line 6)	55,000

To ensure timely payments, the contractor should make sure that there are no mathematical errors and that all the backup information matches the amounts shown on the application face sheet. Once the contractor is sure that the information is put together accurately and that the entire backup is included, he or she will sign the form and have it notarized.

At the beginning of construction, the owner or the architect specifies the procedures for how to submit requests for payment. There may be a review with the owner and the architect before formal submission, or the requisition may be handled through individual reviews. The chosen payment approach affects how many copies of the request will be needed each month—as many as five or as few as one. Each copy must have an original signature and be stamped by a notary public. When the architect receives the requisition, he or she normally passes on applicable sections to the consulting engineers for approval. Each person responsible for signing the requisition tours the site to determine if the work has been completed. There is a certain amount of discretion about determining this since there is a lag time between the requisition and the time when the checks are received. If it is reasonable to assume that certain pieces of work will be complete by the time the checks are received, the architect may approve the requisition.

However, the architect has the discretion to disallow certain costs that the contractor may apply for in that month. There are several reasons why the architect may not want to certify that payment is warranted: if defective work has not been remedied, if third-party claims have been filed, if there is damage caused by the contractor, if the work will not be done in time, or if the quality of the work is continually below what is required in the contract.

Requisitions can represent millions of dollars if a project is going full tilt. Careful preparation is imperative if the contractor wishes to be paid in a timely manner. The requisition is made up of many pieces and looks different depending on the type of contract. In all cases, however, it includes a schedule of values, lien wavers, off-site storage certificates, any approved changes to the contract, and clear indication of retainage. There are many project-specific provisions that must be understood before preparing the request for payment. Most are covered under the specifications, but even there the contractor may find some areas that are unclear. For instance, in the case of changes to the contract, the AIA general conditions allow for reasonable markups but do not specify what is reasonable. The owner normally supplements with his or her own conditions to clarify what is required.

Schedule of Values

As part of the general conditions of the contract, the contractor is required to submit a schedule of values that identifies what each piece of the work is worth (see Figure 12.8). This is used by the owner and the architect as the basis for determining the amount of work in place when the contractor submits progress payment requests. This schedule represents the bids received from the subcontractors plus any costs to be incurred by the contractor in performance of the work.

Stored Material

Sometimes the contractor orders equipment and materials ahead of when they are actually needed on the job. Perhaps a certain piece of equipment, such as an emergency generator, must be ordered long in advance of when it is needed on the site to

Sample schedule of values

Work description	Value	Work description	Subcontractor	Value
General conditions		*Direct work*		
Project manager	$138,500	Site work	J. Derenzo	$ 32,440
MEP coordinator	72,000	Demolition	NASD	440,777
Secretarial	45,000	Earthwork	Flett Co.	2,589
Accounting	14,650	Concrete	Bodgood	234,567
Superintendent	77,000	Masonry	Bertone	145,337
Cutting and repair	14,660	Metals	Capsco	763,466
Site trailer	48,570	Millwork	Waller	257,160
Winter conditions	15,030	Casework	Valley City	1,460,777
Cranes	8,250	Waterproofing	Waldo	47,500
Supplies	16,408	Fireproofing	East Coast	22,670
Cleaning buildings	256,534	Metal wall panels	Cheviot	157,275
Trash chute	19,222	Roofing	Oak	186,880
Dumpsters	60,567	Doors, frames, hardware	West Hartford	413,940
Final cleaning	12,670	Glass and glazing	Salem Glass	141,300
Temporary services	32,450	Curtain-wall restoration	M. L. McDonald	763,099
Legal and professional	9,747	Drywall/rough carpentry	Nardell	998,017
Surveying	3,867	Painting	M. L. McDonald	387,900
Photographs	3,324	Terrazzo	Eastern Floors	93,750
Insurance	53,440	Acoustical ceiling	Cheviot	57,600
Reproductions	30,980	Carpeting, resilient tile	Contours	276,899
Record drawings	2,879	Epoxy flooring	Stonhard	68,100
Deliveries	8,128	Specialties	Automated Solutions	43,582
Office expenses	52,098	Autoclaves	Consolidated	219,800
		Window treatment	Britely	33,350
Total general conditions	**$995,974**	Fixed seating	Krueger	20,815
		Mechanical	E. M. Dugger	2,174,588
		Fume hoods	Kewaunee	201,350
		Pure water system	U.S. Filter	382,990
		Vacuum	Air Energy	62,304
		Mechanical	E. M. Dugger	2,828,174
		Electrical	Broadway	2,466,700
		Temperature controls	Andover	1,067,260
		Total direct costs		**$16,453,056**
Total direct costs	$16,453,056			
Total general conditions	$995,974			
Total cost of the work	$17,449,030			
Contractor's fee	$610,716			
Base contract	**$18,059,746**			

FIGURE 12.8 This schedule of values is for the renovation of a science research lab of 100,000 square feet. These values are the basis of the contractor's cost-control system. The owner uses them to track costs as the invoices are submitted

ensure that it gets there in time. When it arrives, it may have to be stored for some time. This may occur either on the site itself or on some off-site location. The contractor is usually obliged to pay the supplier for this equipment; so although it is not yet installed, the owner may want to authorize either full or partial payment. The owner will want to have clear title to the equipment before these payments are authorized and be assured that the storage methods will protect the equipment until it is installed.

Lien Waivers

Before the owner pays the contractor for work performed, he or she wants to make sure that the contractor is paying the subcontractors in a timely manner. One method of ensuring subcontractor payment is through the lien waiver. So as not to overburden the contractor, the owner can ask for lien waivers for work that was paid for the prior month. By requiring these partial liens, the owner ensures that the prime contractor is paying the subcontractors but does not require that the prime pay the subcontractors before he or she is paid. If the partial liens were required for work being invoiced, either the prime would have to pay the subcontractors before being paid, or the subcontractors would have to waive their legal rights before they were paid.

Retainage

To have some protection regarding the quality and completeness of work as it is being performed, the owner normally holds back a percentage of the work for a period of time. This percentage is usually about 10 percent of the money that has been earned by the contractor. The contractor, in turn, holds this amount back from the subcontractors. On some projects, the money is held throughout the life of the project. In others, especially large projects, the retainage is reduced halfway through the project to 5 percent and sometimes eliminated altogether. Retainage allows the owner to have some leverage over the contractor in the case of failure to pay the subcontractors or failure to complete the job.

Final Payment

Final payment to the contractor will be made after the contractor determines that the work is complete and all other contract matters have been resolved. The owner will require the back-up documentation to support these determinations before releasing the final payment. In many cases, the owner may engage the services of their own legal counsel to review some of this documentation. In addition, it is the architect's responsibility to assist the owner in ascertaining that these documents are in order and that, in fact, the work is complete. Once this is determined, a final certificate for payment can be submitted. The required documentation should be spelled out clearly in the agreement with the contractor and usually includes the following:

- Proof that all outstanding bills for payroll, material, and equipment connected with the work that could be the responsibility of the owner have been paid or otherwise settled. If there are outstanding claims against the project, the contractor must be clear about their nature and if substantial, the owner may ask for a lien bond to protect the owner.
- Waiver of liens from all subcontractors as required by the general conditions and by the mechanics lien laws of the jurisdiction involved

- Completion of the punch list
- Turnover copies of all approved shop drawings and product data
- Filing of all guarantees and warranties and delivery of these and certificates of inspection to the owner
- Submission of O&M manuals, extra parts, and surplus material required by the specifications
- Completion of as-built drawings and specifications
- Training of owner personnel as required by the contract specifications
- Completion of all system and equipment commissioning
- If an OCIP (Owner Controlled Insurance Project)—filing statement of completed operations from each subcontractor

In some cases, there may be a delay in some part of the work. In this case, the owner can authorize a partial final payment and keep as a balance a sum sufficient to complete the delayed work.

CHANGES TO THE WORK

Despite everyone's best efforts, there are always changes in the work. The contract specifically includes procedures for dealing with changes when they occur. How changes are handled is the real test of a team's ability to work effectively. There is a tendency during a change to look for blame, which can be counterproductive to the health of the project and slow resolution of the change. Nevertheless, discussions about responsibility must occur since in some cases the contractor has to absorb the change and in some cases the owner or the architect has to absorb it. For instance, a contractor may have assigned cleaning at the end of the day to a subcontractor. The subcontractor may contend that he or she did not carry the price for doing this work. In this case, the issue is between the subcontractor and the contractor, and neither the owner nor the architect gets involved. The change involves someone's scope of work but no change to the overall job scope.

Because changes happen while the work is progressing, they can be a source of conflict among the owner, the architect, and the contractor. For the owner, any change to the contract is unwelcome because it can mean additional costs in money or time. The architect or the engineer does not like changes because they could mean that the original intent of the design will be compromised. Changes are also disruptive to the contractor, who has planned out the job based on the original scope. For all parties involved, changes mean more work. However, they are a fact of life on a construction project. Whether initiated by the owner, the designer, or the contractor, they become necessary when there are unanticipated conditions encountered during construction.

Unanticipated conditions can be defined in a number of ways:

- Differing site conditions
- Errors or omissions on the drawings or specifications
- Changes in regulatory requirements
- Design changes often initiated by the owner or the architect
- Factors affecting the completion date
- Changes in quantities beyond limits allowed in a unit price contract

Owner-directed changes are the most straightforward to process. There is no dispute about the necessity of the change or the scope because the owner is directing it. Instead, the discussions center around the impact of the change on the schedule and the logistics of the rest of the project, financial impact, and design issues. Changes based on the claim that the plans and specifications are defective or impractical are more difficult to sort out. When making their bid, contractors interpret the plans and specifications in the most economical manner to ensure lower production costs. Owners and architects interpret these documents to ensure the highest standard of performance. Sometimes these interpretations are at odds.

The end results of a change may involve one or all of the following: changed scope, changed price, or changed time. How much of the scope, the price, and the time are affected depends on the specific circumstances of the change. To evaluate this, the AIA has established an accepted procedure that consists of the following steps:

1. The contractor submits a request for information.
2. The architect determines that a change may be needed.
3. The architect asks for pricing through a proposal request.
4. The contractor submits pricing.
5. The architect reviews pricing.
6. The owner approves pricing.
7. The architect issues a change order that is approved by all parties.

Changes can be processed in a variety of ways. The preferred method is the one just described, but sometimes circumstances dictate a different method. Following are three common procedures for processing changes:

1. **Proposal requests.** The contractor is asked to produce pricing based on a description of the scope and any necessary sketches. These are issued by the architect through a proposal request form. When the contractor receives this document, he or she will request pricing from the subcontractors. Once the contractor submits the pricing for the change and the owner approves the pricing and the scope, a change order can be issued. Only after the change order is issued will the work be executed. Use of this form and the procedure that it initiates gives the architect and the owner the opportunity to fully evaluate the change. It also gives the contractor time to adequately price all aspects of the change and make adjustments in his or her own resources to accomplish the change.

2. **Change directives.** A change may need to be executed as soon as possible. Waiting until a definitive price is assembled can actually cost the project more money and more time. In such cases, the contractor is often issued a construction change directive, which takes the place of a proposal request. It describes the change just as the proposal request does and is also accompanied by backup sketches and further explanation. The difference is in the instructions to the contractor. Whereas the proposal request clearly states that it is not a direction to proceed with the work, the change directive instructs the contractor to proceed with the change. Usually there is an estimate of the work prepared first, but this estimate may not take into account all the effects of the change.

3. **Supplemental instructions.** Minor changes in the work that do not affect time or cost can be approved by the architect alone. He or she may pick up an ambiguity in the documents when reviewing them. Instead of waiting for an RFI, the architect may want to clarify the document. This approach normally is used when the architect does not

anticipate any cost or time effect. However, if the contractor feels that there is a cost or time effect, he or she will issue a proposal stating what that effect might be. The procedure then enters the change order stream.

Change Orders

After the contract is signed, any change on the job is approved through the change order process. Change orders are used when there is agreement among owner, architect, and contractor about the amount of the cost adjustment and the contract time. When approved by the owner, the change order becomes part of the contract.

Ideally the actual work in the field takes place after the change orders are executed. Although this does happen, there are often cases when the work must proceed to avoid schedule delays. This puts the owner in a vulnerable position. Unlike the bid situation, there is no competitive pricing in the changes. Because changes happen during construction, the work force is already under contract. The costs, of course, are negotiated; but to minimize conflicts during this time, the contractor must be careful and clear about the costs and the scope of the changes. It is in everyone's best interests to process change orders efficiently. This avoids dragging out issues and creating possible schedule ramifications.

The change order form originates with either the contractor or the architect, depending on the wording of the contract. The form is usually a standard AIA one and includes the following:

- Boxes to be checked for each recipient of the change order
- Project name and address
- Sequential number
- Date when change order is issued
- Description of the change
- Information about the original contract sum and any previous changes
- Amount of money that the contract increases or decreases as a result of the change
- Signature lines for owner, contractor, and architect

After the contractor submits the change order, the architect reviews it for scope and pricing. It is important for the contractor to include all the costs involved with the change before submitting the change order. This way the designer and the owner can understand the whole implication of the change before approving any single component of it. Submitting all the costs together can prove burdensome to the contractor if the work has to precede the approval process. In such cases, some of the subcontractors will have incurred costs and want to be paid. Costs that are not known right away can hold up payment to the subcontractor for work already performed.

Change orders are not only used for changes in price. They also cover changes in the schedule of payments, the completion date, and the plans and specifications. Any of these can be changed with no effect on the cost of the work.

Changes frequently have impacts on other parts of the work that are not directly included in the change, and it is sometimes difficult for the contractor to understand all of them when the change order is being prepared. At the same time, it is only fair for the contractor to be compensated for these impacts. To ensure that the option is open, the contractor should include a clause when preparing the change order that allows for submittal of impact charges.

Change orders generate many of the disputes on a construction project. Therefore, it is important for everyone involved to be clear during contract negotiations about the conditions around these changes. "Who will sign?" "what form will be used?" "what level of detail will be required?" should all be worked out in the original contract negotiations. Costs that will be allowed ought to be discussed in detail as well. Percentages for overhead and profit, general conditions markup, and markup on subcontractor work as well as on the vendors who work for the subcontractors all should be worked out so that they will not be part of the negotiations.

Extension of Time

One of the most difficult changes to price and negotiate is one that asks for an extension of time. There are many reasons why the contractor asks the owner for an extension of time to complete the work. Sometimes this extension is for time only, and sometimes it is accompanied by extra costs. These delays can be excusable; the delay may be caused by conditions outside anyone's control, such as harsh weather. The contractor is entitled to extra time but no extra cost in this case. Extensions of time can also be inexcusable, which means the contractor should have been able to control the situation that led to the delay and therefore will get no time or money compensation. A third category is compensable, which means that the cause of the delay was under the owner's control. In this case, the contractor is entitled to time allowed plus any impact costs.

How time extensions are handled depends on the circumstances. The owner can sometimes be the cause of delays. If the owner organization is not set up adequately to respond to construction situations, response time can be slow. This can occur either because there are too many people in the decision/approval loop or through inexperience in dealing with the size and complexity of a specific project. The owner is responsible for many of the permits that need to be in place. Unless told otherwise at the time of the bid, the contractor prices the work based on timely regulatory approvals and timely access to the site. The owner needs to ensure that this access is clear and all approvals in place. The owner also has to ensure that the work of other contractors or the owner's employees does not interfere with the work of the contractor. Such delays lead to a compensable time extension. The architect can also be the cause of delays. If shop drawings are not approved in a timely manner, if RFIs are not answered adequately, if the drawings have omissions or are not adequately detailed, if samples and mockups are not approved in a timely manner, the contractor may be delayed.

CLAIMS AND DISPUTES

Claims are unresolved issues that occur during construction and remain unresolved after the job is complete. If they are resolved during the life of the job, that resolution can be formalized by a charge order. Since pursuit of claims can be expensive for all parties, the best outcome is for them to be resolved through the change order process. If this is not possible, negotiation of changes is done through arbitration or mediation or, if these fail, litigation. The contract documents require the contractor to let the owner and the architect know as soon as possible, usually within a set number of days, if there is potential for a claim. The first step, after notification of a claim, is for the architect to review the claim and either recommend that it be settled, reject the claim, or suggest a compromise. If the claim still stands after the architect's recommendation, then it either enters arbitration or mediation.

Typically, claims fall into a few general categories. They can be the result of a disagreement about whether a specific item was covered under the contract documents or an extra cost to the contractor. Claims sometimes arise over concealed or unknown conditions when there is disagreement about whether the contractor should have anticipated them. A third category is over delays in the job and disagreements about who caused them.

Contract language can require mediation and/or arbitration depending on how the owner wants to handle disputes. Either method is handled through the procedures and rules set up by the American Arbitration Association (AAA)'s construction industry arbitration rules. The AAA is a nonprofit organization that offers dispute resolution for a variety of businesses. Construction disputes tend to be more technical than those of other businesses, with many facts to research and facets to uncover.

Those who choose to enter into mediation agree to attempt to reach a settlement by direct negotiations between the parties themselves. In this case, the mediator participates impartially in the negotiations, guiding the parties to a mutually acceptable settlement. The obvious advantage is that the claim can be settled with little outside assistance. This may lead to a timelier closure and less money spent settling the claim. Those who enter arbitration, on the other hand, are voluntarily submitting their dispute to a disinterested party for final and binding determination. This is not as desirable and could end up costing a substantial amount of money in administrative costs and take a long time. Dispute resolution is discussed in more detail in Chapter 13.

Conclusion

Job-site administration requires diligence, organization, clear procedures, and an understanding of the importance of consistent record keeping. At the end of the job, a good administrator will have assembled a complete history of the project. The filing system will contain all communications that occurred during the job as well as all the submittals and changes to the job that have become part of the contract documents.

These documents are essential for all parties to the contract. The architect, the owner, and the contractor will all benefit from the ready retrieval of specific documents both during construction and after the project is finished. At the end of the job, these records are turned over to the architect for submittal to the owner. If, after the job is complete, there is a dispute or a court case, these documents can help to resolve the issue in a fair and unbiased manner with less reliance on individual memories.

During the life of the building, these documents, if filed correctly by the owner, help facility managers make decisions about changes to the facility, repairs, and maintenance and understand performance expectations.

Chapter Review Questions

1. Job diaries are subjective accounts of what occurred during the course of the construction workday. True or false?
2. An RFI is a formal request for information necessary to help clarify construction operations. True or false?
3. Weather information is typically reported on a daily report. True or false?
4. Meeting minutes are confidential documents kept internally within the organization that recorded them. True or false?

5. What is the name of the document that authorizes the start of construction?
   a. Notice of award
   b. Notice to proceed
   c. Notice of agreement
   d. Notice of intent
   e. None of the above

6. Which of the following is *not* an example of a project submittal?
   a. Product data
   b. Addenda
   c. Shop drawing
   d. Material samples

7. What does the Hyatt story illustrate?
   a. The importance of proper hotel architecture
   b. The important role of engineering in the design/build process
   c. The importance of thoroughly reviewing shop drawings
   d. The importance of building codes

8. What is the traditional percentage used for owner retainage?
   a. 5
   b. 8
   c. 10
   d. 15
   e. 20

9. Obtaining lien waivers protects the owner in which of the following ways?
   a. It prevents paying for work that has not been completed.
   b. It helps prevent overcharging.
   c. It protects the owner from being subject to a mechanic's lien.
   d. It prevents duplicate or fraudulent invoices.
   e. All of the above are correct.

10. Which of the following is *not* the normal reason for a change in a lump-sum or fixed price contract?
    a. Differing site or unforeseen conditions
    b. Delays caused by contractor inactivity
    c. An increase or decrease in owner requirements
    d. An error in the design documents

11. In a typical application for payment, the contractor has the option of submitting back-up information separately from the application. True or false?

Exercises

1. Investigate the specifications for a project that you are familiar with and prepare a list of all of the submittals required. Note the recipient of each submittal. How many copies are required for each? How many days are allotted for designer review? Owner review?

2. Prepare the meeting minutes for the next meeting you attend. (This may or may not be school-related.) Investigate the different forms that companies use to prepare minutes and adopt the form you feel is best.

3. Visit a local project or company and research a recent change that has occurred. Answer the following questions:
   a. What is the nature of the change?
   b. What caused the change?
   c. How was the change identified? By which party?
   d. How long did it take for the change to be resolved?
   e. What was the impact of the change on the project's scope, budget, and schedule?

13

CONSTRUCTION LAW

**Christopher L. Noble, Esq.,
and Heather G. Merrill, Esq.**

Hill & Barlow

Chapter Outline

Introduction
The Role of Government
     Federal Statutes and Regulations
     State Statutes and Regulations
     Local Ordinances and Bylaws
The Role of Courts
     State and Federal Court Systems
     Jurisdiction
     Common Law Torts
The Role of Contracts
     Contract Formation
     Contract Interpretation
     Statutory Controls
     Damages
     Equitable Relief
     Defenses
Dispute Resolution
Conclusion

Student Learning Objectives

In this chapter you will learn the following:

1. The role of government in the creation of the statutes and regulations that govern the construction process

2. The hierarchy of the U.S. court system and the manner in which the courts interpret statutes, regulations, and local ordinances

3. What must be done to form a legal contract

4. The methodologies employed for interpreting, resolving, and preventing contract disputes

INTRODUCTION

This chapter describes the legal rules that govern the design and construction processes. These rules, which are constantly evolving, have three primary sources: Governments develop and adopt statutes and regulations at the federal, state, and local levels; courts interpret and enforce statutes and regulations and apply common law principles to resolve disputes; and project participants make many of their own rules by entering into contracts for goods and services. Frequently, these participant-developed rules include alternative methods of managing and resolving disputes in an effort to avoid having to go to court during or after construction of the project.

THE ROLE OF GOVERNMENT

Statutes are normally passed by the majority vote of a legislative body at the federal, state, or local level and are approved by the chief elected officer of that governmental unit, such as the president, governor, or mayor. Statutory language is sometimes detailed and specific, but it can also consist of general expressions of legislative policy. Especially in the latter case, many statutes grant rule-making authority to administrative agencies in the executive branch of government. The rules adopted pursuant to this authority are usually called *regulations*. Regulations may set forth such things as the details of compliance with the statutes, what forms must be completed, where to file materials, how approval is granted, and how to appeal unsatisfactory results. Regulations fill in details omitted from the statute, but they must be consistent with it or face possible invalidation by the courts. Every project will be affected in some way by federal, state, and local statutes and regulations.

Federal Statutes and Regulations

The federal government may pass statutes that relate to the health, safety, or welfare of citizens or to interstate commerce. Although this covers a broad arena of issues, a federal statute may be determined to be beyond the power of the federal government if it fails to relate to a power specifically granted in the U.S. Constitution. Most federal laws apply across the board to many industries and commercial activities and, therefore, affect the construction industry only incidentally. These include the National Labor Relations Act (NLRA), the Fair Labor Standards Act (FLSA), the Occupational Safety and Health Act (OSHA), and the Americans with Disabilities Act (ADA).

In general, federal statutes take precedence over state or local laws related to the same subject matter. This is called *preemption*. If the federal government has the right to regulate a particular area and chooses to assume regulation of that area, the state or local government may not do so. Ordinarily, the federal act provides a minimum threshold and permits state or local governments to regulate the area more strictly if they so elect. In certain other areas, such as copyright and patent protection, the federal government may prohibit further regulation.

Some federal acts work hand in hand with state statutes in a symbiotic relationship. One example of this is the ADA, which is a federal statute requiring, among other things, that facilities serving the public be accessible to people with disabilities. Although the ADA and regulations adopted under it contain many guidelines for how this must be accomplished, a number of states have also enacted statutes that provide more guidance with respect to how buildings ought to be designed and constructed to accommodate the needs of individuals with disabilities. New and renovated buildings must comply with both state and federal accessibility rules, and in some cases compliance with one will constitute compliance with the other.

State Statutes and Regulations

States have broad powers of regulation and lawmaking. Many state laws, like federal laws, have broad application and only affect the construction industry incidentally. Certain state laws, however, are particularly designed to regulate the construction industry.

Licensing Laws

Licensing laws establish the qualifications one must possess to practice professions such as architecture and engineering, or to perform work in the plumbing, electrical, and other trades. In some states, but not all, contractors and construction managers are also required to meet certain qualifications and obtain a state license to practice. In general, applicants for a license must meet certain education requirements, must devote a period of time to apprenticeship or practical training, and must pass a written or practical test of skills. Typically, licenses are valid for a year, but may require renewal on a longer or shorter schedule.

Mechanics' Lien Laws

Mechanics' lien laws are another set of state statutes designed to apply specifically to the construction industry. Who may obtain a mechanics' lien, what actions are required to perfect and enforce the lien, and how the public is made aware of the lien are all matters set forth in the mechanics' lien law of each state.

Mechanics' lien laws often vary significantly from state to state. Their general purpose is to permit someone who provides labor and/or materials for a construction project to obtain a lien on the underlying real estate for the value of the goods and services incorporated into the work. These laws are meant to overcome the problem that once the materials are incorporated into the work or the services are performed, the contractors and material suppliers have little leverage to obtain payment—one cannot easily repossess the bricks and mortar once a building is erected. A lien on real estate is a significant weapon in the battle to recover payment. If correctly filed, a mechanics' lien is valid against both the current and future owners of the property. Therefore, the project typically cannot be sold or financed until all outstanding liens are resolved by payment of the underlying debt, by proving that the underlying debt is invalid, or by providing a bond sufficient to cover the debt in the event it is proven to be valid. Ultimately, a lien can be foreclosed and the debt paid from the proceeds of the sale of the real estate.

While the statutory requirements can vary greatly from state to state, most lien laws follow one of several common models. Often, there is a requirement that a notice of contract be filed with a public records office, such as a registry of deeds or city clerk's office. The notice may be required to be filed prior to performing the work or before completion of the work. Sometimes the mere filing of a notice of contract creates the lien. In other states, a certificate must be filed stating the amount owed. In all states, a court action to enforce the lien must be filed within a certain period of time after the filing of the notice of contract, statement of claim, or completion of the work, depending on the state's particular statute. Failure to bring the action within the time required will cause the lien to be automatically dissolved.

Who may be entitled to a mechanics' lien also varies from state to state. In general, contractors, subcontractors, and materials suppliers are entitled to a mechanics' lien. In some states, architects, engineers, and other professionals may be entitled to a lien as well. Familiarity with the mechanics' lien law in the state in which a project is located can be critically important to everyone connected with its design or construction.

State Building Codes

Most states have enacted detailed building codes, either by statute or by regulation. Some states have adopted statewide codes, while others have delegated both adoption and enforcement of codes to local cities, counties, and towns. Most state and local codes are based on one or another national model, such as the Building Officials and Code Administrators International, Inc., Code or the Southern Building Code. A new international building code has recently been drafted by the International Code Council in an effort to further standardize state and local codes.

Local Ordinances and Bylaws

Local statutes, often called *ordinances* or *bylaws*, can have a critical impact on all construction projects. For instance, local zoning ordinances often regulate building dimensions and other design and construction features. Typically, zoning ordinances identify certain areas of the municipality in which particular uses are permitted. Within those areas, or *zones*, there may be great differences in such things as height limitations, lot size requirements, side, front, and rear yard setbacks, and floor area ratios (FARs).

The municipality may require plan review or approval by a planning board; zoning board; board of appeal; board of selectmen; or other municipal board, agency, or official. Special permits, variances, and conditional use permits may be required. At a minimum, the municipal officer charged with approving construction (generally, the building inspector or building department) will be required to review plans to ensure compliance with the zoning and building requirements, as well as with the state or local building code. He or she will also be required to inspect the project during construction and on completion to confirm that it is built in accordance with all of these legal requirements and the previously approved plans.

THE ROLE OF COURTS

Courts are charged with interpreting statutes, regulations, and local ordinances. They also apply *common law principles* to resolve disputes. Common law is the body of law that has developed over time through the courts' interpretation of legal principles. Common law is binding unless and until specifically overruled by the legislature through a statute addressing the particular issue in question.

State and Federal Court Systems

Court systems in the United States are all based on a strict hierarchy. In the federal court system and most state court systems, there are three levels of courts: the trial court, a court of initial appeal, and a court of final appeal. The court of initial appeal is usually called an *appeals court* or, as in the federal system, a *court of appeals*. The court of final appeal is usually called the *supreme court*.

Disputes are resolved initially by a trial court, where a *trier of fact* (either a judge or a jury, depending on the type of case and the election of the parties) listens to testimony and reviews documents regarding the facts of the case and, sometimes, hears opinions from experts in the fields concerned. In a jury trial, the judge is responsible for explaining the law to the members of the jury, who are then charged with deciding how the law applies to the particular facts at hand.

After a trial, either party may appeal the decision to the next higher court. Finally, if either party is not satisfied with the result at the appeals court, it may request a further appeal by the state or federal supreme court. The supreme court of any given jurisdiction is typically very selective in which cases it will accept for review, and must initially determine that the matter is worthy of its review. A minority of cases are granted a hearing at the supreme court level.

Jurisdiction

The federal and state courts run in parallel courses. Most disputes are brought and resolved in state courts. Federal courts have very limited jurisdiction and, unless there is a specific basis for bringing the matter in federal courts, all matters must be tried in the state courts. The most common bases for federal court jurisdiction are when the action is based on a federal statute, when the claim relates to interstate commerce, or when there is diversity between the parties. *Diversity* means that the disputing parties are citizens of different states. The federal courts in such instances are granted jurisdiction so that no one party is disadvantaged by being a "foreigner." In theory, the federal court provides a neutral forum in which the parties may resolve their disputes, despite the fact that it may be located in the home state of one of the parties.

Common Law Torts

American law dates back centuries to the Magna Carta and British law. Since that time, courts have been developing and interpreting principles of law that have been accepted as the foundation of our society. *Torts* (literally, wrongs against people or property) are one of the areas in which the common law has its greatest impact in modern life. Few torts are statutory. There is no law, in most states, that defines negligence. All that we know about what constitutes negligence derives from the common law, that is, the accumulated wisdom of the highest courts of the various jurisdictions over many years. Business torts, such as interference with contractual relations, are also often based on common law principles.

Negligence

Negligence is one of the most common bases of liability in our legal system. *Negligence* is defined as the failure to exercise the degree of care that would be exercised by a reasonably prudent person under similar circumstances. The failure must cause a reasonably foreseeable harm to a reasonably foreseeable plaintiff. For example, if the steps of a building are improperly designed so as to be unsafe, negligence may exist. The first question would be whether a reasonably prudent architect would have designed the steps in such a fashion. If the answer is no, then the next question is whether the harm was reasonably foreseeable (e.g., a fall down the stairs causing a broken leg) and the person injured was reasonably foreseeable (e.g., a visitor to the building). If all of these questions cannot be answered affirmatively, there is no basis for liability. If the architect designed the steps in accordance with accepted practice, the fall may be merely an accident for which no one is legally responsible.

Strict Liability

In some instances, the legislature or courts have determined that a danger is so great that it matters not whether the person acted reasonably under the circumstances. When liability is imposed without fault, it is called *strict liability*. A construction company, for example, is strictly liable for the negligence of its employees while performing their assigned duties, despite the fact that the company may not have any knowledge of or particular involvement in the particular activity. An extremely dangerous activity, such as blasting, may give rise to strict liability for any harm that it may cause, even if the persons conducting the activity did so with due care.

Business torts

Bad faith interference with existing or prospective business relations may give rise to liability, such as when an architect maliciously advises an owner to reject a proposed subcontractor or to terminate a nondefaulting contractor. Some states have also adopted statutes that create tort-like causes of action on account of such things as "unfair or deceptive trade practices."

Defamation

Libel and slander are two types of defamation. In general, *libel* is an untrue written statement causing damage to another, while *slander* is an untrue oral statement. Performance evaluations, press releases, reports to bonding companies, and other project-related communications could, if egregiously untrue, be considered defamatory. For this reason, such communications should always be temperate in tone and based on verifiable facts.

THE ROLE OF CONTRACTS

Governments and courts have the power to impose rules on individuals and companies that do not necessarily have close working relationships with one another. Of course, it takes many such relationships to design and construct a modern building or public work. The primary rules governing these relationships are contained in *contracts*, usually in written form, between and among the project participants. Contracts structure and define the project delivery methods described in Chapter 4. Although the parties and the subject matter may be different, all contracts must be consistent with a common set of legal principles.

Contract Formation

Not every purported agreement is an enforceable contract. A contract may be written or oral, but is only formed when there has been an offer to do or provide something that is accepted by another party and is supported by consideration. In addition, each party to the contract must have the capacity to enter into the contract.

Offer

An *offer* is the first step to forming a contract. One party tells the other, "I will do X for you" or "I will provide Y to you." An offer does not usually need to be made in writing, does not have to be on a particular form, and does not need to clearly state that it is, in fact, an offer. A letter, a verbal statement, or a course of dealing can be enough to establish offer, sometimes to the surprise and corresponding dismay of one party or another.

Acceptance

No contract is formed unless the receiving party has accepted the offer. An offer may usually be accepted verbally, in writing, or by conduct indicating acceptance. For example, if an employer offers a job to a worker, the worker may accept the offer by telephone, in a letter, or simply by appearing for work. Offers may be withdrawn (unless otherwise specifically stated in the offer) at any time prior to acceptance. If someone accepts the offer, but on materially different terms (for example, a contractor offers to build a home for a lump sum of $500,000, but the owner crosses out $500,000 and substitutes $400,000), it would not be an acceptance but merely a counteroffer.

Sometimes parties become involved in what is known as a "battle of the forms" where an offer is tendered on one form (with specific terms) and the acceptance is delivered on another form, agreeing to all the material terms (such as price, description, and timing) but modifying other less important terms. For example, a materials supplier sends a proposal to the construction manager for certain materials on the supplier's standard form, which includes a page and a half of fine print setting out a variety of terms and conditions. The construction manager sends back an acceptance of the quantity, price, description, and delivery dates, but on the construction manager's standard form that includes two pages of fine print contradicting some of the terms contained in the supplier's form (such as what form of requisition is to be used, when payments are due, how notices of breach are delivered). The general rule in such a case is that the acceptance is valid, the contract is formed, and the terms are those contained in the acceptance form, unless disputed in a timely manner.

In construction procurement, an invitation to bid is usually not considered to be an offer, but merely an invitation to make an offer. The bids are considered to be offers, and the contract award is considered to be an acceptance.

Consideration

All contracts must be supported by consideration. *Consideration* is something of value being exchanged on both sides of the transaction. Consideration is often money, but need not be. A young designer may supply architectural services in exchange for publicity and experience. A materials supplier may provide materials to a general contractor in exchange for labor on another project. However, if an electrician provides services without expectation of payment or any other compensation, there is no consideration and, therefore, no contract. In such a case, the electrician is providing the service as a "favor" or "gift" and cannot be sued for breach of contract if he or she fails to perform. (However, if the electrician does the job in a negligent manner, he or she might be liable under a tort theory, as discussed above.)

Capacity

In addition, all parties to a contract must have the capacity to contract. Individuals must be of legal age (in most states, 18) and they must also be of sound mind. For example, a contractor may enter into an agreement to construct a new home for an elderly client. At the time, the contractor notices that the client is forgetful and perhaps eccentric, but thinks nothing of it. At a later date, family members may claim that the client lacked capacity and, therefore, the contract cannot be enforced. The construction professional should make such inquiries as may be necessary to determine that the client has capacity and to document those facts.

In the case of a corporate party, a contract must be authorized by an officer or the board of directors, depending on its relative size and magnitude. That is why, in some cases, an owner or contractor may require the other party to provide a certificate confirming that its board has approved the contract in question.

Contract Interpretation

Unfortunately, it is not always the case that what is written in the contract gives clear direction to the parties or the courts. Sometimes the language can be ambiguous, unclear, or capable of multiple interpretations. For the sake of consistency, courts have developed rules about how contracts will be interpreted.

Parol Evidence Rule

The parol evidence rule relates to when information that is not contained within the "four corners" of the contract will be considered in any dispute. One party may argue as follows: "That may be what the contract says, but that was never what we agreed to do." Unless there is a patent ambiguity on the face of the contract, however, courts will generally not admit evidence of information outside of the contract to resolve the dispute. The court will look first to the language of the contract to resolve the dispute, absent an allegation of fraud or subsequent amendment to the contract.

Plain Meaning

In general, the court will give the words in a contract their *plain meaning*, which usually means their common or usual meaning, rather than a contrived interpretation favoring one position or another. The contract should say what the parties mean in the most clear and simplest manner.

Statutory Controls

Although contracts are largely a private matter between the parties, there are certain important statutes that should be considered when entering into a contract.

Statute of Frauds

The statute of frauds requires certain contracts to be in writing. The statute of frauds varies from state to state, but in most states wills and contracts related to the conveyance of land must be written in order to be enforced. Normally, contracts relating to design and construction are not required to be committed to writing, but it is usually a good idea to do so.

Statute of Limitations

Statutes of limitations set outside dates for commencing litigation. Statutes of limitations may be different for different types of lawsuits. For example, negligence, malpractice, and contract claims may all have different statutes of limitations ranging from one year to ten years or more. Statutes of limitations generally state that they begin to run when the "cause of action accrues." For a contract claim, this would normally be the time of the breach of the contract. For a personal injury claim, it would normally be the date of the injury.

In some cases, the statute of limitations is *tolled* or put on hold. Statutes of limitations for injury to minors are often tolled until the minor reaches the age of eighteen. Statutes of limitations are also tolled if the condition giving rise to the claim is hidden. This is known as the *discovery rule*, which means that until the injured party has discovered, or reasonably should have discovered, the condition giving rise to the claim, the statute of limitations does not begin to run. For example, the roof of a building could leak into an area above a ceiling or behind a wall, but the damage could be initially contained within that area. Water could be collecting and the wooden joists could be rotting, but the building owner might not know, nor have any reason to know, of the problem. Years later, the entire roof and ceiling could collapse from the leak. The statute of limitations on a claim by the owner against the building's architect or contractor would not begin to run until the discovery of such a condition is made or reasonably should have been made.

Statute of Repose

The example just cited gives, or should give, every architect and contractor pause. Can it then be that a lawsuit might not arise for 10 or, for that matter, even 50 years after a building was constructed? How does one protect oneself against such a risk? To answer these questions, a number of states have enacted statutes of repose. A statute of repose is a cousin of the statute of limitations. It usually states that a lawsuit related to defective design and/or construction must be commenced within a certain number of years after the building is completed, a certificate of occupancy is obtained, the public is admitted, or some other fixed milestone occurs. The designer's or contractor's liability is cut off at a particular point and no legal action may be commenced after that date.

Damages

When there is a breach of either a contract or some other common law duty, the law seeks to make the injured party whole. Unfortunately, the remedies a court has at its disposal are few. The primary remedy in every legal dispute is monetary damages. On occasion, when it is clear that money will not solve the problem, the court may exercise its "equitable powers" to order one party to take a certain action or refrain from taking other actions.

Direct Damages

In general, damages for breaches of contract or common law duty relating to a building or structure consist of the cost of repair. Our owner in the roof example given earlier would be entitled to the cost of repairing the collapsed roof and ceiling. However, if the repair cost is so disproportionate to the value of the property as to be unreasonable or wasteful, the courts will instead assess damages based on a diminution of value theory. *Diminution of value* is the difference between the value of what was bargained for and the value of what was received. For example, assume that an owner requires copper piping of a certain grade throughout a building, but the contractor installs copper piping of a different grade, and that the breach is discovered after the building is completed. Replacing the piping would cost three times the value of the plumbing contract because walls and chases would have to be opened and then resealed. In such a case, the court may well award the party suffering the breach the difference between the value of the building with the higher grade piping and the value of the building with the lower grade of piping. This could well be a very different amount than the cost of replacing all the piping.

Consequential Damages

Consequential damages are those costs that result indirectly from a breach, such as lost profits, lost opportunities, or negative publicity. States vary on what constitutes consequential damages (there are many gray areas) and when consequential damages may be recovered. Many design and construction contracts (including the 1997 edition of those published by the American Institute of Architects) contain a waiver of consequential damages. Such a provision should be considered carefully in any negotiation.

Liquidated Damages

Sometimes the parties may agree in advance to the amount of damages payable in case of a breach of contract. The most common form of preagreed damages is a daily amount payable by a contractor as *liquidated damages* in case of contractor-caused delay. Courts will normally enforce such liquidated damages clauses if the daily amount is a reasonable prediction of the damages that the owner might possibly suffer, even if the owner's actual damages are less or more than the preagreed amount.

BOX 13.1

PERINI V. SANDS HOTEL

In 1981, the Sands Hotel organization bought a down-at-the-heels casino a block off the famous boardwalk in Atlantic City, New Jersey. While most of the well-known, profitable casinos in town benefited from boardwalk frontage, this one was not even visible from that well-trafficked strip. To achieve its goal of profitability, the Sands realized that it had to draw a significant number of patrons from the boardwalk. In 1983, the Sands hired Perini Corporation to undertake major renovations to the interior and exterior of the casino, all aimed at attracting more and better heeled patrons. One element of the project was what the Sands called a "new glitzy glass facade on the east side of the building which might act as a magnet to lure a new category of customers—strollers who might leave the boardwalk and walk the long block from the beach to the Sands" (see Figure A).

FIGURE A   The glass facade a few weeks before its scheduled completion date

Source: Courtesy of Steven Arbittier, Esq., of Ballard, Spahr, Andrews & Ingersoll, Philadelphia, PA 19103.

(continued)

BOX 13.1   Continued

The construction contract provided that Perini would be reimbursed for its labor, materials, subcontracts, and other costs, and that it would receive a fee for home office overhead and profit in the amount of $600,000. The cost of the work and the fee were initially capped at a guaranteed maximum price of $16,800,000 (an amount that eventually increased to $24,000,000). At the outset, no specific completion date was established in the contract, but the Sands and Perini subsequently agreed that substantial completion would be achieved on or before May 31, 1984, so that the casino could benefit from the large volume of summer visitors.

The project was plagued by delays, many of which were apparently the fault of Perini and/or its subcontractors. Although most of the work was substantially complete by mid-September 1984, the glass facade and some other components of the project were still not finished by mid-December of that year (see Figure B). Shortly before Christmas, frustrated by the delays and increasing costs, the Sands terminated Perini's contract and completed the work itself.

Perini sued the Sands in the courts of New Jersey to collect money that it claimed was owed. However, the construction contract contained an arbitration clause stating that all claims between the parties would be decided by final and binding arbitration under the Construction Industry Arbitration Rules of the American Arbitration Association. Based on this clause, the Sands obtained an order from the court postponing Perini's lawsuit until the dispute could be heard and acted on by a panel of three arbitrators.

In the arbitration, Perini pressed its payment claim, and also asked for a

FIGURE B   Several months after its scheduled completion date, the glass facade was still not finished

Source: Courtesy of Steven Arbittier, Esq., of Ballard, Spahr, Andrews & Ingersoll, Philadelphia, PA 19103.

determination that the Sands had wrongfully terminated the construction contract. For its part, the Sands made a startling and aggressive claim: that Perini's delays caused the Sands to lose high-rolling gambling customers, not only during the summer but also during the fall and early winter of 1984. Potential customers, said the Sands, could not fill the gambling floors until they were substantially complete, and even then they were dissuaded from walking the "long block from the beach to the Sands" by trucks, cranes, scaffolding, and other disruptions and obstructions caused by Perini's extended construction activities at the project site.

The arbitration proceedings were extensive and included sixty-four days of hearings, twenty-one witnesses, two thousand exhibits, and eleven thousand pages of transcripts. The Sands introduced voluminous statistical evidence in an attempt to demonstrate what its profits would have been if Perini had finished on time. In January 1989, the arbitrators issued their award. They required the Sands to pay nearly $700,000 to Perini and its subcontractors for payments that had been withheld by the Sands. However, they also required Perini to pay the Sands $14.5 million as compensation for the casino's lost profits.

Perini appealed this adverse decision through three levels of the New Jersey court system. Perini argued that the arbitrators' award of "lost profit damages" was excessive, disproportionate to Perini's $600,000 fee, and contrary to the common law principles that would have governed the proceedings if they had been conducted by judges instead of arbitrators. Perini also argued that the Sands should be limited to damages that it suffered before the project

as a whole was substantially complete, and that it should not be held responsible for approximately $4,000,000 in post-substantial completion damages included in the arbitrators $14.5 million award.

Perini's arguments were rejected by the courts at each level. The long battle eventually came to an end in the summer of 1992, when the New Jersey Supreme Court upheld the arbitration award in all respects. The court held that when parties agree to have their disputes decided in arbitration instead of in court, the arbitrators' award should be final and binding except for errors that are "gross, unmistakable, undebatable, or in manifest disregard of the applicable law and leading to an unjust result." The court found no such errors on the part of the arbitrators. In particular, the court stated that lost profits and other so-called "consequential damages" could be awarded if they were "reasonably foreseeable" by the parties. Because Perini knew that the entire reason for the project was to increase the Sands' profits by attracting more patrons from the boardwalk, the consequences of its default could not be characterized as "unforeseeable."

Word of Perini's stunning loss spread throughout the construction industry. Contractors all around the country became alarmed at the magnitude of the damages that, according to the New Jersey Supreme Court, they could be required to pay to owners whose projects were delayed. This issue became a priority for the Associated General Contractors of America (AGC) in its negotiations with the American Institute of Architects over the wording of the upcoming revision to the AIA's widely used General Conditions of the Contract for Construction (AIA Document A201). As a result of the AGC's efforts, the 1997

(continued)

BOX 13.1   Continued

edition of A201 contains the following new provision:

4.3.10 Claims for Consequential Damages
The Contractor and Owner waive Claims against each other for consequential damages arising out of or relating to this Contract. This mutual waiver includes:

1. damages incurred by the Owner for rental expenses, for losses of use, income, profit, financing, business and reputation, and for loss of management or employee productivity or of the services of such persons; and
2. damages incurred by the Contractor for principal office expenses including the compensation of personnel stationed there, for losses of financing, business and reputation, and for loss of profit except anticipated profit arising directly from the Work.

This provision may be deleted from many construction contracts by owners who want to retain the right to be compensated for consequential damages as a result of the contractor's delay. In many other contracts, however, the contractor will be protected against the possibility of suffering Perini's fate (albeit at the cost of giving up its own lost profits and other consequential damages if the project is delayed by the owner). As a result, Perini's $14.5 million loss may ultimately save other contractors many times that amount in consequential damages that they will not be required to pay.

Punitive Damages

Punitive damages are penalties awarded to an injured party over and above its actual damages. Punitive damages must be authorized by statute or by clear common law precedent, and are generally only awarded when to do so would serve an important public purpose. Punitive damages are sometimes awarded where an action is willful, malicious, or reckless, endangers human health or safety, or otherwise constitutes significant abuse. Some statutes that award damages for "unfair or deceptive trade practices" will permit courts to double or triple such damages in egregious cases.

Equitable Relief

When a court orders one party to take, or refrain from taking, a particular action, as opposed to paying money damages, it is called *equitable relief*. In some states, only certain courts may issue equitable relief, and the circumstances in which it will be granted are generally very narrow. Two kinds of equitable relief are important in the construction industry: specific performance and injunctions.

Specific Performance

Specific performance is a type of equitable relief granted when a court finds that a party cannot be made whole simply through the payment of money. Instead, the breaching party must comply with its obligations under the contract. Specific performance is often granted on the sale of land because each parcel of land is considered unique and irreplaceable. Where the contract relates to something unique, extraordinary, or that cannot be elsewhere obtained, specific performance may be appropriate.

Injunction

An *injunction* is an order by a court prohibiting one party from taking certain actions. An injunction might prevent a builder from commencing construction on a suspected Native American burial ground, might prevent an owner from reusing architectural plans for which no license has been granted, or might freeze bank accounts until certain debts have been paid. It is a strong tool, and one that courts use with a great degree of caution and discretion.

The party seeking the injunction must prove that irreparable harm will be caused without the injunction and that equity favors the party's position. If an injunction is granted prior to a trial, it is known as a *preliminary injunction* and is granted only on a showing of a substantial likelihood that the complaining party will win their case when presented at trial. In certain circumstances, an injunction is a necessity and is the only way in which to prevent further harm.

Defenses

When one party breaches a contract, there are certain acceptable excuses or *defenses* for the nonperformance. If the contract was impossible to perform, illegally entered into, or unconscionable (extraordinarily unfair), a party may have an excuse for failing to perform that would eliminate liability. Examples in the construction industry might include the following: a contract for the provision of doors made of a rare hardwood found only in the Amazon and now, unbeknownst to the parties, completely extinct (impossibility); a contract with an unregistered architect or a corporation improperly formed (illegality); or a contract for the construction of a 20-story office tower for a lump sum of $100,000 (unconscionability).

DISPUTE RESOLUTION

Because it takes so many individuals and companies to construct a building, and because the design and construction process is complex and imperfect, disputes are common in the construction industry. As described earlier, the court system provides a venue for the resolution of such disputes. However, judicial dispute resolution is notoriously complicated, expensive, and slow. It is not surprising that other options have emerged to supplement or even replace courts as dispute resolvers. These options are generally grouped together under the term *alternative dispute resolution* (ADR).

One of the most common forms of ADR is arbitration, in which the parties agree to have their dispute heard by a quasi-judicial arbitrator, whose decision (called an *award*) will have the same binding effect as the decision of a judge or jury. If the parties agree in advance that disputes under a particular contract or agreement will be subject to arbitration, they will have waived their right of access to the court system with respect to such disputes.

Arbitration has long been used as a method of solving labor disputes, and it has been included in standard construction industry contracts for nearly one hundred years.

It has the potential of being faster and less expensive than litigation, and carefully selected arbitrators can have a deeper knowledge of industry practices than most judges. Although arbitration can be a very informal process, it is often conducted under detailed rules administered by such organization as the American Arbitration Association. In some cases, these rules can result in arbitration proceedings that are just as complicated, expensive, and slow as equivalent court proceedings. While arbitration is widely used as a method of resolving construction disputes, many other ADR methods have gained in popularity in recent years.

The most widespread and effective ADR technique currently used is *nonbinding mediation*. Mediation is essentially a structured, facilitated negotiation in which a neutral mediator employs a variety of techniques to help the parties reach agreement. Mediators are not normally empowered to impose a binding result, although on occasion the parties might grant the mediator such authority if they cannot overcome an impasse in any other way. In 1997, The American Institute of Architects inserted a provision in all of its standard design and construction contracts requiring the parties to attempt to solve disputes through mediation before turning them over to binding arbitration.

Proponents of ADR have become increasingly creative in designing dispute resolution programs tailored to specific industries and situations. For instance, it is common for standing dispute review boards (DRBs) to be empanelled at the beginning of major construction projects. DRB members often visit the site periodically to become familiar with the progress of the work and to provide assistance in the early stages of disputes. DRBs often issue detailed decisions that, although they may not be binding, are accepted by the parties as thoughtful and fair outcomes.

In the largest projects, DRBs are usually one component of a detailed system of dispute resolution to which all parties agree in their contracts. One measure of the success of such a systems is the immense Central Artery/Tunnel project in Boston, in which virtually no disputes involving the $12+ billion project have reached the Massachusetts court system.

Recently, attention has been given to techniques aimed at preventing disputes from arising in the first place. Perhaps the most widespread of these techniques is *partnering*, a process in which a culture of cooperation and open communication is encouraged through workshops and other exercises facilitated by organizational development professionals. Partnering was popularized by the U.S. Army Corps of Engineers, which has used it successfully to reduce the number and severity of disputes in its infrastructure projects.

There are those who believe that partnering, while potentially useful, is only superficially effective in projects where the contractual terms discourage the very behavior that partnering seeks to foster. Some project sponsors have recently experimented with *project alliances*, in which partnering principles are reflected in commercial and risk allocation arrangements that align interests and encourage cooperation (such as bonuses for all parties if certain project goals are achieved, and penalties for all parties if they are not, with claims between and among the parties being waived or severely restricted). Alliancing is a new method of project delivery with great potential, but it remains to be seen whether or not it will significantly reduce disputes in the rough-and-tumble American construction industry.

Conclusion

Construction law is made up of a specialized set of rules and regulations that govern how people behave in the context of a construction project. Because law is nothing more than an agreed-on set of guidelines by which we live together as a society, construction law is a subset of these agreements. The laws are specific to the circumstances of design and construction but have the same components of laws that govern our everyday life. The government has a specific role to play in developing and adopting these laws at the federal, state, and local levels. The involvement of each is based on the subject matter, but generally federal statutes take precedence over state or local laws. For most matters, the federal government will set minimum thresholds and allow the states and local governments to regulate more strictly.

The courts also have a role to play in these laws—they interpret and enforce existing statutes and regulations. Through their interpretation, a body of common law has unfolded. Common law is the accumulated wisdom of the courts over time and serves as the basis for enforcement of the law. The courts exist at the federal level and at the state level. Most construction-related disputes are heard in state court and resolved there.

Many disputes in construction are brought to the court's attention through some perceived breach of contract. Contracts define people's relationships in a construction project. Several basic elements have to be present in order for the contract to be legal: an offer, an acceptance, some sort of payment, and the legal capacity of each party to make a binding agreement.

Once the enforceability of the contract is established, the courts will use a common established set of guidelines for making their decisions. They consider what is written first and foremost and use the plainest interpretation. They consider any existing statutes as a context, specifically any statutes of limitations that exist for the particular lawsuit. In deciding a case, the courts also address damages. Damages are usually awarded in the form of monetary redress for direct costs, indirect costs, or even punitive penalties, depending on the court's findings.

Although many disputes end up in the courts, more and more parties are turning instead to alternative dispute resolution methods such as arbitration and mediation. In addition, to avoid the costs and bad will that result from dispute resolution of any sort, participants are incorporating preventive measures such as partnering and alternative project delivery strategies into their projects to reduce the risks inherent in the construction projects of today.

Chapter Review Questions

1. The legal rules that govern design and construction processes have evolved from which of the following:
   a. Court interpretation
   b. Federal, state, and local government statutes
   c. Specific rules developed by the project participants
   d. All of the above
2. Regulations developed by the federal, state, or local administration must be consistent with that government's statutory language or the regulations may be invalidated by the courts. True or false?

3. The terms, ordinances, or bylaws are often used to denote a _____.
   a. State statute
   b. Licensing law
   c. Mechanics lien
   d. Local statute

4. The role of the courts is to interpret statutes, regulations, and local ordinances and to apply common law principles to resolve disputes. True or false?

5. What is the major issue to be taken from the case *Perini v. Sands Hotel* described in the sidebar?
   a. The case illustrates preemption—federal statutes take precedence over state statutes.
   b. The findings of binding arbitration are final and if appropriate may include compensation to an owner for loss of use.
   c. When appropriate, a decision by a lower court may be overturned at a higher court.
   d. Binding arbitration is often unfair and overturned by the courts.

6. Torts, literally wrongs against people or property, are typically addressed by federal, state, and local statutes. True or false?

7. A contract which may be written or oral is only formed if which of the following occurred?
   a. An offer has been made
   b. An offer has been accepted
   c. Something of value (consideration) is exchanged
   d. The parties to the contract have the capacity to contract
   e. All of the above

8. Courts will normally enforce a liquidated damages clause if the daily amount is a reasonable prediction of the damages that an owner might suffer. In a liquidated damage clause, the parties agree in advance to the daily amount payable to the owner in the case of contractor-caused delay. True or false?

9. Which of the following is the name for the technique of preventing disputes from arising on a project?
   a. Partnering
   b. TQM
   c. Mediation
   d. Dispute resolution

10. Statutes of Limitations for commencing litigation may be put on hold (tolled) until the discovery of the condition giving rise to the condition is made or reasonably should have been made. True or false?

Exercises

1. Present to the class the findings of a recent construction related court decision. Include the following elements in your presentation:
   a. Summarize the facts of the case
   b. Explain the arguments of the plaintiff
   c. Explain the arguments of the defendant
   d. Summarize the decision made by the court
   e. Will the decision be appealed?

   Note: Engineering News Record regularly reviews recent Engineering and Construction court decisions.

2. Review in detail, section by section, a contract for architectural, engineering, contractor, or construction management services. Prepare a written report which summarizes each contract section to include the purpose of each section and your opinion as to which construction party benefits from the contract language.

Chapter Outline

Student Learning Objectives

In this chapter you will learn the following:

1. How to determine the true cost of an accident

2. The variety of unsafe acts that cause lost workdays

3. The many ways to prevent unsafe acts on the job

4. What to do when an accident occurs

INTRODUCTION

American workers expect safety in the workplace. We have come to expect that the exits will be adequate in number, well marked, and accessible in emergencies. We do not worry about the purity of the air that is pumped into the building as we work, and usually the temperature is comfortable. Lighting is adequate, and power requirements are met safely. The roof does not leak, and the toilets don't clog. Custodians ensure that the trash is collected, the floors cleaned, and the bathrooms sanitized. This is the average office environment for most workers—a comfortable, safe place to perform their work.

In some industries, such as textile, steel, and paper manufacturing, the work itself makes it difficult to meet these basic standards. Construction is a prime example of this type of industry. On a construction site, workers are responsible for cleaning up, toilets are portable units that sit outside, there is often no roof or walls, and the temperature inside is very close to the temperature outside. In such an environment, provisions for health and safety take on new meaning. To meet basic health and safety needs on a construction site, all participants must cooperate. Management and workers, designers, and owners all need to be alert to potential health and safety risks. Constructors are considered primarily responsible for providing a safe environment for their workers and protection for the general public during the construction process. However, everyone associated with the project can assist. Designers can design with an eye to the construction process. Owners can emphasize the importance of safety during the pre-bid stage. Workers can practice safe methods of going about their work. And everyone can be alert to potential hazardous situations as they plan their work and move around the job site.

Construction is a hazardous profession. Climbing high off the ground, digging deep into tunnels and trenches, handling large pieces of material, operating huge equipment, and working with hazardous substances put workers at risk. Managing safety on construction sites is a challenging endeavor, and each project has its own particular set of hazards. There are few standard methods of building, so standard procedures for each activity are difficult to develop. Each activity in itself is often so short that a typical learning curve does not apply. Compounding this, the workers themselves move from job site to job site as their particular trade skills are needed. Each site has particular methods of operating depending on the style of the forepersons and the superintendent and the type of project. In addition, the makeup of the crew is constantly changing, so familiarity with a co-worker's particular work style is often not possible.

Until the Occupational Safety and Health Administration (OSHA) passed the OSH act of 1970, there was little consistency in how these varying factors were handled. This act applies to all businesses but includes specific regulations for construction. OSHA in its essence is a federal standard that sets minimum requirements for health and safety of workers.

The consequences of accidents are many, but the primary one is that someone often gets hurt. Besides the person who suffers the injury, others are affected as well. Worker morale suffers when a co-worker is injured. Worry over the person's welfare, fear of being injured themselves, guilt over not preventing the accident all come into focus. Families of the person injured also suffer. They have to deal with the emotional trauma of having a loved one hurt, must reorganize their life to care for the person, and have to deal with the long-term implications, whether physical, financial, or emotional. Of course, the consequences for the worker are by far the greatest. These include the potential inability to continue working in his or her trade, prolonged pain, increased fear of reinjury, loss of income potential, and, at the very worst, loss of life.

Safety is an attitude. It starts with top management and is reflected on the job site in many ways: through training, housekeeping, toolbox meetings, adherence to safety measures, maintenance of equipment and tools, and intolerance of violations. Accidents remove skilled workers from the job site, break up productive crews, and deplete morale. With increased accidents, insurance costs increase and bonding levels decrease, both of which can result in losing a competitive edge when bidding jobs. Construction work is dangerous, but these dangers can be controlled and sometimes completely eliminated if safety is treated as an integral part of the overall production schedule.

THE COST OF ACCIDENTS

The cost of accidents is high. Companies carry insurance to cover some of these costs (such as medical expenses and workers' compensation), but the real costs are more indirect, difficult to predict, and not covered by insurance (see Figure 14.1). Loss of

Checklists of accident costs	
_____ Lost time of injured worker paid by employer	$_____
_____ Lost time of other employees assisting injured	$_____
_____ Lost time of supervisors and others investigating, attending hearings, processing reports, and so on	$_____
_____ Time required to train new employee	$_____
_____ Damage to equipment or plant	$_____
_____ Product or material damaged or wasted	$_____
_____ Increased production cost	$_____
_____ Limited production of injured during readjustment	$_____
_____ Interruption of work at time of accident	$_____
_____ Payment of penalties	$_____
_____ Cost of renting substitute equipment	$_____
_____ Loss of good will (public or employee)	$_____
_____ All other uninsurable costs	$_____
Total uninsurable cost paid by employer	$_____
Compensation and medical cost paid by insurance company	$_____

FIGURE 14.1   The costs associated with an accident take many forms

productivity and personnel time; damaged property, material, and equipment; cleanup and repair; liability claims; and the cost of retraining replacement workers are all burdens placed on the company that will not be covered by any insurance. These costs eat into the profits on a job. Following are some common indirect costs:

- *Workers' compensation insurance premiums.*   Insurance companies use a measurement tool called an experience modification rate (EMR) to calculate how to charge individual companies. The purpose of an EMR is to collect higher premiums from companies with above-average accident rates and to reduce the costs for companies with below-average rates. The measurement is based on a three-year period and is updated each year. It looks at losses in the years before the current and previous year. In 2007, for example, the years used were 2003, 2004, and 2005. An EMR of 1.0 is classified as normal and reflects a manual tabulation of the workers' compensation premiums for a given job classification. The formula for calculating companies' EMR is based more heavily on the frequency of accidents than on the cost of each claim.
- *Liability.*   Although most state workers' compensation laws limit an employee's ability to file a lawsuit against his or her employer, a company can be faced with a lawsuit in many other ways. If an injury involves a tool or a piece of equipment, the worker can sue the manufacturer, who in turn can sue the company. These are called third-party lawsuits. If another contractor on the site is injured due to a company's negligence, he or she can sue the company directly. The general public

BOX 14.1

CONTRACTOR EXPERIENCE RATING

Construction companies are given an experience rating for the purpose of accurately forecasting the probability of a future worker's compensation loss. A contractor's experience modification rating (EMR) modifies the amount of premium a contractor pays for workers' compensation insurance (see Figure A).

As you can see, a contractor who maintains a strong safety program and therefore exhibits few losses maintains a strong financial advantage over the competition. This system of rating provides a financial incentive to contractors to improve their safety programs. If a rating system were not used, all contractors

would pay at the same premium rate. This is called a manual rating, which simply means that all insured are grouped according to their business operation; the losses of the group are added together, and an average cost is obtained. In this type of system, insurance companies aggressively seek the better-than-average companies, while the less desirable have difficulty attaining insurance.

The dollar value of past losses, number of losses, type of work, and total cost of payroll are all considered in the calculation of a company's EMR. In workers' compensation experience rating, the characteristics of the individual employer are determined

| FIGURE A | The effect of EMR on a contractor's profitability |

Effect of experience modification rating on contractor's profitability

Consider the following three contractors:

    Contractor 1, average safety record, EMR = 1
    Contractor 2, poor safety record, EMR = 1.6
    Contractor 3, excellent safety record, EMR = .83

Contractor	1	2	3
EMR	1	1.6	.83
Payroll	$2.5M	$2.5M	$2.5M
Manual workers' compensation insurance premium	$19.00 (per $100)	$19.00 (per $100)	$19.00 (per $100)
Workers' compensation insurance premium (WCIP)*	$475,000	$760,000	$394,250
% Payroll	19.00	30.40	15.77

*WCIP = (EMR)(Payroll)(Insurance Premium)

(continued)

BOX 14.1   Continued

over a period of usually three years. This experience is compared or contrasted with the expected industry performance, and a rating is calculated. Better-than-average performance nets a credit, while poorer performance nets a debit.

An important fact in calculating a company's EMR is that the frequency of accidents is given greater weight than the dollar value of the loss. This is handled by creating two categories of losses in the calculation: primary and excess. The dollar value of each claim up to $5,000 is included as a primary loss; anything above that is categorized as an excess loss. The primary loss total is given a greater weight than the excess loss total in the experience calculation.

The rating system also considers the type of work and size of the company. These two elements are considered in the calculation of the company's expected losses. The expected losses are compared to the company's actual losses for the three-year period previously discussed. Consider the calculation in Figure B.

FIGURE B   Sample EMR calculation

Sample EMR calculation

Expected losses[1]	Expected excess $76,284	Expected losses $151,737	Expected primary losses $75,453	D-ratio[2] .497

Actual losses[1]	Actual excess $84,824	Actual losses $142,338	Actual primary $57,514	

	W-Factor[3] .22	Tabular ballast value[4] $22,800	Stabilizing value[5] $82,302

Adjusted actual losses   = (Primary losses) + (Weighted excess losses) + (Stabilizing value)
$$= (\$57{,}514) + [(.22)(\$84{,}824)] + (\$82{,}302) = \$158{,}477$$

Adjusted expected losses = (Primary losses) + (Weighted excess losses) + (Stabilizing value)
$$= (\$75{,}453) + [(.22)(\$76{,}284)] + (\$82{,}302) = \$174{,}537$$

$$\text{EMR} = \frac{\text{Adjusted actual losses}}{\text{Adjusted expected losses}} = \frac{\$158{,}477}{\$174{,}537} = .91$$

Notes:

[1] The expected losses are a factor of the type of work and the payroll.

[2] Represents the portion of expected losses that are primary losses.

[3] Weight is given to excess losses.

[4] Stabilizing element is designed to minimize the effect of a single loss.

[5] Stabilizing value = (Expected excess)[1 − (W-Factor)] + (Tabular ballast value)
$$= (\$76{,}284)(1 - .22) + \$22{,}800 = \$82{,}302$$

BOX 14.1   Continued

A company EMR is calculated by dividing actual losses by expected losses. Based on this information, expected standards can be established for both primary and excess losses. Note in Figure B the values for expected excess, expected losses, and expected primary losses. The W-factor, which is the weight given to excess losses, is a factor of the size of the insurer's payroll. The calculation also includes a stabilizing element called tabular ballast value, which is added in to both expected and actual losses. This limits the impact of any single loss. It increases as the expected losses increase. Note that in this calculation excess losses are factored in at 22 percent, while primary losses are considered in full.

Reference

National Council on Compensation Insurance. *ABCs of Revised Experience Rating*. Boca Raton, Fla.: National Council on Compensation Insurance, 1993.

also can file a lawsuit against the company directly if a person is injured due to construction activity.

- *Penalties.*   Companies can be faced with penalties beyond the liability and increased premiums. Federal and state agencies set up guidelines for both employers and employees to follow so that workers will be protected. The most applicable agency for construction is OSHA, which issues standards to protect workers. The standards set by all these agencies are aimed at all workplace environments—from offices to industrial plants. Construction is one of the industries that OSHA is most concerned about because of the inherent dangerous nature of the work.

- *Public relations.*   Serious accidents on construction sites are often shown on the evening news and recounted in newspaper stories. Interviews with families and co-workers reinforce emotional responses to the accident. A company's reputation can be seriously damaged by this sort of coverage. For the remainder of the project, public attention will hover around all activities as workers and management try to normalize production. Motivation to continue will be compromised. Even after the job is complete, the company will find itself in the less than desirable position of having to explain to owners on future jobs the circumstances around the accident. Understandably, owners are reluctant to hire a company with a poor accident record because it puts them in a vulnerable position if there is an accident on their job.

The real cost of accidents is not easy to calculate. However, if you look at some of the statistics on insurance costs alone, the impact starts to emerge. Construction revenue in the United States in 1997 was about $650 billion. Builder's risk and liability insurance averages about 1 percent of direct labor payroll. Workers' compensation insurance averages about 7 percent of direct labor payroll. Direct labor payroll is about 25 percent of total project cost. By using these four figures, we can calculate insurance costs:

$650 billion × 25% = $162 billion in direct labor payroll
Builders' risk and liability insurance − $162 billion × 1% = $1.6 billion
Workers' compensation insurance − $162 billion × 7% = $11.3 billion
Total insurance costs = $12.9 billion

THE CAUSE OF ACCIDENTS

When an accident or near miss happens on a job site, the tendency is to focus on the conditions on the site at that time. Physical evidence can be gathered to back up eye-witness accounts of the incident. Changes can be made to prevent future occurrences. Faulty equipment can be replaced, barriers installed, containers labeled. What is more difficult to predict and then change is the behavior of people on the site. These two factors—people's actions and conditions on the site—are at the heart of safety. When an accident occurs, either or both of these factors will be shown to be the cause. Unsafe acts and unsafe conditions cause accidents. Although simple in concept, the ways in which these two causes can combine are endless.

Unsafe Conditions

Unsafe conditions are hazards that can cause injuries. These hazards can be physical, such as defective tools, unprotected openings, and improper storage of equipment or materials. They also can be environmental, such as contaminants brought onto the site without proper containment. Controlling these unsafe conditions is challenging because they are forever changing as the job progresses. A safe area of construction on a given day can contain many hazards on the following day. Any day a new subcontractor can arrive on the job with new equipment, new tools, and new materials. Where they are stored, how they are moved around the site, who has access to them all create the potential for hazardous conditions. Management can also contribute to these unsafe conditions by not planning the job with safety as a primary consideration or not consistently ensuring that the safety rules and procedures are followed.

In addition to injuries that can occur on the job site, workers are also susceptible to the effects of exposure to hazardous contaminants. Some of these are brought on the site in the form of cleaners or adhesives and, if not properly handled, can cause immediate reactions in the form of respiratory problems, irritated eyes, shortness of breath, or dizziness. Others may be present on the site such as lead or asbestos, or are a by-product of the construction activities, such as mold. Exposure to these are harder to quantify because their effects can surface over time and sometimes do not appear until years later. Nonetheless, the dangers are as real and the costs as high as accidents on site.

In renovation projects, especially in buildings constructed before 1980, asbestos could be present in floor tiles, fireproofing, plaster, pipe insulation, mastic. The health risk in exposure to asbestos is related to the long-term inhalation of fibers that can cause respiratory and lung disease 15–20 years after exposure. Although current practice is to remove these materials in the areas of work by certified workers before construction begins, there is always the danger of uncovering hidden sources. Because of this, workers should be trained to recognize asbestos-containing material, understand how to protect themselves, and understand the specific procedures to follow. OSHA has specific guidelines concerning handling of asbestos materials.

Lead is another hazardous material that could be present in renovation projects. It will be found most often in paint used before 1978 and may be present on woodwork, plaster walls, structural steel members or exterior siding and trim. Workers can be exposed to lead by breathing in lead dust resulting from cutting into a material with lead; by eating, drinking, or smoking in areas where lead has been disturbed; or by handling contaminated objects. Exposure to lead can cause headaches, appetite loss, and sleeplessness and in time lead to serious disability such as memory loss, fatigue, muscle and joint pain, and kidney problems.

Depending on the level of lead present and the type of operations planned, workers may need to protect themselves or the contractor may need to remove the lead before the operation starts. OSHA has specific guidelines concerning permissible levels of exposure. Even in new construction both asbestos and lead along with other hazards such as oil, chemicals, or pesticides could be found in the soil of a new building site. Normally the soil is tested before the project begins and procedures are well established for clean up as part of the operations, but workers may uncover unknown areas of contamination so need to be well trained to react safely.

Another hazard that could be present in renovation projects is mold. Mechanical leaks or deterioration of the exterior envelope—roofing, windows, siding—could allow water to penetrate into the interior of the building, providing an ideal environment for mold. Mold is harbored in cloth, carpet, wood, drywall, and any other materials that are organic in origin. But mold is also a potential by-product of new construction. Materials that are exposed to moisture during construction can be the source of mold infestations. This can cause health risks to the construction workers and, if unabated, to the building occupants. Mold is hazardous to health. It causes allergic reactions, aggravation of the respiratory system, and can worsen already existing conditions such as asthma. Despite these hazards, and unlike asbestos and lead, mold is not regulated. However, contractors can take steps to minimize the growth of mold and prevent moisture from getting to materials by ensuring storage in a dry place and installation in areas that are moisture free. In the event that moisture does get to material, contractors can have procedures in place to dry out the area and material immediately thus reducing the possibility of mold growth.

Unsafe Acts

Unsafe acts are hazards caused by the actions of people on the job site. These actions can be categorized in three ways: things a person should have done (such as informing others about unsafe conditions), should have done differently, or should not have done at all. If a person neglects to inform others about unsafe conditions, he or she is neglecting to act. If the person uses tools or equipment inappropriately or works at heights without proper protection, he or she is acting incorrectly. If the person proceeds into a hazardous area despite warning signs, the person is acting when he or she should not.

One example of an unsafe action is substance abuse. Because of its legal and social ramifications, substance abuse is difficult to contend with on the job site. It can, however, lead to very unsafe actions, even if the actual consumption takes place outside the workplace. Alcohol and drugs can cause workers to take more chances. They increase the potential for injury to the individual or co-worker, increase absenteeism or tardiness, and decrease the quality of workmanship. Alcohol is a legal substance, but overuse can lead to trouble. Drugs fall into two categories: legal and illegal. Legal drugs are those prescribed by a physician. However, the side effects of some of these drugs can cause unsafe behavior on the job. Illegal drugs come in many categories: stimulants, depressants, narcotics, and hallucinogens. All of them affect job performance.

With all the awareness of safety in the workplace today, it might seem simple to have total cooperation from everyone about accident prevention. Sometimes, however, pressures run counter to a safe work environment, especially in construction. During schedule pressures, there is a tendency to increase the speed of individual tasks, which can lead to carelessness. Construction attracts men and women who often have good physical skills, which can sometimes lead to a sense of invulnerability and a willingness to take risks. Construction also has a certain macho mystique, which makes it difficult for workers to always follow safety procedures. Because the typical construction work force mixes different cultures and races, there are likely to be varying styles of behavior and work practices, which can lead to conflicts among workers. If not handled correctly, conflicts can lead to angry confrontations, which in turn can jeopardize safety.

Construction accounts for 6 percent of the work force and 11 percent of the injuries in the United States. According to the Bureau of Labor Statistics, there were 1,186 fatal injuries in 2005 and 160,000 nonfatal injuries and illnesses with a medium of nine days away from work. This is the highest incident rate for all occupations and these lost days stack up to billion of dollars per year in losses.

TYPES OF ACCIDENTS

The leading types of fatal construction accidents are falls, being struck by something, being caught in between something, and being struck by electricity. These account for 90 percent of deaths. In 2005, the top four types of nonfatal accidents were due to contact with an object or equipment, being struck by an object, falls, and over exertion. The examples in Figure 14.2 are a sober reminder of the real dangers in construction and the fatal consequences.

ACCIDENT PREVENTION

Allowing employees to work unsafely leads to accidents. Allowing unsafe conditions to remain leads to accidents. The only rational approach to safety is prevention. Prevention can be accomplished in many different ways. In devising methods of prevention, a clear understanding of the top causes of accidents is important. The Bureau of Labor Statistics accumulates data on accidents that track the type of injuries, the demographics of age, sex and ethnicity, and even the time of day and the day of the week. These statistics can be used to customize and focus the safety program and other preventive measures. The key to accident prevention, however, is consistency and commitment at all levels of management.

Occupational Safety and Health Administration

In 1970, the federal government passed OSH act to ensure that workers have consistently safe work environments. The act provides standards and rules for healthy and safe work environments, tools, equipment, and processes. OSHA conducts investigations to make sure its standards are being followed. Under the act, an employer is required to provide a workplace free from known hazards. If, during an inspection, violations are found, inspectors will likely issue a citation listing the violations and may also impose penalties.

OSHA is directed toward every private employer with one or more employees. The only exception are employers covered by other federal legislation, such as the Atomic

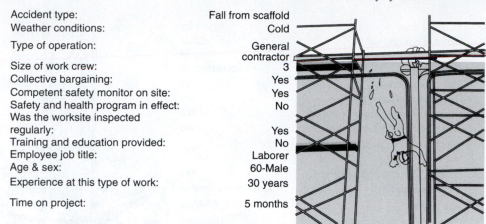

Accident type:	Fall from scaffold
Weather conditions:	Cold
Type of operation:	General contractor
Size of work crew:	3
Collective bargaining:	Yes
Competent safety monitor on site:	Yes
Safety and health program in effect:	No
Was the worksite inspected regularly:	Yes
Training and education provided:	No
Employee job title:	Laborer
Age & sex:	60-Male
Experience at this type of work:	30 years
Time on project:	5 months

BRIEF DESCRIPTION OF ACCIDENT

A laborer was working on the third level of a tubular welded frame scaffold, which was covered with ice and snow. Planking on the scaffold was inadequate; there was no guardrail and no access ladder for the various scaffold levels. The worker slipped and fell head first approximately 20 feet to the pavement below.

ACCIDENT PREVENTION RECOMMENDATIONS

1. Standard guardrails and toeboards must be installed on scaffolds (29 CFR 1926.451(d)(10)).
2. Ice and snow must be cleared from the scaffold to eliminate slippery conditions as soon as possible (29 CFR 1926.451(a)(17)).
3. Access ladders—or the equivalent—must be provided to workers using the scaffold (29 CFR 1926.451(a)(13)).

FIGURE 14.2   These three examples chronicle how injury and death can occur on a construction site

Energy Act. OSHA regulations have many sections. Two pertain to construction—one generally, one specifically. CFR Part 1910 contains general industry safety and health standards; CFR Part 1926 contains the occupational and health standards for the construction industry. Figure 14.3 depicts the table of contents for these two sections, showing the depth of the coverage.

OSHA also allows individual states to establish their own programs for safety to replace the federal guidelines. Presently, 23 states have enacted their own set of regulations, and Connecticut and New York have regulations for public workers only. To qualify as replacements, the state regulations must be equal to or exceed the OSHA standards. The state must also show that it is capable of enforcement.

OSHA ensures compliance with its rules through surprise visits to job sites. It also responds to workers' complaints. If a company is in violation, OSHA issues a citation that requires the company to correct the deficiencies. If an injury or accident occurs, there will be an investigation and usually a fine. Fines range from $1,000 to

Accident type:	Struck by
Weather conditions:	Clear
Type of operation:	Road construction
Size of work crew:	5
Collective bargaining:	No
Competent safety monitor on site:	Yes
Safety and health program in effect:	No
Was the worksite inspected regularly:	Yes
Training and education provided:	Yes
Employee job title:	Concrete finisher
Age & sex:	64-Male
Experience at this type of work:	Unknown
Time on project:	2.5 days

BRIEF DESCRIPTION OF ACCIDENT

Four employees were working near pile driving equipment preparing to drive the first piling. Apparently the two clips on the eye of the hammer hoisting rope slipped, permitting the hammer that was still inside the lead to fall some 45 feet. The hammer struck a large timber on the ground breaking it. One end of the timber struck the employees, fatally injuring one man.

ACCIDENT PREVENTION RECOMMENDATIONS

1. That a minimum of four wire rope clips be used to form eyes in the ends of wire rope of the size used in accordance with 1926.251(c)(5) re: Table H-20.
2. That the employer instruct each employee in the recognition and avoidance of unsafe conditions and the regulations applicable to his work environment to correct or eliminate any hazards or other exposure to illness or injury in accordance with 1926.21(b)(2).

FIGURE 14.2   continued

$70,000, depending on the severity of the incident. Other agencies, such as the Environmental Protection Agency and the Department of Transportation, also get involved in safety. Although they focus on specific aspects of safety, they work cooperatively with OSHA.

In the 35 years since its enactment, the OSH act has had a substantial impact on health and safety. Since OSHA's establishment in 1971, workplace fatalities have been cut by 60 percent and occupational injuries by 40 percent. At the same time, U.S. employment has almost doubled from 56 million to 105 million. Yet despite these efforts, every year 6,000 Americans die from workplace injuries, an estimated 50,000 die from illnesses related to chemical exposures, and 6 million suffer from nonfatal injuries. In an effort to overcome these staggering statistics, OSHA is working with companies to formulate safety programs. It is turning from mere enforcement and policing to partnering with industry to identify, develop, and implement new ways of minimizing accidents.

Accident type:	Electrocution
Weather conditions:	Sunny, clear
Type of operation:	Steel erection
Size of work crew:	3
Collective bargaining:	No
Competent safety monitor on site:	Yes—Victim
Safety and health program in effect:	No
Was the worksite inspected regularly:	Yes
Training and education provided:	No
Employee job title:	Steel erector Foreman
Age & sex:	43-Male
Experience at this type of work:	4 months
Time on project:	4 hours

BRIEF DESCRIPTION OF ACCIDENT

Employees were moving a steel canopy structure using a "boom crane" truck. The boom cable made contact with a 7,200 volt electrical power distribution line electrocuting the operator of the crane; he was the foreman at the site.

ACCIDENT PREVENTION RECOMMENDATIONS

1. Develop and maintain a safety and health program to provide guidance for safe operations (29 CFR 1926.20(b)(1)).
2. Instruct each employee on how to recognize and avoid unsafe conditions, which apply to the work and work areas (29 CFR 1926.21(b)(2))
3. If high voltage lines are not de-energized, visibly grounded, or protected by insulating barriers, equipment operators must maintain a minimum distance of 10 feet between their equipment and the electrical distribution or transmission lines (29 CFR 1926.550(a)(15)(i)).

FIGURE 14.2   continued

Source: U.S. Department of Labor, Occupational Safety and Health Administration.

Safety Programs

The most effective method of reducing accidents in the workplace is through safety programs. OSHA mandates the development of a safety program; but for the program to work, it must have the total support of management. A typical safety program has two components: an overall corporate safety program and a site-specific program (see Figure 14.4).

Corporate programs vary, but in general they have the following components:

- Lay out the responsibility of the top executives in regard to safety
- Identify methods of measuring performance
- Institute control measures through supervisory personnel
- Define reporting requirements in the event of an accident
- Develop safety training for employees
- Institute disciplinary warnings
- Provide incentives for those who achieve high standards of safety

Part 1910	Occupational Safety and Health Standards	Part 1926	Safety and Health Regulations for Construction
Subpart A	General	Subpart A	General
Subpart B	Adoption and extension of established federal standards	Subpart B	General interpretations
		Subpart C	General safety and health provisions
Subpart C	Reserved	Subpart D	Occupational, health, and environmental controls
Subpart D	Walking—working surfaces		
Subpart E	Means of egress	Subpart E	Personal protections and life-saving equipment
Subpart F	Powered platforms, man lifts, and vehicle-mounted work platforms		
		Subpart F	Fire protection and prevention
Subpart G	Occupational and environmental control	Subpart G	Signs, signals, and barricades
		Subpart H	Material handling, storage, use, and disposal
Subpart H	Hazardous materials		
Subpart I	Protective equipment	Subpart I	Tools—hand and power
Subpart J	General environmental controls	Subpart J	Welding and cutting
Subpart K	Medical and first aid	Subpart K	Electrical
Subpart L	Fire protection	Subpart L	Scaffolds
Subpart M	Compressed gas and compressed air equipment	Subpart M	Fall protection
		Subpart N	Cranes, derricks, hoists, elevators, and conveying
Subpart N	Material handling and storage		
Subpart O	Machinery and machine guarding	Subpart O	Motorized vehicles, mechanized equipment, and marine operations
Subpart P	Hand and portable powered tools and other handheld equipment		
		Subpart P	Excavation
		Subpart Q	Concrete and masonry construction
Subpart Q	Welding, cutting, and brazing		
Subpart R	Special industries	Subpart R	Steel erection
Subpart S	Electrical	Subpart S	Underground construction, caissons, cofferdams, and compressed air
Subpart T	Commercial diving operations		
Subpart U	Reserved		
Subpart V	Reserved	Subpart T	Demolition
Subpart W	Reserved	Subpart U	Blasting and use of explosives
Subpart X	Reserved	Subpart V	Power transmissions and distribution
Subpart Y	Reserved		
Subpart Z	Toxic and hazardous substances	Subpart W	Rollover protective structures, overhead protection
		Subpart X	Ladders
		Subpart Y	Commercial diving operations
		Subpart Z	Toxic and hazardous substances

FIGURE 14.3 Table of contents for OSHA CFR Part 1910 and Part 1926

A strong corporate safety program is the foundation of the site safety program. To be effective over time, the corporate program should have constant feedback from the sites concerning critical areas for training and any ideas about more effective methods of prevention.

The site safety program specifically explains the work that must be done at the site both before the project starts and during construction itself. During a startup phase, planning is done. The safety team is identified and assembled at this time. It usually

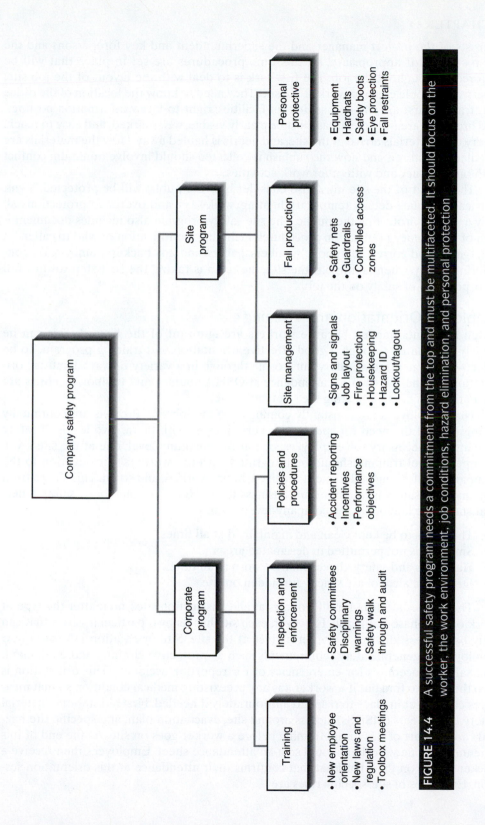

FIGURE 14.4 A successful safety program needs a commitment from the top and must be multifaceted. It should focus on the worker, the work environment, job conditions, hazard elimination, and personal protection

Company safety program

Corporate program

Site program

Training
- New employee orientation
- New laws and regulation
- Toolbox meetings

Inspection and enforcement
- Safety committees
- Disciplinary warnings
- Safety walk through and audit

Policies and procedures
- Accident reporting
- Incentives
- Performance objectives

Site management
- Signs and signals
- Job layout
- Fire protection
- Housekeeping
- Hazard ID
- Lockout/tagout

Fall production
- Safety nets
- Guardrails
- Controlled access zones

Personal protective
- Equipment
- Hardhats
- Safety boots
- Eye protection
- Fall restraints

consists of the project manager and the superintendent and key forepersons and the shop steward if appropriate. At this time procedures are set in place that will be enforced throughout the job. The first task is to deal with the layout of the job site. Every day people come to work at the site. They need to know the location of the office and trailers, first aid stations, sanitation facilities, right-to-know information postings, and breakout areas. These areas must be clearly visible, well marked, and easy to reach. Every day materials arrive at the site, and debris is hauled away. How the materials are handled and stored and how the rubbish is collected should involve minimum conflict with one another and with other work activities.

The layout of the site must also consider how the public will be protected. Signs, barricades, police details, temporary lighting, walkways, and overhead protections all play a part in protecting the public. The site safety program also includes documentation of emergency notification procedures, including identification of who to call in an emergency and correct telephone numbers, pagers, and any backup numbers. By considering safety when laying out the site, the team is taking the first step toward full incorporation of safety on the job.

Employee Orientation and Training

Often accidents happen because workers are ignorant of the hazard. This can be largely eliminated through a good effective orientation and training program. To be effective, the message of safety must come through in a variety of ways. First-day orientation, on-the-job training, attendance at OSHA courses, and toolbox meetings are all methods of communicating the safety message.

New employees are constantly coming onto the job site. Projects are continually changing, and the need for specific workers changes with them. Two levels of safety training are necessary for employees: one at the company level, one at the site level. Company-level training should be integrated with the workers' introduction to the company itself, along with benefit received, hours worked, and so on. This shows from day one that safety is an important business tenet. Here are some basic safety tenets that should be laid out at the company-level training:

- The site is to be kept clean and maintained at all times.
- Smoking is not permitted in designated areas.
- Hard hats and safety glasses shall be worn at all times.
- Drugs and alcohol are strictly forbidden on site.

These rules are true for all workers at all construction sites, no matter the type of work or the phase of the job. However, each site has its own particular issues that can only be addressed when a worker arrives at the site. Site orientation informs a new employee of general safety requirements such as protective clothing and equipment, and safety procedures for emergencies or for reporting accidents. This orientation is also the time to find out if a worker has any preexisting medical condition so that measures can be put in place to respond appropriately if needed. First aid stations, material safety data sheets (MSDSs), access around site, evacuation plan, and specific site hazards are all part of this initial training before a worker goes on site. At the end of this orientation, a new worker should sign an attendance sheet. Employees then receive a sticker to put on their hard hat that confirms their attendance at this orientation session. Examples of site-specific rules are

- Respirators are required with the use of hazardous substances.
- Lifelines are required on elevated areas within six feet of the edge if no other restraints are in place.
- Restraint of equipment is required within two feet of the edge of excavations.

OSHA requires employers to teach workers how to recognize and avoid unsafe conditions. It also requires review of regulations regarding equipment they are using and conditions they will work in. Companies should not make assumptions regarding a new employee's level of knowledge about his or her job until they ask specific questions and observe the person to ensure that he or she understands how to operate safely and correctly. In addition, new employees need to understand potential exposures to chemicals, how to interpret MSDSs, where to get them, how to prevent exposures, and procedures to follow if exposed. Even if an employee has been on the job for some time, he or she should periodically review these basic rules and procedures. Changing conditions can make even the most seasoned worker unsure about correct safety measures.

Safety training occurs in a number of ways. Ideally, a worker is exposed to training through a variety of sources. Unions often sponsor training programs, the company itself should have a company program, OSHA offers different levels of training, and on-the-job training should be a continuing process. Whichever combination of these is used, the key is consistency among all employees. Thus, workers are able to understand safe practices as they move from site to site. Workers who have knowledge about safety stand a better chance of avoiding accidents.

As part of an accident prevention program, hazard communication is especially important. Accidents often happen because people are unaware of the hazard. Substances used in construction such as adhesives, lubricants, and sealants can cause harm if handled improperly. It is the responsibility of every employer to ensure that workers have access to information about each hazardous substance that is brought on site and be trained in the correct method of handling it. OSHA requires that the company maintain MSDSs in their offices. Posters announcing the availability of this information should be prominently displayed at the site.

An effective hazard communication program normally includes the following:

- MSDSs on file at the site for all chemicals
- A predetermined labeling system for all containers of chemicals
- Employee training for how to handle chemicals
- A written program that explains all the items in this list

Any subcontractor who brings hazardous substances on the site has to abide by the safety rules set up by the general contractor. This ensures that all workers, no matter whom they work for, are aware of all hazardous substances.

Safety Meetings

There are generally two levels of safety meetings that occur on a job site. The safety committee meets monthly to direct and monitor the effectiveness of the safety program. Issues dealt with during these meetings include the following:

- Report of any accident or near miss with review of corrective action
- Review of new regulatory activity
- Results of project safety audits

FIGURE 14.5 A toolbox meeting is a safety meeting held at the job site. Forepersons often run them, typically focusing on the safe accomplishment of current work

Source. Courtesy of Beacon Skanska Construction Company, Boston.

The other safety meetings are the weekly toolbox meetings (see Figure 14.5). These are conducted by the forepersons and are brief. They generally focus on spreading information about specific safety hazards. Any accidents or near misses during the week are discussed, as are updated information about hazardous substances and a review of safety procedures related to upcoming activities. These talks are conducted by the forepersons and are usually 15 minutes or so. They are most successful if held the same time each week, allow some time for questions, and vary in their method of presentation. Topics should be very specific to what the crew is doing now or in the near future. Topics covered in these toolbox meetings include the following:

Equipment and tool safety
    Lock out/tag out
    Ladders
    Power tool use
Personal safety
    Heat stress
    Hearing protection
    Confined space
    Hazardous materials
Safety and fire
    Use of portable extinguishers
    Procedures for evacuation

Preventive Devices

In addition to training, the safety program identifies preventive devices that can be used on site to eliminate hazards. The more these measures can provide safe conditions for the workers, the more productive the worker can be. Following are some common protective devices:

- *Fall protection.* This is required when workers are above six feet in areas with sides and edges open, such as open-sided floors, wall openings, roofing, hoist areas, working surfaces with holes, edges of excavations, and form work. Protections include guardrails, safety nets, personal fall restraints, covers, and controlled access zones.
- *Personal protective equipment.* All construction sites require some sort of personal protective equipment. Hard hats are the most common, along with safety goggles. Personal fall restraints are required for working on higher elevations. If work is above water, as in bridge building, life jackets are required.
- *Fire protection.* To keep flammables and combustibles from causing harm, they need to be kept in special containers. Fire extinguishers should be available as well.
- *Signs, signals, and barricades.* These give information to workers and sometimes to the public about hazardous conditions when those conditions cannot be eliminated. Flag-waving garments, traffic control, visible signs and signals, and barricades are all examples (see Figure 14.6).

Owner and Architect Roles

Both owners and designers spend considerable time on the job site. Awareness of unsafe conditions and behavior is important. Wearing safety gear while on site, with proper footwear, gives the message that safety is a requirement for everyone on the site. Pointing out areas where hazards exist increases the number of eyes looking out for safety. In addition, owners and designers have a legal and moral responsibility to report unsafe situations and to take action—that is, stop the work—if the contractor does not immediately address the situation.

Owners are regulated by OSHA and work to maintain their own good safety records. Thus, an owner does not want his or her record tarnished by the actions of a contractor who comes onto the owner's property to do work. One effective way to minimize this risk is to look closely at the contractor's safety record before hiring him or her. Not only does this minimize the chances that an accident will occur, but it also reduces payment of excessive insurance costs. It is no coincidence that contractors with good safety records also have increased productivity and better quality construction.

Some owners actually issue their own set of specific safety rules for contractors working on their site. In addition to OSHA requirements, owners may add other, more specific rules. For instance, an owner may require a fire watch for all welding operations or may have specific procedures for confined space entries. In addition, an owner may have certain emergency procedures that a contractor will need to follow. Some owners also have specific hazardous conditions. Hospitals, research laboratories, and industrial plants all produce their own hazardous conditions. Contractors working in or adjacent to these sites must be made aware of any potential hazards.

Liability concerns have traditionally kept designers out of any deep involvement with safety during construction. Safety has traditionally been part of the means and

FIGURE 14.6   Barricades are used to protect the public from the hazards of construction. They can also be used to disseminate project information

Source. Photo by Margot Balboni, Geoscapes.

methods, which are the responsibility of the contractor. However, worker safety requires support from the design team as well as from the contractor. Designers need to be educated about safety requirements and keep them in mind during the design process—for example, considering the installation of underground utilities; mechanical, engineering, and plumbing system layouts; and precast placements. If, during construction, there are conflicts between design and safety considerations, designers must be willing and able to provide guidance to the contractor. During a lawsuit, designers will be brought into the suit through third-party claims. The degree of designer responsibility for safety depends on the nature of the contract. Factors such as the right to stop work, authority to issue change orders, degree of actual supervision, and control of the work are all contractual responsibilities that are used in court to define designers' liability. It is therefore in a designer's best interest to design for construction safety.

Identification of Hazards

The key to identification of hazards is regular, consistent inspection of the job site. The superintendent should do this with assistance from the foreperson and shop stewards. The tours are conducted daily for some things and weekly for others. A consistent systematic inspection yields information that over time can inform safety programs. In the short term, the inspections uncover unsafe conditions and practices. Documentation of these inspections is important to meet regulatory requirements and insurance regulations; and if an accident occurs, they can provide a historic context.

To help develop its safety training, a company can use job hazard analysis. By looking in depth at any job activities with a history of causing injuries, a company can develop safe procedures to control or eliminate the hazards. These procedures can then be used in training and fed back to the corporate safety committee to make adjustments in the company's safety program.

Enforcement

Beyond training, a company needs to follow up with enforcement. Much enforcement is through example: if a supervisor is not consistent with rules and procedures, the workers will not be either. An unkempt site sends a message of laxness. If visitors are allowed in without wearing proper protection, workers may learn that rules are made to be broken. If violations do occur, the site must have a consistent notification procedure, whether to an individual employee or to a subcontractor on the job.

OSHA enforces its regulations principally through surprise inspections. When inspectors find violations, they may issue citations listing them. Employers have the right under this law to contest these violations, and an independent board will hear the complaint. The board assumes the employer is innocent, thereby putting the burden of proof on OSHA inspectors. There have been many employer complaints about the bureaucratic nature of OSHA and the "one-size-fits-all" method of inspections. Regardless of a company's strong safety record, OSHA handles enforcement in a consistent manner. This has led to tensions between the agency and contractors. OSHA recognizes this and has launched a program that offers clear choice for the contractor. For firms with strong and effective health and safety programs, OSHA is offering a partnership that stresses prevention and will give incentives to companies that have good management programs. Incentives include low priority for inspections, focused inspections on only the most serious hazards when they do occur, priority assistance, and appropriate regulatory relief.

IF AN ACCIDENT OCCURS

If an accident occurs on the job site, the key to an effective response is "Be prepared." Preparation means planning beforehand for the types of emergencies that could occur on your particular site. Digging tunnels creates a set of possible emergencies different from those associated with building bridges. OSHA requires this plan to be written down and mandates that individual workers be familiar with the parts of the plan related to their work. Emergency procedures must include at least the following:

- Who and how to call for help
- Method of sounding the alarm to evacuate the area

BOX 14.2

OSHA INSPECTIONS

OSHA conducts inspections on a routine basis, in response to written complaints by workers, or in the aftermath of an accident.

Upon arrival at the job site, the inspector will produce official credentials from the U.S. Department of Labor in the form of a photo ID with a serial number. This ID can be verified through a local OSHA office. If the inspector does not offer this ID, the employer should ask to see it.

There are three parts to an OSHA inspection: the preconference, the walkaround site inspection, and the closing conference. The preconference should be conducted in a private location and attended by the person in charge at the time. Anyone in authority at a job site should be well versed in the requirements of inspections to avoid being caught off guard. At the preconference, the inspector will explain the reason for the visit and, if in a response to a written complaint, will produce the correspondence. Although the employer has the right to ask for a warrant before the inspection can take place, this is probably not the best position to take unless the inspection seems groundless. At this conference, the inspector will ask to review various logs that are kept by the employer. These include safety rules and the corporate safety program, record of toolbox meetings, location and availability of material data sheets, and use of personal protective equipment. The inspector will also ask the person in charge to select an employee to accompany the officer during the inspection.

The walk-around inspection will focus on the reason behind the inspection but will probably also entail a general inspection for workplace hazards. The compliance officer will talk with various employees and will probably take photographs. During this walk around, the accompanying employee should take notes about all areas inspected, who was interviewed, and what was discussed. The employee should take photos similar to those of the inspector, as part of an overall photographic record of the inspection.

At the closing conference, the inspector will review any areas of perceived violations and may offer technical advice about how to correct the deficiencies. The inspector will impose a time limit for implementation of the corrections and will provide information about possible fines. The person in charge and the employee who accompanied the inspector should be at this closing conference. It is important to understand fully the areas of concern and to ask very specific questions of the inspector. Directly after the inspector leaves, the employee who attended the walk around should write a report about what transpired.

If the inspection results in a citation, then the inspector will write the citation and send it to the person in charge. The citation will include a description of the violation and the amount of the fine, if any. It will also include a time limit by which the violation must be corrected. If the employer intends to protest the citation, the objection must be declared within 15 days of receipt of the citation. This objection will then be heard before an independent appeals board.

- Escape routes and procedures in the event of an evacuation
- Method of accounting for everyone after the evacuation
- Designation of a person to administer first aid
- Location of the first aid kit
- Rescue methods in the event of a specific type of accident
- Designation of a person who will perform the rescue
- What to do if a chemical spill occurs

If an accident occurs that has resulted in an injury, the first task is to call emergency medical personnel. Depending on the location, these personnel may include paramedics, the local emergency response team, or the fire department. The emergency action plan should designate specifically who to call. Once all pertinent information is given to these people, the site should be cleared to provide access for emergency vehicles. If first aid must be administered before the emergency personnel arrive, it should be done only by trained and designated persons.

Accident Investigation

Accident investigation ascertains the facts that have led up to and caused the accident. With this information, future accidents of a similar nature can be avoided. All investigations look at the cause of the accident, keep detailed records of the facts, and determine if there was deviation from normal procedures. Even if an accident is a near miss (no injuries or property damage), it should be treated as seriously as if it were real. Corrective measures should follow, as should related discussions at the weekly toolbox meetings and the monthly safety meeting.

Procedures for investigating an accident include the following:

- Clear the scene of all nonessential personnel and rope off the area
- Protect the scene, leaving everything as is
- Photograph or videotape the scene
- Interview those involved separately and as soon as possible after the occurrence

After an accident, emotions are high, and the environment may be chaotic. An interviewer should be careful when interviewing witnesses. It is important to establish authority and to move through the questions methodically and calmly. Being very clear when asking questions and rechecking what is said helps to establish the facts of the incident and weed out the emotional responses that are natural at this time.

Conclusion

How safety is attended to on construction sites depends on individual attitudes toward it. No matter what the attitude, however, safety is required by law. There are also humanitarian and economic reasons for attending to safety. It is no coincidence that safe jobs are productive jobs. Accidents cut down on productivity and increase insurance costs and claims; they can even mean the difference between winning the next job or losing it. Owners are interested in working with contractors who have good safety records. No one wants to attract the negative attention to a job that comes with a serious accident.

There are many ways to prevent accidents. It takes a commitment from top management that then filters down to individual workers in the field. Everyone has a responsibility for safety. It can only be effective if people are trained to spot hazardous conditions and if the hazardous conditions are addressed quickly and consistently.

Even with the best of intentions, however, accidents can happen. When they do, it is important that everyone knows his or her role. First aid kit locations, emergency numbers, procedures for aiding injured workers, protection of the accident scene must be addressed before there is a reason to use them. Finally, the cause of the accident should be determined and, if possible, eliminated so that it does not occur again.

Reference

AGC. *Managing the Risk of Mold in the Construction of Buildings.* Developed by the Mold Litigation Task Force of the Association of General Contractors (AGC, Inc.). March 2003.

Chapter Review Questions

1. EMR stands for experience modification rate and is a measure of the frequency of accidents that a company experiences. It is used in the calculation of workers' compensation insurance premiums. True or false?
2. The use of material safety data sheets (MSDSs) is of prime importance in which aspect of a safety program?
   a. Employee orientation
   b. Personal protection devices
   c. Hazard communication
   d. Toolbox meetings
   e. All of the above
3. Material safety data sheets must be prominently displayed at the job site. True or false?
4. Which of the following would go the farthest in the reduction of job-site accidents?
   a. Increasing the frequency of toolbox meetings
   b. Upgrading the quality and availability of personal protection devices
   c. Increasing the number of safety training sessions
   d. Improving new worker orientation sessions
   e. Writing or improving a comprehensive safety program
5. What should a toolbox meeting discuss?
   a. Specific hazards that workers face at this time on the project
   b. Details about any recent accident or near miss
   c. Updated information about hazardous materials now in use
   d. A review of safety procedures in relation to new activities about to occur
   e. All of the above
6. The formula for calculating a company's EMR weighs the total cost of all the company's accidents more heavily than the frequency of accidents. True or false?
7. An OSHA fine is best described as which type of cost?
   a. Insurance
   b. Penalty
   c. Liability
   d. Public relations
   e. None of the above
8. Aggressive construction scheduling often leads to unsafe working conditions. True or false?

9. Contractors with good safety records are typically more expensive and exhibit lower job site productivity. True or false?
10. Proper emergency procedure planning should be conducted before the beginning of construction and include which of the following?
    a. Escape routes in the event of evacuation
    b. Location of first aid equipment
    c. Who and how to call for help
    d. What to do if a chemical spill occurs
    e. All of the above

Exercises

1. Research a safety-related topic from one of the following categories and prepare a written report and/or an oral presentation to the class.
   Safety training
       Subjects of safety meetings
       Toolbox meetings
       Safety careers and training
       New worker orientation
   Human factors
       Ergonomics
       Drug-free workplace
       Worker attitudes
   Safety economics
       True cost of an injury
       Safety incentives for contractors
       Safety facts and costs
       Workers' compensation
       Insurance industry
       Safety versus profitability
   Miscellaneous safety topics
       Implementing a safety program
       Safety techniques
       OSHA requirements
       Fire prevention
       Tool maintenance
       Personal protective equipment
       Work in a confined area
       Fall protection
2. Research a construction accident and discuss the following:
   a. What was the cause of the accident?
   b. What are the economic impacts of this accident on the worker and his or her family? The employer? The owner? The government and the taxpayer?
   c. Examine the safety plan that was in effect and discuss what aspects of the plan addressed the cause of this accident and what could be done to prevent the accident from happening again.
   d. If you were the project superintendent, what future toolbox meeting topic(s) might you suggest?

Appendix

Construction Project Management WebSites

The following list provides websites that contain valuable construction-related information. The list was originally compiled by Elizabeth Holmes and updated by the authors.

American Council for Construction Education
http://acce-hq.org/

American Concrete Institute
http://www.aci-int.org

American Construction Inspectors Association
http://www.ACIA.com

American Consulting Engineers Council
http://www.acec.org

American Institute of Architects
http://www.aiaonline.com/

American Institute of Constructors
http://www.aicnet.org/

American Institute of Steel Construction
http://www.aisc.org/

American Iron and Steel Institute
http://www.steel.org

American National Standards
  Institute (ANSI)
http://web.ansi.org/

American Road and Transportation Builders
  Association
http://www.ARTBA.org

American Society for Testing and Materials
http://www.astm.org

American Society of Civil Engineers
http://www.asce.org/

American Society of Heating, Refrigerating &
  Air Conditioning Engineers (ASHRAE)
http://www.ashrae.org

American Society of Mechanical Engineers
http://www.asme.org

American Society of Professional Estimators
http://www.aspenational.com

American Subcontractors Association
http://www.asaonline.com/

Associated Builders and Contractors
http://www.abc.org/

Associated General Contractors of America
http://www.agc.org/

Associated Schools of Construction
http://www.ascweb.org

Association for the Advancement of Cost
  Engineering
http://www.aacei.org/

BOCA Online
http://www.bocai.org/

Builder Online
http://www.builderonline.com/

Building Online
http://www.buildingonline.com/

Building Owners and Managers Association
  (BOMA)
http://www.boma.org/

Commerce Business Daily
http://www.ld.com/cbd/today/index-ssi/

Construction Industry Institute
http://www.construction-institute.org

Construction Management Association of America
http://www.access.digex.net/~cmaa/index.html

Construction Management Research Group
http://www.pse.sbu.ac.uk/cmrg/

Construction Marketing Network
http://www.cmarket.net

Construction Specifications Institute
http://www.csinet.org/

Construction Net
http://www.constructionnet.org

Design-Build Institute of America
http://www.dbia.org/

Electronic Blue Book
http://thebluebook.com

ENR's Cost Indexes
http://www.enr.com/cost/cost1.asp

Engineering News-Record Headline News
http://www.enr.com/

Facilities Net
http://www.facilitiesnet.com

Green Building Council
http://www/usgbc.org/

Institute for Research in Construction
http://www.nrc.ca/irc/irc.html

International Cost Engineering Council
http://www.icoste.org/

International Organization for Standardization
(ISO)
http://www.iso.ch/

National Association of Home Builders
http://www.nahb.com

National Association of Women in Construction
http://www.nawic.org/

National Center for Construction Education
and Research
http://www.nccer.org

National Concrete Masonry Association
http://www.ncma.org

National Fire Protection Association
http://www.nfpa.org

National Society of Project Engineers
http://www.NSPE.org

Occupational Safety and Health
Administration
http://www.osha.gov

Project Management Forum
http://www.pmforum.org

Project Management Institute
http://www.pmi.org

R.S. Means
http://www.rsmeans.com

Small Business Administration
http://www.sbaonline.sba.gov/

Society of Cost Estimating and Analysis
http://www.sceaonline.net

Sweet's System Online
http://www.sweets.com

Thomas Register of American
Manufacturers
http://www.thomasregister.com

United States Department of Labor
http://gatekeeper.dol.gov/

Welcom Library—Project Management
Solutions
http://207.158.209.41/library/index.html

Index